June 15–16, 2012
Beijing, China

I0044239

Association for Computing Machinery

Advancing Computing as a Science & Profession

ISMM'12

Proceedings of the 2012 ACM SIGPLAN

International Symposium on Memory Management

In cooperation with:

ACM SIGPLAN

Sponsored by:

Microsoft Research, Oracle Labs, AZUL Systems, and IBM Research

Association for
Computing Machinery

Advancing Computing as a Science & Profession

The Association for Computing Machinery
2 Penn Plaza, Suite 701
New York, New York 10121-0701

ISBN: 978-1-4503-1350-6 (Digital)

ISBN: 978-1-4503-1734-4 (Print)

Additional copies may be ordered prepaid from:

ACM Order Department
PO Box 30777
New York, NY 10087-0777, USA

Phone: 1-800-342-6626 (USA and Canada)
+1-212-626-0500 (Global)
Fax: +1-212-944-1318
E-mail: acmhelp@acm.org
Hours of Operation: 8:30 am – 4:30 pm ET

Printed in the USA

2012 International Symposium on Memory Management

It is with great pleasure that we welcome you to the ACM SIGPLAN 2012 International Symposium on Memory Management (ISMM'12). This year continues ISMM's tradition as the top venue for presenting research results on memory management.

This year ISMM'12 received 30 submissions out of which the program committee selected 12 to appear in the conference. These papers cover diverse and interesting aspects of memory management including multicore, program analysis, and mechanisms such as read and write barriers.

We used a double-blind reviewing process, an external review committee (XRC) to add reviewer expertise, and a rebuttal process, all of which worked smoothly and efficiently. Each program committee (PC) member reviewed seven or eight papers in a four-week time period. In turn, the authors were given a rebuttal period of three days, during which they could answer reviewer questions. The rebuttal was not limited in content, but was limited in length.

The XRC followed the effort started in 2008 to increase the breadth of the reviewer pool and the depth of reviewer expertise. Unlike PC members, XRC reviewers did not attend the PC meeting. The XRC provided expert reviews, but was established ahead of time, rather than on an ad-hoc basis. Each XRC member was assigned three to four papers to review. This light reviewing load encouraged XRC members to focus on producing especially careful critiques. All submissions received at least three PC reviews and at least one XRC review. All PC and XRC members had the opportunity to revise their reviews based on the rebuttal and based on discussions prior to and during the PC meeting. The XRC played no part in the final decision-making for non-PC submissions.

All non-PC papers were discussed at the PC meeting on March 23, 2012, in Seattle. All PC members attended the entire meeting. PC members who had a conflict with a submission left the room during the discussions of their conflict papers. The software also prevented conflicted PC members from reading reviews or knowing the reviewers of conflicted papers. Only the committee members who reviewed the paper made the acceptance decisions. We discussed all non-PC papers. All authors were notified of the decisions by email on March 23.

PC co-authored submissions were allowed, and we received four and three were accepted. The XRC provided four to five reviews for each of these submissions and met on a conference call on March 22, 2012. These papers were held to the customary higher standard. The General Chair, Martin Vechev, handled the conflicts of interest with the Program Chair. He assigned the reviewers and led the telephone discussions of these papers. Only XRC members who reviewed PC co-authored submissions participated in the call and in the final decision.

We were very happy with blind reviewing, rebuttal, and the XRC mechanism. In particular, handling PC submissions with non-PC reviewers in a separate meeting worked quite well. In the discussion of each paper, the program chair asked a PC member to summarize the paper, its strengths and weaknesses, and the authors' response. In some cases the authors' response strongly influenced the final decision.

Thank you for your interest and support of ISMM'12. We hope you enjoy Beijing.

Kathryn S. McKinley
ISMM'12 Program Chair
Microsoft Research
Redmond, Washington, USA

Martin Vechev
ISMM'12 General Chair
ETH Zurich
Zurich, Switzerland

Table of Contents

Session 4: Caches and Analysis
Session Chair: Zhenlin Wang *(Michigan Technical University)*

2012 International Symposium on Memory Management

General Chair: Martin Vechev *(ETH Zurich)*

Program Chair: Kathryn S McKinley *(The University of Texas at Austin and Microsoft Research)*

Local Arrangements Chair: Chen Ding *(University of Rochester)*

Program Committee: Steve Blackburn *(Australian National University)*
Dave Detlefs *(Microsoft)*
Laurent Daynès *(Oracle Labs)*
Chen Ding *(University of Rochester)*
David Gay *(Google)*
David P Grove *(IBM T.J. Watson Research Center)*
Maria Jump *(King's College)*
John Regehr *(University of Utah)*
Zhenlin Wang *(Michigan Technological University)*
Christian Wimmer *(Oracle Labs)*
Greta Yorsh *(ARM)*
Qin Zhao *(Google)*

External Review Committee: Emery Berger *(University of Massachusetts, Amherst)*
Daniel Frampton *(Australian National University)*
Chandra Krintz *(University of California, Santa Barbara)*
Simon Marlow *(Microsoft Research)*
Maged Michael *(IBM T.J. Watson Research Center)*
Nick Nethercote *(Mozilla)*
Tomas Petricek *(University of Cambridge)*
Filip Pizlo *(Apple)*
Xipeng Shen *(College of William and Mary)*
Michael Spear *(Lehigh University)*
Witawas Srisa-an *(University of Nebraska)*
Eran Yahav *(Technion)*

ISMM 2012 Sponsor & Supporters

Sponsor:

Supporters:

Microsoft Research

ORACLE

AZUL SYSTEMS

IBM Research

Why Is Your Web Browser Using So Much Memory?

Robert O'Callahan

Mozilla
robert@ocallahan.org

Abstract

Browsers are the operating systems of the Web. They support a vast universe of applications written in a modern garbage-collected programming language. Browsers expose a rich platform API mostly implemented in C++. Browsers are also consumer software with low switching costs in an intensely competitive market. Thus in addition to standard requirements such as maximizing throughput and minimizing latency, browsers have to consider issues like "when the user closes a window while watching Task Manager, they want to see memory usage go down". Browsers have to compete to minimize memory usage even for poorly written applications. In this talk I will elucidate these requirements and describe how Firefox and other browsers address them. I will pay particular attention to issues that we don't know how to solve, and that could benefit from research attention.

Categories and Subject Descriptors D.3.4 [*Processors*]: Memory Management

General Terms Languages, Reliability

Keywords Memory Management, Web Browser

ISMM'12, June 15–16, 2012, Beijing, China.
ACM 978-1-4503-1350-6/12/06.

Memory Management for Many-Core Processors with Software Configurable Locality Policies

Jin Zhou and Brian Demsky

University of California, Irvine
{jzhou1,bdemsky}@uci.edu

Abstract

As processors evolve towards higher core counts, architects will develop more sophisticated memory systems to satisfy the cores' increasing thirst for memory bandwidth. Early many-core processor designs suggest that future memory systems will likely include multiple controllers and distributed cache coherence protocols. Many-core processors that expose memory locality policies to the software system provide opportunities for automatic tuning that can achieve significant performance benefits.

Managed languages typically provide a simple heap abstraction. This paper presents techniques that bridge the gap between the simple heap abstraction of modern languages and the complicated memory systems of future processors. We present a NUMA-aware approach to garbage collection that balances the competing concerns of data locality and heap utilization to improve performance. We combine a lightweight approach for measuring an application's memory behavior with an online, adaptive algorithm for tuning the cache to optimize it for the specific application's behaviors.

We have implemented our garbage collector and cache tuning algorithm and present results on a 64-core TILEPro64 processor.

Categories and Subject Descriptors   D.3.4 [*Programming Languages*]: Processors—Memory management(garbage collection)

General Terms   Languages, Performance

Keywords   Garbage Collection, Many-Core

1. Introduction

Microprocessor manufacturers have recently developed several many-core processors. Tilera ships a 64-core TILEPro64 microprocessor and recently announced a 100-core processor [36]. Intel has developed the 48-core Single-chip Cloud Computer(SCC) processor [23]. Examination of these early many-core processors provides the following insights into future mainstream processors:

- **Sophisticated Caches:** Existing caches are largely transparent to developers. Cache scalability limitations will force future processors to include cache systems that place more burden on developers. The SCC embodies one extreme approach — it does not provide hardware cache coherence. Mainstream processors are less likely to take such an extreme approach be-

cause of market forces that require backwards compatibility with existing code in applications, libraries, and operating systems. Moreover, the existence of processors that provide cache coherence for 64 cores demonstrate that this problem can be solved for moderate core counts. We believe that mainstream processors will likely adopt a moderate approach — sophisticated cache-coherence protocols that will guarantee coherence, but require tuning for optimal performance.

Future many-core processors will likely provide mechanisms for software to tune cache behavior. For example, the TILEPro64 development tools provide an API that supports several software configurable caching modes for each page.

- **Multiple Controllers:** Future processors will likely include multiple controllers to provide sufficient memory bandwidth. For example, the TILEPro64 processor has four memory controllers that are connected to a mesh of cores through an on-chip network, while the AMD Magny Cour processor has two memory controllers. Optimizing performance on these architectures requires balancing memory accesses across the controllers.

- **Communication Channels:** Future processors may provide additional communication mechanisms beyond cache-coherent shared memory. For example, both the TILEPro64 and SCC processors have a mesh network that connects the tiles. Low-latency messaging provides an opportunity to rethink how we partition the work of marking objects during garbage collection.

These changes will have profound effects on software development. Optimizing programs will require developers to carefully manage the location of data and computation, and tune cache policies. Garbage collectors for future memory systems will need to be both highly parallel and memory system aware to achieve acceptable performance. Earlier work on parallel garbage collection [5, 14, 17, 18, 20, 22, 28] largely targeted SMP systems in which all processors have uniform memory access.

While our implementation focuses on the TILEPro64 processor, we believe that our techniques will generalize to other processors in the future. Our approach primarily targets the following hardware features — software configurable caches and multiple memory controllers. Software configurable caching could be implemented in an x86 compatible chip. The operating system would interact with these features normally and provide reasonable defaults to run existing legacy applications. As scaling broadcast-based cache coherence beyond a handful of cores is known to be difficult, future caches are more likely to be configurable distributed caches that are easier to scale. The issues related to multiple memory controllers exist in current x86 processors such as the AMD Magny Cour.

1.1 NUMA-Aware Parallel Garbage Collector

This paper presents a Non-Uniform Memory Architecture (NUMA)-aware, many-core parallel garbage collector that is architected as a master/slave distributed system with a master core coordinating the actions of all other cores.

We have designed our collector with careful consideration of the memory system. Our collector turns off cache coherence to eliminate the overhead of inter-cache coherence traffic. A key design principle is to have each core independently manage its own memory partition in the common case. On modern architectures this both minimizes coordination overheads and leverages the improved performance that is available through the local memory system.

Modern collectors combine many techniques to optimize performance including generational collection, mark-sweep collection, and mark-compact collection. This paper focuses on mark-compact collection as this component proves challenging for both preserving locality and parallelization. Our collector can be used to optimize the collection of the old generation in generational collectors. We did not implement concurrent collection — a straightforward adaptation of the virtual memory based approach used by the Compressor collector [24] could be used to support concurrent collection. Note that there is a tradeoff here — concurrent collection necessarily incurs cache coherence overheads.

1.2 Adaptive Cache Tuning

Application behaviors and load balancing in the garbage collector can cause mismatches between the application's access patterns and cache homing policies. To further tune an application's performance on many-core processors, our system adaptively tunes caching policies in response to measurements of the application's memory behavior. Our approach has four components:

- **Estimate Memory Accesses:** Tuning the cache policies for memory pages requires estimating how often each core accesses each memory page. Current processors do not provide explicit hardware support for fine-grained memory profiling of all pages. We present a low-overhead technique that leverages the TLB miss handler to estimate memory accesses.

- **Generate Tuned Caching Policies:** Our approach uses a set of heuristics to analyze the collected memory access statistics to discover opportunities for optimizing caching policies. Each heuristic is designed to identify a specific performance issue and adjust the caching policy to correct the issue.

- **GC Compensation:** One issue is that the collector moves objects — our system adjusts data collected before the garbage collection to compensate for moving objects.

- **Dynamically Adjust Caching Policies:** At the end of garbage collection, our system adjusts caching policies.

1.3 Contributions

This paper makes the following contributions:

- **NUMA-Aware Collector:** It presents a collector that optimizes both allocation and collection for NUMA architectures.

- **Incoherent Garbage Collection:** Applications may have drastically different memory access patterns than the garbage collector. Caching policies that work well for the application may work poorly for the garbage collector. We have designed our garbage collector to support collection without requiring hardware cache coherence during collection. During collection we turn off hardware cache coherence to avoid cache coherence traffic. Note that the data is still cached during garbage collection — there is simply no hardware-provided guarantee of coherence if multiple cores access the same data.

- **Hybrid Heap Organization:** It presents a hybrid heap organization approach that balances (1) partitioning the heap to support independent collection, (2) maintaining locality in a NUMA memory system, and (3) defragmenting the entire heap

to ensure post-GC that most free partitions are contiguously located at the top of the heap to avoid introducing artificial constraints on the size of objects that can be allocated.

- **Adaptive Cache Coherence Policies:** It presents an approach for dynamically adapting cache coherence policies in response to actual memory access patterns.

- **Evaluation:** It presents our evaluation of the garbage collection and the cache tuning approach on a 64-core TILEPro64 microprocessor on several benchmarks.

The paper is structured as follows: Section 2 describes the TILEPro64 memory system. Section 3 presents the collector. Section 4 presents our approach to dynamically tune caching policy for the system. Section 5 presents our evaluation of the approach. Section 6 discusses related work; we conclude in Section 7.

2. The TILEPro64 Memory System

The TILEPro64 contains 64 cores arranged in a grid. Each core is connected to a mesh network that provides communications for the memory system and application-level messaging. Each core has a local L1 and L2 cache. The TILEPro64 uses a directory-based distributed cache that maintains consistency across the L2 caches.

Directory-based cache coherence protocols were originally designed for multiprocessor systems — Tilera has made significant changes to optimize these protocols for many-core processors. Each cache line has a home core — the home core for a cache line maintains the directory for that line. The collection of L2 caches effectively serves as a large, distributed L3 cache. The distributed L3 cache respects the cache inclusion principle — if any L2 cache on the entire chip contains a copy of a cache line, there must also be a copy of that line in the cache line's home core's L2 cache.

The home core for a cache line is software configurable at the page granularity. The hardware supports four different policies: (1) software can specify a core to home all of the cache lines on a given page, (2) software can specify that the home for cache lines on the page is computed by hashing the base address of the cache line (*hash-for-home*), (3) software can specify the page is cached incoherently, or (4) software can specify the page is not cached. Hash-for-home distributes the homes for a page's cache lines across many cores to avoid cache hot spots by load balancing memory accesses across several caches. The cache policy for a page is stored in its page mapping in the page table and loaded into core's translation lookaside buffer (TLB) on a TLB miss.

The L2 cache is write-through to the distributed L3 — all writes are forwarded immediately to the home core. The home core then uses the directory to invalidate all shared copies of the cache line, performs the write, and then replies that the write has completed.

2.1 Caching Policy Considerations

The directory-based, distributed caching system has a number of performance implications that software developers must consider:

- **Effective Reduction of Cache Size:** Every cache line in the local cache that is remotely homed occupies two cache lines — one in the local core's L2 cache and one in the remote core's L2 cache. Remote homing provides significant performance benefits by avoiding expensive off-chip memory accesses, but it effectively shrinks the size of the cache.

- **Home Core Capacity Constraints:** The cache inclusion property of the home core's L2 cache can have significant impacts. If a large, hot data structure is homed on a single core, the inclusion property means that the size of that core's cache limits how much of the data structure can be simultaneously cached by the entire processor at a given time. Large data structures should therefore be cached hash-for-home.

4

- **Extra Latency:** Accessing memory locations that are homed on remote cores may require communicating with remote cores. Of course, despite the extra on-chip latency to fetch the data from the L3 copy, the huge advantage is that it saves expensive off-chip bandwidth and reduces substantially higher off-chip latencies. On the TILEPro64, we measured the following load latencies: a load that hits in the local L2 takes 8 cycles, a load that hits in a remote L2 takes 36 cycles, a load that misses the L2 for locally homed memory takes 80 cycles, and a load that misses the L3 for remotely homed memory takes 123 cycles.

- **Hot Spots:** Cache controllers have limited capacity for servicing requests. This capacity is split between requests from remote cores and the local core. If too many cores access memory that is homed on one core, the core's cache can be a bottleneck. In the TILEPro64, there are as many controllers as there are cores, so in general the load is distributed. The situation is significantly better than in centralized L3 caches where the L3 is a catastrophic hot spot.

2.2 Performance Impact of Caching Policies

A simple experiment reveals the potential impact of tuning the cache policy for an application's behavior. We developed a microbenchmark that allocates a two-page-long (128KB) array and then each core executes a loop that scans through the array reading a single word in each cache line. In this microbenchmark, every read will miss in the core's local cache and then be forwarded to a remote core. The *fixed remote location* version homes each of the two pages on a dedicated core while the *hfh* version uses the hash-for-home policy for the two pages.

With 60 cores, hash-for-home speeds up accesses to these two pages by $4\times$ relative to the fixed remote location version. These results show that memory access patterns that create hot spots cause scaling problems and that the appropriate use of hash-for-home effectively addresses hot spots by distributing accesses to the same page across many caches. The results show cache hot spots for reads even though the local core keeps a local cached copy because of capacity misses in the local core's cache.

Hash-for-home is the default caching mode on the TilePro64 and tends to work well for shared data. While hash-for-home is sometimes needed to avoid cache hot spots and capacity constraints, memory accesses under hash-for-home are likely to incur the overhead of communicating with a remote core. Moreover, as remotely homed cache lines occupy a cache line in both the local core's cache and the home core's cache, hash-for-home effectively reduces the cache size as compared to locally homed cache lines.

3. NUMA-Aware Collector

Our collector has a master/slave architecture. One core is statically designated as the master — it coordinates the phases of the collector and distributes large (megabytes) blocks of memory to the allocators on the individual cores. In our implementation, the master also participates as any core in addition to its coordination activities. The collector is designed such that the coordination overhead is not significant. We have not observed scaling issues in our experiments using the collector on a 64-core TILEPro64 processor. Note that in our implementation, one core serves as both the master and a participant in the computation. If processors should ever become available with a sufficient number of cores to cause the coordination workload to become significant, dedicating a core to serve as the master can further scale the implementation.

Our collector has the following three phases:

1. **Mark Live Objects:** The collector marks the live objects.

2. **Planning Phase:** The collector next plans how to compact the live objects.

3. **Update Heap:** The collector finally compacts the live objects and updates references in one sweep through the heap.

Our collector uses the TILEPro64's on-chip network to send messages to coordinate garbage collection. For example, when a core does not have sufficient space in its local partition of the heap to process an allocation request, it sends a request to the master core to garbage collect the heap. The master core notifies all cores that garbage collection has been requested with a message. When the cores reach a garbage collection safe point, they send a response. When the master receives all responses, it sends a message to all cores to begin the mark phase of garbage collection. Note that low-latency messaging can be replaced with shared-memory queues.

3.1 Heap Organization

The compaction phase in many mark-compact collectors globally compacts objects towards the bottom of the heap. It is sequential and must be parallelized. The key parallelization challenge is that the compaction phase reads from locations that it later overwrites.

A more serious problem is that the traditional approach to heap compaction is poorly suited for NUMA memory systems. Traditional compaction moves objects to new memory locations that are potentially located on different memory controllers and mixes objects allocated by different cores. This means that thread-local data is likely to be migrated to memory whose cache lines are homed on some other core. This will likely both increase the garbage collection time and slow down the execution of the mutator.

Several parallel collectors address this issue by partitioning the heap into processor or core local heaps [20]. As the processor core count increases to hundreds of cores, this partitioning approach can fragment the free space into very tiny regions. While plenty of free space may be available in aggregate, sufficiently large contiguous free blocks may not exist. Our heap organization is a hybrid approach — it partitions the global heap into contiguous core local heaps for locality while still compacting the global heap to recover large contiguous blocks of free memory.

Our collector partitions the shared heap into N disjoint partitions, where N is significantly larger than the number of cores — each partition is assigned to a core and the core is then the *host core* for that partition. Each partition is an integer multiple of the page size. We create many more partitions of the heap than the number of cores to provide the allocator with the flexibility to allocate memory where it is needed while still maintaining locality. In our collector design, large objects can cross partition boundaries. Therefore, as long as the allocator can keep several contiguous partitions free, small partitions do not prevent the collector from allocating large objects. As small partitions make it more likely that contiguous partitions will be free at the heap top, smaller partitions can actually help with allocating larger objects.

While cores can allocate memory from any partition, each core only garbage collects its own heap partition. It marks only objects in this partition and compacts the live objects in this partition. However, a core may compact objects into another core's partition as necessary to balance the object load.

After garbage collection, free memory partitions are configured such that the cache lines for the memory partition are homed on the partition's host core. The physical addresses for all memory partitions correspond to the closest memory controller. Our collector preferentially allocates objects into the local partition. However, it will allow cores to allocate objects into other partitions when necessary to balance heap usage or to support large objects.

We next describe how the heap's partitions are mapped onto cores. Figure 1 presents a mapping of the heap partitions to the cores of a 3×3 mesh multi-core processor with $N = 27$ partitions. The mapping stripes the address space across the cores. The mapping ensures that adjacent partitions in the virtual address space

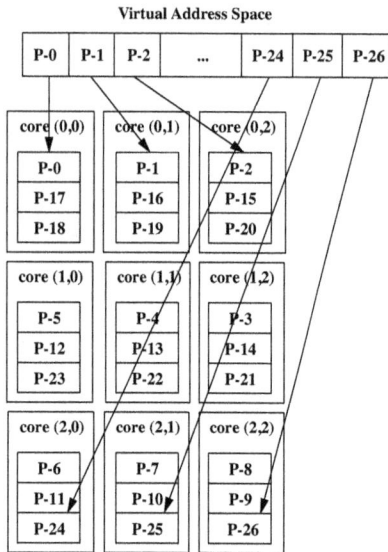

Figure 1. Heap Mapping

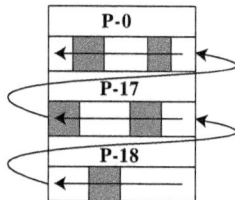

Figure 2. Garbage Collection Strategy on Core 0,0

are hosted on nearby cores. This mapping when combined with our compaction strategy provides large contiguous blocks of free memory at the top of the address space while at the same time allowing all cores to independently compact their heap partitions.

Our collector takes a modified compaction approach — each core compacts the heap within the heap partitions that are hosted on the local core when possible. The arrows in Figure 2 shows the strategy for the example heap mapping. The strategy preserves locality while still generating large contiguous free blocks of memory that are suitable for large objects at the heap top. We use a combination of three techniques to generate large free blocks of memory at the top of the heap (1) mapping several memory blocks to each core in a striped fashion around the cores, (2) having cores compact to their lowest blocks, and (3) load balancing objects across cores during garbage collection. Our goal of dividing up the heap while also globally compacting the heap is shared by the Abuaiadh collector [3] — our approach has the advantages of requiring significantly less synchronization (we only synchronize to load balance) and maintaining locality for NUMA systems.

3.2 Mark Phase

Each core runs its own collector to mark the objects in its partitions. The collector on each core begins the mark phase by scanning its local heap roots. When the core processes a reference, it checks whether the reference is local. If the referenced object resides in the local heap partition and it has not already been discovered, it is placed in the mark queue. If the object is located in another core's heap partition, the collector sends a `mark` message with the reference to the core that owns the partition that contains the object. When a core receives a `mark` message from another core, it checks whether the object has been marked. If not, it adds the object to

its mark queue. Each core executes a loop that dequeues object references from the mark queue, and then scans all of the references in that object. When the mark queue is empty, the collector on the core notifies the master and then continues to poll the queue until the master detects termination.

If an object is referenced by many other objects, the core hosting the partition that contains the object can potentially receive a large number of `mark` messages for the object. Each core therefore implements a small, fixed-size hashtable that caches recently sent object references. If a reference to a remote object hits in this cache, a `mark` message has already been sent for this object and the core elides sending a duplicate `mark` message.

The shape of the object graph can limit parallelism while tracing the heap [7]. Our collector design makes a tradeoff — we minimize synchronization cost and coherence traffic, but could hypothetically lose some potential parallelism during marking. It is unclear how large of a problem this is in practice. In both extremes, heaps with lots of parallelism and heaps with no parallelism, minimizing synchronization costs is optimal.

3.2.1 Hybrid Fixed/Variable-Length Mark Codes

The traditional approach to efficiently track live objects is to use a mark bitmap in which there is a mark bit for each allocation unit. This approach loses information about the sizes and numbers of objects that comprise a contiguous live block of memory.

The Compressor collector extends the traditional approach to also encode object sizes and uses a bit per each word and encodes both the mark and the object size using those bits [24]. While writing such a mark is O(1), reading the marked size requires finding the trailing mark bit and is therefore O(object size).

Our variation uses a hybrid fixed/variable length encoding that has O(1) overhead. We allocate 2 bits in the mark bitmap for each (32 byte) allocation unit in the heap. Note that for objects that are longer than one allocation unit, we can also use the bits assigned to the other allocation units that store the object. In general, the number of bits used to encode an object's length is constrained by the object's length. A pure variable length encoding makes the encoding and decoding process complex. We therefore use variable length codes up to 6 bits long. Figure 3 presents the 6-bit variable length code. The left column presents the bit pattern (X's indicate do not care values) and the right column presents the encoded length. Encoding and decoding these 6-bit values is efficiently implemented as array lookups. For objects that are 16 allocation units or longer in length, there are at least 32 bits available for encoding the length. For these longer objects, we compute the mark bit pattern with a single addition using the formula $(110001b << 18) + (length - 16)$.

Our basic approach can be used for a number of different length coding approaches. For example, it is possible to modify our variable length encoding approach to use 1 bit per allocation unit if we give up on encoding some object sizes (some small object sizes would have to be rounded up to the next largest encodable size).

Bit encoding	Object size in allocation units
00XXXX	free
01XXXX	1
1000XX	2
100100	3
100101	4
100110	5
100111	6
. . .	. . .
110000	15

Figure 3. Hybrid Fixed/Variable-Length Coding (X is don't care)

3.2.2 Detecting Termination of Mark Phase

We next describe how we detect the termination of the mark phase. The complication is that even after a core has completed scanning all live objects that it knows about, a `mark` message that contains the address of a newly discovered live object in its partition can arrive. Blackburn et al. [9] have noted that this corresponds to the well-known problem of distributed algorithm termination [13].

The mark phase has terminated only when all cores have finished scanning all of their known live objects and there are no `mark` messages in flight. When a core notifies the master that its mark queue has emptied, it informs the master of the number of `mark` messages it has sent and the number it has received. When the total number of sent and received mark messages match and all cores report that their mark queues are empty, the mark phase may have terminated. However, this check is not sufficient to guarantee termination, as the collected information does not necessarily represent a snapshot of the system's state.

To verify that the collected data represents a valid snapshot, when the master has collected notifications that indicate the mark phase may have terminated, it initiates a snapshot verification. The master sends a verification message to all other cores and each core responds with a message that includes (1) whether the core is halted and (2) the number of `mark` messages it has sent and received. If the responses don't match, the master repeats the process. Correctness is straightforward: if the responses from the verification round match the previous notifications, the collected data must have been a valid snapshot of the system for the period of time from the last empty queue notification until the master sent the first verification message. Since the number of sent and received messages match in the snapshot, no messages can be in flight. The combination of no messages in flight and all cores having completed local marking in the snapshot guarantees that the mark phase has terminated.

3.3 Compaction

The compaction phase of a garbage collector must both move the objects to their new locations and update all of the references to the new object locations. Memory bandwidth is a key constraint for many-core processors — a key component of garbage collector design is to minimize memory accesses. To minimize memory accesses, we therefore use a single-pass compaction phase in a similar fashion to the Compressor collector [24].

Our collector first plans how to compact the heap using relatively small mark tables and then does the update in a single pass over the heap. The planning phase computes new locations for all live objects. It reads the mark bitmap to compute where to move objects and does not access the actual heap.

The collector constructs a forwarding table to store a mapping from old object locations to new object locations. An object's index in this table is computed by dividing the offset of the object's old address from the heap base address by the allocation unit size.

3.3.1 Sharing Forwarding Pointers

While we currently use a forwarding pointer per object (a 12.5% space overhead), it is possible for multiple objects to share the same forwarding pointer. To be more concrete, consider an example in which groups of four allocation units share the same forwarding pointer table entry. Observe that the mark bitmap contains enough information to compute the forwarding pointer of an object from the forwarding pointer of a neighboring object later in the heap. The compaction phase needs only a small modification — it must ensure that objects that share a forwarding pointer are moved to the same block. When it compacts, it writes the forwarding pointer as before — potentially overwriting forwarding pointers for previous objects that share the same pointer. After the planning phase is finished, each forwarding table entry corresponds to the forwarding

pointer for the highest-addressed live object in the four allocation units that share the table entry. To lookup a forwarding pointer for an object o, the algorithm looks up the shared forwarding pointer and the mark bits for the allocation units that share a forwarding pointer. It then shifts the mark bits left to make the bits corresponding to the object o the highest. It then computes the number of bytes between object o and the last object that shares the same forwarding pointer and subtracts this number from the forwarding pointer. This computation can be made efficient by precomputing it for all mark bit patterns and storing it in a table (sharing a forwarding pointer between 4 allocation units only requires a table with 256 entries).

3.3.2 Partition Balancing

Our locality-preserving strategy can lead to fragmentation at the partition granularity in the shared heap. Figure 4 presents an example fragmented heap. The problem is that some cores may have more live objects and as a result fill their highest partitions while other cores have space left in their lower partitions. The resulting heap then does not have large contiguous free blocks of memory available for large objects. Additionally, some cores are left with no free space in their local heap partitions for new objects.

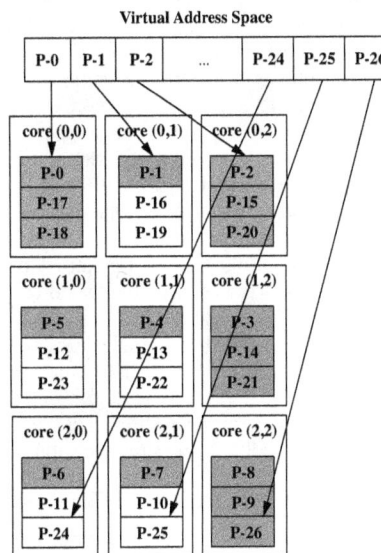

Figure 4. Fragmentation Problem

Our collector uses a partition balancing algorithm in the compaction planning phase to balance objects across cores while minimizing cross-core fragmentation. During the mark phase, each core computes the total size of the live objects in its heap partitions and sends this information to the master collector. When the mark phase completes, the master collector uses these sizes to estimate the average number of heap partitions each core will fill during compaction.

We use this average as an initial upper bound on each core's planning phase. Some cores will come under this average while other cores will go over the average. Note that cores that go under average likely have less work and should finish earlier. Moreover, these cores know exactly what memory they will use when they begin to plan for compacting their last block, and therefore immediately return the unused memory at that point. Synchronization during the actual heap update phase described in Section 3.3.3 ensures that the core compacting objects out of a memory region has finished with the region before a core begins compacting objects into the region.

Cores that exceed the average threshold by a tunable threshold will compact their extra objects into the blocks of other cores.

When a core exceeds the local compacting threshold, it requests more memory from the master core — it sends a message that includes (1) the total size of the objects remaining to be compacted and (2) the minimum amount of memory needed for the next object.

When the master core receives a memory request from a core that ran out of space, it searches its heap table to find space. It begins by first searching the table entries for neighboring cores for space. If space is not available from the neighboring core's heap partitions, it performs a global search in the table. If no memory is available from a core that has returned memory, it stores the request to wait for another core to return memory. If after all cores return their memory sufficient memory is still not available, the master core will hand out memory blocks above the compaction limit. Note that in practice cores will rarely have to wait for another core as (1) cores that return memory have less work to do than cores that need memory and (2) cores preemptively return memory before they start compacting into their last block.

3.3.3 Heap Update Pass

When all cores have notified the master that the planning phase has completed, the master sends messages to instruct all cores to begin the heap update phase. Each core begins by updating the object references in its data structures and then compacts and updates the object references in its heap partitions in one sweep. The core looks up forwarding pointers using the shared table.

There is one complication — due to partition balancing cores may need to compact objects into another core's heap partitions. Cross core compaction can begin as soon as the other core has finished evacuating objects from the destination partition. When a core needs to compact an object into another core's partition, it sends a request to the other core. The second core will respond to this request when it has finished copying objects from the given partition. Although cross core compaction creates dependences between cores, we only cross core compact to lower blocks. Therefore the length of any dependence chain cannot exceed the maximum number of filled blocks assigned to a single core. In practice, we expect that cores will rarely have to wait for another core as the second core has significantly less work to do to reach the point that it finishes copying objects from a partition than the work the first core must do to reach the point it needs the partition.

3.4 Garbage Collection Without Cache Coherence

Our collector has been designed to function correctly even without cache coherence. This allows the collector to avoid incurring cache coherence overheads introduced by the homing policies used by the application. We turn off cache coherence before starting collection and then turn cache coherence back on at the end of collection — both changes require a cache flush. Assuming that the live set of objects is large comparable to the cache size, cache flushes have minimal cost in this case as the data in the cache from the mutator is likely to be evicted before the collector accesses it.

A key point to address is the issue of memory consistency due to turning off cache coherence. The mark and planning phases trivially have no cache consistency issues due to rigorous partitioning of the memory. Consistency for the heap update phase is more subtle. Before a core finishes copying objects from a memory partition, no other core has accessed that partition. Therefore, there are no memory consistency issues for reading the objects. We maintain the invariant that before a core copies objects into a cache line located another core's heap region, no other core has ever written to that cache line since the cache flush at the beginning of the collection. Therefore, any copies of these cache lines in the core that owns the heap region must be clean. We rely on the fact that the core will never write clean cache lines back out to memory to ensure consistency. These clean cache lines are then invalidated in the final cache

flush before they can cause any consistency issues for the mutator. Multiple cores may evacuate objects into the same heap partition due to partition balancing — this does not pose a consistency issue as they will never evacuate objects into the same cache line because we align their memory regions to cache line boundaries.

3.5 Two-Level Memory Allocator

The challenge for the allocator is to tune data locality and heap fragmentation. We use the standard two-level allocation design: the top-level manages the competing concerns of data locality and heap utilization when allocating large memory blocks. The core-local second-level allocators then allocate small memory blocks at minimal overhead. The top-level allocator executes on the master core. The master core maintains a table to track all heap partitions in the system and uses this table to allocate space to second-level allocators. It uses the following allocation strategy to manage both locality and heap utilization concerns:

1. **Local Search:** The top-level allocator first attempts to give the second-level collector a block of memory from the local core's heap partitions. If the local core runs out of space, it falls back to the neighboring core search.

2. **Neighboring Core Search:** The top-level allocator next attempts to give the second-level allocator a block of memory from one of the neighboring core's partitions. The top-level allocator first searches for a free memory partition on the eight neighboring cores. It chooses the partition that is lowest in the heap. If this search fails it falls back to the global search.

3. **Global Search:** Some applications can present an uneven allocation load — a few threads can potentially allocate most of the objects. The global allocator allows these threads to allocate objects into the memory blocks of any other cores on the chips.

We observed that many of our benchmarks triggered global search even though these benchmarks have even allocation loads. The problem is that some threads may run faster than others and thus consume memory faster. In such a situation, pure local search triggers more GCs and is problematic for performance.

Another issue that becomes important with large core counts is clearing memory — it is important to clear memory on demand to spread the required memory traffic over a longer time period. The TILEPro64 like many processors contains instructions that clear an entire cache line without reading from main memory. The second-level allocator uses this instruction to clear memory in blocks of 4,096 bytes. This both spreads memory clearing over a longer time period and avoids cache misses on newly allocated objects.

3.6 Supporting Large Objects

Our presentation of the cache-aware collector has assumed that applications only allocate objects that are smaller than a heap partition. Although our current implementation does not support large objects, we next discuss how the design could support objects that are larger than a heap partition.

Each core collector would maintain a local large object list to track its local large objects and the master collector would maintain a global list to track all large objects in the system. This list is always relatively short as the total number of large objects must be fewer than the number of heap partitions in the system.

During the compaction phase, a core collector scans its local heap partitions to compact all its live objects to the bottom of its heap partitions. The possibility arises that the beginning of a heap partition may contain the end or middle of a large object that began in another heap partition. The compactor would recognize such heap partitions to skip over the space taken by large objects.

Large objects are never copied. If a large object is below the compaction line it is simply left in place and objects are compacted into the memory around it. If a large object is above the compaction line, the large object would be compacted by remapping its pages.

Although large objects can be split across heap partitions, objects are only ever split across contiguous partitions. As a result, we could generate normal accesses in the program code.

4. Adaptive Cache Tuning

Our collector attempts to keep the data a core accesses on the core when possible. Load balancing during collection, uneven allocation rates, or remote allocation can hurt this locality. However, in many applications one thread allocates shared data structures that other threads frequently access. Writes to such data structures can cause a hot spot in the home core's cache. Even though local caches make copies of cache lines, reads can cause similar issues from misses due to capacity constraints in either the local or home core's cache.

In this section, we present an automatic cache tuning technique that measures usage patterns and automatically tunes homing policies to minimize hotspots and remote accesses.

4.1 Overview of Tuning Approach

We use the following approach to tune caching policies:

1. **Continuous Monitoring of Memory Accesses:** Our system extends the virtual memory system to estimate how often each core accesses each page. Every core collects statistics on its own memory accesses.

2. **Compensate Measurements for Garbage Collection:** The collector moves objects in the heap to reduce fragmentation. Our system automatically compensates for the collection process and uses the pre-collection statistics to estimate memory accesses for the post-collection heap.

3. **Compute Tuned Caching Policies:** The master core analyzes the post-collection memory access estimates to tune caching policies for each page.

4. **Update Caching Policies:** Updating caching policies requires stopping all application threads to ensure cache coherence. We therefore update policies during the collection process. After garbage collection is completed, we update the page tables to modify the caching policies. To maintain cache coherence our system flushes the caches on all cores when it changes policies. While our prototype only updates policies during garbage collection, it is of course possible to update cache policies at other points by just stopping and restarting the execution. Note that our approach is applicable to non-managed languages like C — supporting such languages simply requires stopping the execution occasionally to adapt caching policies.

4.2 Estimating Memory Accesses

Measuring an application's memory behavior is the first step for tuning the cache configuration. While modern processors provide hardware support for a wide range of performance counters, these mechanisms typically do not provide sufficient detail to tune caching policies at the page granularity. We therefore leverage the virtual memory system to collect the necessary information.

Tuning cache policies only requires approximate information — rough estimates of memory accesses by cores are sufficient. The TILEPro64, like MIPS, uses a software-managed translation lookaside buffer (TLB). When a lookup of a virtual address misses in the TLB, these chips take a software interrupt and the miss handler loads the missing page entry into the TLB. Our measurement system piggybacks on the software TLB miss handler. Our measurement approach can be adapted for architectures with a large hardware-managed TLB by using large 4MB pages for the heap and protecting individual page table entries.

One naïve strategy for estimating page accesses is to approximate them with TLB miss counts. This strategy has a significant problem. A given number of memory access to many pages will produce more TLB misses than the same number to a few pages. Therefore, it can be difficult to estimate accesses using this method.

We instead use a waiting time-based strategy to estimate how often a thread accesses a given page. The basic idea is that the average time between events that occur frequently is smaller, and therefore the time one has to wait to observe an event can be used to estimate how often the event occurs.

The measurement process begins by clearing the TLB entries for the application's heap from the core's TLB table and records the current time using the clock cycle granularity hardware timing register. The core then resumes execution of the application's thread. During execution, when the application accesses a page in the heap for the first time after the measuring process is initialized, it will miss in the TLB cache and cause a software interrupt, and the TLB interrupt handler will record the time of the miss. When the measuring process finishes, it has computed waiting times for all pages that were accessed during the measuring process.

Our implementation triggers the measuring process many times between garbage collections using the timer interrupt. We compute the average waiting time for page accesses over the many measurements. The distribution of events affects the relation between the measured waiting time and the total number of events.

We model memory accesses to a page as a Poisson process. Poisson processes model events that occur independently of one another such as radioactive decay events. Under these assumptions, the event rate is $\lambda' = \frac{1}{t_{\text{wait}}}$. Alternatively, modeling memory access as periodic gives a rate estimation of $\lambda = \frac{1}{T} = \frac{1}{2t_{\text{wait}}}$, a factor of two difference. We believe that the differences arising from the distributions are acceptable as our cache tuning heuristics only needs approximate information and often makes decisions based only on relative rates.

4.3 Compensating for Garbage Collection

During the time window that we reconfigure the caching policy for a page, we must ensure that no cache contains a cache line for that page. In practice this requires stopping the application's execution on all cores. Therefore, a natural time to adapt the caching policies is when the garbage collector stops the world.

One challenge with this approach is that garbage collectors typically move objects around. The garbage collection process can split the objects from one page across two pages or can merge objects from different pages. Our collector uses the memory access statistics we have collected pre-garbage collection to estimate the memory access statistics of the heap after garbage collection.

We assume that each byte in a page is equally accessed. If a set of objects S with a size of m_{obj} bytes is moved from a page p with a total size of m_p and total access rate λ, we assume that the set S was responsible for $\frac{\lambda m_{\text{obj}}}{m_p}$ of that rate. We estimate the access rate to a page p on core i as $\lambda'_{pi} = \sum_{q \in P} \frac{\lambda_{qi} m_{\text{bytes transferred from } q \text{ to } p}}{m_q}$. Each compacting thread computes the new estimated access λ'_{pi} for all cores for each page p that it compacts into.

4.4 Caching Policies

We have implemented two static policies as references and two adaptive policies that tune the caching behavior in response to the actual application behavior:

- **All-hash:** The `all-hash` policy sets hash-for-home caching for all pages in the heap. This policy avoids hot spots. If only a few cores are actively making use of memory, this policy allows them to effectively use the caches of other cores. The downside of this policy is that all accesses are remote and nearly all cache lines effectively occupy two cache line slots (one in the local cache and one in the home cache).

- **Locally-homed:** The `locally-homed` policy homes each partition on the core that collects that partition. Each core preferentially allocates objects from its partition. This cache policy can cause pathological behavior for hot pages — such pages can overwhelm a core's cache with both the volume of remote requests and the working set may not fit in the home cache.

- **Hottest:** Homing data on the core that accesses it is more space efficient in the cache and provides faster access. However, as an application executes, data structures may migrate between threads. The hottest policy monitors page accesses and homes pages on the core that recently accessed the page the most.

- **Adaptive:** Pages that are accessed by many cores can become hot spots — if several such pages are homed on a single core, the accesses can overwhelm the core's cache and the total cached size of those pages at one time is limited to the cache of that core. Therefore, the `adaptive` policy only homes a page on a core if that core accesses the page the most and performs more than a quarter of the page's total accesses. Otherwise, it selects the hash-for-home policy for the page.

5. Evaluation

We implemented our collector and adaptive cache tuning framework in our Java compiler and runtime system, which contains approximately 130,000 lines of Java and C code. The compiler generates C code that runs on the TILEPro64 processor. The source code for our benchmarks and compiler is available on the web[1]. We executed our benchmarks on a 64-core 700MHz TILEPro64 processor. We only used 62 as 2 cores are dedicated to the PCI bus.

5.1 Benchmarks

Many traditional garbage collection benchmarks are sequential. Two modern GC benchmark suites, DaCapo and SPECjbb2005, do include multi-threaded benchmarks. We include results for SPECjbb2005. Several platform constraints prevent using the DaCapo benchmarks. Our runtime was designed to support modifications to the low-level memory management system — it runs directly on the bare hardware without an OS. An additional limitation is that our Tilera card does not contain a hard drive. Compiler limitations further limit the benchmarks we can compile.

We are unaware of any JVM or Java garbage collectors for the TILEPro64 chip and the effort to port the code generator and runtime of an existing JVM to the TILEPro64 is prohibitive. We therefore implemented the parallel mark compact collector described by Flood et al. [18] as a baseline. This collector employs dynamic work stealing during the mark phase and balances compacting load.

Benchmark	Description
SPECjbb2005 [2]	Simulates middle tier business logic
MixedAccess	Update shared and local trees and local array
GCBench [11]	Builds arrays and trees
FibHeaps [1]	Fibonacci heap
LCSS [29]	Longest Common SubSequence
Voronoi [12]	Compute and merge Voronoi diagrams
BarnesHut [12]	N-body simulation
TSP [12]	Traveling salesman problem
RayTracer [33]	Renders a large scene with objects in parallel

Figure 5. Benchmark Descriptions

Figure 5 lists our benchmarks. Finding GC benchmarks that have a very large object allocation load and scale well has proven

difficult. We therefore modified the other benchmarks (except SPECjbb2005) to execute multiple copies of the same computation. We report results for four versions:

- **fdsz:** The fdsz collector implements the mark compact collector described by Flood et al. [18]. This collector does not preserve locality and therefore we used the hash-for-home cache policy.

- **h4h:** The h4h version uses our collector and the hash-for-home homing policy for all cache lines.

- **local:** The local version uses our collector and locally homes each core's memory partitions.

- **hottest:** The hottest version uses our collector and homes pages on the core that accesses them the most.

- **adapt:** The adapt version uses our collector and the adaptive homing algorithm.

5.2 GC Performance

We split our evaluation into two components: the first part evaluates SPECjbb and the second part evaluates the remaining benchmarks.

5.2.1 SPECjbb

We first present results for SPECjbb. SPECjbb is unique among our benchmarks in that it runs for a fixed time period and measures transaction throughput. We present results for 2 cores, 4 cores, 8 cores, 16 cores, and 32 cores — the number of worker threads is one less than the number of cores. The live set of objects for this benchmark is proportional to the number of workers threads — the benchmark allocates one warehouse for each worker thread. We selected 4 heap sizes for SPECjbb — S is $1.5\times$ the minimal heap size, M is $2\times$, L is $3\times$, and H is $4\times$. We omit results for 62 cores for all heap sizes and 32 core versions for L and H heap sizes as the necessary heap space exceeds the 32-bit virtual address space.

Figure 6 presents normalized throughputs. The versions of the benchmark that use our collector (h4h, local, hottest, and adapt) perform significantly better than the fdsz collector. Note that there is a smaller difference between the h4h homing policy and the other versions of our collector. Much of the data accessed is newly allocated objects local to a core, and these versions allocate those objects primarily in memory that is locally homed.

Figure 7 presents the average time each collector takes to collect the heap once. All versions of our collector are between $2\times$ and $8.6\times$ faster than the fdsz collector. There are two primary reasons: (1) the fdsz collector incurs significant cache coherence overheads as its heap is h4h and (2) the fdsz collector makes multiple sweeps through the heap. All versions of our collector have similar performance as cache coherence (and therefore homing) is turned off during garbage collection.

Figure 8 presents the percentage of execution time each execution spends in the garbage collector as a function of the heap size. Note that because the fdsz collector makes sweeps through the entire heap including dead objects, its overhead to collect the heap grows with the heap size (larger heap sizes can result in fewer collections). While our collector's execution time is also sensitive to the heap size due to the mark bitmap, it has a negligible constant. We see that as the heap size increases our collector spends significantly less time.

Cache policies tuned for the application may work poorly for the collector. For example, an application may home a page of memory on another core than the collecting core. To address these potential performance issues, we turn off cache coherence during garbage collection. To measure the benefit of turning off cache coherence, we executed the benchmarks with cache coherence left on during collection. Figure 9 presents the garbage collection speedup due to turning off cache coherence. We see the smallest benefits for the local version — this version of the collector primarily accesses

---

[1] Tilera specific interface code is not included due to licensing issues, but the garbage collector is included.

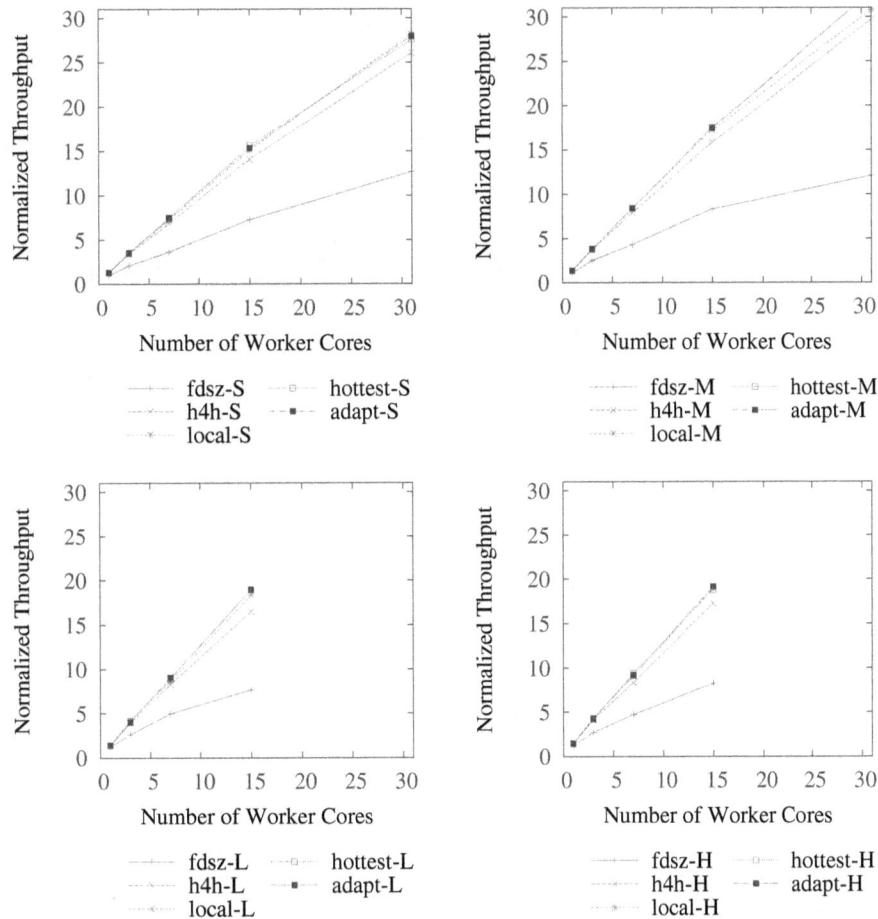

Figure 6. Throughput Normalized to 1-threaded FDSZ-S Version (higher is better)

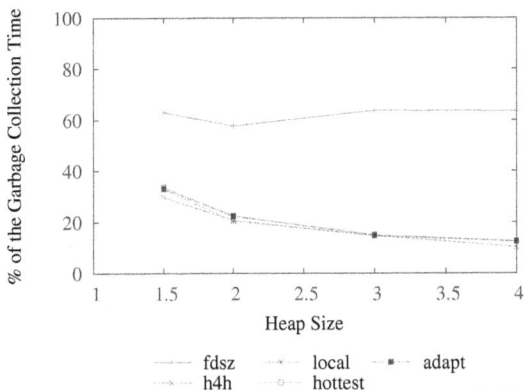

Figure 8. Percentage Time Spent in GC (15 worker cores versions)

Threads	h4h	local	hottest	adapt
1	12.5%	2.6%	11.0%	11.0%
3	15.6%	2.7%	15.0%	14.3%
7	20.3%	3.6%	30.8%	29.5%
15	21.4%	4.2%	42.4%	39.1%
31	24.1%	4.6%	47.4%	47.6%

Figure 9. Speedup from Turning Off Coherence During GC

		GC		APPLICATION	
		LOCAL	REMOTE	LOCAL	REMOTE
incoherent	h4h	151,113,750	135	154,434,824	71,517,748
	local	156,356,673	132	177,962,266	31,418,911
	hottest	157,920,761	283,812	223,777,594	19,795,376
	adapt	148,728,773	286,122	225,405,657	16,897,063
coherent	fdsz	17,665,795	97,889,718	65,902,083	32,575,816
	h4h	22,425,566	98,401,064	141,708,183	66,618,789
	local	136,820,278	9,993,122	176,170,786	29,276,631
	hottest	32,960,861	80,392,653	178,312,884	16,129,789
	adapt	31,298,317	75,769,027	168,107,310	16,134,823

Figure 10. Memory Access Counts

pages that are already homed locally, and therefore incurs minimal cache coherence overheads (it performs remote accesses only for GC data structures and load balancing). The other versions obtain significant speedups that grow with the number of cores.

Figure 10 presents the total memory access counts from the hardware performance counters for the medium heap, 31 worker core versions. These results show that: (1) cache incoherent GC greatly reduces the remote accesses during GC and (2) that the hottest and adapt versions perform fewer remote accesses during the application execution. Our incoherent GC does not perform remote accesses during GC — the recorded remote accesses are for statistics and for memory access profiling. The fdsz version performs relatively fewer application memory accesses as it spends more of its limited execution time in the garbage collector.

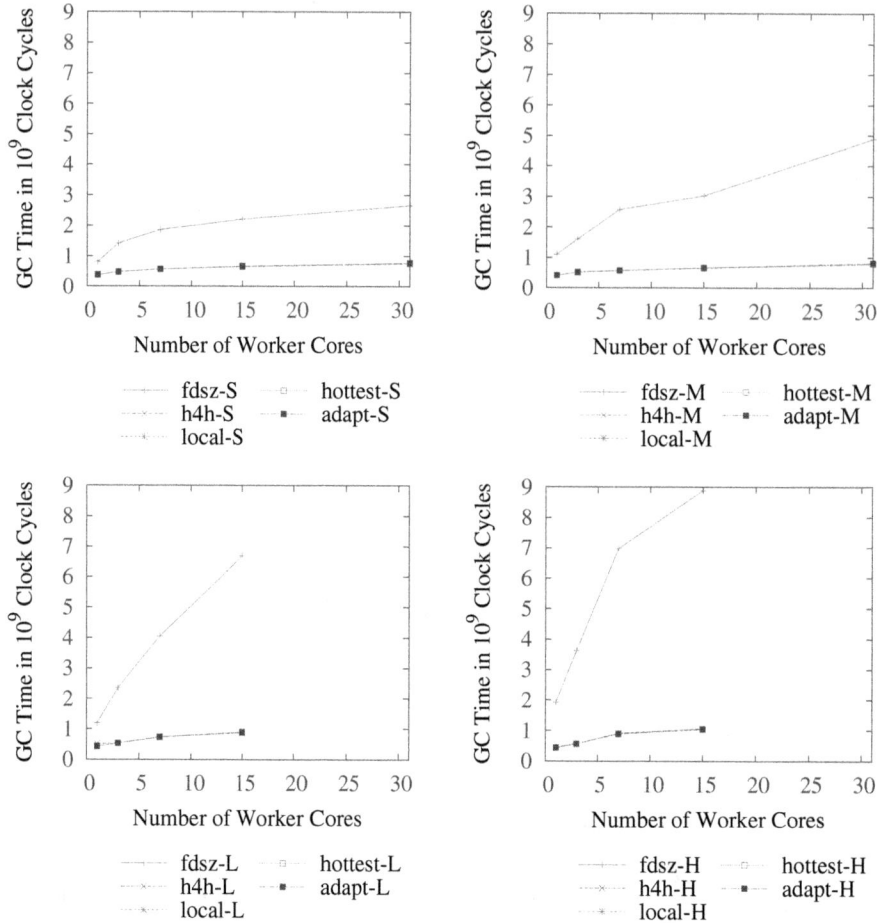

Figure 7. Average GC Time Per Collection (lower is better)

5.2.2 Other Benchmarks

Benchmark	Version	2	4	8	16	32	62
Mixed-Access	fdsz	32.43	68.89	79.22	251.68	232.47	439.46
	h4h	6.86	6.79	8.84	9.94	10.27	13.42
	local	5.55	5.62	7.43	13.30	23.47	45.61
	hottest	5.27	5.60	6.29	7.01	8.22	10.11
	adapt	5.30	5.60	6.40	7.33	8.15	9.01
GCBench	fdsz	5.26	9.14	16.07	30.35	63.11	108.47
	h4h	1.52	1.67	2.01	2.29	3.07	4.51
	local	1.40	1.41	1.52	1.55	1.78	2.27
FibHeaps	fdsz	0.75	0.88	1.01	1.08	1.24	1.44
	h4h	0.47	0.49	0.50	0.50	0.64	0.77
	local	0.41	0.43	0.41	0.41	0.53	0.55
BarnesHut	fdsz	9.41	11.32	13.22	14.54	16.17	19.10
	h4h	5.28	5.48	5.52	5.72	6.34	7.57
	local	5.07	5.37	5.25	5.24	5.65	6.51
LCSS	fdsz	2.58	3.00	3.47	3.83	4.37	5.20
	h4h	1.98	2.03	2.10	2.16	2.43	2.80
	local	1.98	1.95	1.94	1.94	2.03	2.26
TSP	fdsz	1.52	1.56	1.52	1.57	1.63	1.84
	h4h	1.36	1.42	1.52	1.38	1.40	1.49
	local	1.34	1.32	1.38	1.35	1.38	1.40
Voronoi	fdsz	1.20	1.39	1.75	2.04	2.90	4.78
	h4h	0.95	0.98	1.07	1.04	1.12	1.40
	local	0.90	0.94	0.91	0.92	0.95	1.12
RayTracer	fdsz	4732.28	4365.18	2646.02	1274.70	578.96	305.73
	h4h	3882.02	3674.44	2141.16	1073.34	554.46	308.73
	local	4313.14	3995.34	2023.85	1112.94	641.88	458.75
	hottest	3961.88	3828.35	2013.39	1041.31	524.44	309.27
	adapt	4298.56	3731.31	1925.55	992.21	523.69	284.71

Figure 11. Execution Times in 10^9 Clock Cycles. Lower is better.

Figure 11 presents execution times for the remaining benchmarks. The top of each column gives the number of cores for Figures 11, 12, and 14. We omit results for the hottest and adapt versions of the benchmarks other than MixedAccess and RayTracer as those benchmarks only access data allocated on the local core (they have similar performance to local). Nearly all versions are faster with our collectors than fdsz. We see a few exceptions for RayTracer. RayTracer has a large scene that is shared by all threads. The local version attempts to home the large scene on one core and therefore creates a hot spot while the fdsz version uses the hash-for-home policy that effectively resolves this problem. The h4h versions are slower than the local versions for benchmarks other than RayTracer because these benchmarks primarily access locally allocated data and therefore do not exhibit hot spots. Figure 12 presents the total time spent in garbage collections. Our collectors scaled significantly better than fdsz as core counts increase.

Figure 13 presents a breakdown of time spent in our collector. On average, the mark phase takes 47.1% of the time, the planning phase takes 12.0%, and the update phase takes 40.9%.

We also measured the speedups from turning off cache coherence during garbage collection. Figure 14 presents the garbage collection speedup from turning off cache coherence. We see smaller speedups for local versions because they make relatively few remote accesses. Turning off cache coherence incurs the overhead of flushing the cache and DTLB twice — this overhead is hard to overcome for small collections with relatively few remote accesses.

12

Benchmark	Version	2	4	8	16	32	62
Mixed-Access	fdsz	17.10	31.95	64.92	121.91	224.69	428.83
	h4h	1.16	1.13	1.16	1.20	1.66	2.04
	local	1.16	1.14	1.12	1.18	1.30	1.47
	hottest	1.16	1.16	1.18	1.25	1.58	2.09
	adapt	1.17	1.16	1.19	1.26	1.56	2.08
GCBench	fdsz	4.50	8.19	15.03	29.13	61.53	106.23
	h4h	0.77	0.81	0.94	0.96	1.21	1.66
	local	0.77	0.78	0.83	0.91	1.13	1.55
FibHeaps	fdsz	0.33	0.46	0.57	0.61	0.74	0.87
	h4h	0.05	0.05	0.05	0.05	0.15	0.20
	local	0.05	0.05	0.05	0.06	0.14	0.17
BarnesHut	fdsz	5.04	6.72	8.25	9.75	11.28	14.08
	h4h	0.93	1.14	1.17	1.26	1.68	2.51
	local	0.95	1.16	1.10	1.18	1.58	2.12
LCSS	fdsz	1.10	1.50	1.84	2.24	2.67	3.30
	h4h	0.51	0.52	0.55	0.57	0.70	0.94
	local	0.52	0.53	0.54	0.56	0.62	0.81
TSP	fdsz	0.18	0.21	0.21	0.24	0.29	0.52
	h4h	0.06	0.06	0.06	0.06	0.07	0.10
	local	0.06	0.06	0.06	0.06	0.07	0.10
Voronoi	fdsz	0.52	0.70	1.04	1.31	2.15	3.96
	h4h	0.28	0.27	0.28	0.29	0.32	0.35
	local	0.28	0.28	0.28	0.29	0.32	0.43
RayTracer	fdsz	67.57	71.85	60.34	32.30	35.34	25.32
	h4h	1.96	1.81	2.01	2.40	3.52	7.80
	local	1.96	1.80	2.03	2.38	3.51	7.80
	hottest	2.00	1.82	2.05	2.46	3.56	7.92
	adapt	2.00	1.83	2.05	2.46	3.58	7.92

Figure 12. Total GC Time in 10^9 Clock Cycles. Lower is better.

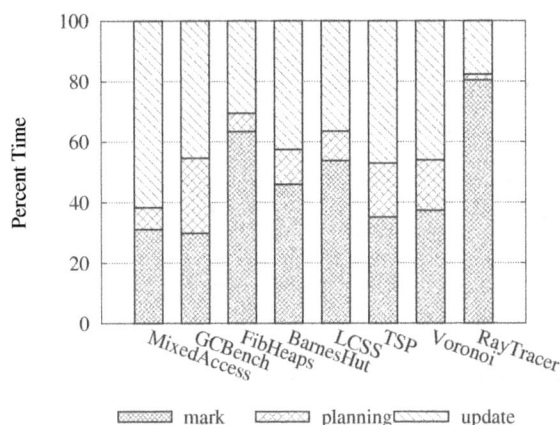

Figure 13. Breakdown of Time Spent in Collector

Benchmark	Version	2	4	8	16	32	62
Mixed-Access	h4h	10.2%	16.9%	19.6%	20.8%	11.7%	18.0%
	local	0.3%	0.6%	0.7%	0.3%	-4.8%	-7.3%
	hottest	9.3%	9.1%	8.3%	7.2%	2.2%	3.3%
	adapt	7.4%	7.8%	8.7%	7.9%	2.1%	1.9%
GCBench	h4h	10.2%	16.0%	21.8%	22.5%	14.3%	12.2%
	local	-0.8%	2.3%	3.9%	1.1%	-5.8%	-15.7%
FibHeaps	h4h	10.3%	18.5%	19.7%	22.1%	16.3%	20.3%
	local	5.5%	11.9%	8.5%	6.7%	2.9%	13.3%
BarnesHut	h4h	10.5%	14.1%	19.3%	22.3%	19.5%	14.6%
	local	-0.7%	-4.6%	5.5%	2.9%	-7.5%	-13.0%
LCSS	h4h	5.9%	10.8%	10.8%	12.1%	11.0%	9.0%
	local	0.0%	0.2%	0.6%	-0.4%	-4.2%	-6.6%
TSP	h4h	7.6%	13.2%	17.8%	17.3%	16.3%	14.0%
	local	-3.3%	0.0%	1.6%	0%	-7.5%	-7.6%
Voronoi	h4h	11.0%	17.2%	19.3%	23.1%	25.1%	14.1%
	local	0.7%	1.8%	2.8%	2.0%	1.5%	0.5%
RayTracer	h4h	6.3%	8.2%	3.6%	-1.8%	-14.1%	-12.6%
	local	-0.6%	-0.7%	-7.4%	-8.3%	-16.2%	-13.1%
	hottest	2.3%	6.7%	4.6%	1.3%	-2.2%	1.2%
	adapt	2.9%	6.8%	3.5%	1.2%	-5.0%	-0.5%

Figure 14. Speedup from Turning Off Coherence

5.2.3 Measurement Overhead

We performed an experiment to quantify the overhead of our sampling-based memory profiling technique. We implemented two versions of each benchmark: a baseline version that does not collect memory profile data and a memory profiling version that collects memory profile data but does not use it. We were unable to measure the sampling overhead using our normal sample rate because the overhead was too small relative to the measurement noise. We therefore used a profiling version that collects profiling data at 4,000 times our normal sampling rate (every 10,000 instructions) to estimate the overhead. We measured the overhead on FibHeaps and BarnesHut as 0.002% and 0.01%, respectively.

5.2.4 Discussion

The evaluation results in Figures 6, 7, 11 and 12 provide some idea of the degree each of our techniques is responsible for the performance gain. The differences between the fdsz version and the h4h version roughly shows the benefits gained by our garbage collection architecture (the h4h version distributes data across all cores much like the fdsz version). The differences between the adapt version and the h4h/local/hottest versions shows the impact of different caching policies. In general, it appears that adapt policy tends to do approximately as well as the local policy for the benchmarks that depend on locality such as SPECjbb and as well as the h4h policy for the benchmarks that create cache hotspots such as Ray-Tracer. In the MixedAccess microbenchmark, the adapt policy does better than either the local policy or the h4h policy.

6. Related Work

Imai and Tick proposed a work stealing parallel copying collector [22]. Attanasio et al. [5] explored several parallel garbage collection algorithms including both generational and non-generational versions of copying and mark-and-sweep collectors. Cheng and Blelloch [14] developed a real-time GC, in which load balancing is achieved by employing a single shared stack among all threads. Li et al. present a parallel compacting algorithm that manages dependences to compact heaps [25]. Ossia et al. [28] developed a parallel, incremental, and mostly concurrent garbage collector. Their load balancing mechanism called work packet management is similar to Imai's work pools, but their garbage collector partitions the global pool into sub-pools to reduce the atomic operations. None of these approaches address the memory locality concerns that have become important with recent processors. The Azul pauseless collector [16] and C4 collector [35] are designed for platforms that provide relatively uniform memory access.

Bacon et al. [6] developed a parallel collector based on reference counting that uses a cycle detection to collect cyclic garbage.

Load balancing between threads is a common theme in these collectors. Many algorithms incur synchronization overheads to ensure load balancing. Our approach avoids the need for dynamic load balancing during collection (and its synchronization overhead) by using a collection and allocation strategy that balances the work.

Endo et al. [17] developed a parallel mark-and-sweep collector based on work stealing. Their work does not address memory fragmentation. Oancea et al. [27] presented a parallel tracing algorithm which associates the worklist to the memory space. Similarly to our approach, it also partitions the heap into regions. However, it does not statically map heap partitions to cores or processors. Instead, it binds worklists to heap partitions and lets the processors steal worklists. This work ignores fragmentation over the shared heap, which makes it difficult to support larger objects. Shuf et al. [32] presented a region-based traversal algorithm that can reduce GC time by using regions to improve the locality of heap traversals.

The region-based approach is similar in aspects to our work, but it is used in a different with different goals.

Cell GC [15] adapts the Boehm-Demers-Weiser garbage collector for the Cell processor. It offloads the mark-phase to the synergistic co-processors to free the host processor for other computations.

Marlow et al. present a block-based, parallel copying collector [26]. This collector copies objects first and then uses blocks to structure parallelization of scanning objects. This collector does not attempt to keep objects in the memory that is local to the allocating core and has to use separately allocated memory for objects larger than the block size. Immix is a region-based, parallel collector that uses defragmentation to defragment space within a region [10]. Unlike our collector, it is not designed to support objects that are larger than a region. Anderson explores the use of private nurseries to limit cache-coherence traffic over the bus [4]. They find that bus traffic becomes problematic with as few as 4 cores.

R-NUCA explores OS control of cache placement on tiled processors [21]. The motivation for this work is avoiding hardware support for cache coherence. We address a different problem — they only determine whether a page is shared while we tune the caching policy for the memory traffic to a shared page. Software control of cache policies has been studied in other contexts. Sherwood [31] used TLB entries to map pages to regions of the cache. Explicit regions provide an alternative to garbage collection [19].

Ungar and Adams implemented a Smalltalk virtual machine on a Tile64 chip [37]. Their implementation contains special support for read-mostly objects to minimize the overhead incurred by cache coherence. The Barrelfish operating system supports using system-specific knowledge to schedule related tasks to improve cache behavior through cache warming [30]. The Hoard allocator [8] uses thread local heaps to avoid false sharing of cache lines.

In the context of garbage collection, algorithms that use feedback to dynamically switch collectors have been proposed [34].

7. Conclusion

Tuning applications for many-core processors requires careful attention to memory locality. Developers need to simultaneously manage memory accesses locality and balance the memory accesses evenly across both the caching system and multiple memory controllers. We have implemented two techniques that automatically improve the memory behavior of applications on many-core processors. Our garbage collector balances data locality concerns with heap utilization and fragmentation concerns to achieve good performance while maintaining the abstraction of a single large heap. We developed a dynamic technique that measures an application's memory behavior and tunes the caching system on the fly to optimize performance. Our experience on our benchmarks indicates that our approach can significantly improve performance due to improved locality, parallelism, and load balancing. Moreover, many-core chips of the future should expose some of the memory allocation policies to the software system as there is significant performance variability depending on the use case.

Acknowledgments

This research was supported by the National Science Foundation under grants CCF-0846195 and CCF-0725350. We would like to thank the anonymous reviewers for their helpful comments.

References

[1] nobench. http://www.cs.york.ac.uk/fp/nobench/, 2007.

[2] http://www.spec.org/jbb2005/, 2011.

[3] D. Abuaiadh, Y. Ossia et al. An efficient parallel heap compaction algorithm. In *OOPSLA*, 2004.

[4] T. A. Anderson. Optimizations in a private nursery-based garbage collector. In *ISMM*, 2010.

[5] C. Attanasio, D. Bacon et al. A comparative evaluation of parallel garbage collector implementations. In *LCPC*, 2001.

[6] D. F. Bacon, C. R. Attanasio et al. Java without the coffee breaks: A non-intrusive multiprocessor garbage collector. In *PLDI*, 2001.

[7] K. Barabash and E. Petrank. Tracing garbage collection on highly parallel platforms. In *ISMM*, 2010.

[8] E. D. Berger, K. S. McKinley et al. Hoard: A scalable memory allocator for multithreaded applications. In *ASPLOS*, 2000.

[9] S. M. Blackburn, R. L. Hudson et al. Starting with termination: A methodology for building distributed garbage collection algorithms. In *ACSC*, 2001.

[10] S. M. Blackburn and K. S. McKinley. Immix: A mark-region garbage collector with space efficiency, fast collection, and tutator performance. In *PLDI*, 2008.

[11] H. Boehm. GCBench. http://www.hpl.hp.com/personal/Hans_Boehm/gc/gc_bench.html, 1997.

[12] B. Cahoon and K. S. McKinley. Data flow analysis for software prefetching linked data structures in Java. In *PACT*, 2001.

[13] K. M. Chandy and L. Lamport. Distributed snapshots: Determining global states of distributed systems. *TOCS*, 1985.

[14] P. Cheng and G. E. Blelloch. A parallel, real-time garbage collector. In *PLDI*, 2001.

[15] C.-Y. Cher and M. Gschwind. Cell GC: Using the Cell synergistic processor as a garbage collection coprocessor. In *VEE*, 2008.

[16] C. Click, G. Tene et al. The pauseless GC algorithm. In *VEE*, 2005.

[17] T. Endo, K. Taura et al. A scalable mark-sweep garbage collector on large-scale shared-memory machines. In *SC*, 1997.

[18] C. H. Flood, D. Detlefs et al. Parallel garbage collection for shared memory multiprocessors. In *JVM*, 2001.

[19] D. Gay and A. Aiken. Memory management with explicit regions. In *PLDI*, 1998.

[20] R. H. Halstead, Jr. MULTILISP: A language for concurrent symbolic computation. *TOPLAS*, 1985.

[21] N. Hardavellas, M. Ferdman et al. Reactive NUCA: Near-optimal block placement and replication in distributed caches. In *ISCA*, 2009.

[22] A. Imai and E. Tick. Evaluation of parallel copying garbage collection on a shared-memory multiprocessor. *TPDS*, 1993.

[23] Single-chip Cloud Computer. http://techresearch.intel.com/UserFiles/en-us/File/SCC_Sympossium_Mar162010_GML_final.pdf, 2010.

[24] H. Kermany and E. Petrank. The Compressor: Concurrent, incremental, and parallel compaction. In *PLDI*, 2006.

[25] X.-F. Li, L. Wang et al. A fully parallel LISP2 compactor with preservation of the sliding properties. In *LCPC*, 2008.

[26] S. Marlow, T. Harris et al. Parallel generational-copying garbage collection with a block-structured heap. In *ISMM*, 2008.

[27] C. E. Oancea, A. Mycroft et al. A new approach to parallelising tracing algorithms. In *ISMM*, 2009.

[28] Y. Ossia, O. Ben-Yitzhak et al. A parallel, incremental and concurrent GC for servers. In *PLDI*, 2002.

[29] W. Partain. The nofib benchmark suite of Haskell programs. In *Proceedings of the 1992 Glasgow Workshop on Functional Programming*, 1993.

[30] A. Schüpbach, S. Peter et al. Embracing diversity in the Barrelfish manycore operating system. In *MMCS*, 2008.

[31] T. Sherwood, B. Calder et al. Reducing cache misses using hardware and software page placement. In *ICS*, 1999.

[32] Y. Shuf, M. Gupta et al. Creating and preserving locality of Java applications at allocation and garbage collection times. In *Proceedings of the 17th ACM SIGPLAN Conference on Object-Oriented Programming, Systems, Languages, and Applications*, 2002.

[33] L. A. Smith, J. M. Bull et al. A parallel Java Grande benchmark suite. In *SC*, 2001.

[34] S. Soman, C. Krintz et al. Dynamic selection of application-specific garbage collectors. In *ISMM*, 2004.

[35] G. Tene, B. Iyengar et al. C4: The continuously concurrent compacting collector. In *ISMM*, 2011.

[36] Tilera. http://www.tilera.com/.

[37] D. Ungar and S. S. Adams. Hosting an object heap on manycore hardware: An exploration. In *DLS*, 2009.

The Myrmics Memory Allocator: Hierarchical, Message-Passing Allocation for Global Address Spaces

Spyros Lyberis   Polyvios Pratikakis
Dimitrios S. Nikolopoulos *

Institute of Computer Science (ICS),
Foundation for Research and Technology (FORTH)
{lyberis,polyvios,dsn}@ics.forth.gr

Martin Schulz   Todd Gamblin
Bronis R. de Supinski

Center for Applied Scientific Computing (CASC),
Lawrence Livermore National Laboratory
{schulzm,tgamblin,bronis}@llnl.gov

Abstract

Constantly increasing hardware parallelism poses more and more challenges to programmers and language designers. One approach to harness the massive parallelism is to move to task-based programming models that rely on runtime systems for dependency analysis and scheduling. Such models generally benefit from the existence of a global address space. This paper presents the parallel memory allocator of the Myrmics runtime system, in which multiple allocator instances organized in a tree hierarchy cooperate to implement a global address space with dynamic region support on distributed memory machines. The Myrmics hierarchical memory allocator is step towards improved productivity and performance in parallel programming. Productivity is improved through the use of dynamic regions in a global address space, which provide a convenient shared memory abstraction for dynamic and irregular data structures. Performance is improved through scaling on many-core systems without system-wide cache coherency. We evaluate the stand-alone allocator on an MPI-based x86 cluster and find that it scales well for up to 512 worker cores, while it can outperform Unified Parallel C by a factor of 3.7–10.7×.

Categories and Subject Descriptors   D.4.2 [*Operating Systems*]: Storage Management—Allocation/Deallocation strategies;   D.4.7 [*Operating Systems*]: Organization and Design—Distributed systems, Hierarchical design

Keywords   Parallel Memory Allocator, GAS

1. Motivation

The many-core era poses substantial challenges for programmers to harness the processing power of emerging hardware architectures. A dominant hardware paradigm is the cache-coherent shared memory machine, often paired with thread-based programming models. However, the complexity of hardware cache coherency protocols and the inefficiency of shared-memory programming models may limit this paradigm's lifetime, restricting coherency to a subset of cores on a processor or eliminating it altogether.

The main reason for this trend is that hardware cache coherency protocols do not scale as the number of on-chip cores increases. Further, at larger core-counts, verifying the hardware against timing-sensitive failures, such as race conditions, becomes so difficult that some researchers advocate abandoning cache coherency altogether [18]. However, programming non-coherent architectures can be tedious and difficult. Significant programmer expertise is required to structure code around message-passing protocols, and errors in these programs are notoriously hard to debug.

Cache-coherent, shared memory architectures with high core counts are, against general belief, also hard to program. The dominant shared-memory programming model uses threads, which resemble sequential programs and "feel" easier to programmers. However, threading requires the programmer to reason about implicit communication and interactions through shared memory. This complex, tedious and error-prone process makes threaded programs hard to test, debug and maintain. In general, writing good-quality, race-free, well performing and scalable multithreaded code is challenging [24].

Many commercial and academic programming models attempt to increase programmer productivity by abstracting away the difficult parts of parallelization and communication. However, notable examples like Intel TBB [23], OpenMP [28], and Cilk [5, 12] target cache-coherent architectures that do not scale well to high core counts. The most well-known programming models oriented towards non-coherent architectures belong to the Partitioned Global Address Space (PGAS) family of languages, such as Unified Parallel C [10], Titanium [17], X10 [8, 15], Co-array Fortran [27] and Chapel [7].

To schedule and to manage parallel tasks, existing PGAS and distributed programming models require strict control of the task footprint in memory. To meet this requirement, they restrict the use of dynamic memory in the program by making all dynamic allocation local to a task [11], or by statically limiting the available dynamic memory[1]. Conversely, an MPI program that uses dynamically allocated data structures, such as trees, must manually marshal and unmarshal them for communication. The programmer must allocate adequate space before a transfer takes place, and must rewrite any pointers after the transfer. Essentially, programmers implement the near equivalent of a PGAS or RPC runtime within the application. Therefore, dynamic memory management in the existing non-coherent programming models tends to be either:

---

* Also with the School of Electronics, Electrical Engineering and Computer Science, Queen's University of Belfast.

---

[1] The Berkeley UPC 2.14.0 we used in the evaluation imposes a static limit of 64 MB per thread for dynamically allocated memory.

- *Easy and expensive,* because the runtime does not know about application-specific structures and must assume the worst; or

- *Efficient and difficult,* because the programmer must control all transfers and synchronization — MPI, the *de facto* winner, is like "assembly" for parallel programming.

We bridge this gap by providing the programmer a middle ground. We propose a distributed memory allocation system that supports control of communication at a much higher level of abstraction than MPI-like programming. For this purpose, we borrow a well-known and well-studied construct in memory management literature: region-based memory management [30]. Regions are intuitive. They have been used to increase locality and to accelerate bulk allocation and deallocation. Successful coherent implementations of regions include stand-alone libraries and built-in programming language support. Regions offer the best of both worlds because they preserve the shared-memory abstraction while providing a mechanism to describe the desired structure of memory and control the locality and placement of memory objects. Gay and Aiken [13] have measured up to 58% faster execution times on memory-intensive benchmarks that use region-based memory management versus a conventional garbage collector.

Regions can be used to augment parallel programming models to express dynamic data structures more intuitively and efficiently. By allocating structure members in the same region, the programmer can express accessing, locking or transferring the whole structure simply by referring to the region itself. This capability enables reduced communication overhead for transferring complex, irregular, pointer-based data structures, which can be tightly packed by an underlying region-based memory allocator.

The contributions of this work are:

1. We design a distributed, Global Address Space (GAS), region-based memory allocator for non-coherent machines, which targets both MPI clusters and future many-core architectures with no support for cache coherency. To our knowledge, we are the first to introduce distributed region-based memory allocation.

2. We implement our algorithms in a runtime library that offers region-based GAS on large supercomputers, hiding MPI communication from the programmer.

3. We evaluate our techniques and implementation using representative benchmarks.

Our experimental results demonstrate that our distributed, region-based memory allocator can improve program performance by a factor of 3.7–10.7× compared to equivalent Unified Parallel C programs without support for regions.

The rest of the paper is organized as follows. Section 2 outlines the Myrmics runtime system and its stand-alone memory allocator. Section 3 presents the lowest software layer, the SLAB allocator, which manages a set of discrete heaps. Section 4 explains how the SLAB allocator is used to realize regions of the programming model. Section 5 discusses how multiple memory allocator instances cooperate to serve requests in parallel. Section 6 describes the development of benchmarks for the stand-alone version of the Myrmics memory allocator. We also measure benchmark runs in an MPI cluster and compare the Myrmics allocator to UPC.

2. The Myrmics Memory System

This paper presents the memory allocation system of the *Myrmics* runtime system, a task-based runtime for non-coherent many-core architectures. Myrmics uses distributed scheduler cores to manage memory and schedule parallel tasks on worker cores, as in other task-based programming models [2]. The Myrmics runtime is work-in-progress, but its memory allocator system is fully usable

in a stand-alone fashion with an MPI backend. For the remainder of the paper, we will use the term "scheduler" to refer only to the memory allocation functionality of the Myrmics scheduler cores.

In the Myrmics runtime system, programs are written as collections of possibly recursive tasks. Each task is atomic and cannot communicate with other tasks during its execution. However, the tasks define their memory footprint and the runtime guarantees that this memory is made available locally to the core that will execute the task code before the execution starts. The runtime resolves task dependencies and ensures the tasks will have exclusive access to the memory that they request. The programming model has been proved to execute parallel programs in a deterministic order [29].

In this work we present the stand-alone Myrmics memory allocator, which does not handle task dependency analysis or scheduling. Instead, parallel programs using the stand-alone allocator are written as follows:

- A number of *worker* cores run the application code. Each worker executes as a separate MPI process.

- A number of *scheduler* cores cooperate to serve requests from workers to implement a global address space. Each scheduler also executes as a separate MPI process.

- Workers do not make local heap calls; instead, they send requests to a designated scheduler, which answers with objects that have unique system-wide addresses.

- Workers may send or receive data to/from other workers only by specifying heap objects that have been allocated previously by a scheduler. Data sent in this way is visible on the other end at the same addresses.

- Objects can be arbitrarily allocated in *regions,* which are used by workers for efficient bulk transfers of multiple objects. Regions can be hierarchical in nature, supporting sub-regions.

A large chunk of virtual address space is memory mapped at all worker cores during the initialization phase. Allocation in this space is done in parallel by the scheduler cores. The Myrmics memory allocator, therefore, implements a *global address space,* much like the shared-memory aspects of the PGAS languages. Scheduler cores are organized in a hierarchy and cooperate using messages to serve the worker cores, which run the parallel application. Workers run only a small part of the allocator functionality and communicate with schedulers to service all allocation and data transfer requests. Any allocation in a worker core returns a globally unique pointer for new objects or a globally unique region ID for new regions and sub-regions.

Worker cores can access any memory location in the global address space, but the data for the location must first be received. To receive the data, workers use data objects and regions in point-to-point communication calls. A sender and a receiver worker both specify which objects or regions they want to exchange. The Myrmics memory allocator ensures that data is sent to the correct locations. The receiver can then safely access the data at the same memory addresses as the sender. This mechanism enables pointer-based data structures to be traversable using the same pointers locally, assuming all needed data has been transferred. In the stand-alone memory allocator, the application must ensure that all needed data is requested before any pointers are accessed.

To scale to a large number of cores, Myrmics runs the main parts of the runtime, including its distributed memory allocator, on multiple dedicated scheduler cores. We use dedicated scheduler cores to optimize for locality of the runtime's metadata, remove allocator-related communication from the application's critical path, and amortize much of the allocator's cost.

This work bridges the gap between limited use of dynamic memory in PGAS systems and manual message-passing distributed programming, by providing support for distributed, region-based dynamic memory management and implementing a global address space from dynamic regions. Regions, also called *arenas* [16], are growable memory pools that contain objects or other sub-regions. Traditionally, regions are used for fast allocation and deallocation of objects that share the same lifetime, and to control and improve locality. We reuse this abstraction to enable distributed programs to use dynamic memory without requiring explicit data marshaling and unmarshaling or restricting the scope of dynamically allocated objects.

The Myrmics memory allocator allows the programmer to create regions and sub-regions, allocate objects dynamically within them, and use arbitrary pointers to create dynamic data structures. The distributed allocator guarantees a global address space among all cores so any region can be transferred to any core without translating any pointers in the allocated data. Consider, for instance, a dynamically linked list: to transfer the whole list in MPI, the program would have to traverse it, serialize the "next" pointers, to send each data item, and re-establish the pointers after the transfer. Conversely, a UPC program would also traverse the list and send each item, while using an expensive "fat" pointer to the next element. In comparison, the Myrmics memory allocator allows the programmer to allocate the whole list in a region (and possibly sub-regions). Thus, the whole region can automatically be packed and sent efficiently. After the transfer, the receiver can traverse the list using the existing, all-local, list pointers.

3. SLAB Allocator

3.1 Overview

The lowest layer of the Myrmics memory management system is the SLAB allocator. It manages the dynamic allocation and freeing of memory objects of any size organized in *slabs*, which are packed groups of same-sized objects.

SLAB allocation is a well-established method [6], widely employed for memory allocation in operating system kernels. Its primary advantages are that it has a simple implementation — allowing fast, constant-time allocate and free operations — and that it avoids external fragmentation because the kernel allocates a small variety of object sizes. Typically, an operating system will also benefit from caching objects that use slabs. For instance, if all allocations and frees of mutexes happen from the same set of memory addresses, then reinitialization of all fields of a freshly allocated mutex is often unnecessary.

In the taxonomy of memory allocation policies [21], SLAB allocation belongs to the simple segregated storage family. To minimize the code and to maximize cache efficiency, we use the same allocator for runtime system heap management and to implement the system calls for application heap management. The Myrmics allocator differs from existing segregated storage allocators in several ways. First, we observe that the runtime kernel uses only a few size classes. Applications in general tend not to use too many classes[2]; we target high-performance applications that tend to have even more disciplined memory requirements. Therefore, we relax the requirement that size classes must be a power of two and instead we support as many classes as requested with the restriction that every size must be aligned to the size of a cache line, such as 64 B. This versatility reduces fragmentation and usually leads to better cache utilization. Second, since we target message-passing archi-

tectures, we design the slabs so that their metadata are carefully separated from the data, which increases the efficiency of hardware transfers and facilitates moving whole regions with fewer operations.

3.2 Design

The system uses two configurable sizes for the basic quantities of allocation. The *slab size,* set to 4 KB, is the basic unit used internally in each allocator instance to allocate a chunk of memory. The *page size,* set to 1 MB, represents the basic unit at which different allocator instances trade free address ranges. It is also the basic unit at which schedulers request memory from the operating system (or directly from the hardware, when the Myrmics allocator is used in bare-metal setups). Whenever a memory allocation request is completed, the requested size is adjusted upwards to a 64-B aligned *slot size*. Objects belonging to the same slot size are serviced from the same set of slabs.

To index memory, the allocator uses a custom 8-degree Trie library, which is tuned to fit into the minimum 64-B slot size. Tries support fast, constant-time searches. We prefer them over hash tables for their deterministic performance as well as their added abilities to offer approximate searches and ordered walks. Three different tries are used in the allocator: the *Used Trie* holds an entry for each full or partial slab that is in use, keyed by the slab starting address. The *Partial Trie* holds the head of a linked list for each slot size that is currently active, keyed by the slot size. The *Free Trie* holds an entry for each free range of slabs available in the allocator, keyed by the starting address of the range. We employ a number of performance optimizations, such as *(i)* preallocating empty slabs for commonly used slot sizes, *(ii)* avoiding frequent Trie updates through lazily returning free slabs and *(iii)* eliminating the referencing of intermediate slabs to support efficient allocation and freeing of arbitrarily large slot sizes.

Each allocator supports multiple *slab pools* that operate independently using their own sets of slabs. Moreover, upon creation of each pool, we specify which other pool will be used for its metadata. The separation of metadata from data is crucial to support efficient region-based communication. The "recursion" of slab pool metadata stops at the runtime kernel slab pool, which handles its own metadata, as we explain below.

The SLAB allocator, including the trie library, occupies roughly 4,000 lines of C code.

3.3 Usage for Runtime Kernel Heap

In order for Myrmics to be portable to distributed memory machines — which may have no operating system, as with accelerator processors — we use the same SLAB allocator for the application and for the runtime kernel heap management, through the use of separate slab pools. The kernel heap slab pool is an exception, in the sense that its metadata are kept in the same slab pool along with the heap data under allocation. This combination is not straightforward. For example, allocating a new 64-B object in the kernel may require new 64-B trie nodes that are recursively allocated by the same code path into the same memory space. Specifically, this behavior may run into two problems: where to allocate the dynamically allocated metadata (like trie nodes) for the kernel heap pool and how to bootstrap the system.

To solve the first problem, we treat the kernel heap slab pool specially, by imposing additional constraints for preallocating empty slabs. For all object sizes necessary for the allocator data structures, we ensure that a minimum of empty slabs is left after any allocation is finished. If there are too few, we raise a flag, and as soon as the (possibly recursive) allocation/free requests are served we replenish the empty slabs from the Free Trie as needed. This procedure guarantees that we can satisfy any kernel slab pool

---

[2] Johnstone and Wilson [21] measured that for typical applications 90% of all objects allocated were of just 6.12 different sizes, 99% of all objects were of 37.9 sizes, and 99.9% of all objects were of 141 sizes.

```
// Region management
rid_t sys_ralloc(rid_t parent, int level_hint);
void  sys_rfree(rid_t region);

// Object management
void *sys_alloc(size_t size, rid_t region);
void  sys_free(void *ptr);
void  sys_realloc(void *old_ptr, size_t new_size,
                  rid_t new_region);
void  sys_balloc(size_t size, rid_t region,
                 int num_objects, void **objects);

// Communication
void  sys_send(int peer_worker_id,
               rid_t *regions, int num_regions,
               void **objects, int num_objects);
void  sys_recv(int peer_worker_id,
               rid_t **regions, int num_regions,
               void ***objects, int num_objects);
void  sys_barrier();
```

Figure 1. The stand-alone Myrmics memory allocator API

request solely from the preallocated empty slabs by setting bitmap bits and without perturbing trie structures, which could require further allocator requests. Thus, we allow allocator requests to recurse as needed, knowing that they can be fulfilled without further recursion when they reach the lowest pool.

We bootstrap the kernel heap slab pool by initially assigning the needed number of preallocated empty slabs in a linear fashion. During boot, kernel heap allocations receive objects from the predefined slabs and the kernel tracks which slots are allocated. To leave the bootstrap mode, we perform normal allocation calls for all tracked objects, which set up all needed data structures with new linearly allocated objects. Eventually, this process converges[3] and when all objects are accounted for, the system is bootstrapped and the linear allocation is abandoned in favor of the normal one.

4. Local Memory Allocation

4.1 Overview

The intermediate layer in the Myrmics memory allocator uses the SLAB allocator to support hierarchical regions that are local to a scheduler instance. Figure 1 lists the basic set of system calls that implement the programming model application interface. The user allocates a new region with the `sys_ralloc()` call under an existing parent region or the default top-level root region. A unique, non-zero *region ID*, which represents the new region, is returned. We explain the use of the optional `level_hint` in Section 5. A region is freed using the `sys_rfree()` call, which destroys the region, all objects belonging to it and its children regions.

A new object is allocated by the `sys_alloc()` system call, which returns a pointer to its base address. The object may belong to any user-created region or the default top-level root region, represented by region ID 0. Objects are destroyed by the `sys_free()` call and can also be resized and/or relocated to other regions by the `sys_realloc()` call. Since the programming model requires all memory allocation to be done through system calls that induce worker-scheduler communication, we also provide the `sys_balloc()` call, which allocates a number of same-sized ob-

---

[3] It converges because kernel objects are smaller than 4 KB: most allocations complete using the empty slabs and only a few need new slabs that require new trie nodes.

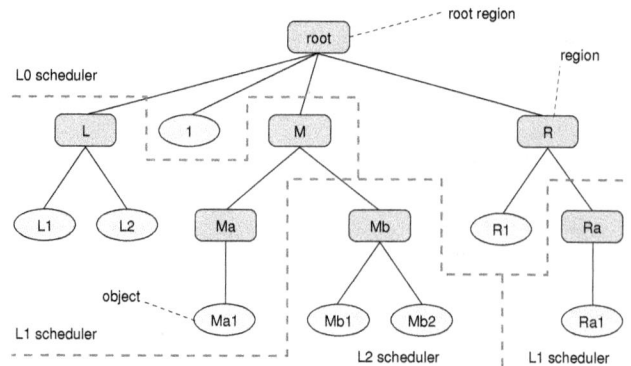

Figure 2. An example of a Region Tree. Dotted lines show how the Region Tree can be split among multiple schedulers.

jects in bulk and returns a set of pointers. This call minimizes communication for common cases like the allocation of table rows.

We globally construct a *Region Tree,* such as the one shown in Figure 2, based on the relationship of user-allocated regions and objects. When the application starts, only the default "root" region exists. A scheduler core handles a part of the global region tree. This portion includes whole regions and any objects that belong to them, but not necessarily all of their descendants. The latter may belong to another scheduler core deeper in the hierarchy.

4.2 Design

We use a new slab pool to build each local region when it is created. We dedicate the equivalent of a separate heap to each region for many reasons. Our model hinges on communicating whole regions rather than individual objects, and the transfer of regions should therefore be as compact as possible. Packing region objects in dedicated slabs helps to isolate them from other regions and to enable communication on slab-based quantities. Further, a future design choice of migrating region responsibility among schedulers becomes feasible because different slab pools have carefully separated metadata. Allocating a new slab pool per region increases fragmentation, because partially filled and preallocated empty slabs are dedicated for the new region. We consider this tradeoff to be acceptable since many future object allocations in the region will happen quickly and will be compacted with other region objects, increasing communication efficiency and locality of region objects.

Apart from the creation of a new slab pool and the basic bookkeeping for the part of the Region Tree that is local, each scheduler contains four main data structures, which are also based on the same trie library. The first two are the *Used Ranges* and the *Free Ranges* Tries. The former tracks which local region uses which ranges of slabs. The latter contains ranges of slabs that the allocator can give to local slab pools that request more memory. These tries enable the allocator to determine in constant time which region is responsible for freeing an arbitrary pointer or which is the nearest set of free slabs to give to a slab pool under pressure, in order to keep region addresses as compact as possible.

For similar reasons, and using similar code paths, we use two more tries: the *Used Region IDs* tracks which region IDs are handled locally and the *Free Region IDs* contains the IDs that can be assigned to new regions. These tries enable quick translation of the globally unique, programmer-visible region IDs to the slab pools and region data structures, which are internal to each scheduler.

We use an adaptive mechanism that is based on watermarks to control the limit of external fragmentation. Initially, when the allocator is not under memory pressure, the number of slabs that

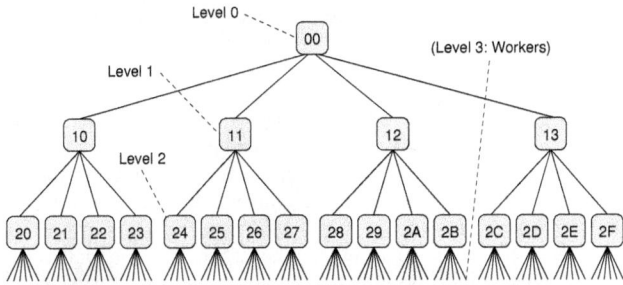

Figure 3. Organization of three scheduler levels, with a 4→1 scheduler-to-scheduler ratio. Assuming a 8→1 scheduler-to-worker ratio, each level 2 scheduler owns eight workers (not shown).

populate a new region's free pool is set to the high watermark. If and when many regions are requested by the application, the allocator reclaims increasing numbers of free slabs from the regions that have free memory above the current threshold. These are then used for the new regions. This process stops when all local regions have free memory equal to the low watermark, at which point the scheduler will communicate with its parent to request more pages. This policy reduces communication and balances increased locality of region objects with increased fragmentation.

4.3 Complexity

The local region layer adds a single trie lookup to most common-case operations for allocating and freeing objects. We consult the Used Ranges or Used Region IDs Tries to translate the pointer or region ID of the programming model API to a slab pool.

To allocate a new region, when the local allocator has enough memory and region IDs, it takes a new region ID from the Free Region IDs Trie and a range of slabs from the Free Ranges Trie. We create a new slab pool, initializing all related structures described in Section 3. In the case of increasing memory pressure between the high and low watermarks, local regions are visited — starting from the one last visited — possibly to trim free slabs. If we have already performed this process and still need more memory, we use inter-scheduler communication to request more memory.

Freeing regions is fast and independent of the number of allocated objects. We destroy the region slab pool by discarding its data structures altogether and returning all used and free slab ranges to the scheduler Free Ranges Trie. The programming model assumes that if the region has children regions, all of them are also destroyed. Thus, the complexity of hierarchical region freeing grows linearly with the number of children regions.

Transferring regions adds a new intra-scheduler operation on top of those required by the programming model API. *Region packing* accumulates a list of starting addresses and sizes that correspond to the memory usage of a region. The list encompasses all region objects as well as all children region objects. For each region involved, all slabs in the pool that are full or partially full are traversed in order[4] and a list is built by coalescing adjacent slabs on the fly, further increasing communication efficiency.

The local regions layer is 2,000 lines of C code.

---

[4] The Used Trie enables fast traversals by remembering the last visited node and following the appropriate turns on the trees to find the next one.

5. Distributed Allocation

5.1 Overview

A single memory allocator instance can service a limited number of requests from workers efficiently. All memory allocation calls involve scheduler-worker communication, so we must keep the latency of these operations low. As we have not yet implemented the rest of the runtime system, we do not know the full impact of other important scheduler duties, such as task arguments dependency analysis. Thus, the memory allocation system must scale to a high number of schedulers, the number and organization of which we will finalize in the future.

We organize the multiple scheduler instances, which contain only the memory allocator and basic interprocessor communication mechanisms, in a tree hierarchy, as Figure 3 shows. The tree has one top-level scheduler with a configurable number (equal to the *scheduler-to-scheduler ratio*) of next-level children. The scheduler tree descends for some levels. We attach multiple worker cores (equal to the *scheduler-to-worker ratio*) to each lowest-level scheduler. Processor cores can communicate directly only with cores that are one level above or below them in the hierarchy. This restriction targets future mesh-based, many-core hardware messaging layers by localizing communication patterns. It also helps to expose hardware locality constraints to the software architecture.

We divide work between schedulers based on the regions that are local to them. Figure 2 shows an example of how we can split the Global Region Tree among four schedulers. The mechanisms that we described in Section 4 handle all objects that belong to local regions. Worker access to objects and regions that are not local to the lowest-level scheduler incurs inter-scheduler communication so that the scheduler that is responsible for the region can handle the request. In Myrmics, the scheduling system primarily attempts to minimize this cost. The workers closest to the schedulers that handle the related regions should run the tasks. Another alternative, which we leave for future work, would migrate region metadata among schedulers in order to balance the load of irregular cases.

5.2 Design

The highest layer of the memory allocator is an expandable, generic, asynchronous, event-based server. If an incoming event refers to a local region, the server immediately processes it and responds. Otherwise, the server forwards the event to its parent or child schedulers. Replies from other schedulers are intercepted if they refer to pending actions for which the local scheduler awaits reply. Otherwise we forward them to the original requesters. Finally, we support reentrant events with saved local state for more complex situations in which we can handle part of the request locally or the final response should be assembled from multiple remote responses.

We assign regions to schedulers using both an optional level hint from the programmer and load-balancing criteria. The application may know how many levels of regions it will create, so it can help position the new region at an appropriate level within the region hierarchy, which the runtime translates to a scheduler level. Thus, we use the hint to estimate the "vertical" positioning of a region on the scheduler hierarchy. If the user does not supply a level hint, we assign new regions to lower-level schedulers. We use load balancing to determine the "horizontal" positioning; a non-leaf scheduler that must assign a new region to one of its children does so by selecting the one with the lowest region load. Schedulers periodically exchange upstream load information messages, whenever the previous reported load differs by a configurable threshold. Thus, higher-level schedulers always know the load status of their entire subtrees with a programmable degree of certainty.

The top-level scheduler initially owns all memory and all region IDs. During boot, middle- and low-level schedulers request chunks of both from their parent schedulers. The chunk, which represents a high watermark, is proportional to the total number of descendant schedulers. When a scheduler cannot service more requests by the internal balancing mechanism described in Section 4, or when a local request brings the free pools below a low watermark, the scheduler requests and receives more memory and/or region IDs from its parent. Extra memory pages and/or IDs are piggybacked to the last request to bring the scheduler back to the high watermark level without additional messages. Memory among schedulers is always traded in whole 1-MB page boundaries.

Schedulers know how to route requests for remote regions and objects by extending the Used Ranges and Used Region IDs Tries of non-leaf schedulers to include which child is responsible for the next hop. We tightly couple this mechanism to the memory and region ID assignment described above, so the information is readily available and does not require extra communication.

5.3 Complexity

When a worker core issues a memory allocation request that its leaf scheduler cannot handle, the request must pass through a number of schedulers in the hierarchy before they reach the the scheduler that can handle it. For each hop, we access the Used Ranges or Used Region IDs Tries to determine if (part of) the request can be handled locally. If not, but the tries contain an entry, we forward the request to the appropriate child scheduler, which is either directly responsible or knows to which of its children to delegate the request. If the address or region ID is not in the tries, we forward the request to the parent scheduler. Finally, if the top-level scheduler does not contain a corresponding entry, then we propagate error handling responses down the tree to indicate a programmer error. Programmer errors include freeing an invalid pointer and allocating an object in a nonexistent region. Thus, all non-local memory allocation requests incur a cost that is logarithmically proportional to the distance to the responsible scheduler in network hops. This cost is generally low since we assign tasks to workers as close to the data as possible.

The boundary cases of scheduler responsibilities present slightly more complex cases. In the example of Figure 2, creating region Mb as a child of region M requires a few additional messages between the two schedulers, since the L1 scheduler cannot fully complete the delegation to a child region for which the region ID is unknown at creation time. Handling of this and similar cases, such as deleting boundary regions or hierarchically packing regions that multiple schedulers own, is straightforward but generally requires more inter-scheduler communication. We create reentrant, stateful events that track each scheduler's local progress, until the operation completes successfully.

The distributed memory layer is written in 3,000 lines of C code.

6. Evaluation

6.1 Benchmark design

To evaluate the Myrmics memory allocator, we developed a number of microbenchmarks as well as two larger, application-quality benchmarks. We used a number of small test programs to test the allocator and to verify its correctness. Apart from these, we also present the results on four benchmarks: (i) a non-MPI, single-core, random object allocator that analyzes the fragmentation inside a region slab pool, (ii) a parallel, region-based, Barnes-Hut N-body simulation application, (iii) a parallel, region-based, Delaunay triangulation application and (iv) a comparison to Unified Parallel C for dynamically allocated lists.

In this section, MPI processes request all memory in advance from the Linux kernel, through large `mmap()` calls. This memory is subsequently managed by the memory allocator by intercepting all glibc allocation calls: we use a single runtime kernel slab pool for both the allocator and for MPI. The runtime kernel slab pool is private per processor, but we do not otherwise separate address spaces or vary privilege levels. For the stand-alone Myrmics allocator, the API of Figure 1 provides three calls. The `sys_send()` and `sys_recv()` calls take a target MPI rank and a variable number of region IDs or object pointers as arguments. Internally, we translate these arguments to lists of addresses and sizes (by packing regions and querying pointers) and then wrap around the respective `MPI_Send()` and `MPI_Recv()` calls. Also, a `sys_barrier()` call performs an MPI barrier among all worker cores.

All MPI-based measurements are done on the Lawrence Livermore National Laboratory *Atlas* cluster. Atlas has 1,152 nodes, each of them equipped with four Dual core AMD Opteron 2.4 GHz processors and 16 GB of main memory. The machines are interconnected with an Infiniband DDR network.

6.2 Fragmentation measurements

Our first benchmark, a serial program, allocates and frees objects within a single region. The application tracks all allocated pointers and randomly either allocates an additional object or frees a randomly chosen existing object. Figure 4a presents an execution for single-sized 192-B objects, with a 60% probability of allocating a new one and 40% probability to free one. The dotted gray line shows the application-requested size of all active objects with units on the left Y axis. The right Y axis shows the number of full and partial slabs. While the total number of objects grows, the allocator can compact most objects into full slabs; the number of partially filled slabs is kept constantly low.

Full slabs are demoted to partial ones whenever a free is performed. Figure 4b, in which we vary the alloc/free probability in phases, shows this issue more clearly. The phases can be allocation-intensive or free-intensive as indicated by the slope of the application size curve. When frees are more common, full slabs become partial as they develop "holes" of 192 bytes. When the application returns to an allocation-intensive phase, first all holes in the partial slabs are discovered and plugged. We observe that this behavior is consistent with our prime concern to keep a region as packed in full slabs as possible, so that a region communication operation can access few address/size pairs.

In Figure 4c, the application runs with the same alloc/free phases, but uses six object sizes randomly during allocation. Three sizes are aligned to the slab size (64, 1024 and 4096 bytes), and the other three are not (192, 1536 and 50048 bytes). Behavior is similar to the previous measurements, although the large objects (4096 and 50048 bytes) consume correspondingly more full slabs and thus the ratio of full to partial slabs is much greater.

6.3 Barnes-Hut N-Body simulation

The second benchmark is a 3D N-body simulation application that calculates the movement of a number of astronomical objects in space as affected by their gravitational forces. To avoid $O(N^2)$ force computations, the Barnes-Hut method approximates clusters of bodies that are far enough from a given point by equivalent large objects at the clusters' centers of mass.

From the many variations of the Barnes-Hut method in the literature, we choose to start with the Dubinski 1996 approach [9], which is a well-known MPI-based implementation. This approach dynamically allocates parallel trees, parts of which are transferred among processors. Thus, it is a prime candidate for region-based memory allocation. Dubinski employs index-based structures with non-trivial mechanisms to allow for efficient transfer, pruning and

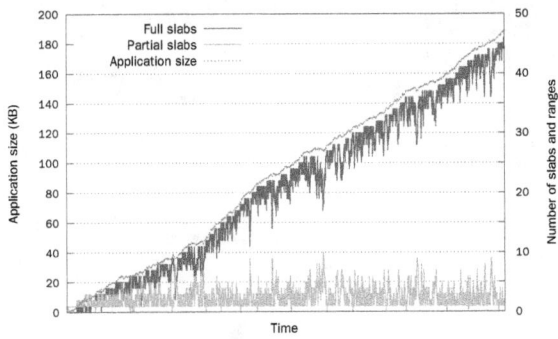

(a) Fragmentation, 192-B objects, 60% allocs, 40% frees

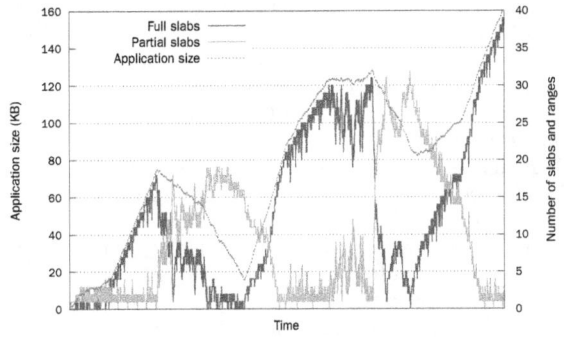

(b) Fragmentation, 192-B objects, varying probabilities

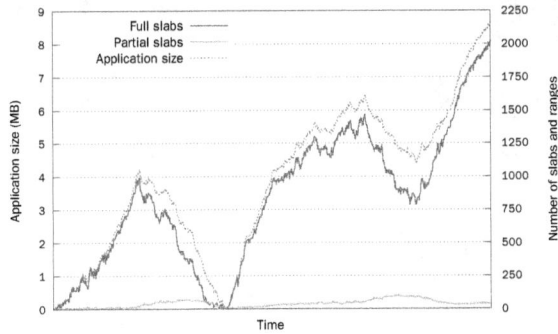

(c) Fragmentation, 6 object sizes, varying probabilities

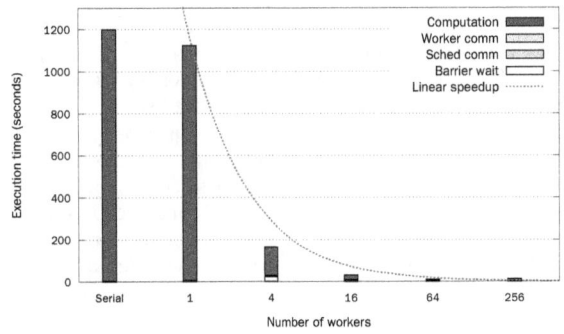

(d) Delaunay, 5M points, Single scheduler

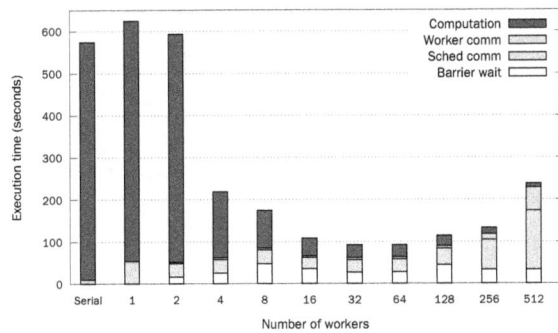

(e) Barnes-Hut, 1.1M bodies, Single scheduler

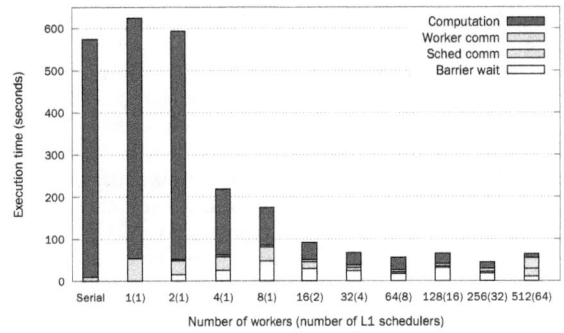

(f) Barnes-Hut, 1.1M bodies, Multiple schedulers

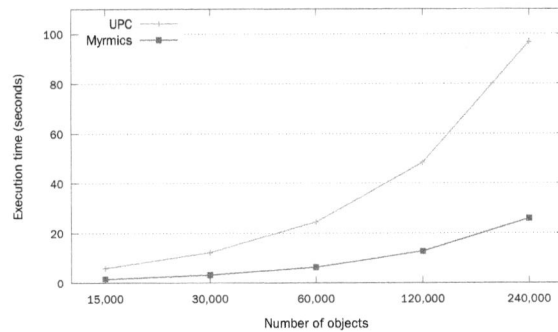

(g) UPC, 16 workers, varying number of objects

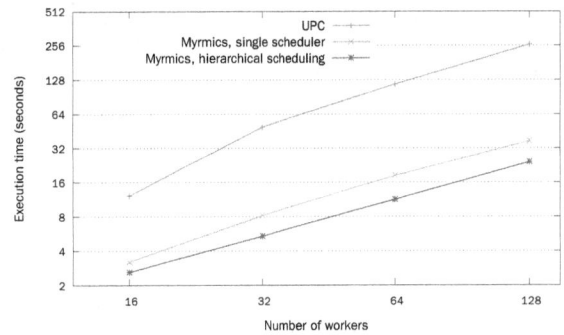

(h) UPC, 30K objects, varying number of workers

Figure 4. Evaluation of the Myrmics memory allocator using an MPI communication layer

grafting of subtrees over MPI. Our programming model supports a much more intuitive, pointer-based implementation in which we can easily graft trees since pointers retain their meaning after data transfers. MPI-based applications commonly resort to complex, "assembly-like" techniques to marshal data efficiently for transfers. The Myrmics allocator automates this tedious task.

In our benchmark, each worker core builds a local oct-tree in each simulation step for each body that it owns. We build the tree with each level belonging to a different memory region. The bounding box of the local bodies is communicated in pairs with all other workers, which compute based on that portion (*i.e.*, number of levels) of the local tree that must be sent to the communicating peer. We send the respective regions en masse. After we fetch and graft the portions of the remote trees, we perform the force simulation and body movement in isolation. A recursive bisection load-balancing stage in which we split processors into successively smaller groups follows each simulation step. We cut and exchange bodies along the longest dimension, balancing the load based on the number of force calculations that each body performed in the previous iteration. The recursive bisection load-balancer requires that the number of worker cores is a power of two.

Figure 4e presents application scaling on up to 512 worker cores with a single scheduler core. For each run, stacked bars show the average time of each worker. Time is spent either communicating with other workers ("Worker comm"), communicating with the scheduler via any other API call ("Sched comm") or doing local work ("Computation"). The first bar, marked "Serial" on the X axis, shows a single-core run in which the scheduler and a single worker are on the same processor. The next bar shows the scheduler and the single worker on separate processors. This distribution increases the cost of scheduler communication for the same work from 2% to 8%. For more worker cores, scaling is irregular, which is a data-dependent feature of the recursive bisection load balancer and the Barnes-Hut cell opening criterion, which needs more tree levels when any cell dimension exceeds certain quality constraints. Replacing the cell opening criterion gives much smoother scaling results, but unfortunately sacrifices simulation accuracy. A second observation concerns the scheduler communication time. As the application scales, each worker requires fewer allocations for its own tree, but the scheduler services more workers and its latency increases. This increase becomes a problem as early as in 32 cores, after which it grows worse. Last, worker communication becomes a bottleneck after 256 cores and overtakes the simulation time at 512 cores. Thus, the given problem size cannot scale further, which is a known limitation of this Barnes-Hut algorithm [9].

Figure 4f verifies our hypothesis that we can successfully distribute the memory allocation on multiple schedulers. In these experiments, up to eight workers are dedicated to a single scheduler. When multiple schedulers are present, they are organized in a two-level tree with a single top-level scheduler. The parenthesized number in the X axis specifies the number of leaf schedulers that we use. As expected, the scheduler communication time drops consistently as the application scales up to 128 workers. After that, the increased work needed to fetch all remote trees also involves the scheduler to pack all the remote regions; this work appears as scheduler communication time.

6.4 Delaunay triangulation

Our third benchmark, a Delaunay triangulation algorithm, creates a set of well-shaped triangles that connect a number of points in a 2D plane. Delaunay triangulation is a popular research topic with many serial and parallel algorithms. We base our code on the implementation of the serial Bowyer-Watson algorithm by Arens [1]. The algorithm adds each new point into the existing triangulation, deletes the triangles around it that violate the given quality constraints and

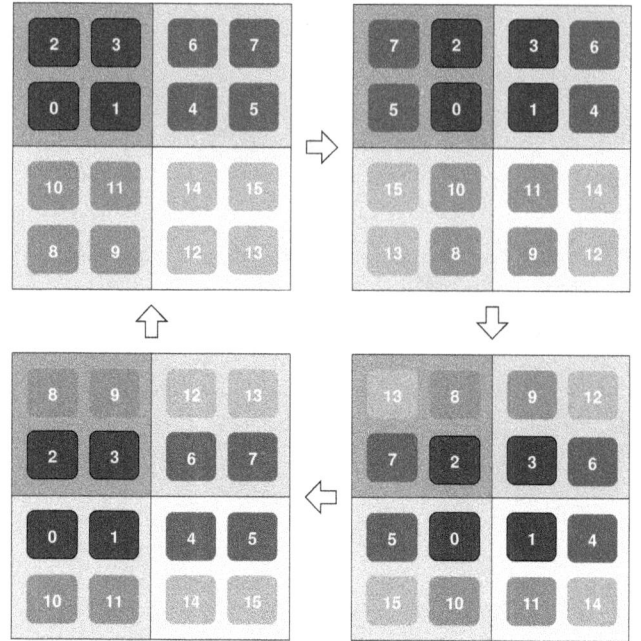

Figure 5. Parallelization of the Bower-Watson algorithm on four cores. Each core works on four sub-quadrants, which successive rotations to the right, down, left and up communicate among cores.

re-triangulates the convex cavity locally. We use the optimization that Arens described to walk the neighboring triangles in order to determine the triangles that build the cavity quickly.

The Bowyer-Watson algorithm is difficult to parallelize, so it is an active research topic; Linardakis [25] wrote an extensive survey. State of the art distributed memory approaches combine algorithms of great complexity, such as graph partitioning and multiple passes that handle the borders of the decomposition. Understanding and modifying these algorithms to use regions effectively is beyond the scope of testing and evaluating the memory allocator, so we follow a simpler parallelization approach.

Our benchmark uses a grid decomposition to divide the 2D space statically into a number of regions equal to four times the number of worker cores. Each region holds the triangles with circumcenters within its bounds. All regions are at the lowest level of a hierarchy with a degree of four; *e.g.*, the top-level master region owns the whole space and its four children own one fourth of the space. Initially, after we create all regions, the space is empty except for placeholder triangles that form the borders. A single core begins the triangulation process by inserting a small number of points up to a limit. We dynamically allocate all triangles into the appropriate last-level regions of the hierarchy, according to the triangle centers. When we have inserted enough points to create an adequate number of triangles, the core delegates the four quadrants to three other cores and to itself and the algorithm recurses with four times more workers.

Apart from the first step, in which a single core owns the entire space, points near the borders of the space owned by a core may need to modify triangles that belong to other cores. Our algorithm postpones the processing of these points, when three *re-triangulation* phases occur. Figure 5 shows the concept used with four active cores. The *main triangulation* is in the top-left, where each core owns a quadrant of space comprised of four sub-quadrants, which are the regions one level below in the region hierarchy. The first re-triangulation uses communication with other cores and rotates the four sub-quadrants to the right. For example, a point that needs triangles from regions 3 and 6 would be postponed in the main triangulation, but handled successfully by the blue core in the first re-triangulation. The two next re-triangulations rotate the sub-quadrants down and left, while a fourth rotation brings the sub-quadrants upwards back to their original position, in order to be split to more workers[5].

Figure 4d shows the results for a triangulation with 5 million points. The dotted line represents the ideal scaling. We find that the scaling is superlinear due to the increased caching effects that the division of work has over the approximately 650 MB dataset. This memory locality effect is also apparent from the difference between the serial run and the one in which a single worker communicates with a single scheduler. In contrast to the Barnes-Hut runs, the two-process run is faster despite the MPI communication.

6.5 Comparison to Unified Parallel C

With our fourth benchmark, we compare the Myrmics memory allocator to Unified Parallel C (UPC) [10]. We use the Berkeley UPC 2.14.0 for these measurements. For the most faithful comparison possible, we instruct the UPC compiler to use its MPI backend for interprocess communication.

Each worker core (in Myrmics) or thread (in UPC) begins by dynamically building a linked list of objects. After all cores are done, an all-to-all communication pattern happens in multiple stages, separated by barriers. In each stage, a pair of workers exchange their lists, the receiving core modifies all objects and the lists are swapped back to their original owners.

In UPC, we allocate the list nodes in the shared address space of each thread using the upc_alloc() call. In the exchange phase, each thread fetches a list node locally with upc_memget() for the node, modifies it and returns it to its owner with upc_memput(). In Myrmics, each worker creates a region and then allocates all list nodes inside it, which supports a more efficient exchange. To fetch a remote list, a worker fetches the whole region. We traverse the list nodes by following the pointers locally. When the whole list is modified, we send the region back in one operation.

Figure 4g shows how the benchmark performs in UPC and Myrmics. For both implementations, we use 16 worker cores/threads; in Myrmics a 17th core runs the scheduler. All list nodes are 256 B (including the shared pointer to the next node), as dynamic memory allocation requests for typical applications are on average less than 256 B [4]. The X axis shows the number of objects that are allocated for each worker list. Myrmics performs 3.7–3.9 times better. Sending or receiving the whole list in one call more than compensates for communication between the scheduler and worker, which happens for every memory allocation, and region packing, while we must communicate the list nodes one by one in UPC.

Figure 4h shows that the benchmark scales to more than 16 workers; the time scale on the Y axis is logarithmic. We keep the list size constant at 30,000 objects per core. We could not use larger problem sizes due to UPC's limits on total shared memory available. When using a single scheduler core, Myrmics outperforms UPC by a factor of 3.8–7.0×. The scheduler overhead can be further improved when using hierarchical scheduling, which makes Myrmics 4.6–10.7× faster than UPC.

7. Related Work

Serial region-based memory management. Tofte and Talpin introduced managing memory in regions for serial programs in 1997 [30] as a programming discipline to facilitate mass deallocation of dead objects in languages, replacing the garbage collector.

Memory is managed as a stack of regions and static compiler analysis determines when regions can be scrapped in their entirety, thus avoiding the expensive operations of freeing or garbage-collecting dead objects individually. Gay and Aiken implement RC [13], a compiler of an enhanced version of C for dynamic region-based memory management that supports regions and sub-regions. RC focuses on safety: reference counts are kept to warn about unsafe region deletions or to disable them. The authors claim up to 58% improvement over traditional garbage collection-based programs. Berger et al. [3] verify that region-based allocation offers significant performance benefits, but the inability to free individual pointers can lead to high memory consumption.

Parallel region-based memory management. To our knowledge, our work is the first to introduce parallel region-based allocation. Titanium [17] uses "private" regions for efficient garbage collection, in the same way as serial region-based allocators do. There is some tentative support for "shared" regions, which are implemented inefficiently with global, barrier-like synchronization of all cores. Gay's thesis [14] provides some details on the Titanium shared regions and briefly mentions a sketch of a truly parallel implementation as future work. Parallel regions in Myrmics must not be confused with the X10 language regions [8], which are defined as array subsets and not as arbitrary collection of objects.

Partitioned Global Address Spaces. PGAS languages are specifically designed to offer parallel semantics by differentiating between local and global memory accesses. Unified Parallel C (UPC) [10] is a popular example: it extends C by providing two kinds of pointers: private pointers, which must point to objects local to a thread, and shared pointers, which point to objects that all threads can access but may have affinity to specific cores. The Berkeley UPC compiler [20], which is a reference implementation, translates UPC source code to plain C code with hooks to the UPC runtime system, which manages shared memory aspects. Other well-known PGAS languages are X10 [8, 15], which defines lightweight tasks (activities) that run on specific address spaces (places), Co-Array Fortran [27], which extends Fortran 95 to include remote objects accessible through communication, Titanium [17], which extends Java to support local and global references and Chapel [7], which is a language written from scratch that aims to increase high-end user productivity by supporting multiple levels of abstractions.

Our programming model resembles PGAS since we base communication on data structures. Myrmics, however, does not pin object and region locality to cores; a task can specify any accesses and the runtime attempts to schedule the task close to the data.

Shared memory parallel allocators. For thread-based, shared-memory architectures, Hoard [4] is considered one of the best parallel memory allocators. Hoard implements a small number of per-processor local heaps, which are backed by a global heap when they run out of memory, which is backed in turn by the operating system virtual memory system. While Hoard focuses on increased throughput, Michael [26] improves on multi-threaded, lock-based allocators by presenting a scalable lock-free allocator that guarantees progress even when threads are delayed, killed or deprioritized by the scheduler. MAMA [22] is a recent high-end parallel allocator that introduces client-thread cooperation to aggregate requests on their way to the allocator. McRT-malloc [19] follows a different approach, by implementing a software transactional memory layer to support concurrent requests; threads maintain a small local array of bins for specific, small-sized slots and they revert to accessing a public free list to get more blocks; larger slot sizes than 8 KB are directly referred to the Linux kernel.

Our work resembles, in many respects, parallel memory allocators that use heap replication. Our schedulers trade address ranges hierarchically and serve requests from these ranges. In the MAMA

---

[5] Our algorithm assumes each point can be triangulated within two adjacent sub-quadrants and requires the number of workers to be a power of four.

paper, the authors describe a three-way tradeoff for memory allocators: they can only feature two of the benefits of space efficiency, low latency or high throughput. The Myrmics memory system sacrifices space efficiency (memory is hoarded by multiple schedulers and preallocated for region usage) but offers high throughput, low latency and also compactness for memory objects inside regions.

8. Conclusion

This work presents the design, implementation and evaluation of the hierarchical memory allocator of the Myrmics runtime system. To our knowledge, our implementation is the first distributed region-based memory allocator. As the number of available cores continually scales, we must evolve programming models towards easier, or more automated parallelization. Scalable memory allocation is a basic prerequisite for this transformation. Hierarchically organized region-based memory allocation is an interesting approach with many benefits for parallel programmers. It offers the programmer better control over memory management, abstracts tedious communication primitives, and allows the programmer to expose locality constraints naturally to the scheduling subsystems.

Acknowledgments

The research leading to these results has received funding from the European Union 7th Framework Programme [FP7/2007-2013], under the ENCORE (grant agreement n° 248647) and TEXT (grant agreement n° 261580) Projects.

This article (LLNL-CONF-545875) has been authored in part by Lawrence Livermore National Security, LLC under Contract DE-AC52-07NA27344 with the U.S. Department of Energy. Accordingly, the U.S. Government retains and the publisher, by accepting the article for publication, acknowledges that the U.S. Government retains a non-exclusive, paid-up, irrevocable, world-wide license to publish or reproduce the published form of this article or allow others to do so, for U.S. Government purposes.

References

[1] C. Arens. The Bowyer-Watson Algorithm; An efficient Implementation in a Database Environment. Technical report, Delft University of Technology, January 2002.

[2] E. Ayguadé, N. Copty, A. Duran, J. Hoeflinger, Y. Lin, F. Massaioli, X. Teruel, P. Unnikrishnan, and G. Zhang. The Design of OpenMP Tasks. *IEEE Transactions on Parallel and Distributed Systems*, 20(3): 404–418, 2009.

[3] E. D. Berger, B. G. Zorn, and K. S. McKinley. Reconsidering Custom Memory Allocation. In *OOPSLA '02: Proc. 2002 ACM SIGPLAN Conference on Object-Oriented Programming Systems, Languages and Applications*, pages 1–12.

[4] E. D. Berger, K. S. McKinley, R. D. Blumofe, and P. R. Wilson. Hoard: A Scalable Memory Allocator for Multithreaded Applications. *SIGPLAN Not.*, 35:117–128, November 2000.

[5] R. Blumofe, C. Joerg, B. Kuszmaul, C. Leiserson, K. Randall, and Y. Zhou. Cilk: An Efficient Multithreaded Runtime System. In *PPoPP '95: Proc. 5th ACM SIGPLAN Symposium on Principles and Practice of Parallel Programming*, pages 207–216.

[6] J. Bonwick. The Slab Allocator: An Object-Caching Kernel Memory Allocator. In *USTC '94: Proc. 1994 USENIX Summer Technical Conference*, pages 87–98.

[7] B. L. Chamberlain, D. Callahan, and H. P. Zima. Parallel Programmability and the Chapel Language. *IJHPCA*, 21(3):291–312, 2007.

[8] P. Charles, C. Grothoff, V. A. Saraswat, C. Donawa, A. Kielstra, K. Ebcioglu, C. von Praun, and V. Sarkar. X10: An Object-Oriented Approach to Non-Uniform Cluster Computing. In *OOPSLA '05: Proc. 20th Annual ACM SIGPLAN Conference on Object-Oriented Programming, Systems, Languages, and Applications*, pages 519–538.

[9] J. Dubinski. A Parallel Tree Code. *New Astronomy*, 1(2):133–147, 1996.

[10] T. A. El-Ghazawi, W. W. Carlson, and J. M. Draper. UPC Language Specifications v1.1.1. October 2003.

[11] K. Fatahalian, D. R. Horn, T. J. Knight, L. Leem, M. Houston, J. Y. Park, M. Erez, M. Ren, A. Aiken, W. J. Dally, and P. Hanrahan. Sequoia: Programming the Memory Hierarchy. In *SC '06: Proc. 2006 ACM/IEEE Conference on High Performance Networking and Computing*.

[12] M. Frigo, C. E. Leiserson, and K. H. Randall. The Implementation of the Cilk-5 Multithreaded Language. In *PLDI '98: Proc. 1998 ACM SIGPLAN Conference on Programming Language Design and Implementation*, pages 212–223.

[13] D. Gay and A. Aiken. Language Support for Regions. In *PLDI '01: Proc. 2001 ACM SIGPLAN Conference on Programming Language Design and Implementation*, pages 70–80.

[14] D. E. Gay. *Memory Management with Explicit Regions*. PhD thesis, UC Berkeley, Berkeley, CA, USA, 2001.

[15] D. Grove, O. Tardieu, D. Cunningham, B. Herta, I. Peshansky, and V. Saraswat. A Performance Model for X10 Applications. In *X10 '11: Proc. ACM SIGPLAN 2011 X10 Workshop*.

[16] D. R. Hanson. Fast Allocation and Deallocation of Memory Based on Object Lifetimes. *Software Practice and Experience*, 20:5–12, January 1990.

[17] P. N. Hilfinger, D. O. Bonachea, K. Datta, D. Gay, S. L. Graham, B. R. Liblit, G. Pike, J. Z. Su, and K. A. Yelick. Titanium Language Reference Manual, Version 2.19. Technical Report UCB/EECS-2005-15, EECS Berkeley, November 2005.

[18] J. Howard, S. Dighe, Y. Hoskote, S. R. Vangal, and D. Finan. A 48-Core IA-32 Message-Passing Processor with DVFS in 45nm CMOS. In *ISSCC '10: Proc. 2010 IEEE International Solid-State Circuits Conference*, pages 108–109.

[19] R. L. Hudson, B. Saha, A.-R. Adl-Tabatabai, and B. C. Hertzberg. McRT-Malloc: A Scalable Transactional Memory Allocator. In *ISMM '06: Proc. 2006 International Symposium on Memory Management*, pages 74–83.

[20] P. Husbands, C. Iancu, and K. Yelick. A Performance Analysis of the Berkeley UPC Compiler. In *ICS '03: Proc. 17th International Conference on Supercomputing*, pages 63–73.

[21] M. S. Johnstone and P. R. Wilson. The Memory Fragmentation Problem: Solved? *SIGPLAN Notices*, 34:26–36, October 1998.

[22] S. Kahan and P. Konecny. "MAMA!": A Memory Allocator for Multithreaded Architectures. In *PPoPP '06: Proc. 11th ACM SIGPLAN Symposium on Principles and Practice of Parallel Programming*, pages 178–186.

[23] A. Kukanov and M. Voss. The Foundations for Scalable Multi-Core Software in Intel Threading Building Blocks. *Intel Technology Journal*, 11(4), Nov. 2007.

[24] E. A. Lee. The Problem with Threads. *Computer*, 39(5):33–42, May 2006.

[25] L. Linardakis. *Decoupling Method for Parallel Delaunay Two-Dimensional Mesh Generation*. PhD thesis, College of William & Mary, Williamsburg, VA, USA, 2007.

[26] M. M. Michael. Scalable Lock-Free Dynamic Memory Allocation. *SIGPLAN Notices*, 39:35–46, June 2004.

[27] R. W. Numrich and J. Reid. Co-Array Fortran for Parallel Programming. *SIGPLAN Fortran Forum*, 17:1–31, August 1998.

[28] OpenMP ARB. OpenMP Application Program Interface, v. 3.1. www.openmp.org, July 2011.

[29] P. Pratikakis, H. Vandierendonck, S. Lyberis, and D. S. Nikolopoulos. A Programming Model for Deterministic Task Parallelism. In *MSPC '11: Proc. 2011 ACM SIGPLAN workshop on Memory Systems Performance and Correctness*, pages 7–12.

[30] M. Tofte and J.-P. Talpin. Region-Based Memory Management. *Information and Computation*, 132(2):109 – 176, 1997.

GPUs as an Opportunity for Offloading Garbage Collection *

Martin Maas, Philip Reames, Jeffrey Morlan, Krste Asanović, Anthony D. Joseph, John Kubiatowicz

University of California, Berkeley

{maas,reames,jmorlan,krste,adj,kubitron}@cs.berkeley.edu

Abstract

GPUs have become part of most commodity systems. Nonetheless, they are often underutilized when not executing graphics-intensive or special-purpose numerical computations, which are rare in consumer workloads. Emerging architectures, such as integrated CPU/GPU combinations, may create an opportunity to utilize these otherwise unused cycles for offloading traditional systems tasks. Garbage collection appears to be a particularly promising candidate for offloading, due to the popularity of managed languages on consumer devices.

We investigate the challenges for offloading garbage collection to a GPU, by examining the performance trade-offs for the mark phase of a mark & sweep garbage collector. We present a theoretical analysis and an algorithm that demonstrates the feasibility of this approach. We also discuss a number of algorithmic design trade-offs required to leverage the strengths and capabilities of the GPU hardware. Our algorithm has been integrated into the Jikes RVM and we present promising performance results.

Categories and Subject Descriptors   D.3.4 [*Processors*]: Memory management (garbage collection);   I.3.1 [*Hardware Architecture*]: Parallel processing

General Terms   Design, Experimentation, Languages, Performance, Algorithms

Keywords   parallel garbage collection, mark and sweep, SIMT, GPU, APU

1.   Introduction

Graphics Processing Units (GPUs) have been part of commodity systems for more than a decade. While frameworks such as CUDA and OpenCL have enabled GPUs to run general-purpose workloads, their additional compute power is rarely utilized other than by graphics-intensive applications (e.g. games), special-purpose computations (e.g. image processing) or scientific simulations (e.g.

fluid dynamics). In the absence of such workloads, the GPU is underutilized on most systems.

Today, we are seeing the first chips that integrate CPUs and GPUs into a single device. These changes open up a whole new set of application scenarios since they eliminate the copying overhead that is traditionally associated with moving data between the CPU and a dedicated GPU. We expect future hardware to move even further in this direction by providing a shared address space and possibly cache-coherence between CPU and GPU.

This development entails an opportunity to move traditional systems workloads to the GPU. Garbage collection appears to be a particularly good candidate for this, since garbage-collected languages such as C# and Java account for a significant portion of code running on consumer devices. Offloading their GC workloads to the GPU allows us to harvest the GPU's unused compute power, leaving the CPU free to perform other tasks such as JIT compilation, garbage collection for other memory spaces, or running mutator threads (if the GPU is used by a concurrent garbage collector).

Garbage collection is a workload that is arguably well-suited for running on the GPU, especially once the copy overhead between CPU and GPU disappears. Graph traversals (a key component of many garbage collectors) have already been efficiently demonstrated on GPUs [12].

Recent work by Veldema and Philippsen [21] has shown that garbage collection for GPU programs can be efficiently performed on the GPU itself. We take the next step and ask whether it is feasible to offload garbage collection workloads from conventional programs running on the CPU, and what it takes to achieve this goal. In this, we explore a different direction in choice of algorithm, as well as design trade-offs that are specific to our scenario. Garbage collection on the GPU is a challenging problem due to the GPU's SIMD-style programming model, and the need to design algorithms that make explicit use of available parallelism and memory bandwidth, while avoiding serialization of execution. The contributions of our work are as follows:

- We present an analysis of the heap graphs of several Java benchmarks, to evaluate the theoretic feasibility of using the GPU for garbage collection (Section 3).

- We prototype a GPU-based garbage collector integrated into the *Jikes Research Virtual Machine* [1] (Section 4), a Java VM maintained by the research community.

- We show a new algorithm, and variations thereof, for performing the mark phase of a mark & sweep garbage collector on the GPU. Our algorithm differs from previous work by using a frontier queue approach instead of a data-parallel algorithm. We also discuss trade-offs and optimizations to make it efficient on a GPU.

The objective of this work is not to present a single tuned implementation. The implementation presented in Section 4 is mainly for the purpose of illustrating a particular point in the design space. Our

* Research supported by Microsoft (Award #024263) and Intel (Award #024894) funding and by matching funding by U.C. Discovery (Award #DIG07-10227). Additional support comes from Par Lab affiliates National Instruments, Nokia, NVIDIA, Oracle, and Samsung. Philip Reames was also supported by the National Science Foundation (Award #CCF-1017810).

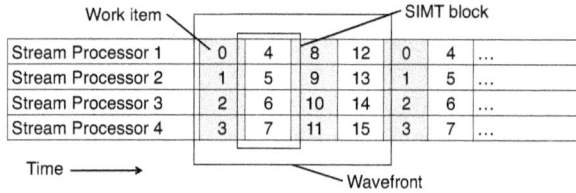

Figure 1. Scheduling of work-items for a fictional compute unit with 4 stream processors and a wavefront size of 16.

main goal is to assess whether using the GPU to offload garbage collection is feasible and to identify obstacles that need to be overcome. The GPU space is evolving rapidly and a compelling application workload such as garbage collection might influence the direction of that evolution.

After giving a brief introduction to the GPU hardware and programming model, the first part of our work (Section 3) consists of analyzing a selection of program heap graphs from the DaCapo benchmark suite [6] to determine whether heaps of real-world applications exhibit sufficient regular parallelism to take advantage of the GPU. We then present the implementation of our GPU-based collector (Section 4). This is followed by a discussion of design choices for our mark algorithm (Section 5), and experimental results (Section 6). We close with a discussion of the implications of our work, on current and future hardware (Section 7).

2. GPU Programming Model

This section provides a general introduction to the hardware and programming model of a GPU. Note that throughout this paper, we use the terminology from *OpenCL*; the terminology used by *CUDA* (the other major framework) is synonymous.[1]

GPUs provide a SIMT (*Single Instruction Multiple Thread*) programming model. SIMT is an extension of SIMD (Single Instruction Multiple Data) with support for hardware execution masking to handle divergent control paths within an instruction block. Computation is described in terms of a program *kernel* which is executed by a number of *work-items* (a.k.a. threads).

The basic building block of a GPU is a *streaming multiprocessor* (SM), or *compute unit*, which contains a single instruction decoder and a number – typically between 8 and 64 – of *stream processors* (SP). The stream processors execute the same instruction in lockstep, but with different register contexts (each of them stores the registers and a small amount of memory for each of its work-items). Within the compute unit, stream processors share access to a *Local Data Store*, a small fast block of dedicated memory.

Work-items are grouped into *wavefronts* (Figure 1); each wavefront typically contains four times the number of stream processors. The work-items of the wavefront are interwoven such that each stream processor executes the same instruction four times – once for each quarter of the wavefront. To handle divergence of control flow within a wavefront (e.g. one work-item takes a branch while another work-item does not), the hardware will perform masked execution. Both sides of the branch will be executed, but only some of the work-items will be enabled. For good performance, it is critically important to minimize the amount of divergence.

Wavefronts are in turn grouped into *workgroups*; 256 to 1,024 work-items per workgroup are common. When a given wavefront stalls because of memory access, another ready wavefront begins executing. Context switches between wavefronts are extremely fast

(usually a single cycle) since each work-item in the entire workgroup retains its dedicated registers at all times. To maximize memory bandwidth, a kernel should maximize the number of wavefronts that are able to perform independent memory accesses.

GPUs have a number of compute units which share access to a memory region known as *global memory*. On today's devices, the number of compute units varies from 2-4 on a low-end device to as many as 12-40 in high-end devices. For discrete GPUs (such as graphics cards), global memory is dedicated hardware on the device; for integrated GPUs (where CPU and GPU share the same package), it will often be a reserved area of the main system memory. The discrete approach has the advantage of much faster access times, but requires slow (on the order of 8GB/s) explicit copies between CPU and GPU, using DMA over the PCIe bus. In current-generation parts, neither approach participates in the cache-coherency protocol of the CPU; this means that communication between CPU and GPU must be done explicitly through the OpenCL interface.

3. Preliminary Analysis

Garbage collection in general – and the mark phase of a mark & sweep garbage collector specifically – is a memory-bound problem. As such, the main challenge of any implementation is to process and issue memory requests at a sufficiently high rate to fully utilize the available memory bandwidth. As we will discuss more in Section 5, being able to process a large number (i.e. hundreds) of objects in parallel is essential for meeting this goal on a GPU.

The core of our mark algorithm is a highly parallel queue-based breadth-first search. Objects to be processed are added to a *frontier queue*. For each item in the queue, we take it off, mark the object, and then add each outbound reference to the queue. This processes objects in order of increasing distance from the root set (i.e. increasing *depth*). At each depth, there is a fixed *width* (or *beam*) of nodes available for processing. If this available width is greater than the number of work-items, we can keep the entire device busy and make efficient progress through the traversal.

Any practical collector can do no better than an ideal collector which examines every object at a given depth in a single iteration. To understand this theoretical best case garbage collector on real programs, we examined the heap structure of benchmarks from the DaCapo 9.12 [6] benchmark suite. We examine two attributes of heap graphs: their general shape (i.e. depth, width per iteration, etc.) and the distribution of outbound references across objects. The latter has a significant performance impact on GPUs due to the divergence problem described previously (Section 2).

The data collection for this section was performed using an instrumented Jikes garbage collection plan. (We also repeated the analysis using a plugin for the Oracle HotSpot VM, but do not report the results since they were similar). All collection was done using the optimizing compiler; optimization affects the frequency of collection and thus the heap graphs' shapes. We ran the small and default configurations of a subset of the benchmarks.[2]

For further details about the structure of common Java heaps, we recommend Barabash and Petrank's paper [5]. They analyze heap depth and approximate shape for a previous release of the DaCapo benchmarks, as well as several Java SPEC benchmarks.

3.1 Structural Limits on Parallelism

We first examined the general shape of the heap graphs as traversed by the ideal collector. We were interested in determining whether

---

[1] For further reading, the AMD OpenCL Programming Guide [3] and the OpenCL v1.2 Specification [15] provide all the detail one might require.

[2] We are only reporting a subset of the benchmark suite since several benchmarks did not work on a vanilla Jikes RVM running on our evaluation system. This is a known problem and unrelated to our garbage collector.

DaCapo Benchmark - avrora (small)

DaCapo Benchmark - luindex (small)

DaCapo Benchmark - lusearch (small)

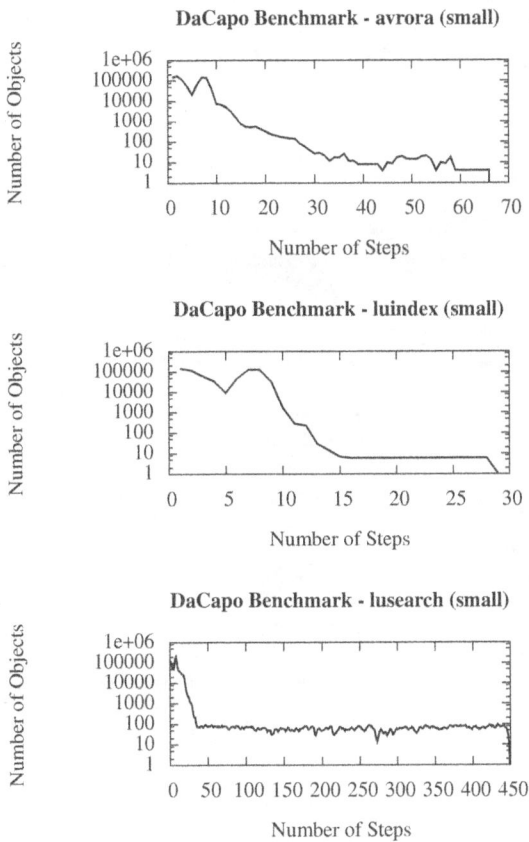

Figure 2. Number of objects at each depth during an idealized breadth-first traversal starting from the root set. The figures were chosen to exemplify classification by degree of parallelism.

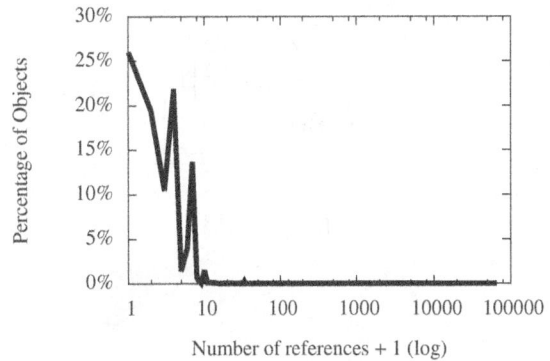

Figure 3. Distribution of the number of references within objects on the heap. The majority of objects have few outbound references, but some rare objects have hundreds or thousands.

there were structural limits that would prevent the degree of parallel processing that the GPU requires for efficiency.

A selection of the graphs generated from the DaCapo benchmarks is shown in Figure 2; these graphs were picked to be representative of the three categories of graph shape we identified. The figures show the number of objects reachable – marked or unmarked – from a given step of the ideal breadth-first traversal starting at the root set. For presentation purposes, we picked the deepest traversal found within a couple of runs of each benchmark, as these are likely to be the least advantageous for the GPU.

All of the benchmarks begin with a short section of extreme parallelism. The first step is limited to the size of the root set (typically 600-1,000 objects), but the next few steps expand rapidly. Once this startup section is completed, our benchmarks fell into three categories. Some of the benchmarks – such as `luindex` – then complete within a small number of additional steps. A few – such as `avrora` – had moderate length sections of structurally limited parallelism. Unfortunately, there were also a few benchmarks – such as `lusearch` – which had long narrow sections ("tails") following the parallel beginning. A width of 30 to 80 represents at most 1/3 of the available parallelism on the GPU. As the number of available work-items per workgroup increases with time, this fraction may drop precipitously.

Since no hardware can execute an infinite number of threads, we repeated the analysis above with maximum step widths of 128, 256, 1,024, and 32,768. As expected, decreasing the number of items processed in each iteration increased the effective depth of the graph, but did not change the overall shape or categorization of any of the benchmarks.

Despite the limited parallelism towards the end of some collections, we conclude that heap graphs are sufficiently parallel for the purposes of garbage collection on a GPU. However, if one wants to minimize collection latency, having a mechanism to deal efficiently with long narrow tails in the heap graph is critical; we discuss our solution in Section 5.4. An alternative approach would be to insert artificial shortcut edges into the heap graph. Barabash and Petrank describe this strategy in detail [5].

3.2 Distribution of Outbound References

Prompted by Veldema and Philippsen's [21] findings, the second issue we examined was the distribution of the number of outbound references within each object. When processing one object per thread in a SIMT environment where each thread loops over the outbound references within its object, this distribution is critical to understanding and controlling divergence.

Our findings show that while the vast majority of objects have a small out-degree – 26% of objects have no outbound references (other than their class pointer), 76% have four or fewer, and 98% have 12 or fewer – the distribution has a very long and noisy tail. A small fraction of objects (less than 0.01%) have hundreds to thousands of outbound references. It is worth noting that our analysis does not distinguish between objects and arrays of references; we have manually confirmed that some of the high double-digit out-degree nodes are, in fact, objects.

The distribution of the number of references within objects can be seen in Figure 3. Given that the results across benchmarks are fairly uniform, we chose to present the distribution across all the collections of all the benchmarks for which we collected results.

Even leaving aside the extreme tail of the distribution, the distribution of references between objects means that blindly looping over the number of references will result in unacceptable divergence of threads. We discuss one solution for distributing references between work-items in Section 5.2.

4. Offloading Garbage Collection

In this section, we present challenges for offloading garbage collection to the GPU and discuss as well as measure different performance trade-offs. To substantiate our claims, we implemented a proof-of-concept GPU-based garbage collector for the *Jikes Research Virtual Machine* [1] (a Java Virtual Machine maintained by

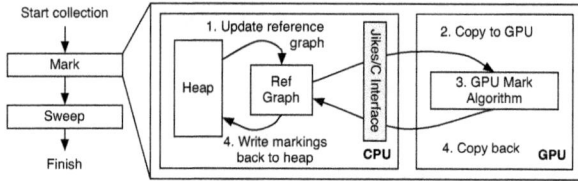

Figure 4. Overview of the collector integration.

the research community). This allows us to investigate performance trade-offs for full executions of real Java programs, by performing a series of macro and micro benchmarks.

4.1 High-level Overview

We modified Jikes' `MarkSweep` garbage collector to offload its mark phase to the GPU. The steps performed by the collector are shown in Figure 4. Our mark phase is performed on a *reference graph* data structure, a self-contained version of the heap that only contains references but no other fields (an implementation detail which we discuss in the next sections). This structure is kept up-to-date during program execution or filled in on each collection. We then invoke our collector in a native call which sets up our mark kernel and runs it on the GPU. The CPU is idle until the mark completes (a production-grade implementation would perform other tasks during this time). Upon completion, execution returns to Jikes and the markings are transferred back into the heap. The sweep phase is then performed by Jikes. Note that the intermediary copying steps are merely an implementation detail of our prototype, and not inherent in our approach.

While a real-world collector will have to offload the sweep phase as well, we think that Veldema et al. have sufficiently covered this aspect in their work, so we focus on the mark phase for brevity. A complete collector would perform the sweep phase on the GPU (immediately after the mark algorithm) and only copy the resulting free lists back to the Jikes RVM.

4.2 Object Layout

The difficulty of integrating our collector into Jikes was exacerbated by the VM's object layout. To identify the reference fields within each object, it is necessary to look up their offsets in an array that is stored with the type information of the current class. This adds up to three levels of indirection (type information block, type info, offset array), and incurs a significant performance penalty on the GPU, due to the lack of caching. We therefore require a different object layout, which lays out the references of an object consecutively and contains the object's number of references in the object header. The layout introduced by the Sable VM [8] achieves this requirement with minimal overhead [9] by laying out reference fields to the right of the object header, and non-reference fields to the left.

4.3 Reference Graph

While high-end GPUs may provide up to 3 GB of global memory, today's consumer GPUs often only have 256-512 MB. Even though our test platform (see Section 6.1) can access the system's main memory, it can only map 128 MB at a time.[3] This became problematic, as this size was too small to hold the heaps of several DaCapo benchmarks (when including Jikes' memory spaces).

For the purposes of evaluation, we solved this problem by building a condensed version of the heap which we call a *reference graph*. The reference graph is stored in a separate space and contains an entry for each object on the main heap, consisting of a

---

[3] This value was determined experimentally.

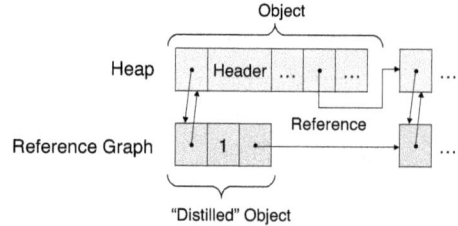

Figure 5. The reference graph structure.

pointer to the original object, the number of references, and a consecutive list of all outbound references as pointers into the reference graph (Figure 5). Arrays are represented in the same way. This emulates the object layout presented in Section 4.2, but reduces the size of the heap such that it fits on the GPU. Due to the lack of caching on the GPU, this approach does not give a performance advantage, while it allows us to evaluate our collector on real-world heaps that otherwise would have been too large to fit on the GPU.

We found that the reference graph approach gave us a sufficient reduction in size to evaluate the DaCapo benchmarks on our collector. The following table shows the cumulative sum of heap sizes across all collections within a run, as well as the equivalent numbers for the reference graph.[4] This allows us to estimate that the reference graph approach reduces the size of our graph by about 75% on average:

	# GCs	Cum. Heap	Cum. Graph	Ratio
avrora	9	256 MB	80 MB	31.2%
jython	114	10499 MB	3301 MB	31.4%
luindex	7	178 MB	35 MB	19.8%
lusearch	77	7078 MB	515 MB	7.3%
pmd	14	809 MB	233 MB	28.9%
sunflow	39	2935 MB	658 MB	22.4%
xalan	23	1686 MB	456 MB	27.1%

We experimented with two different approaches to building and maintaining the reference graph. Both of them allocate a node in the reference graph whenever a new object is allocated.

- The most basic approach fills in the reference graph immediately before performing a collection. It performs a linear scan through the distilled objects in the reference graph, follows the references of each corresponding original object, and copies the pointers for the corresponding distilled objects to the reference graph (Figure 5).

- The reference graph can also be built while running the mutator threads: this turns every reference write into a double-write to two locations, which can be implemented as either a write barrier or issuing a second write instruction in the compiler. We prototyped the simpler write barrier approach.

While these approaches obviously differ in performance, we refrain from performing a deeper analysis, as this problem is somewhat orthogonal to our approach and current hardware trends are indicating that the memory available to the GPU will soon be large enough to store the entire heap.

4.4 Launch Overhead

Equipped with the reference graph, our collector calls into a C function which initializes OpenCL, copies (or maps) the reference graph to the GPU and launches the mark kernel. Launching a kernel execution incurs both a fixed startup cost, and a variable cost

---

[4] We used a heap size of 100 MB for all of these runs.

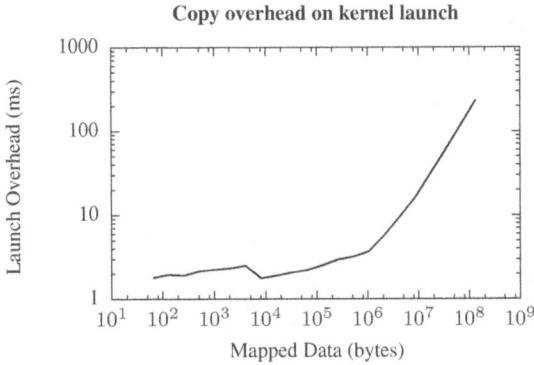

Figure 6. Kernel launch latency presented as a function of the amount of data being mapped onto the GPU (in ms).

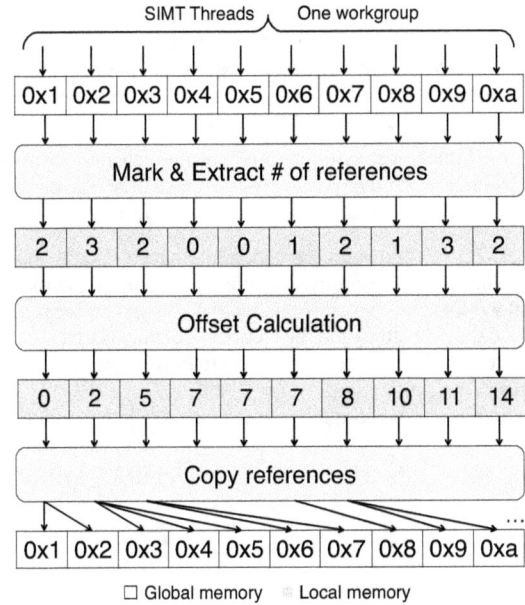

Figure 7. Structure of the baseline algorithm.

related to the kernel itself and the size of memory being mapped to the GPU. We incur these costs once per garbage collection. To analyze their impact, we measured the launch latencies of two microbenchmarks: an empty kernel, and our mark algorithm (Section 5) when run on a single object. Each experiment was repeated 20 times and we present the average latencies.

- The results from the first microbenchmark show that the first invocation of a kernel incurs an overhead (around 1 ms) which is not repeated for successive runs. We believe this to be the time to copy the kernel itself. For the remaining runs, the overhead hovers between 0.33 ms and 0.62 ms. The execution time of the empty kernel was always below 0.01 ms (i.e. negligible).

- The results from the second benchmark show that overhead scales roughly linearly with mapped memory for sizes above 2 MB (Figure 6). Below that threshold, the overhead is dominated by the fixed cost. We want to note that there is substantial variation in results, particularly for larger sizes. The range of times for 128 MB was from 181 ms to 292 ms.

While our test platform supports zero-copy mapping between CPU and GPU, the device drivers available for Linux do not currently support this feature. The Windows drivers do, but we chose to run our experiments on Linux for consistency with the rest of our results. We therefore incur a copy-overhead, which can be seen in the linear scaling for large memory sizes; this resembles the behavior on traditional (discrete) GPU architectures. We argue that the majority of this overhead will go away once zero-copy mapping is supported (except for some cache write-back costs).

The remaining launch time can be largely discounted for purposes of assessing validity, as long as the number of kernel launches is small. Launch times have been trending downward at a steep rate and we expect them to decrease further, since this is clearly a general problem for many GPU workloads. For this reason, we exclude launch overheads from the execution times of our kernels.

4.5 Copy-back Overhead

After performing the mark phase on the GPU, our collector incurs an additional overhead from copying the marked reference graph back into main memory and transcribing the mark bits into the original heap structure. This is necessary for the integration with Jikes, but would not occur in a real-world collector that integrates both mark and sweep phase: after finishing the sweep phase on the GPU, the collector would simply move the resulting free-list to the CPU, ideally in a low-overhead, zero-copy operation. For this reason, we ignore this overhead for the purpose of our evaluation.

5. Algorithm and Optimizations

The core part of our collector consists of an algorithm that performs a parallel mark phase on the GPU, using n work-items (on our platform, $n = 256$). Our approach is based on maintaining a *frontier queue* that contains pointers to objects to be processed; we do not differentiate between arrays and objects. The kernel processes these elements in a loop: at each iteration, it removes up to n pointers from the queue, marks them, and adds the address of any referenced objects to the end.

Veldema and Philippsen [21] identified synchronization as a core problem of such an approach: in an implementation where each work-item accesses the queue in an atomic operation, execution would be serialized and therefore very inefficient. Based on this observation, they discard the queue-based approach and instead show a data-parallel implementation that flips to the CPU after every iteration, to spawn a new set of work-items.

We avoid the problem of serialization by calculating in on-chip memory the total number of elements to remove and add to the queue, as well as their offsets. This avoids the need for per work-item atomic operations on the critical regions of the queue. At the same time, it avoids flipping between CPU and GPU, since we found the associated launch overhead to be too significant for this approach (Section 4.4).

Our algorithm is implemented as an OpenCL kernel which executes the code in Algorithm 1 (discussed below) in a loop until the frontier queue is empty. For the purposes of this explanation, assume that *in_queue* and *out_queue* are pointers to the parts of the queue where we are extracting elements from and where we store new elements, respectively. On each iteration, we remove up to n pointers from *in_queue* and examine the corresponding objects in parallel. We then mark all objects that have not been marked before and copy their references to the end of *out_queue*. This is done in three steps (Figure 7):

1. For all objects, read the number of references and whether the object has been marked. Objects that have already been marked are treated like an object with zero references.

2. Compute the offsets that the references of each object will have in *out_queue*, using either a prefix sum or histogram (discussed in Section 5.1). For the ease of exposition, assume the prefix sum approach for now, which lays out the references of an object consecutively, one object after another.

3. Copy all references within the objects to their new location in the frontier, using the previously calculated offsets to determine where to store the first reference of each object.

Only between iterations do we update the queue's start- and end-offsets. This can be done by a single work-item per workgroup, since all work-items know the number of elements that are removed from the queue (l below) and the number of elements that are added to the queue (which is given by the offset calculation – e.g. the right-most entry of the prefix-sum).

The following paragraphs give a more detailed description of the algorithm that is executed by each work-item. Note that id is the offset of each individual work-item within the workgroup.

Algorithm 1 One step of the GPU mark phase.

---

function MARK_PHASE (id, in_queue, out_queue)
1: $x[work\_group\_size] \leftarrow (0, \ldots, 0)$
2: $l \leftarrow \min(length(in\_queue), work\_group\_size)$
3: **if** $id \geq l$ **then** return
4:
5: $header \leftarrow mark(in\_queue[id], mark\_bit)$
6: **if** $\neg marked(header)$ **then**
7:     $refcount \leftarrow ref\_count(header)$
8: **else**
9:     $refcount \leftarrow 0$
10: **end if**
11: $x[id] \leftarrow refcount$
12:
13: $offset \leftarrow compute\_offsets(id, x, l)$
14:
15: **for** $i = 0$ to $refcount - 1$ **do**
16:     $refptr \leftarrow in\_queue[id] + i + HEADER\_SIZE$
17:     $out\_queue[offset + i] \leftarrow *refptr$
18: **end for**

Lines 1-3 set up the necessary data structures and drop out of the function if there is no work to do for the work-item. Notably, x is allocated in the local scratchpad memory and used to efficiently calculate the offsets into the output queue.

Lines 5-11 implement the first part of the algorithm. It retrieves the object's header, in order to extract the marking and the reference count. It then stores the reference count in x.

Line 13 calculates the offsets for writing into the output queue. We implemented several options, which are discussed in Section 5.1. The presented algorithm uses a simple prefix-sum to determine the offset for each object in the output queue, and stores the object's references in consecutive slots after this offset. The next section discusses this aspect in detail.

Lines 15-18 describe the last part of the algorithm. The references are copied one-by-one into their dedicated locations in the output queue. The output calculation in the previous step ensures that no two references are written into the same slot, avoiding the requirement for synchronization or locking. In the given code, the fixed constant *HEADER_SIZE* represents the offset of the first reference from the beginning of the object header.

It is important to note that the *mark* operation does not need to use an atomic operation. Setting the mark bit is an idempotent operation and there is no correctness concern if a single object is processed multiple times. The slight performance loss due to redundant work – if an unmarked object gets added to the frontier

multiple times and processed within the same iteration – is vastly outweighed by the cost of atomic operations.[5].

The described version of the algorithm performs no coordination between workgroups and can thus only exploit one compute unit per device. In Section 7.4 we expand on it and discuss load balancing and synchronization concerns in detail. We present a naïve proof-of-concept solution in Section 5.5.

5.1 Offset Calculation

Our first strategy for calculating the offsets for the output queue used Blelloch's prefix-sum algorithm from [11]. With this approach, all references of an object are stored in consecutive slots in the queue, and the offset of an object's first reference is the total number of references from work-items with a lower id than the one processing that object (Figure 8). When performed in local memory, the complexity of this approach is $O(\log n)$ parallel addition and local memory operations.

However, we discovered that this approach often takes up 40-50% of the kernel's total execution time, arguably due to the large number of accesses to local memory. We therefore implemented a different approach, based on a histogram. In this layout, the first references from all work-items with at least one reference appear first, followed by the second references, third references, etc.

Offsets for this layout are calculated by generating a histogram that counts the number of work-items that have at least one reference, at least two references, etc. The histogram is generated using atomic operations in local memory, by atomically counting the number of work-items with an object having $i = 1, 2, \ldots$ references or more. The sum of the first $i - 1$ entries of the histogram gives the global offset of the part of the output array where the i'th references begin (Figure 8). The atomic counting operation also gives each work-item a unique local offset into the i'th part, where it will write its reference. The following code replaces the last part of Algorithm 1, starting from line 13.

Algorithm 2 Histogram approach for the offset calculation.

1: $hist \leftarrow (0, \ldots, 0)$
2: $global\_offset \leftarrow 0$
3: $atomic\_max(\&max\_refcount, refcount)$
4: **for** $i = 0$ to $max\_refcount - 1$ **do**
5:     **if** $i < refcount$ **then**
6:        $local\_offset \leftarrow atomic\_increment(\&hist[i], 1)$
7:        $refptr \leftarrow in\_queue[id] + i + HEADER\_SIZE$
8:        $out\_queue[global\_offset + local\_offset] \leftarrow *refptr$
9:     **end if**
10:     (*memory barrier*)
11:     $global\_offset += hist[i]$
12: **end for**

This uses $O(max\_refcount)$ parallel atomic operations, where *max_refcount* is the maximum number of references among the objects currently processed by any of the work-items. Since the atomics are executed in local memory, they do not slow down global memory access and are comparatively fast. An additional advantage of this approach is that we are writing to consecutive items in the queue, which is efficient on our hardware.

---

[5] At least on AMD hardware, atomic operations are up to 5x slower than normal accesses, because they use the *complete path* vs the *fast path* for memory access [3] In the compiler available with the current version of the SDK (AMD APP SDK v2.6), using any atomic operation on global memory causes *all* global memory accesses to use the complete path. In practice, this has led us to avoid atomic operations wherever possible.

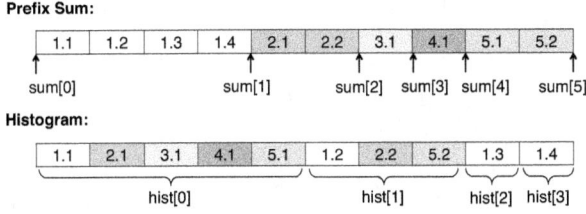

Figure 8. Different approaches for calculating offsets. $m.n$ describes the n'th reference of the m'th object (i.e. work-item).

5.2 Reducing Divergence

As discussed in Section 3, the majority of objects have a small out-degree (i.e. few references), while a few objects have a large numbers of references. In the algorithm above, each work-item loops over all references within the object it handles. This behavior is problematic for SIMT execution: when one work-item encounters a high-degree node, the remainder of the workgroup will stall until that work-item has completed its task. This results in low utilization of available parallelism and wastes available memory bandwidth.

To avoid this case, we extended our algorithm to let each work-item process at most a fixed number of references for each object (currently 16). This minimizes the worst case divergence in the loop. Objects that are longer than this are then stored on a non-blocking stack and (in the same iteration of the algorithm) processed in parallel. This is done by letting all work-items process one reference each in parallel, a very efficient way to perform a large copy operation. Like Veldema and Philippsen, we consider this an essential optimization. Our approach bears resemblance to theirs, but processes large arrays (and objects) immediately and does not require a new kernel launch.

5.3 Vectorized Memory Accesses

We explored the possibility of using vector reads to decrease the number of individual memory requests. OpenCL supports 4-wide vector types, which allow reading 128 bits at a time. We rewrote our algorithm to use vector loads to access the header and the first three references at the same time (and then read references in groups of four). This made it necessary to lay out the objects in such a way that headers are aligned to 128 bit boundaries, which we achieved by introducing additional padding to our reference graph.

Vector reads can lead to extra work, as the algorithm may read more references than necessary. Overall, however, we expected a speed-up due to the reduced number of memory requests.

5.4 Cut-off for Long, Narrow Heaps

As we show in our heap analysis (Section 3), some workloads exhibit very long narrow tails (stemming from e.g. linked lists). From a performance perspective, it is beneficial to detect such cases and return execution to the CPU. We believe that without the ability to saturate the memory pipe with many requests, the GPU loses out to the CPU due to the CPU's much lower average memory latency as a result of caching. The CPU benefits from any spatial locality of the memory graph that may exist, whereas the GPU does not. The CPU also benefits from the fact that the (very small) active section of the queue ends up in L1 cache.

We therefore implemented a mechanism that returns execution to the CPU once the size of the queue drops below a certain threshold. As a safeguard, we require a minimum number of iterations on the GPU to complete before returning.

Veldema and Philippsen identified a similar optimization, but in a different context: their discussion focuses on avoiding context switches to and from the GPU. To handle linked lists, their algorithm runs multiple iterations on the GPU without switching to the CPU. This optimization does not apply to our approach.

5.5 Multiple Compute Units

In order to achieve high throughput, it is desirable to leverage all of the GPU's compute units. For the purposes of our evaluation, we chose a naïve proof-of-concept approach to run the algorithm on the two compute units that our platform provides: we first divide the root set into two halves and hand one of them to each compute unit. Each compute unit then runs the algorithm independently, without any load balancing or synchronization. This approach has two drawbacks:

- If the initial partitioning results in an uneven distribution of work, one compute unit may be idle for most of the execution.
- We may perform redundant work in cases where the two compute units race to mark an object.

While this results in a negative performance impact, our approach is nonetheless correct: marking a node is an idempotent operation and can be performed multiple times without harm. Better results can be achieved by using dynamic load balancing between compute units – we discuss this aspect in Section 7.4.

6. Evaluation

In this section, we present the results of experiments we ran to evaluate the performance of our mark algorithm. We first describe our evaluation platform and then use microbenchmarks to highlight strengths and weaknesses of our algorithm and collector implementation. We then examine the performance of our implementation on real-world application benchmarks from the DaCapo 9.12 benchmark suite. We conclude with a brief discussion of additional overheads that were excluded from the previous subsections.

6.1 Test Platform

Our test platform was an AMD E-350 APU[6] which is one of the first chips that integrate a CPU and GPU into a single device (Intel's Sandy Bridge architecture has a similar integrated GPU, but it is not programmable). The E-350 targets low-end laptops and tablets.

The system was configured with 3.5 GB of DDR3 1066 RAM. The APU's "Bobcat" CPU is a dual core running at 1.6 GHz with a 512 KB L2 cache [2]. Its "Brazos" GPU is running at 492 MHz with 2 compute units, 16 stream processors, an 8 KB L1 cache per compute unit, and a 64 KB L2 cache per GPU [3]. Measurements show that the caches are disabled for accesses to local and shared memory. The CPU and GPU share memory and a single memory controller on which they compete for bandwidth; we experimentally determined that the GPU can only map 128 MB in any given kernel invocation. All experiments were conducted on Fedora Linux (kernel version 2.6.35.14-103).

6.2 Microbenchmark Results

To explain the performance of the baseline algorithm and explore potential optimizations, we used a set of simple microbenchmarks. These benchmarks were handwritten and do not run through the Jikes environment. This approach was chosen to get pure forms of the heap graphs; even a small Java program creates enough internal objects to obscure the microbenchmark results.

Table 1 presents the execution times of the microbenchmarks for a set of different configurations of the garbage collector.

---

[6] *Accelerated Processing Unit* (APU) is a term coined by AMD to describe their integrated CPU/GPU solution marketed as *AMD Fusion*.

	Size	CPU	GPU	GPU+P	GPU+V	GPU+F	GPU+D	GPU+VD	GPU+2CU
Single Item	28 bytes	0.001	0.027	0.027	0.028	0.028	0.027	0.028	0.028
Long Linked List	156 KB	0.151	94.604	74.400	83.451	0.360	96.279	85.412	84.173
256 Parallel Linked Lists	39 MB	129.723	140.465	192.823	118.982	140.783	142.556	120.984	102.092
2560 Parallel Linked Lists	117 MB	1074.920	415.553	572.153	350.523	416.389	421.589	356.986	194.317
Very Wide Object	3.92 KB	0.018	1.862	1.077	1.696	1.861	0.218	0.221	0.220
VP Linked List	4 MB	0.150	77.462	60.950	68.123	0.317	78.757	69.802	68.843
VP Array of Objects	20 MB	1.347	5.361	6.308	3.516	5.378	5.843	3.095	1.693

Table 1. Average mark times for microbenchmarks. All times are in ms and do not include overheads. CPU is a baseline CPU implementation. GPU is our baseline algorithm using the histogram approach. GPU+P is the variant using prefix-sum. GPU+V is the vectorization of that algorithm. GPU+F falls back to the CPU if a narrow tail is encountered. GPU+D has special support for large objects to prevent divergence. GPU+VD combines vector and divergence. GPU+2CU enables both compute units for the GPU+VD configuration.

Methodology We ran our microbenchmarks on the following configurations: *CPU* is our implementation of a serial single CPU mark phase. *GPU* is the baseline algorithm described previously. *GPU+V* is the vectorization of that algorithm (Section 5.3). *GPU+D* is the variant with special support for large objects to prevent divergence (Section 5.2). *GPU+F* is a variant which falls back to the CPU once the queue length drops below a threshold and a minimum number of iterations have run (Section 5.4); we use 20 as the threshold and 5 as the minimum number of iterations. We report the sum of the GPU and CPU runtime. *GPU+P* uses the prefix-sum approach instead of the histogram (Section 5.1), for comparison. *GPU+2CU* contains the first two optimizations but also uses both compute units.

Each configuration was run for 20 iterations and the average runtime is reported; variation between runs was extremely low.

Benchmark Descriptions For each benchmark, we also provide the overall size of the reference graph that is associated with it:

- **Single Item** (28 bytes) - This benchmark consists of a single item in the heap, with a corresponding pointer in the root set. The purpose of this benchmark is to measure the overhead (excluding copy overhead) of the algorithm. As would be expected, the startup cost for the GPU variants are similar. The CPU is an order of magnitude faster since the data is already in cache.

- **Long Linked List** (156 KB) - This benchmark consists of a single long linked list with 10,000 elements. This case is the worst for the GPU since it cannot exploit any parallelism in the graph. All of the GPU implementations perform badly, but the one with the option to fall back to the CPU fares best. It runs the minimum number of iterations on the GPU, then returns to the CPU for the majority of the execution. Unfortunately, the few iterations it does run on the GPU prove quite expensive.

- **256 Parallel Linked Lists** (39 MB) - This benchmark consists of 256 parallel linked lists with 10,000 elements each. The root set contains a pointer to each linked list. The effect of this is that each work-item within the workgroup can operate independently, which allows the GPU implementations to perform relatively well, some even beating the CPU by a small amount.

- **2560 Parallel Linked Lists** (117 MB) - This benchmark extends the previous by adding more linked lists. Due to our hardware's limited amount of mappable memory, we shortened each list to 3,000 elements each. This case can arguably be seen as the best for the GPU since there is abundant parallelism and little locality between objects in the queue. This microbenchmark is the only one where the GPU solidly outperforms the CPU.

- **Very Wide Object** (3.92 KB) - This benchmark consists of a single array containing 1,000 individual objects. This is an extreme case designed to illustrate the effects when SIMT divergence is not addressed.

Discussion These benchmarks allow us to evaluate the impact of the optimizations discussed in the previous section.

- **Histogram** (Section 5.1) - Comparing the GPU and GPU+P results shows the difference in performance characteristics of the histogram and prefix styles of offset calculations. The prefix sum implementation performs well for cases in which a small subset of the work-items perform useful work, while the histogram fares better when many work-items are active. On real-world benchmarks (not presented), the histogram is clearly better, but it may be worth exploring a combination of both approaches (e.g. by switching dynamically between them).

- **Divergence Handling** (Section 5.2) - This causes a slight slowdown for those benchmarks that do not contain objects with large numbers of references. For benchmarks that do (such as *Very Wide Object* above), the performance improvement is substantial (a 89% improvement). For real workloads, we believe divergence handling to be a critical and necessary optimization.

- **Vectorization of Loads** (Section 5.3) - This optimization shows an improvement on most of the microbenchmarks we report. The improvements range from 12% to 40% for all benchmarks except the *Single Item* case. This case is hinting at a more general problem which is that vectorization can (and does) hurt performance in some cases: if the vectorization causes memory words to be read that are not used, and if memory bandwidth is already running at the hardware limit, vectorization can slow down the algorithm. However, from our experiences, this seems to be a rare case.

- **Falling back to the CPU for narrow tails** (Section 5.4) - Our implementation of fallback has a barely perceptible negative impact on performance for most benchmarks. However, for cases where the GPU would perform extremely poorly (such as the *Long Linked List* microbenchmark), it recovers some, but not all, of the performance lost. There is still a significant amount of time spent on the GPU to handle narrow sections before the cut-off is invoked; we believe this to be a necessary evil to prevent temporary drops in parallelism from triggering overly eager fall-back.

- **Multiple Compute Units** (Section 5.5) - Despite our naïve approach, we still obtain perceptible improvements by using both compute units. It is important to note that this improvement is not guaranteed: using a second compute unit can hurt performance if the first unit would otherwise get additional bandwidth and the second unit is performing only redundant work.

Comparison with related work The last two benchmarks are modeled closely after those presented by Veldema and Philippsen for evaluating their GPU mark algorithm. Unfortunately, the results are not directly comparable due to different experimental setups. We would like to note that their results were collected on a sig-

	Jikes MS	Serial CPU	Baseline GPU	Optimized GPU	Opt GPU + 2CU	GPU Slowdown	Opt Speedup
lusearch	1566.10	1084.18	11739.50	2404.18	1490.96	1.38	7.69
pmd	211.98	356.09	1651.66	634.24	357.49	1.69	4.55
sunflow	1422.54	401.36	3446.52	724.92	554.25	1.38	6.25
xalan	809.79	423.31	2836.33	1088.78	750.12	1.77	3.85

Table 2. Cumulative mark times for DaCapo benchmarks (default sizes). All times are in ms and do not include overheads. *Optimized GPU* uses vectorization and divergence handling. *Jikes MS* is the unmodified `MarkSweep` collector. *Serial CPU* is a CPU implementation using the reference graph. The last two columns show the slowdown over the best CPU implementation and the improvement from optimizations.

nificantly more powerful GPU. Nonetheless, our mark algorithm appears to fare well in comparison.

- **VP Linked List** (4MB) - This benchmark consists of 16 linked lists of 8,192 element each, of which all but one is immediately garbage. Only one of the linked lists is traced by the mark phase. As a result, this is structurally very similar to the *Long Linked List* benchmark above.

- **VP Arrays of Objects** (20MB) - This benchmark consists of 1,024 arrays, each containing exactly 1,024 objects. Only the first 64 arrays are retained. All others immediately become garbage and are not traced.

It should be noted that we do not report launch overheads, while Veldema and Philippsen report complete execution times. Furthermore, they perform 8 collector runs while we only measure one.

6.3 DaCapo Benchmarks

We measured the performance of our GPU-based collector for real-world application benchmarks from the DaCapo 9.12 benchmark suite. The results are shown in Table 2.

Methodology In these results, the *Optimized GPU* implementation includes the vectorization and divergence handling optimizations (*Opt GPU+2CU* also uses both compute units). Both the optimized and unoptimized results use the histogram method for offset calculation. Neither version includes the long-tail cutoff (to avoid the issue of confusing what is actually running on the GPU). The *Jikes MS* column is an unmodified instance of Jikes' `MarkSweep` collector. The second column is a trivial CPU implementation which operates on the reference graph. We present these numbers to offset any minor locality advantage the reference graph structure may give us. The final two columns present the slowdown of the GPU over the best of the two CPU implementations and the improvement resulting from optimization of the GPU algorithm.

The Jikes RVM was configured with a maximum heap size of 192 MB - the largest we could map on the GPU even with the reference graph. We do not report collection times for `avrora` or `luindex` since neither consistently triggers a collection at the heap size we are using. All results were generated running the benchmarks with their default configurations and using the "converge" (-C) option provided by the suite. We report the cumulative time of all garbage collections conducted during the final iteration.

Discussion As can be seen from the results in Table 2, our GPU mark implementation is within a factor of two for all of the benchmarks we report. As a reminder to the reader, we are conservatively comparing against the better of Jikes' `MarkSweep` and our own CPU implementation working off the reference graph. When comparing only against the `MarkSweep` collector, our implementation fares significantly better; the GPU outperforms Jikes on 3 of 4 benchmarks. We consider this to be a highly encouraging result.

We would like to note that these performance results are extremely sensitive to the heap size. As the heap size increased, the relative performance of our GPU implementation to Jikes increased

sharply. We present the largest heap sizes supported by our evaluation platform, but even those are small for real program heaps. We suspect that relative performance would continue to improve as the heap size increases.

6.4 Overheads of Our Implementation

In the preceeding discussion, we excluded the copy overhead and kernel launch overhead for any of the GPU configurations; we report kernel execution only[7].

Our reference graph implementation adds some additional overhead outside the mark phase. Allocating each object requires that a corresponding reference graph node be allocated as well; this introduced mutator overhead of approximately 40% in an allocation stress test microbenchmark. This overhead is less pronounced in the DaCapo results, but is still significant, varying between 7% and 25%. It should be mentioned that this overhead could presumably be reduced by adding this functionality through the compiler, rather than adding an extra function call.

Using the basic approach of filling in the entire reference graph before every collection adds a major overhead to each collection, taking several times as long as the mark phase on the CPU (arguably due to a highly untuned implementation). The double-write approach eliminates this at the cost of an additional 11% runtime overhead in the microbenchmark (for a cumulative total of 57%).

Some collector overhead is also added in copying markings from the reference graph back to the heap in preparation for running an unmodified Jikes sweep phase.

Let us emphasize that all overheads discussed in this subsection are artifacts of either the copying of data to the GPU (Section 4.4) or our need to reduce the size of the space being collected (Section 4.3). Neither is intrinsic to the problem and both are likely to be eliminated by hardware changes in the near future.

7. Discussion

While our numbers imply that our GPU-based garbage collector is 40-80% slower than our CPU-based collector and therefore not directly competitive in terms of performance, our experimental results nonetheless answer the questions we set out to investigate. We identified the key points for offloading garbage collection to the GPU, some of which are surprising in hindsight. We were also able to assess the suitability of today's GPUs for garbage collection, as well as making predictions on how future hardware will further improve the situation.

7.1 Lessons from the Mark Algorithm

Somewhat counter-intuitively, the primary goal for garbage collection on the GPU is not to parallelize the computational steps of the algorithm but to maximize the hardware's ability to schedule memory requests. The key challenge is to ensure that each work-item can effectively generate and handle memory requests. It is therefore crucially important to avoid serialization of execution (as en-

---

[7] For Jikes, we only report the mark phase, `scan` in Jikes terminology.

sured by our queue approach), but also to reduce divergence between threads (Section 5.2). The numbers presented in Section 3 confirm that common heap graphs exhibit the rare but long objects and arrays which cause this divergence.

In our algorithm, the number of outstanding requests is limited by the maximum size of a workgroup (which depends on the hardware). Notably, this is different from the number of streaming processors in the GPU: while the number of streaming processors limits the throughput in terms of instructions per cycle, the workgroup size limits the number of work-items that can be in-flight at a given time, and therefore the number of outstanding memory requests that can be issued. We already see this size increasing in high-end parts, implying that future generations will be increasingly good at memory-bound problems such as garbage collection. The same is true for the number of memory channels: While our APU features only two channels, high-end parts often provide eight.

As with many GPU algorithms, it is only feasible to run the mark algorithm on the GPU if the number of objects to mark is sufficiently large. For small collections, the launch-overhead dominates the entire collection time, in which case it is beneficial to run the collection on the CPU in the first place. Predicting the size of a collection is non-trivial, but heuristics could be applied.

7.2 Lessons from the Reference Graph

Our reference-graph approach is orthogonal to the problem of performing garbage collection on the GPU: we assume that in the near future, GPUs will be capable of mapping the entire heap, perhaps even cache-coherent with the CPU. However, we noticed that the reference graph gave us significantly better performance for a CPU collector: our untuned *Serial CPU* collector beat the optimized Jikes collector on several occasions, arguably due to increased cache locality. We therefore briefly discuss performance trade-offs for using the reference graph in a conventional GC.

Our numbers from Section 6.4 indicate that keeping the reference graph up-to-date when running the mutator seems to be the most promising approach. We believe that modifying the compiler to issue duplicate writes whenever a reference is written will lead to a significantly lower performance impact than we are incurring with our naïve, write-barrier based approach. An alternative approach consists of splitting each object into two parts, one only containing the references, the other containing the non-references. This avoids the need for duplicating data and substantially improves collector locality, at the cost of access locality.

We did not investigate this approach further but found it worth mentioning as we found the trade-offs intriguing.

7.3 Estimation of Performance Limits

To estimate the potential of our approach, we need to quantify how the performance of our implementation compares to the theoretical best case on the given hardware. To do so, we present two weak, but independent, constructions of a lower bound on execution time for the *2,560 Parallel Linked List* benchmark from Section 6. We then discuss performance measurements that lead us to believe that the actual bound is even tighter.

The first bound can be constructed by examining the minimum time required to touch every memory location in the reference graph exactly once. As constructed, the reference graph contains only the edges in the heap graph and some minor padding. While there may be a more compact representation, we believe that this is a reasonable first order approximation for a minimum-size representation of the heap graph. Using only the size of the benchmark (117 MB) and the peak memory bandwidth for our device (9 GB/s), we can establish a lower bound for GPU execution of ∼12.7 ms.

For the second bound, we can consider the minimum number of dependent loads from main memory and the stall latency implied by

each. Without the presence of caches, each step of the list traversal requires at least one round trip to main memory. As a result, a lower bound on the run-time of the algorithm is given by *depth* × *stall_penalty_in_cycles* × 1/*gpu_frequency*. We benchmarked a stall latency of 256 cycles under load and the benchmark requires a minimum of 3,000 dependent loads (one per linked-list element). Taken together, this gives us a lower bound of ∼ 1.5 ms. For this benchmark, the bound is not particularly tight, but we present it nonetheless since it reflects structural features of the heap graph that cannot be avoided (Section 3).

Together, these two approaches gives us a bound that is about 15x better than our best measured performance on the GPU.

We also examined the sustained memory bandwidth achieved by our implementation over an entire execution of the mark phase and compare it against the peak memory bandwidth available on the device. For our benchmark, the optimized dual compute unit configuration achieves a sustained bandwidth of 3.016 GB/s, or roughly one third of peak. As expected, the single compute unit version of the same code achieves roughly 1/2 of the bandwidth at 1.72 GB/s. It is worth noting that these are measurements of our actual implementation and thus may not reflect an actual bound due to errors in the implementation or missed optimizations. As an illustrative example, disabling the vectorization and divergence handling for the dual compute unit code gives a higher sustained bandwidth (4.317 GB/s), but lower overall performance. (We believe this to be due to the fact that the native memory request size is 2 words. In some cases, reading the two words separately can result in separate requests being issued and artificially inflate bandwidth). An additional caution is that the profiler is known by the vendor to provide unreliable results under some circumstances.[8]

Taking these points together, we believe our algorithm to be within a moderate constant factor of optimal on our hardware.

7.4 Load Balancing on Multiple Compute Units

As explained in Section 5.5, our current implementation statically distributes the load between the two compute units on the device. We believe that static load balancing will not suffice for a real implementation (or even our own implementation on a device with more than two compute units). Given that we expect to see the number of compute units grow in future-generation parts, this is an urgent concern. With this in mind, we experimented with a number of options for synchronization between compute units.

Today, GPUs are primarily used for regular numeric computations. The traditional approach to irregular (imbalanced) computations has been to either pre-partition data into regular components or to defer irregular work to the CPU. Synchronization and load balancing between compute units is an underexplored area.

Graph traversal is a highly irregular computation. The analogy of pre-partitioning (and re-partitioning) for graph traversal is to stop the GPU kernel after regular intervals, have the CPU inspects all queues, load balance if necessary, and then relaunch the kernels. This is related to the option chosen by Veldema and Philippsen [21]. As they showed, it can be used effectively, but incurs significant overhead since kernel launch and termination are expensive synchronization actions (see Section 4.4 for discussion of launch overheads). Additionally, this solution would interfere with our goal of leaving the CPU available for other processing. Potential alternatives include:

- Using global atomics to synchronize through shared memory. As discussed previously and documented by Elteir et al. [7], global operations are prohibitively expensive on AMD hardware. It may be viable on hardware from other vendors or future generations of GPUs.

---

[8] As noted in the Developer Release Notes for AMD APP SDK v2.6.

- Using on-device hardware counters to construct a fast software lock. After a trial implementation, we were forced to conclude that the counters were not appropriate for our goals.

- Having each compute unit copy content from the other compute unit's queue into its own if its queue length drops below its number of work-items. This scheme does not use any form of synchronization and thus cannot update the source queue safely. As a result, redundant work can and will be performed. From preliminary results, it appears that the overhead caused by the inspection outweighs any benefit provided by the load balancing. We did not explore this idea further.

Based on our investigation, the only dynamic load balancing scheme that seems currently viable is to use the CPU for coordination as suggested by Veldema and Philippsen [21]. This is unsatisfactory and we see a need for future work in this area.

7.5 Assessment of Garbage Collection on Current GPUs

Our results show that it is possible, with a significant overhead, to build a GPU-based garbage collector on current hardware. The numbers from the microbenchmarks show that an optimized GPU mark algorithm can, for the best case, significantly outperform a mark algorithm running on the CPU. However, our results for the DaCapo benchmarks show that the mark phase for real-world workloads is 40-80% slower than on the CPU (but sometimes outperforms Jikes' `MarkSweep` collector).

We noted that the copy-overheads for the heap (or reference graph) can quickly reach or exceed the order of magnitude of an actual collection on the CPU, even if CPU and GPU are on a single chip. We therefore argue that, to make GPU-based garbage collection feasible, we have to wait for architectures (or, in our case, drivers) that support zero-copy mapping between the two devices. However, these devices are appearing at the moment.

At the same time, the overhead from maintaining the reference graph will have to be reduced as well. We expect that GPUs will soon allow mapping enough memory to store the entire heap, so that minimal changes to Jikes' object model should be sufficient to run our collector without the reference graph.

Once these overheads disappear, there is no intrinsic reason why GPUs could not be used for garbage collection in the near future. A particularly interesting application area is the use in concurrent garbage collectors: if it is possible to generate a snapshot of a part of the heap (which may well have the form of our reference graph), it could be offloaded to the GPU and collected in isolation from the mutators running on the main CPU.

7.6 Future Directions in Hardware

During our work, we discovered a number of situations where we were severely limited by the capabilities of the hardware. Oftentimes these were "quirks" rather than fundamental limitations of GPUs, and we believe that, as more non-numeric workloads (such as GC) appear, vendors could quickly address them.

As discussed is Section 7.4, support for dynamic load balancing is a particular problematic area. Given the ongoing efforts by GPU vendors to generalize their applicability, we expect that better support will be forthcoming in future revisions of hardware and software. We also note that the specific issues we encountered were vendor-specific and might not apply to other vendors' devices.

Another area of potential improvement is the provisioning of dedicated memory-bandwidth for the individual components of integrated GPUs; AMD Fusion APUs have the disadvantage that the performance of an application running on the CPU is directly tied to the memory behavior of the corresponding code on the GPU and vice versa. While some dynamic provisioning is certainly desirable, a priority reservation per device would help to improve performance isolation.

A different aspect that causes problems on current-generation hardware is the vastly different model in AMD and NVIDIA GPUs, which requires fundamentally different mechanisms, optimizations and trade-offs (e.g. memory coalescing is much more important on NVIDIA GPUs than it is on AMD hardware). With a more serious entrance from Intel into the GPGPU market, this may well leave us with three fundamentally different GPU models. While it would be possible to auto-tune a collector to the individual platform before running it, a broad adaption of GPU-assisted garbage collection would require a more unified programming model.

Somewhat orthogonally, we also believe that GPU-like support for parallelism might become increasingly integrated into the CPU itself. This would make it easier to implement an approach such as ours directly on this parallel hardware on the CPU. However, current-generation CPUs lack support for `scatter` and `gather` instructions, which would be crucial for such an approach.

Overall, we believe that hardware is heading in a direction that is beneficial to our approach: the number of supported work-items per workgroup is increasing, more memory is becoming available to the GPU, CPU/GPU integration is becoming more common (eliminating copy-overhead) and cache-coherence between CPUs and GPUs is on the horizon. We therefore believe that the work we show in this paper will be particularly relevant for the next generation of hardware and may show an appealing application of those devices beyond graphics-intense and special-purpose workloads.

8. Related Work

The idea of performing garbage collection on the GPU is not a contribution of this paper. Jiva and Frost describe the basic approach in a patent application in 2010 [13], while Sun and Ricci [20] describe the idea as part of a larger vision of using GPUs to speed-up a variety of traditional operating system tasks. However, to our knowledge, none of them has published an appropriate algorithm or publicly disclosed a working GPU-based collector.

While the recent work by Veldema and Philippsen [21] explores the implementation of a mark & sweep garbage collector on the GPU, their work differs from ours in a number of important points. First and foremost, their goal was not to use the GPU to accelerate garbage collection for programs running on the CPU, but to provide garbage collection facilities for CUDA-like programs written in a Java dialect and running on the GPU. Additionally, our mark algorithm bears little resemblance to theirs.

There have been a few recent papers proposing potential non-numeric applications for GPUs. Naghmouchi et al. [18] investigated using GPUs for regular expression matching. Smith et al. [19] evaluate GPUs as a platform for network packet inspection.

Several groups have investigated efficient algorithms for performing breadth-first-search on a GPU. One of the first publications in this space was the work by Harish and Narayanan [10] who presented the first algorithm to perform an efficient breadth-first-search on the GPU. However, this approach was based on visiting every node at every iteration, and was less efficient than the most efficient CPU implementation at that time. Their approach was improved by Luo et al. [16] who used an approach based on hierarchical queues to achieve better performance. Recent work by Hong et al. [12] improved the performance even further. Veldema and Philippsen's [21] approach resembles the work by Harish and Narayanan [10], whereas ours takes the approach of Luo et al. [16] and Hong et al. [12]

Another body of work that is related to ours describes the use of other parallel architectures or heterogeneous platforms to perform garbage collection. An example for this is the work by Cher and Gschwind which demonstrates how to use the Cell processor to accelerate garbage collection [22]. Barabash and Petrank cover the problem of garbage collection on highly parallel platforms from a more general perspective and perform a heap analysis similar to ours [5]. An early paper by Appel and Bendiksen [4] covers garbage collection on vector processors and our approach has been influenced by some of their ideas.

There is, of course, a multitude of work in the general space of garbage collection. A general introduction can be found in [14]. While we are focusing on mark & sweep garbage collection, the state of the art collectors are usually parallel generational-copying collectors. A good example for such a collector is given in [17].

9. Conclusion

GPUs are often underutilized when not executing graphics-intense or special-purpose numerical computations. We showed that it is possible to offload garbage collection workloads to the GPU, to use these otherwise unused cycles.

We presented and evaluated a prototype of a GPU-based collector for real-world Java programs. We first examined heap graphs from the DaCapo benchmark suite to show that there are no structural features that would prevent the effective parallelization that is required by a GPU. We then implemented a queue-based mark algorithm on the GPU, as well as a number of optimizations. We integrated this algorithm into a collector for the Jikes RVM.

Reflecting the direction of current hardware trends, we used an integrated GPU/CPU device as our evaluation platform. With minor adjustments to reflect the limits of current-generation parts, we showed that a GPU implementation of the mark phase is nearly performance-competitive with a tuned CPU implementation.

We identified two hardware features which are essential for garbage collection on GPUs: eliminating copy overhead (zero-copy) and enabling the GPU to access the entire physical address space of the CPU. We also highlight fast synchronization between compute units on the GPU and the memory subsystem as areas where hardware changes would be profitable to better support garbage collection. Current hardware trends indicate that each of these areas is likely to improve rapidly in the near future.

Acknowledgments

We would like to thank David Sheffield for providing us with insights to developments in hardware architectures and GPUs in particular. Thanks is also owed to Eric Brewer for his feedback on early drafts of this paper, and to our colleagues at UC Berkeley for proof-reading and advice. Last but not least, we would like to thank the anonymous reviewers for their comments.

References

[1] B. Alpern, S. Augart, S. M. Blackburn, M. Butrico, A. Cocchi, P. Cheng, J. Dolby, S. Fink, D. Grove, M. Hind, K. S. McKinley, M. Mergen, J. E. B. Moss, T. Ngo, V. Sarkar, and M. Trapp. The Jikes Research Virtual Machine project: Building an open-source research community. *IBM Systems Journal*, 44(2):399–417, 2005.

[2] AMD. AMD Embedded G-Series Platform: The world's first combination of low-power CPU and advanced GPU integrated into a single embedded device. http://www.amd.com/us/Documents/49282_G-Series_platform_brief.pdf.

[3] AMD. AMD Accelerated Parallel Processing (APP) SDK OpenCL Programming Guide. http://developer.amd.com/sdks/AMDAPPSDK/assets/AMD_Accelerated_Parallel_Processing_OpenCL_Programming_Guide.pdf.

[4] A. W. Appel and A. Bendiksen. Vectorized garbage collection. *The Journal of Supercomputing*, 3:151–160, 1989.

[5] K. Barabash and E. Petrank. Tracing garbage collection on highly parallel platforms. *SIGPLAN Not.*, 45:1–10, June 2010.

[6] S. M. Blackburn, R. Garner, C. Hoffmann, A. M. Khang, K. S. McKinley, R. Bentzur, A. Diwan, D. Feinberg, D. Frampton, S. Z. Guyer, M. Hirzel, A. Hosking, M. Jump, H. Lee, J. E. B. Moss, A. Phansalkar, D. Stefanović, T. VanDrunen, D. von Dincklage, and B. Wiedermann. The DaCapo Benchmarks: Java Benchmarking Development and Analysis. *SIGPLAN Not.*, 41:169–190, October 2006.

[7] M. Elteir, H. Lin, and W.-C. Feng. Performance Characterization and Optimization of Atomic Operations on AMD GPUs. In *2011 IEEE International Conference on Cluster Computing (CLUSTER)*, pages 234 –243, Sept 2011.

[8] E. M. Gagnon and L. J. Hendren. SableVM: A Research Framework for the Efficient Execution of Java Bytecode. In *In Proceedings of the Java Virtual Machine Research and Technology Symposium*, pages 27–40, 2000.

[9] R. J. Garner, S. M. Blackburn, and D. Frampton. A comprehensive evaluation of object scanning techniques. In *Proceedings of the International Symposium on Memory Management*, ISMM '11, pages 33–42, New York, NY, USA, 2011.

[10] P. Harish and P. J. Narayanan. Accelerating large graph algorithms on the GPU using CUDA. *Technology*, 4873:197–208, 2007.

[11] M. Harris. Parallel Prefix Sum (Scan) with CUDA. *GPU Gems*, 3 (April):851–876, 2007.

[12] S. Hong, S. K. Kim, T. Oguntebi, and K. Olukotun. Accelerating CUDA graph algorithms at maximum warp. In *Proceedings of the 16th ACM Symposium on Principles and Practice of Parallel Programming*, PPoPP '11, pages 267–276, New York, NY, USA, 2011.

[13] A. S. Jiva and G. R. Frost. GPU Assisted Garbage Collection, 04 2010. URL http://www.patentlens.net/patentlens/patent/US_2010_0082930_A1/en/.

[14] R. Jones and R. D. Lins. *Garbage Collection: Algorithms for Automatic Dynamic Memory Management*. Wiley, Sept. 1996.

[15] Khronos Group. OpenCL 1.2 Specification. http://www.khronos.org/registry/cl/specs/opencl-1.2.pdf.

[16] L. Luo, M. Wong, and W.-m. Hwu. An effective GPU implementation of breadth-first search. In *Proceedings of the 47th Design Automation Conference*, DAC '10, pages 52–55, New York, NY, USA, 2010.

[17] S. Marlow, T. Harris, R. P. James, and S. Peyton Jones. Parallel generational-copying garbage collection with a block-structured heap. In *Proceedings of the 7th International Symposium on Memory Management*, ISMM '08, pages 11–20, New York, NY, USA, 2008.

[18] J. Naghmouchi, D. P. Scarpazza, and M. Berekovic. Small-ruleset regular expression matching on GPGPUs: quantitative performance analysis and optimization. In *Proceedings of the 24th ACM International Conference on Supercomputing*, ICS '10, pages 337–348, New York, NY, USA, 2010.

[19] R. Smith, N. Goyal, J. Ormont, K. Sankaralingam, and C. Estan. Evaluating GPUs for network packet signature matching. In *International Symposium on Performance Analysis of Systems and Software, 2009. ISPASS 2009*, pages 175 –184, April 2009.

[20] W. Sun and R. Ricci. Augmenting Operating Systems With the GPU. Technical report, University of Utah, 2010.

[21] R. Veldema and M. Philippsen. Iterative data-parallel mark & sweep on a GPU. In *Proceedings of the International Symposium on Memory Management*, ISMM '11, pages 1–10, New York, NY, USA, 2011.

[22] C. yong Cher and M. Gschwind. Cell GC: using the Cell synergistic processor as a garbage collection coprocessor. In *VEE '08: Proceedings of the 4th ACM SIGPLAN/SIGOPS International Conference on Virtual Execution Environments*, pages 141–150. ACM, 2008.

Barriers Reconsidered, Friendlier Still! *

Xi Yang[†], Stephen M. Blackburn[†], Daniel Frampton[†], Antony L. Hosking[‡]

[†]Australian National University   [‡]Purdue University

[†]{Xi.Yang, Steve.Blackburn, Daniel.Frampton}@anu.edu.au   [‡]hosking@cs.purdue.edu

Abstract

Read and write barriers mediate access to the heap allowing the collector to control and monitor mutator actions. For this reason, barriers are a powerful tool in the design of any heap management algorithm, but the prevailing wisdom is that they impose significant costs. However, changes in hardware and workloads make these costs a moving target. Here, we measure the cost of a range of useful barriers on a range of modern hardware and workloads. We confirm some old results and overturn others. We evaluate the microarchitectural sensitivity of barrier performance and the differences among benchmark suites. We also consider barriers in context, focusing on their behavior when used in combination, and investigate a known pathology and evaluate solutions. Our results show that read and write barriers have average overheads as low as 5.4% and 0.9% respectively. We find that barrier overheads are more exposed on the workload provided by the modern DaCapo benchmarks than on old SPECjvm98 benchmarks. Moreover, there are differences in barrier behavior between in-order and out-of-order machines, and their respective memory subsystems, which indicate different barrier choices for different platforms. These changing costs mean that algorithm designers need to reconsider their design choices and the nature of their resulting algorithms in order to exploit the opportunities presented by modern hardware.

Categories and Subject Descriptors D.3.4 [*Programming Languages*]: Processors—Memory management (garbage collection), Run-time environments

General Terms Experimentation, Languages, Performance, Measurement

Keywords Write barriers, Memory management, Garbage collection, Java

1. Introduction

Software read and write barriers are small code fragments transparently inserted into a program by the compiler or interpreter to mediate run-time accesses to memory. By observing and/or intercepting a program's accesses, they allow the run-time system to: a) present richer memory abstractions, and b) transparently implement aggressive memory management strategies. For example, array bounds checks enforce memory safety and read and write barriers are used to ensure correctness of concurrent garbage collection. The creative possibilities opened up by the mediating role of barriers are large. However, because barriers add instructions to the

---

* This work supported by grants ARC DP0666059 and NSF CCF-0811691.

program, any opportunities they present are held in tight check by performance concerns. Because their overhead is often hard to measure, in practice it is typically *perceptions of overhead* that curtail the creative use of barriers.

Software barriers are particularly interesting today because of the growing use of garbage collected languages, and simultaneously, significant disruption to hardware trends. These developments invite deeper investigation into barrier costs because they indicate both a growing dependence on barriers and a growing need for creative memory management strategies that might minimize the impact of disruptive and complex hardware changes. Furthermore, as hardware evolves the folklore surrounding software barrier costs must also be re-examined.

We measure the mutator cost of a range of barriers on a range of hardware and Java workloads. We find that: a) modern benchmarks expose the overheads of barriers more than older benchmarks did, b) write barrier costs are lower on modern machines, and c) barrier overheads can be sensitive to microarchitecture. We consider commonly used barriers as well as more fundamental barriers from which other barriers can be composed. This strategy allows us to tease apart the sources of overhead and will guide future implementers in understanding important influences on barrier overhead.

We compare our findings with the prior study by Blackburn and Hosking [5]. We took some care to optimize each barrier. Using similar hardware, we measured a much lower overhead for a read barrier of 8.5%, down from 15.9%, which we largely attribute to our optimization of the barrier code. The prior work was published before the DaCapo benchmarks became available [11]. We found that the newer benchmarks expose the barrier overheads more than the older ones, so the results in the previous study are understated. We found that on a modern i7-2600 processor, read and write barriers have average overheads as low as 5.4% and 0.9% respectively. We were surprised to see that the overhead of the read barrier on the in-order Atom is almost the same as on the aggressive out-of-order i7 processor. On the other hand the write barrier overhead on the Atom is twice that of the i7. We also examine a barrier pathology [14] that is known to exist in a popular commercial Java virtual machine (JVM). Our study of this pathology for card marking barriers shows it to be very real. We evaluate a number of possible solutions to this pathology.

These changing costs mean that algorithm designers need to reconsider their design choices and the nature of their resulting algorithms in order to exploit the opportunities presented by modern hardware.

2. Related Work

In 2004 Blackburn and Hosking [5] measured the cost of barriers on hardware of that era, including both x86 and PowerPC. Our methodology is essentially the same. Here, we focus on modern x86 platforms, and consider a broader range of benchmarks and additional useful barriers. We explore barrier costs more precisely using hardware performance counters. Our results using similar hardware broadly confirm theirs, but we observe a number of interesting differences in behavior on current platforms, such as a greatly reduced read barrier overhead. Details appear in Section 5.

Previous direct studies of barrier overheads used less direct approaches to studying barrier cost. Zorn [26] timed the cost of barrier implementations in a tight loop and then used heap access profiles for several large Lisp programs to estimate the total cost of the barriers executing in those programs. These ranged from 2% to 6% for inlined fast path write barriers, and up to 20% for read barriers. Because Lisp is dynamically-typed the overhead includes the cost of dynamically filtering out non-pointer accesses.

Real-time copying collectors commonly use an indirection barrier (for both reads and writes) so that all accesses forward to the most recent copy of the object in constant time [12]. Bacon et al. [4] measured the cost of this style of barrier as 4% on average and 10% maximum for the SPECjvm98 benchmarks. To obtain these results they applied standard optimizations (such as common-subexpression elimination) and special-purpose optimizations (such as barrier-sinking, which moves the barrier to the point of use, so allowing the null-check for the access to combine with that for the barrier).

There is much other related work looking at the effects of different barriers on both mutator and collector execution [2, 3, 9, 13, 18–21, 24, 25]. Some use hardware and/or operating system support. As in Blackburn and Hosking [5], we focus here on pure software techniques. Blackburn and McKinley [6] detail the impact of barriers on compile times and code quality. Hirzel et al. [17] designed a region-based collector to avoid the need for barriers entirely so as to eliminate their overhead. Hellyer et al. [16] study the locality effects of barriers in concurrent collectors.

3. Barriers

We now describe each of the barriers we evaluate. We first describe the most simple barriers, which we term *primitive* barriers, before describing *compound* barriers, which combine primitive barriers to build more sophisticated barriers. We consider both because primitive barriers have the attraction of being easier to analyze, while compound barriers may be more interesting because of their broader application.

In practice, barriers also occur when array elements are written, arrays are copied, and in a number of other more obscure circumstances. Table 2 shows the relative frequency of the important cases. Depending on the barrier semantics, an array copy (System.arrayCopy) can be greatly optimized, and need not consist of naïve element-by-element application of the simple barrier. In our performance analysis, we apply array copy optimizations aggressively. For simplicity, in this section we present only the code for barriers corresponding to putfield and getfield bytecode operations.

3.1 Primitive Barriers

Figure 2 presents Java and x86 assembly code for each of the primitive barriers. Each of the Java code segments belongs in the context of the skeleton code shown in Figure 1. We assume that a read barrier must load at least the reference value held in the source (src) object's slot and return the (equivalent, possibly modified) reference (i.e., the read barrier substitutes for the load). In contrast, we assume that the actual store of the target (tgt) reference is performed separately from the write barrier (i.e., the write barrier is additional to the store). Figure 2, and subsequent figures showing barrier code, present only the barrier operations (without showing the actual heap load/store).

```
 1  @Inline
 2  public ObjectReference objectReferenceRead(
 3      ObjectReference src,
 4      Address slot)
 5  {
 6      ObjectReference value;
 7      value = slot.loadObjectReference;
 8      /* barrier-specific code here */
 9      return value;
10  }
```

(a) Read

```
 1  @Inline
 2  public final void objectReferenceWrite(
 3      ObjectReference src,
 4      Address slot,
 5      ObjectReference tgt)
 6  {
 7      /* barrier-specific code here */
 8  }
```

(b) Write

Figure 1: Skeleton code for generic read and write barriers.

Card The card marking barrier is widely used to identify intergenerational pointers in a generational garbage collector. It consists of an unconditional store of a byte to a computed offset in a card table. We improved over the previous version of the card marking code [5] by making the card base constant, reducing the barrier from three instructions to two. At collection time, the card table is scanned to identify the location of regions (cards) that contain mutated reference fields. The size of each card (2^9 bytes in our case) dictates how precise the card table is. A more precise card table has a large footprint but reduces the scanning load at collection time. The card marking barrier is widely used in commercial Java virtual machines (JVMs) and is popular primarily because of its simplicity and the fact that it is unconditional. The barrier has a number of potential pathologies which we explore in detail in Section 5.3. Moreover, frequent unconditional stores generate significant write traffic, so if write bandwidth is scarce, the card marking barrier may perform poorly. The collection-time cost of the barrier is a function of the size of the table, which is typically linear in the size of the heap. If the heap is very large the scanning overhead may be considerable. This overhead is imposed on every nursery collection, so discouraging small nurseries, which may otherwise be a desirable choice.

Object The object barrier is also used in generational collection and also conservatively records areas containing mutated reference fields. However, it works by remembering objects whose reference fields were mutated rather than remembering regions of memory (cards). The barrier is conditional. It checks the header of the object being mutated and only remembers the object if a bit is set in the header to indicate that the object has not yet been remembered. The barrier slow path then clears the bit so that the object is not remembered again. The collector scans each remembered object and re-sets its not-remembered bit. A simple optimization allocates new objects with the bit clear, which means they will not be needlessly remembered. We optimized Jikes RVM's implementation of the check for the non-remembered bit (HeaderByte.isUnlogged()) to use the x86 TEST instruction, reducing the four lines of assembly code reported in Blackburn and Hosking [5] down to two.

Because it remembers objects rather than cards, the object barrier is more precise than the card marking barrier. Because it is conditional, the object barrier generates much less write traffic. The first method call within the slow path (line 2) is very small and is explicitly inlined with an @Inline pragma. By contrast, the

```
1 LOG_CARD = 9;
2 offset = src.rshl(LOG_CARD);
3 Gen.cardBuffer.store((byte)1, offset);
4
```
```
1 SHR     EAX      9
2 MOVB    1048576[EAX] 1
3
4
```

(a) Card

```
1 if (HeaderByte.isUnlogged(src)) {
2   HeaderByte.markAsLogged(src);
3   modbuf.insertOutOfLine(src)
4 }
```
```
1 TEST    -8[EBX] -128
2 JEQ     45
3
4
```

(b) Object

```
1 if (!Gen.inNursery(slot) &&
2   Gen.inNursery(tgt))
3   remset.insert(slot);
4
```
```
1 CMP     EDX     -1530920960
2 JGE     0
3 CMP     EAX     -1530920960
4 JGE     38
```

(c) Boundary

```
1 REGION_SIZE = 32*1024*1024;
2 if (tgt.toAddress().NE(Address.zero()))
3   if (src.xor(tgt).GE(REGION_SIZE))
4     remset.insert(slot)
```
```
1 TEST    EAX     EAX
2 JEQ     0
3 XOR     EBX     EAX
4 CMP     EBX     33554432
5 JGE     36
```

(d) Zone

```
1 return value.and(^3);
2
3
4
```
```
1 AND     EDX     -4
2
3
4
5
```

(e) Read

```
1 if (value.and(1).NE(0))
2   return insertNOP(src);
3 return value;
4
```
```
1 TEST    EAX     1
2 JNE     35
3
4
5
```

(f) Conditional Read

Figure 2: Primitive barriers, showing Java source for the barrier and x86 assembler for the fast path.

second method is larger and is explicitly forced out of line with the @NoInline pragma. The barrier slow path therefore includes a couple of instructions and a call. We show later (in Table 4) that the object barrier only remembers an object once every thousand times it is invoked. In the presence of a good branch predictor, the object barrier's very low take-rate may help mitigate the fact that the barrier is conditional. This very low take-rate may also argue for forcing the entire slow path out of line, reducing i-cache pressure, however we have not explored this.

Boundary The boundary barrier remembers the address of any reference that crosses a fixed address boundary in a particular direction. This can be used as an inter-generational barrier when the nursery is strictly higher or lower than the mature heap in the address space. If the nursery is in high memory then null references are automatically ignored by the barrier. At collection time all of the remembered reference fields are scanned by the collector. Unlike card marking and the object barrier, this barrier will log duplicates when the program changes a given field repeatedly. Table 4 shows that on average the boundary barrier remembers fields 19 times as often as the object barrier remembers objects.

Zone The zone barrier uses exclusive or to test for and remember all references that cross power-of-two-aligned regions of the address space. In our example we use a large 32 MB zone. So the address space is broken into 32 MB zones on 32 MB alignment boundaries. Before checking whether the reference crosses boundaries, we check whether the target is null. This is because 42% of references that cross boundaries are due to null-assignments to reference fields. Table 4 shows that the zone barrier remembers pointers very frequently, 390 times as often as the object boundary.

Read The unconditional read barrier is a very simple bit-masking barrier, masking the two low-order bits of the reference value before it is returned to the caller. The motivation for such a barrier is that it can be used to cleanse addresses that have had their low-order bits tainted. In a system such as a JVM where all addresses are guaranteed to be at least word-aligned this barrier safely allows 'stealing' of the low order bits. Although this barrier is very simple, reads occur an order of magnitude more frequently than writes

```
1 return value.and(^3);
2
3
4
```
```
1 AND     EDX     -4
2
3
4
5
```

(a) Read

```
1 Word old = slot.load();
2 if (!old.and(3).isZero())
3   slowPath(slot, tgt);
4
```
```
1 AND     EDI     -4
2 MOV     EAX     ESI
3 TEST    [EBX]   1
4 JNE     105
5
```

(b) Write

Figure 3: The bit-stealing barrier, showing Java source for the barrier and x86 assembler for the fast path.

(see Table 2), so it has far greater potential to slow the program down. This barrier has been implemented in hardware on a number of mainstream RISC architectures that require memory operations to be word-aligned, but is not supported on x86.

Conditional Read The conditional read barrier will remember the loaded reference if the reference has its low order bit set. When run in isolation, the test will always fail, so the slow path will never be executed. However, the compiler cannot identify this fact, so the test is not optimized away. We made an improvement over the conditional barrier used by Blackburn and Hosking [5]. They used value.and(1).NE(1) where we use value.and(1).NE(0). Our code is faster for two reasons: a) it compiles down to the TEST instruction rather than an immediate mode comparison, and b) by reversing the sense of the comparison, the taken case (line 3 of the Java code) does not require a branch.

3.2 Compound Barriers

These barriers combine one or more of the primitive barriers to form more complex barriers.

Bit-Stealing The bit-stealing barrier 'steals' one or both of the low order bits of references in a context where the bits are unneeded because references are guaranteed to be word-aligned. The Java and assembler code for this barrier is shown in Figure 3. The barrier consists of both a write barrier that sets the bits under some condition, and a read barrier that masks the bits out before use. The read barrier is identical to the unconditional read barrier of Section 3.1. The bit-stealing barrier is analogous to the object barrier, but instead of conditionally remembering modified objects it conditionally remembers modified fields. It is therefore precise rather than conservative. Once the field is remembered, a low order bit is set ensuring that it is not re-remembered until the bit is cleared again at the next collection. Like the object barrier, the bit-stealing barrier does not remember duplicates.

Hybrid Object/Region The hybrid barrier presented by Blackburn and Hosking [5] simply uses the object barrier for stores to scalar objects and the boundary barrier for stores to arrays.

4. Methodology

We use similar methodology to that introduced by Blackburn and Hosking [5]. In particular, we use the ignore remsets feature they added to MMTk, which allows us to implement and measure the overhead of barriers. In this section, we present the software, hardware, and measurement methodologies we use, in particular highlighting areas where we differ from their previous barrier overhead study.

Measurement Methodology We implement all barriers in MMTk [10], based on JikesRVM's [1] production configuration that uses a generational Immix [7] collector. By default the generational collector relies on a write barrier to remember references from the mature space to the nursery, allowing an efficient partial trace of the heap. However, the need to gather this remembered set for correctness limits the experiments that can be performed. We use the approach of Blackburn and Hosking [5], where the effect of a nursery collection is simulated by performing a full trace and *only* collecting the nursery. This removes the requirement of gathering the remembered set for correctness, making it possible to measure other systems, including a baseline no-barrier system.

Our focus is on barrier overheads, and so we report mutator time, rather than total or garbage collection time. This is particularly important when using the ignore remset approach, because the full trace to simulate the remembered set may be quite expensive. We use a 32MB fixed size nursery, which performs well for our benchmarks. We execute with a generous heap size: 6× the minimum required for each individual benchmark, so nursery allocation and collection dominates. We run each benchmark 20 times (20 invocations) and report the average. We also report 95% confidence intervals for the average using Student's t-distribution.

Controlling Non-Determinism To reduce perturbation due to dynamic optimization and to maximize the performance of the underlying system that we improve, we use a *warmup replay* methodology, which was recently committed to Jikes RVM, and is a refinement to the pseudoadaptive approach used by Blackburn and Hosking [5]. Before executing any experiments, we gathered compiler optimization profiles from the 10th iteration of each benchmark. When we perform an experiment, we execute one complete iteration of each benchmark without any compiler optimizations, so as to load all the classes and resolve methods. We next apply the benchmark-specific optimization profile after which no further compilation occurs. We then measure and report the subsequent iteration. This methodology greatly reduces non-determinism due to the adaptive optimizing compiler and improves underlying perfor-

mance compared to the prior replay methodology which is used by Blackburn and Hosking [5].

To reduce the non-determinism introduced by the operating system's scheduler on multicore machines, we run using a single core (except for our microbenchmark results that investigate contention when using a card marking barrier).

Metrics We use performance counters to help understand barrier costs. We measure execution time, retired instructions, and instruction cache misses. We report percentage overhead for each of these measures (Δt, Δi, and Δi_{miss}) relative to the *no barrier* configuration. As an indicative measure of how costly the instructions added by each barrier are, we also report $\Delta t/\Delta i$.

Hardware and Software Environment We use three IA32 architectures to explore the role microarchitecture has on barrier overhead: 1) a recent Intel Core i7 2600 processor, 2) an in-order Atom D510, and 3) an older Pentium 4 (P4) D 820 machine (similar to the machine used in the previous study). The i7 represents the current mainstream multicore processor. Unlike the P4, which has a deep superscalar pipeline, the i7 has a more modest out-of-order pipeline with a powerful memory subsystem. The Atom tries to improve energy efficiency by using a simpler in-order pipeline. Table 1 shows the parameters of these three architectures.

Operating System We use Ubuntu 10.04.01 LTS server distribution running with a 64-bit (x86_64) 2.6.32-24 Linux kernel.

Benchmark Properties A key way we improve on previous work is the use of a more comprehensive, modern set of benchmarks. We draw the benchmarks from the DaCapo suite [11], the SPECjvm98 suite [22], and pjbb2005 [8] (a fixed workload version of SPECjbb2005 [23] with 8 warehouses that executes 10,000 transactions per warehouse). We use benchmarks from both 2006-10-MR2 and 9.12 Bach releases of DaCapo to enlarge our suite and because a few 9.12 benchmarks do not execute on Jikes RVM.

Table 2 shows the frequency of operations that may trigger barriers, expressed as a number of operations per millisecond. We include results for reference field and array load/store operations as well as array copy operations, which may invoke a special barrier to avoid performing a naïve element-by-element copy in a loop. The results show both that these statistics vary considerably between benchmarks, and also that the benchmarks used in the previous study are not representative. In particular, we see that the four benchmarks with the lowest reference `putfield` rates are all found within the seven SPECjvm98 benchmarks.

5. Results

We now report the barrier overheads, starting with a detailed evaluation of the costs on modern architectures before discussing microarchitectural sensitivity and examining a case study in pathological write barrier performance.

5.1 The Cost of Barriers on Modern Architectures

We start by examining the cost of read and write barriers on modern hardware. Table 3 summarizes these results and reproduces corresponding numbers from Blackburn and Hosking [5]. All numbers except for the right-most column ($\Delta t/\Delta i$) are expressed as percentage overhead compared to a base case with no barrier. We include 95% confidence intervals in grey beneath the corresponding mean. We include a column P4⋆ that uses a set of benchmarks similar to Blackburn and Hosking [5] as well as similar hardware.

Note that our data differs from Blackburn and Hosking [5] in at least three significant respects, each of which is covered in detail in Section 4: a) our benchmarks are larger and newer, b) our hardware is newer (excepting P4 which approximates the P4 used in the

Architecture	Pentium 4	Atom D510	i7-2600
Model	P4D 820	Atom D510	Core i7-2600
Technology	90nm	45nm	32nm
Clock	2.8GHz	1.66GHz	3.4GHz
Cores × SMT	2 × 2	2 × 2	4 × 2
L2 Cache	1MB × 2	512KB × 4	256KB × 4
L3 Cache	none	none	8MB
Memory	1GB DDR2-400	2GB DDR2-800	4GB DDR3-1066

Table 1: Processors used in our evaluation.

Benchmark	Reference Fields		Reference Arrays			
					Arraycopy	
	Get/μs	Put/μs	Load/μs	Store/μs	Call/μs	Elem/μs
compress	117.41	0.00	0.01	0.00	0.00	0.00
jess	61.98	2.08	42.87	1.99	1.33	9.34
db	75.10	0.66	26.03	5.77	0.00	0.60
javac	69.51	5.86	7.08	0.77	0.00	0.01
mpegaudio	37.34	0.92	60.15	0.00	0.00	0.00
mtrt	68.58	0.69	37.37	0.93	0.00	0.00
jack	52.60	8.86	12.86	2.06	0.01	0.09
SPECjvm mean	*68.93*	*2.72*	*26.62*	*1.64*	*0.19*	*1.43*
antlr	75.21	1.99	1.95	0.19	0.00	0.01
avrora	40.83	1.73	5.71	0.01	0.00	0.00
bloat	81.11	19.12	12.96	0.30	0.00	0.00
eclipse	51.42	2.18	11.97	2.93	0.08	1.75
fop	43.53	1.50	6.17	0.06	0.00	0.02
hsqldb	79.73	6.09	17.40	1.68	0.00	0.28
jython	64.88	6.48	18.45	3.13	0.11	1.07
luindex	61.77	4.90	18.79	0.46	0.00	0.03
lusearch	69.81	6.31	4.61	0.17	0.00	0.00
pmd	63.04	8.02	13.31	0.92	0.01	0.03
sunflow	69.49	3.18	19.13	0.01	0.00	0.00
xalan	60.27	2.82	5.28	1.49	0.00	0.01
DaCapo mean	*63.43*	*5.36*	*11.31*	*0.95*	*0.02*	*0.27*
pjbb2005	42.47	7.94	13.01	1.96	0.00	0.02
min	*37.34*	*0.00*	*0.01*	*0.00*	*0.00*	*0.00*
max	*117.41*	*19.12*	*60.15*	*5.77*	*1.33*	*9.34*
Total mean	**64.31**	**4.57**	**16.76**	**1.24**	**0.08**	**0.66**

Table 2: Frequency of reference field and reference array operations by benchmark and benchmark suite.

Barrier	*Prior [5]*			Current Overheads					
	P4	*AMD*	*P4$_\star$*	P4	Atom		i7		
	Δt	*Δt*	*Δt*	Δt	Δt	Δt	Δi	Δi$_{miss}$	Δt/Δi
Card	*0.8*	*1.0*	*1.8* ±0.4	2.2 ±0.4	1.8 ±0.3	0.9 ±0.8	1.3 ±0.1	6.9 ±1.5	0.70
Object	*1.2*	*1.8*	*0.8* ±0.4	1.8 ±0.4	1.3 ±0.3	1.6 ±0.7	2.0 ±0.1	5.7 ±1.2	0.81
Boundary	*1.3*	*2.2*	*1.5* ±0.7	2.2 ±0.6	2.5 ±0.3	1.7 ±0.8	2.7 ±0.1	10.2 ±1.3	0.65
Zone	*4.8*	*5.1*	*7.1* ±0.5	9.0 ±0.5	9.3 ±0.5	9.6 ±0.8	8.5 ±0.1	28.8 ±1.4	1.12
Read	*5.0*	*8.1*	*4.1* ±0.5	4.6 ±0.5	5.5 ±0.3	5.4 ±0.8	8.5 ±0.2	11.9 ±2.4	0.64
Cond Read	*15.9*	*21.2*	*9.2* ±0.6	9.4 ±0.6	9.1 ±0.5	10.1 ±0.8	20.9 ±0.1	37.2 ±1.7	0.48
Bit Steal			*7.0* ±0.4	7.1 ±0.5	7.8 ±0.4	8.3 ±0.9	12.8 ±0.4	21.2 ±2.3	0.65
Hybrid	*1.3*	*1.8*	*0.9* ±0.4	2.1 ±0.4	1.8 ±0.3	1.7 ±1.1	2.2 ±0.1	9.1 ±1.4	0.78

$\star$ Running on current system with a subset of benchmarks similar to that used by Blackburn and Hosking [5].

Table 3: Summary of barrier overheads on various platforms, expressed in percentages in terms of time (Δt), instructions (Δi), and i-cache misses (Δi$_{miss}$). For comparison, measurements from Blackburn and Hosking [5] are reproduced in italics in the second and third columns. For each average, the corresponding 95% confidence interval is printed in small grey font.

Benchmark Suite	Object							Boundary							Zone						
	Take Rate		Original Slow			NOP Slow			Take Rate		Original Slow			NOP Slow			Take Rate		Original Slow			NOP Slow
	/μs	%	Δt	Δi	Δi_{miss}	Δt	Δi	Δi_{miss}	/μs	%	Δt	Δi	Δi_{miss}	Δt	Δi	Δi_{miss}	/μs	%	Δt	Δi	Δi_{miss}	Δt Δi Δi_{miss}
SPECjvm mean	0.019	0.1	1.0	1.4	4.6	0.8	1.0	11.6	0.0	0.4	0.7	1.7	7.5	1.3	1.4	12.6	7.3	51.7	7.6 7.5 38.6			3.1 3.6 18.5
geomean			0.9	1.4	4.1	0.8	1.0	9.0			0.7	1.7	6.9	1.3	1.4	12.0			7.5 7.3 36.5			3.1 3.5 16.8
DaCapo mean	0.010	0.1	1.8	2.2	6.7	2.0	1.7	7.3	0.4	2.8	2.3	3.1	12.6	3.0	2.5	12.7	6.0	31.4	11.4 9.8 28.0			5.3 4.5 18.6
geomean			1.8	2.2	6.4	2.0	1.7	6.8			2.3	3.1	12.1	2.9	2.4	12.5			10.7 9.3 26.0			5.2 4.4 17.3
Total mean	0.015	0.1	1.6	2.0	6.1	1.6	1.5	8.6	0.3	1.9	1.8	2.7	10.7	2.5	2.2	12.7	6.5	39.0	10.1 8.9 30.9			4.5 4.2 18.4
geomean			1.6	2.0	5.7	1.6	1.5	7.4			1.7	2.7	10.2	2.5	2.2	12.4			9.6 8.5 28.8			4.4 4.2 17.0

Table 4: Summary of take-rate and cost of slow path for conditional barriers on the i7.

prior work), and c) our JVM is newer and faster. Furthermore, on the i7 we present performance counter data for instructions retired (Δi), and i-cache misses (Δi_{miss}), and confidence intervals for our average of 20 runs. Each of these differences reflects the passage of eight years of improvements in software, hardware and evaluation methodology since the previous study and is a source of motivation for our study.

Tables 6 and 7, which appear at the end of the paper, provide substantially more detailed data, including per-benchmark results, all measured on the i7.

5.1.1 Primitive Barriers

Each primitive barrier is described in Section 3.1. The baseline for our comparison is a system with no barrier. The first six rows of Table 3 summarize performance results for each of the primitive barriers (detailed results are in Table 6). For each barrier, the tables report the percentage increase in execution time (Δt), retired instructions (Δi), and instruction cache (i-cache) misses (Δi_{miss}). Table 3 also presents $\Delta t/\Delta i$, which indicates each barrier's ability to be absorbed by instruction-level parallelism (ILP).

Card Card marking shows an average performance hit of just $0.9\% \pm 0.8\%$ on the i7 processor. Retired instructions increase by just 1.3% and i-cache misses are only 6.9% higher. The performance overhead is consistent with Blackburn and Hosking [5], and is explained by the increase in retired instructions. The increase in i-cache misses is higher, but not enough to result in a significant performance overhead. The performance overhead for card marking is significantly higher on the P4 ($2.2\% \pm 0.4\%$) and Atom ($1.8\% \pm 0.3\%$), which both have much lower memory bandwidth than the i7 and much smaller caches. This doubling in overhead between the i7 and Atom is the strongest architectural sensitivity we see for any of the barriers.

Unlike card marking, the object, boundary, and zone barriers are all conditional. Thus, their performance depends heavily on the rate at which their slow path is taken. Table 4 summarizes the take-rates of these write barriers and the impact of taking the slow path. Detailed results are presented in Table 7. For each of the three barriers, we present the rate at which the barrier is taken, both in terms of execution frequency and in percentage rate of slow paths taken per execution of the barrier. We also present overhead statistics as in Table 3 for the barrier with the regular slow path (Original Slow) and with a call to an empty function (NOP Slow).

Object The object barrier has an average performance overhead of $1.6\% \pm 0.7\%$ on the i7. Although a little higher than the card marking barrier, the 0.7% difference between the barriers is smaller than the confidence intervals on either barrier. On the i7, the number of retired instructions increased by 2.0% and the relative change in CPI is very similar to card marking. Perhaps unsurprisingly, we found that the i-cache locality is strongly affected by inlining of

the slow path. When the slow path is forced inline the performance overhead grows to 2.6% and the i-cache misses increase by 20%, compared to 5.7% for the out of line case.

Boundary The boundary barrier has a performance overhead of $1.7\% \pm 0.8\%$ on the i7 — not statistically different from the object or card marking barriers. The take-rate for boundary is an order of magnitude higher than for object, but in absolute terms is low, at around 2%.

Each of these three primitive write barriers records mutated reference fields, but they represent different points in a mutator/collector tradeoff space. Card marking has the highest collection-time overhead, generates the most write traffic and, as we will show in Section 5.3, has some problematic performance pathologies. Yet its performance is not significantly better than either of the other barriers. In the case of card marking, the collector must scan each marked card. The object barrier is similar, but a little more targeted, because it requires each remembered object to be scanned at collection time. By contrast, the boundary barrier is precise — it remembers the address of each modified field, so it requires no scanning at collection time.

Zone The zone barrier is more general than the others because it records mutations crossing multiple boundaries (in both directions). However, this generality comes at a considerable cost, with a $9.6\% \pm 0.8\%$ performance overhead on the i7. This overhead is explained by its slow path take-rate of 39% — more than two orders of magnitude higher than the object barrier! As shown in Figure 2, we explicitly check whether the target address is null before checking whether the boundary is crossed (in a system where young objects are in high memory, a null looks like a mature object). This check is necessary because we found that 42% of taken slow paths were due to nulling of object fields! A standard generational barrier will only remember the mature-to-nursery pointers. Table 4 shows that when we replaced the slow path with a call to an empty function the average overhead reduced to 4.4%. This reduction is due both to the removal of parameter marshaling overhead and the cost of actually executing the code that stores the remembered pointer field. This result differs considerably from the overhead of just 5% reported by Blackburn and Hosking [5].

The overheads of these three conditional write barriers are quite different for different benchmark suites. The average overheads of DaCapo are 1.8%, 2.3%, 10.7% for object, boundary, and zone barriers, respectively. These are much higher than SPECjvm98, at 0.9%, 0.7%, and 7.5%, respectively. The explanation lies in the high rate of reference writes in DaCapo, revealed in Table 2 . The DaCapo reference write rate is about $2\times$ higher than SPECjvm98. One DaCapo benchmark, bloat, has $7\times$ more frequent reference writes than the average for SPECjvm98.

We now examine the two primitive read barriers.

Read The unconditional read barrier has an overhead of 5.4% on the i7 despite a 8.5% increase in retired instructions. The fraction $\Delta t/\Delta i$ is just 0.64, indicating that much of the instruction overhead is absorbed by instruction level parallelism (ILP). Interestingly, on the ILP-limited Atom the performance overhead is only 5.5%.

Conditional Read The conditional read barrier has a 10.1% overhead with a 20% increase in retired instructions. The fraction $\Delta t/\Delta i$ is 0.48, which is the lowest of all the barriers we measure. We see a 9.2% overhead on the P4, which is significantly lower than the 15.9% and 21.2% previously reported by Blackburn and Hosking [5] for the P4 and AMD, respectively. We attribute this improvement to our tuning of the barrier to use a compare to zero rather than immediate mode compare to 1 (cf. Section 3.1).

Summarizing our analysis of primitive barriers, we find that among the write barriers, card marking has the lowest overhead on i7, but only by 0.7%, which is not statistically significant. Furthermore, card marking does not perform well on the Atom or P4. The difference between them is very likely due to the substantially better memory subsystem of the i7. The object barrier is attractive because it outperforms card marking on the Atom and P4 and unlike the previous findings, it dominates boundary and hybrid.

5.1.2 Compound Barriers

Section 3.2 describes each of the compound barriers. The last two rows of Table 3 (and the right-most two column groups of Table 6: Bit Steal and Hybrid) give performance results for each of the compound barriers, relative to the base case where no barriers are used.

Bit Steal Recall from Section 3.2 that the bit steal barrier combines the (unconditional) read barrier with a write barrier that remembers any unlogged reference fields (determined by the 'stolen' low order bit of the reference), and marks the reference as logged by *atomically* updating it. Retired instructions increase by 12.8% while time increases by only 8.3%. I-cache miss rates also increase by 21%, in line with the overheads for the primitive conditional write and unconditional read barriers.

Hybrid The hybrid barrier shows an average performance overhead of 1.7% on the i7 processor. Retired instructions increase by 2.2% and i-cache misses increase by 9.1%. The performance overhead remains fairly consistent with Blackburn and Hosking [5], and is explained by the increase in retired instructions. However, unlike the prior findings, hybrid does not dominate object and boundary. The detailed results in Table 6 show that the worst case performance of hybrid (**max**) is worse than that for object and boundary. It is therefore hard to argue for hybrid over object or boundary on the basis of our analysis using modern benchmarks and modern machines.

5.2 Microarchitectural Sensitivity

We evaluated three different microarchitecture in this study: an aggressively out-of-order machine (P4), an in-order machine (Atom), and a modern out-of-order machine (i7). As shown in Table 1, compared with the i7, both the P4 and Atom have outdated memory subsystems. Not only do they have much smaller caches, but they also suffer low memory bandwidth. Nevertheless, it is surprising that the barrier performance is relative stable among the three diverse microarchitectures. However, there are a number of trends revealed in Table 3.

Among the barriers, card marking is the most memory intensive because it unconditionally executes a store (it does not have a slow path) which may cause a cache miss. Although the object barrier's fast path contains a load to check the source header, the header byte is likely already to be in the cache. Thus, the performance of

Barrier	Overall	Pathology
Card Bytemap	0.88 ±0.78	378.0 ±51.6
Card Wordmap	0.91 ±0.75	372.4 ±48.4
Card Wordmap NT	3.58 ±0.77	40.1 ±24.7
Card Conditional Set	2.44 ±0.83	26.7 ±5.9
Object	1.57 ±0.74	1.0 ±5.1

Table 5: Card marking overheads on the i7 in average and pathological contexts, expressed as percentages. We show four variations of card marking barriers, plus an object barrier. The barriers have successively lower overhead in the pathological setting.

card marking will depend more heavily on the memory subsystem. As shown in Table 3, the overhead of card marking on the more powerful i7 is much less than for the other two architectures.

In contrast, read barriers have different behavior. On the slow in-order Atom, read barrier overheads are always marginally better than that of the state-of-the-art i7. This is also due to the differences in memory subsystem. Unlike the write barriers, our read barriers do not have any memory accesses, so their cost should be similar on all three machines. But, the Atom's cache is 16 times smaller than the i7's, so the impact of the extra read barrier instructions is buried in the higher cache miss rates for the Atom. The P4 has a similar memory subsystem to the Atom (for similar miss rates), but it is much more aggressively out-of-order so it can more readily hide the read barrier overheads. The i7 can similarly hide the read barrier overhead, but its lower cache miss rate offers less opportunity to hide read barriers behind cache misses. Indeed, memory-bound operations like the write barriers benefit more from the i7's larger caches.

The Atom is noticeably worse on the boundary barrier than the other architectures. We speculate that the cause of this slowdown may be that the boundary barrier uses two `CMP REG IMM` instructions where the immediate value is 32 bits long. The Atom is known to perform poorly with instructions greater than 4 bytes because of its low instruction fetch-rate [15].

5.3 A Case Study in Barrier Pathology

We now explore and evaluate a known barrier pathology along with several potential solutions to the pathology. Table 5 shows the performance of four different card marking implementations and the object barrier. We show the overall performance when run against our suite of 20 benchmarks and the performance when run on a microbenchmark designed to highlight the pathology.

Card marking is often advocated as a very low-cost unconditional write barrier (indeed it is cheap according to our results and those of Blackburn and Hosking [5]), but it does suffer from at least two known pathologies. The first is that the work of scanning the cards is a function of heap size and thus small nurseries perform poorly because of the fixed cost of scanning the cards dominates. The second arises when multiple threads perform frequent concurrent updates to the same or adjacent cards, resulting in cache contention on the cache line holding the metadata for those cards [14]. We focus now on this second pathology.

One proposed solution is to use conditional card marking, marking a card only if it is not already marked. This eliminates unnecessary writes (and any associated contention) at the expense of an additional read. Table 5 shows that whereas the average overhead of card marking is 0.88% ± 0.78%, conditional card marking is more than twice as expensive at 2.4% ± 0.83%. The simple object barrier discussed earlier is cheaper at $1.57\% \pm 0.74\%$ overhead. Another suggested solution is to use a non-temporal store instruction when marking a card, allowing the write to occur without affecting the cache. Unfortunately, Table 5 reveals that this has unacceptably high overhead of $3.58\% \pm 0.77\%$. Thus, using non-temporal instructions to avoid cache contention in card marking is less preferable than conditional card marking, but using a cheaper alternative such as the object barrier also avoids the pathology.

To illustrate the gains to be had, we use a synthetic micro-benchmark designed to trigger card mark contention. This benchmark creates multiple worker threads, each of which has a thread-local buffer that is continually written to in a tight loop. If the buffer objects themselves are located on different cache lines — but lie within the same or adjacent cards — then the card marking barrier can introduce contention. This microbenchmark is drawn from the real world example of a work-stealing scheduler, where each worker thread is managing task objects in a thread-local buffer.[1] Table 5 shows that this pathology can cause dramatic slowdowns, with the byte-map card barrier suffering 378% overhead, meaning that the system runs nearly $5\times$ slower. While all of the proposals to reduce contention are reasonably effective when compared to the original byte-map card marking, in practice the object barrier handles this case better than any of the card approaches.

6. Conclusion

This paper presents a detailed and up-to-date quantitative study of barrier costs. Because barriers are a key building block for memory management algorithms and enable opportunities for algorithmic creativity, properly understanding their cost is essential. Reprising the previous study of Blackburn and Hosking [5], we deepen and renew the results using modern workloads, modern hardware, and more rigorous methodology. The use of modern workloads is critical because the prior study was done with the simplest of Java workloads. The use of modern hardware is important because there has been substantial upheaval in computer architecture in the eight years since the previous work. Applying more rigorous methodology is essential because it clarifies the significance of some important results. By using performance counters we were able to shed more light on why barriers perform differently. We have also examined an important write barrier pathology and evaluated four alternative solutions.

Significant changes in computer architecture and increasing demand for managed languages are likely to put renewed pressure on researchers to develop interesting memory management solutions for diverse settings. Our work fortifies the algorithmic toolkit available to researchers embarking on this route by quantifying barrier costs in detail.

References

[1] B. Alpern, D. Attanasio, J. J. Barton, M. G. Burke, P.Cheng, J.-D. Choi, A. Cocchi, S. J. Fink, D. Grove, M. Hind, S. F. Hummel, D. Lieber, V. Litvinov, M. Mergen, T. Ngo, J. R. Russell, V. Sarkar, M. J. Serrano, J. Shepherd, S. Smith, V. C. Sreedhar, H. Srinivasan, and J. Whaley. The Jalapeño virtual machine. *IBM System Journal*, 39(1), Feb. 2000. doi: 10.1147/sj.391.0211.

[2] A. W. Appel. Simple generational garbage collection and fast allocation. *Software: Practice and Experience*, 19(2):171–183, Feb. 1989. doi: 10.1002/spe.4380190206.

[3] A. Azagury, E. K. Kolodner, E. Petrank, and Z. Yehudai. Combining card marking with remembered sets: How to save scanning time. In *ACM International Symposium on Memory Management*, pages

10–19, Vancouver, Canada, Oct. 1998. doi: 10.1145/286860.286862.

[4] D. F. Bacon, P. Cheng, and V. T. Rajan. A real-time garbage collector with low overhead and consistent utilization. In *Proceedings of the Thirtieth Annual ACM Symposium on the Principles of Programming Languages*, pages 285–294, New Orleans, LA, Jan. 2003. doi: 10.1145/604131.604155.

[5] S. M. Blackburn and A. Hosking. Barriers: Friend or foe? In *ACM International Symposium on Memory Management*, pages 143–151, Vancouver, Canada, Oct. 2004. doi: 10.1145/1029873.1029891.

[6] S. M. Blackburn and K. S. McKinley. In or out? Putting write barriers in their place. In *ACM International Symposium on Memory Management*, pages 175–184, Berlin, Germany, June 2002. doi: 10.1145/512429.512452.

[7] S. M. Blackburn and K. S. McKinley. Immix: A mark-region garbage collector with space efficiency, fast collection, and mutator locality. In *ACM Conference on Programming Language Design and Implementation*, pages 22–32, Tuscon, AZ, June 2008. doi: 10.1145/1375581.1375586.

[8] S. M. Blackburn, M. Hirzel, R. Garner, and D. Stefanović. pjbb2005: The pseudoJBB benchmark. URL http://users.cecs.anu.edu.au/~steveb/research/research-infrastructure/pjbb2005.

[9] S. M. Blackburn, R. E. Jones, K. S. McKinley, and J. E. B. Moss. Beltway: Getting around garbage collection gridlock. In *ACM Conference on Programming Language Design and Implementation*, pages 153–164, Berlin, Germany, June 2002. doi: 10.1145/512529.512548.

[10] S. M. Blackburn, P. Cheng, and K. S. McKinley. Oil and water? High performance garbage collection in Java with MMTk. In *Proceedings of the 26th International Conference on Software Engineering*, pages 137–146, Scotland, UK, May 2004. doi: 10.1109/ICSE.2004.1317436.

[11] S. M. Blackburn, R. Garner, C. Hoffman, A. M. Khan, K. S. McKinley, R. Bentzur, A. Diwan, D. Feinberg, D. Frampton, S. Z. Guyer, M. Hirzel, A. Hosking, M. Jump, H. Lee, J. E. B. Moss, A. Phansalkar, D. Stefanović, T. VanDrunen, D. von Dincklage, and B. Wiedermann. The DaCapo benchmarks: Java benchmarking development and analysis. In *ACM SIGPLAN Conference on Object-Oriented Programming, Systems, Languages, and Applications*, pages 169–190, Oct. 2006. doi: 10.1145/1167515.1167488.

[12] R. A. Brooks. Trading data space for reduced time and code space in real-time garbage collection on stock hardware. In *ACM Conference on Lisp and Functional Programming*, pages 256–262, Austin, Texas, Aug. 1984. doi: 10.1145/800055.802042.

[13] P. J. Caudill and A. Wirfs-Brock. A third-generation Smalltalk-80 implementation. In *ACM Conference on Object–Oriented Programming Systems, Languages, and Applications*, pages 119–130, Portland, OR, Nov. 1986. doi: 10.1145/28697.28709.

[14] D. Dice. False sharing induced by card table marking, Feb. 2011. URL https://blogs.oracle.com/dave/entry/false_sharing_induced_by_card.

[15] A. Fog. The microarchitecture of Intel, AMD and VIA CPUs. An optimization guide for assembly programmers and compiler makers. Copenhagen University College of Engineering, June 2011.

[16] L. Hellyer, R. E. Jones, and A. L. Hosking. The locality of concurrent write barriers. In *ACM International Symposium on Memory Management*, pages 83–92, Toronto, Canada, June 2010. doi: 10.1145/1806651.1806666.

[17] M. Hirzel, A. Diwan, and M. Hertz. Connectivity-based garbage collection. In *ACM Conference on Object–Oriented Programming Systems, Languages, and Applications*, pages 359–373, Anaheim, California, Nov. 2003. doi: 10.1145/949305.949337.

[18] A. L. Hosking and R. L. Hudson. Remembered sets can also play cards. In J. E. B. Moss, P. R. Wilson, and B. Zorn, editors, *OOPSLA Workshop on Garbage Collection in Object-Oriented*

---

[1] Indeed, Doug Lea has reported this pathology in his work on concurrent data structures for the `java.util.concurrent` library.

Systems, Oct. 1993. URL `ftp://ftp.cs.utexas.edu/pub/garbage/GC93/hosking.ps`.

[19] A. L. Hosking and J. E. B. Moss. Protection traps and alternatives for memory management of an object-oriented language. In *Proceedings of the Fourteenth ACM Symposium on Operating Systems Principles*, pages 106–119, Asheville, North Carolina, Dec. 1993. doi: `10.1145/168619.168628`.

[20] A. L. Hosking, J. E. B. Moss, and D. Stefanović. A comparative performance evaluation of write barrier implementations. In *ACM Conference on Object–Oriented Programming Systems, Languages, and Applications*, pages 92–109, Vancouver, Canada, Oct. 1992. doi: `10.1145/141936.141946`.

[21] P. Sobalvarro. A lifetime-based garbage collector for Lisp systems on general-purpose computers. Technical Report AITR-1417, MIT AI Lab, Feb. 1988. Bachelor's thesis.

[22] SPEC. *SPECjvm98, Release 1.03*. Standard Performance Evaluation Corporation, Mar. 1999. URL `http://www.spec.org/jvm98`.

[23] SPEC. *SPECjbb2005 (Java Server Benchmark), Release 1.07*. Standard Performance Evaluation Corporation, 2006. URL `http://www.spec.org/jbb2005`.

[24] D. M. Ungar. Generation scavenging: A non-disruptive high performance storage reclamation algorithm. In *ACM Software Engineering Symposium on Practical Software Development Environments*, pages 157–167, Apr. 1984. doi: `10.1145/800020.808261`.

[25] P. R. Wilson and T. G. Moher. A card-marking scheme for controlling intergenerational references in generation-based garbage collection on stock hardware. *ACM SIGPLAN Notices*, 24(5):87–92, May 1989. doi: `10.1145/66068.66077`.

[26] B. Zorn. Barrier methods for garbage collection. Technical Report CU-CS-494-90, University of Colorado, Boulder, Nov. 1990.

Benchmark	Card			Object			Boundary			Zone			Read			Cond Read			Bit Steal			Hybrid		
	Δt	Δi	Δi_miss	Δt	Δi	Δi_miss	Δt	Δi	Δi_miss	Δt	Δi	Δi_miss	Δt	Δi	Δi_miss	Δt	Δi	Δi_miss	Δt	Δi	Δi_miss	Δt	Δi	Δi_miss
compress	0.0	0.0	-0.8	-0.1	0.0	-1.5	0.0	0.0	2.4	-0.1	0.0	7.3	-9.3	13.7	4.4	-4.6	37.3	14.4	-9.2	16.0	9.5	0.0	0.0	-0.8
jess	2.8	1.2	15.5	1.3	1.5	16.5	1.0	2.0	21.5	12.4	10.1	90.6	20.9	17.0	17.8	23.7	32.9	56.8	31.9	28.6	41.6	2.3	1.8	25.8
db	1.3	1.5	3.1	1.4	2.3	4.1	1.3	3.3	6.7	15.6	19.7	52.2	9.9	25.0	12.1	13.2	43.6	14.0	11.0	28.8	10.4	1.5	3.3	2.5
javac	2.1	1.8	5.7	3.6	3.1	6.5	3.0	3.0	10.4	8.9	6.8	19.5	6.4	6.9	13.2	10.3	14.4	40.1	9.7	10.5	18.8	3.1	2.9	5.8
mpegaudio	0.4	0.2	-0.4	0.2	0.3	-2.0	-0.2	0.3	-0.1	3.9	2.5	31.1	3.2	6.7	17.7	8.2	19.2	41.1	3.5	7.1	13.1	0.3	0.3	-2.0
mtrt	0.0	0.4	21.2	-0.3	0.5	19.4	0.0	0.6	23.6	1.6	1.3	37.2	8.5	9.6	73.5	13.6	27.3	141	9.2	10.6	81.0	0.4	0.6	24.6
jack	0.5	1.6	6.7	0.5	2.4	-11.0	0.1	2.8	-11.8	11.1	12.4	32.0	1.5	4.3	-12.5	4.2	10.9	7.8	5.4	7.7	3.8	1.5	2.5	0.1
SPECjvm mean	1.0	1.0	7.3	1.0	1.4	4.6	0.7	1.7	7.5	7.6	7.5	38.6	5.9	11.9	18.0	9.8	26.5	45.0	8.8	15.6	25.5	1.3	1.6	8.0
	±0.2	±0.0	±1.8	±0.2	±0.0	±0.9	±0.2	±0.0	±0.9	±0.2	±0.0	±1.2	±0.2	±0.2	±4.6	±0.3	±0.0	±1.2	±0.6	±0.7	±3.3	±0.8	±0.0	±1.1
geomean	1.0	1.0	7.0	0.9	1.4	4.1	0.7	1.7	6.9	7.5	7.3	36.5	5.5	11.7	15.8	9.5	26.0	39.9	8.2	15.3	23.2	1.3	1.6	7.5
antlr	-3.3	0.7	4.9	-2.4	1.2	2.8	-5.0	1.2	5.1	-4.3	1.6	10.6	-2.5	5.6	9.1	1.0	10.9	25.0	-0.8	7.1	13.0	-4.9	1.2	0.1
avrora	0.4	0.7	-0.8	2.6	0.8	7.0	0.0	1.6	-0.3	5.0	3.1	13.5	3.5	8.2	10.7	6.1	18.7	32.1	3.2	9.5	9.5	-1.0	0.8	-5.4
bloat	1.0	4.2	3.8	6.8	8.2	6.1	8.3	11.8	7.4	52.7	43.8	37.2	5.8	11.6	7.9	21.1	35.0	32.7	18.7	25.3	20.3	8.6	9.1	9.2
eclipse	0.3	0.6	1.4	-0.7	1.5	-2.6	-0.5	1.3	6.0	7.0	8.1	3.2	3.6	6.1	2.0	4.9	12.1	22.3	3.7	7.7	9.1	2.0	1.2	5.3
fop	1.8	0.6	8.2	5.1	1.3	6.1	2.0	1.3	8.1	6.9	3.0	11.8	2.8	5.3	7.8	7.8	18.0	24.5	5.9	7.1	12.9	1.7	1.4	0.2
hsqldb	2.8	1.8	8.0	3.6	2.5	6.2	5.4	4.4	7.3	9.8	7.8	15.8	7.8	7.5	14.4	12.6	16.9	38.8	12.0	11.2	17.6	5.4	3.4	7.8
jython	1.0	1.6	16.4	2.2	2.4	22.3	2.7	3.5	40.4	16.0	13.0	105	13.8	17.7	23.5	18.8	28.8	66.2	17.1	21.4	66.7	2.9	2.7	60.4
luindex	0.7	1.0	12.8	0.9	0.5	9.3	0.6	0.9	7.1	3.9	2.5	26.5	5.2	7.7	18.0	8.0	14.2	49.0	7.1	8.9	20.7	0.9	0.5	9.8
lusearch	1.7	2.1	7.0	1.4	2.6	7.7	5.1	3.6	17.3	12.8	9.1	24.5	3.7	7.7	8.3	9.0	15.6	29.6	6.9	10.8	18.6	3.1	2.5	10.6
pmd	1.4	2.3	6.5	3.3	3.0	17.5	4.9	4.1	24.9	13.4	13.4	28.3	6.7	6.0	10.5	9.5	16.9	36.1	10.1	11.0	27.8	4.4	3.4	24.0
sunflow	0.1	-0.7	17.4	1.5	0.9	0.1	2.5	1.2	22.3	11.5	10.7	39.8	4.3	7.2	0.8	14.8	17.9	62.6	7.2	8.1	30.6	1.5	0.9	9.1
xalan	1.3	1.8	1.6	-2.7	1.5	-2.4	1.9	2.6	6.1	1.9	1.3	19.6	13.6	5.7	12.9	16.5	19.5	26.6	12.7	11.7	11.9	-1.1	2.5	1.7
DaCapo mean	0.8	1.4	7.3	1.8	2.2	6.7	2.3	3.1	12.6	11.4	9.8	28.0	5.7	8.0	10.5	10.8	18.7	37.1	8.7	11.6	21.6	2.0	2.5	11.1
	±1.0	±0.2	±1.3	±0.9	±0.2	±1.3	±1.0	±0.2	±1.5	±1.1	±0.2	±1.7	±1.0	±0.2	±1.2	±1.0	±0.2	±2.0	±1.0	±0.2	±1.8	±1.1	±0.2	±1.5
geomean	0.8	1.4	7.1	1.8	2.2	6.4	2.3	3.1	12.1	10.7	9.3	26.0	5.6	8.0	10.3	10.7	18.5	36.4	8.5	11.5	20.7	1.9	2.5	10.0
pjbb2005	1.5	1.9	2.8	3.8	3.0	9.1	2.4	4.1	9.5	11.1	7.5	12.0	3.0	8.9	4.9	6.5	15.3	28.0	6.0	10.6	12.4	2.3	3.2	9.5
min	-3.3	-0.7	-0.8	-2.7	0.0	-11.0	-5.0	0.0	-11.8	-4.3	0.0	3.2	-9.3	4.3	-12.5	-4.6	10.9	7.8	-9.2	7.1	3.8	-4.9	0.0	-5.4
max	2.8	4.2	21.2	6.8	8.2	22.3	8.3	11.8	40.4	52.7	43.8	105	20.9	25.0	73.5	23.7	43.6	141	31.9	28.8	81.0	8.6	9.1	60.4
Total mean	0.9	1.3	7.0	1.6	2.0	6.1	1.8	2.7	10.7	10.1	8.9	30.9	5.6	9.4	12.8	10.3	21.3	39.4	8.6	13.0	22.5	1.7	2.2	9.9
	±0.8	±0.1	±1.5	±0.7	±0.1	±1.2	±0.8	±0.1	±1.3	±0.8	±0.1	±1.4	±0.8	±0.2	±2.4	±0.8	±0.1	±1.7	±0.9	±0.4	±2.3	±1.1	±0.1	±1.4
geomean	0.9	1.3	6.9	1.6	2.0	5.7	1.7	2.7	10.2	9.6	8.5	28.8	5.4	9.3	11.9	10.1	20.9	37.2	8.3	12.8	21.2	1.7	2.2	9.1

Table 6: Overheads (%) in time, instructions, and i-cache misses for the primitive barriers on the i7. The the first six column groups summarize the performance for each barrier, showing percentage increase in execution time (Δt), retired instructions (Δi), and instruction cache misses (Δi_{miss}) compared to the base case where no barriers are used. The right-most two column groups give results for the compound barriers. The figures in grey beneath the corresponding arithmetic mean report 95% confidence intervals.

Benchmark	Object								Boundary								Zone							
	Take Rate		Original Slow			NOP Slow			Take Rate		Original Slow			NOP Slow			Take Rate		Original Slow			NOP Slow		
	/μs	%	Δt	Δi	Δi_{miss}	Δt	Δi	Δi_{miss}	/μs	%	Δt	Δi	Δi_{miss}	Δt	Δi	Δi_{miss}	/μs	%	Δt	Δi	Δi_{miss}	Δt	Δi	Δi_{miss}
compress	0.000	0.2	-0.1	0.0	-1.5	0.0	0.0	-1.2	0.0	1.3	0.0	0.0	2.4	0.0	0.0	1.8	0.0	39.8	-0.1	0.0	7.3	-0.2	0.0	1.7
jess	0.001	0.0	1.3	1.5	16.5	0.7	1.0	10.0	0.1	0.2	1.0	2.0	21.5	2.5	1.5	19.9	18.9	52.4	12.4	10.1	90.6	9.2	7.1	60.7
db	0.000	0.0	1.4	2.3	4.1	1.9	1.7	4.9	0.0	0.0	1.3	3.3	6.7	1.2	2.8	5.6	15.0	86.1	15.6	19.7	52.2	2.7	7.2	9.0
javac	0.124	0.8	3.6	3.1	6.5	3.1	2.1	9.4	0.1	0.3	3.0	3.0	10.4	4.4	2.5	15.1	3.7	24.5	8.9	6.8	19.5	5.1	4.0	15.7
mpegaudio	0.000	0.0	0.2	0.3	-2.0	0.1	0.2	-1.0	0.0	0.0	-0.2	0.3	-0.1	-0.2	0.2	1.1	3.6	98.5	3.9	2.5	31.1	0.5	0.8	0.1
mtrt	0.003	0.0	-0.3	0.5	19.4	0.2	0.3	74.6	0.0	0.0	0.0	0.6	23.6	0.2	0.6	38.6	1.1	14.6	1.6	1.3	37.2	0.6	0.7	37.8
jack	0.001	0.0	0.5	2.4	-11.0	-0.3	1.8	-15.4	0.2	0.8	0.1	2.8	-11.8	1.1	2.2	6.1	8.9	46.4	11.1	12.4	32.0	3.9	5.1	4.2
SPECjvm mean	0.019	0.1	1.0	1.4	4.6	0.8	1.0	11.6	0.0	0.4	0.7	1.7	7.5	1.3	1.4	12.6	7.3	51.7	7.6	7.5	38.6	3.1	3.6	18.5
geomean			0.9	1.4	4.1	0.8	1.0	9.0			0.7	1.7	6.9	1.3	1.4	12.0			7.5	7.3	36.5	3.1	3.5	16.8
antlr	0.003	0.1	-2.4	1.2	2.8	-4.0	0.9	2.6	0.0	0.2	-5.0	1.2	5.1	-5.4	1.0	4.0	0.2	3.7	-4.3	1.6	10.6	-3.9	1.4	5.5
avrora	0.000	0.0	2.6	0.8	7.0	-0.2	0.7	-1.6	0.2	8.7	0.0	1.6	-0.3	2.8	1.2	7.4	0.9	33.4	5.0	3.1	13.5	3.1	1.4	14.4
bloat	0.009	0.0	6.8	8.2	6.1	7.9	7.6	2.2	0.0	0.0	8.3	11.8	7.4	10.7	10.2	11.3	26.3	61.1	52.7	43.8	37.2	17.6	18.2	19.5
eclipse	0.004	0.0	-0.7	1.5	-2.6	1.0	1.7	-5.5	0.0	0.4	-0.5	1.3	6.0	-0.8	1.3	3.0	4.2	34.2	7.0	8.1	3.2	5.3	5.0	0.3
fop	0.005	0.2	5.1	1.3	6.1	6.6	0.9	5.4	0.0	0.5	2.0	1.3	8.1	1.4	1.1	5.8	0.8	28.9	6.9	3.0	11.8	7.1	1.8	7.3
hsqldb	0.025	0.1	3.6	2.5	6.2	5.1	1.8	10.5	2.1	8.9	5.4	4.4	7.3	4.5	2.9	14.9	5.2	19.6	9.8	7.8	15.8	6.7	4.9	18.0
jython	0.001	0.0	2.2	2.4	22.3	1.1	1.5	40.7	1.0	3.7	2.7	3.5	40.4	2.0	2.3	27.6	16.5	68.4	16.0	13.0	105.2	6.2	5.7	80.3
luindex	0.000	0.0	0.9	0.5	9.3	1.1	0.2	7.1	0.1	0.6	0.6	0.9	7.1	1.0	0.6	19.5	2.7	18.8	3.9	2.5	26.5	2.1	1.1	9.6
lusearch	0.001	0.0	1.4	2.6	7.7	1.4	1.8	7.0	0.5	3.5	5.1	3.6	17.3	4.8	3.0	16.1	6.1	42.2	12.8	9.1	24.5	5.9	4.3	20.5
pmd	0.058	0.3	3.3	3.0	17.5	2.9	2.5	11.0	0.7	3.3	4.9	4.1	24.9	5.2	3.4	18.9	5.5	27.5	13.4	13.4	28.3	6.2	6.2	23.7
sunflow	0.014	0.1	1.5	0.9	0.1	1.1	-0.2	7.2	0.0	0.2	2.5	1.2	22.3	1.0	0.4	14.6	0.1	1.1	11.5	10.7	39.8	1.9	0.5	12.9
xalan	0.003	0.0	-2.7	1.5	-2.4	0.0	1.4	1.3	0.4	3.9	1.9	2.6	6.1	8.4	2.2	9.9	3.6	38.3	1.9	1.3	19.6	5.7	4.0	10.9
DaCapo mean	0.010	0.1	1.8	2.2	6.7	2.0	1.7	7.3	0.4	2.8	2.3	3.1	12.6	3.0	2.5	12.7	6.0	31.4	11.4	9.8	28.0	5.3	4.5	18.6
geomean			1.8	2.2	6.4	2.0	1.7	6.8			2.3	3.1	12.1	2.9	2.4	12.5			10.7	9.3	26.0	5.2	4.4	17.3
pjbb2005	0.054	0.3	3.8	3.0	9.1	1.1	2.2	3.0	0.4	1.9	2.4	4.1	9.5	3.0	3.4	12.5	7.0	40.6	11.1	7.5	12.0	4.5	5.4	16.4
min	0.000	0.0	-2.7	0.0	-11.0	-4.0	-0.2	-15.4	0.0	0.0	-5.0	0.0	-11.8	-5.4	0.0	1.1	0.0	1.1	-4.3	0.0	3.2	-3.9	0.0	0.1
max	0.124	0.8	6.8	8.2	22.3	7.9	7.6	74.6	2.1	8.9	8.3	11.8	40.4	10.7	10.2	38.6	26.3	98.5	52.7	43.8	105.2	17.6	18.2	80.3
Total mean	0.015	0.1	1.6	2.0	6.1	1.6	1.5	8.6	0.3	1.9	1.8	2.7	10.7	2.5	2.2	12.7	6.5	39.0	10.1	8.9	30.9	4.5	4.2	18.4
geomean			1.6	2.0	5.7	1.6	1.5	7.4			1.7	2.7	10.2	2.5	2.2	12.4			9.6	8.5	28.8	4.4	4.2	17.0

Table 7: Effect of take-rate and slow path cost for conditional barriers on the i7.

Eliminating Read Barriers through Procrastination and Cleanliness

KC Sivaramakrishnan   Lukasz Ziarek   Suresh Jagannathan

Purdue University

{chandras, lziarek, suresh}@cs.purdue.edu

Abstract

Managed languages typically use read barriers to interpret forwarding pointers introduced to keep track of copied objects. For example, in a multicore environment with thread-local heaps and a global, shared heap, an object initially allocated on a local heap may be copied to a shared heap if it becomes the source of a store operation whose target location resides on the shared heap. As part of the copy operation, a forwarding pointer may be established in the original object to point to the copied object. This level of indirection avoids the need to update all of the references to the object that has been copied.

In this paper, we consider the design of a managed runtime that eliminates read barriers. Our design is premised on the availability of a sufficient degree of concurrency to stall operations that would otherwise necessitate the copy. Stalled actions are deferred until the next local collection, avoiding exposing forwarding pointers to the mutator. In certain important cases, procrastination is unnecessary – lightweight runtime techniques can sometimes be used to allow objects to be eagerly copied when their set of incoming references is known, or when it can be determined that having multiple copies would not violate program semantics.

We evaluate our techniques on 3 platforms: a 16-core AMD64 machine, a 48-core Intel SCC, and an 864-core Azul Vega 3. Experimental results over a range of parallel benchmarks indicate that our approach leads to notable performance gains (20 - 32% on average) without incurring any additional complexity.

Categories and Subject Descriptors   D.4.2 [*Operating Systems*]: Storage Management – Allocation/Deallocation strategies, Garbage collection; D.3.3 [*Programming Languages*]: Language Constructs and Features – Concurrent programming structures

General Terms   Algorithms, Design, Experimentation, Management, Measurement, Performance

Keywords   barrier elimination, private heaps, parallel and concurrent collection, cleanliness, concurrent programming, functional languages

ISMM'12,   June 15–16, 2012, Beijing, China.
Copyright © 2012 ACM 978-1-4503-1350-6/12/06. . . $10.00

1. Introduction

Splitting a program heap among a set of cores is a useful technique to exploit available parallelism on scalable multicore platforms: each core can allocate, collect, and access data locally, moving objects to a global, shared heap only when they are accessed by threads executing on different cores. This design allows local heaps to be collected independently, with coordination required only for global heap collection. In contrast, stop-the-world collectors need a global synchronization for every collection. In order to ensure that cores cannot directly or indirectly access objects on other local heaps, which would complicate the ability to perform independent local heap collection, the following invariants need to be preserved:

- No pointers are allowed from one core's local heap to another.

- No pointers are permitted from the shared heap to the local heap.

Both invariants are necessary to perform independent local collections. The reason for the first is obvious. The second invariant prohibits a local heap from transitively accessing another local heap object via the shared heap. In order to preserve these invariants, the mutator typically executes a *write barrier* on every store operation. The write barrier ensures that before assigning a local object reference (source) to a shared heap object (target), the local object along with its transitive closure is lifted to the shared heap. We call such writes *exporting writes* as they export information out of local heaps. The execution of the write barrier creates *forwarding pointers* in the original location of the lifted objects in the local heap. These point to the new locations of the lifted objects in the shared heap. Since objects can be lifted to the shared heap on potentially any write, the mutator needs to execute a *read barrier* on potentially every read. The read barrier checks whether the object being read is the actual object or a forwarding pointer, and in the latter case, indirects to the object found on the shared heap. Forwarding pointers are eventually eliminated during local collection.

Because the number of reads are likely to far outweigh the number of writes, the aggregate cost of read barriers can be both substantial and vary dramatically based on underlying architecture characteristics [6]. Eliminating read barriers, however, is non-trivial. Abstractly, one can avoid read barriers by eagerly *fixing* all references that point to forwarded objects at the time the object is lifted to the shared heap, ensuring the mutator will never encounter a forwarded object. Unfortunately, this requires being able to enumerate all the references that point to the lifted object; in general, gathering this information is very expensive as the references to an object might originate from any object in the local heap.

In this paper, we consider an alternative design that completely eliminates the need for read barriers *without* requiring a full scan of the local heap whenever an object is lifted to the shared heap. The design is based on two observations. First, read barriers can be clearly eliminated if forwarding pointers are never introduced. One way to avoid introducing forwarding pointers is to *delay* operations that create them until a local garbage collection is triggered. In other words, rather than executing a store operation that would trigger lifting a thread local object to the shared heap, we can simply *procrastinate*, thereby stalling the thread that needs to perform the store. The garbage collector must simply be informed of the need to lift the object's closure during its next local collection. After collection is complete, the store can take place with the source object lifted, and all extant heap references properly adjusted. As long as there is sufficient concurrency to utilize existing computational resources, in the form of available runnable threads to run other computations, the cost of procrastination is just proportional to the cost of a context switch.

Second, it is not necessary to always stall an operation that involves lifting an object to the shared heap. We consider a new property for objects (and their transitive closures) called *cleanliness*. A clean object is one that can be safely lifted to the shared heap without introducing forwarding pointers that might be subsequently encountered by the mutator: objects that are immutable, whose elements are only referenced from the stack, or whose set of incoming heap references is known, are obvious examples. The runtime analysis for cleanliness is combined with a specialized write barrier to amortize its cost. Thus, procrastination provides a general technique to eliminate read barriers, while cleanliness serves as an important optimization that avoids stalling threads unnecessarily.

The effectiveness of our approach depends on a programming model in which (a) most objects are clean, (b) the transitive closure of the object being lifted rarely has pointers to it from other heap allocated objects, and (c) there is a sufficient degree of concurrency in the form of runnable threads; this avoids idling available cores whenever a thread is stalled performing an exporting write that involves an unclean object. In this paper, we consider an implementation of these ideas in the context of MultiMLton [17], a scalable, whole-program optimizing compiler and multicore-aware runtime system for Standard ML [15], a mostly functional language whose concurrent programs typically enjoy these properties. Our technique does not rely on programmer annotations, static analysis or compiler optimizations to eliminate read barriers, and can be completely implemented as a lightweight runtime technique.

This paper provides the following contributions:

- A garbage collector design that has been tuned for mostly functional languages in which there is typically a surfeit of concurrency (in the form of programmer-specified lightweight threads) available on each core, to realize a memory management system that does not require read barriers.

- A new object property called *cleanliness* that enables a certain (albeit broad) class of objects to be safely lifted to the shared heap without requiring a full traversal of the local heap to fix existing references to them, reducing the frequency of thread stalls as a result of procrastination.

- An extensive evaluation of the collector performance on three multicore platforms; a 16 core AMD Operton server, Intel's 48 core Single-chip Cloud Computer (SCC), and Azul System's 864 core Vega 3 processor. The results reveal that eliminating read barriers on these platforms can lead to significant performance improvements.

The paper is organized as follows. In the next section, we present additional motivation that quantifies the cost and benefit of read barriers in our system. The overall design and implementation of the collector is provided in Section 3. Section 4 describes our treatment of cleanliness. The modifications to our write barrier to support cleanliness analysis and delayed writes are presented in

```
1  pointer readBarrier (pointer p) {
2    if (!isPointer(p)) return p;
3    if (getHeader(p) == FORWARDED)
4      return *(pointer*)p;
5    return p;
6  }
```

Figure 1: Read barrier.

Section 5. Details about the target platforms we use in our experiments is given in Section 6. Experimental results are presented in Section 7. A comparison to related work is given in Section 8, and Section 9 presents conclusions.

2. Motivation

In this section, we quantify the cost/benefit of read barriers in our system. The context of our investigation is a programming model that is mostly functional (our benchmarks are written in the asynchronous extension [24] of Concurrent ML [18]), and that naturally supports large numbers of lightweight user-level threads. We have implemented our garbage collector for MultiMLton [17], a parallel extension to MLton [16], that targets scalable, many-core platforms.

In our implementation, lightweight threads are multiplexed over kernel threads, with one kernel thread pinned to every core. Each core has a local heap, and a single shared heap is shared among all of the cores; the runtime system enforces the necessary heap invariants described earlier. In our experiments, we fixed the heap size to 3X the minimum heap size under which the programs would run.

MultiMLton performs a series of optimizations to minimize heap allocation, thus reducing the set of read barriers actually generated. For example, references and arrays that do not escape out of a function are flattened. Combined with aggressive inlining and simplification optimizations enabled by whole-program compilation, object allocation on the heap can be substantially reduced.

The compiler and runtime system ensure that entries on thread stacks never point to a forwarded object. Whenever an object pointer is stored into a register or the stack, a read barrier is executed on the object pointer to get the current location of the object. Immediately after an exporting write or a context switch, the current stack is walked and references to forwarded objects are updated to point to the new location of lifted objects in the shared heap. Additionally, before performing an exporting write, register values are saved on the stack, and reloaded after exit. Thus, as a part of fixing references to forwarding pointers from the stack, references from registers are also fixed. This ensures that the registers never point to forwarded objects either. Hence, no read barriers are required for dereferencing object pointers from the stack or registers. This optimization is analogous to "eager" read barriers as described in [4]. Eager read barrier elimination has marked performance benefits for repeated object accesses, such as array element traversals in a loop, where the read barrier is executed once when the array location is loaded into a register, but all further accesses can elide executing the barrier.

Whenever an object is lifted to the shared heap, the original object's header is set to FORWARDED and the first word of the object is overwritten with the new location of the object in the shared heap. Before an object is read, the mutator checks whether the object has been forwarded, and if it is, returns the new location of the object. Hence, our read barriers are conditional [5, 6].

Figure 1 shows the pseudo-C code for our read barrier. MLton represents non-value carrying constructors of (sum) datatypes us-

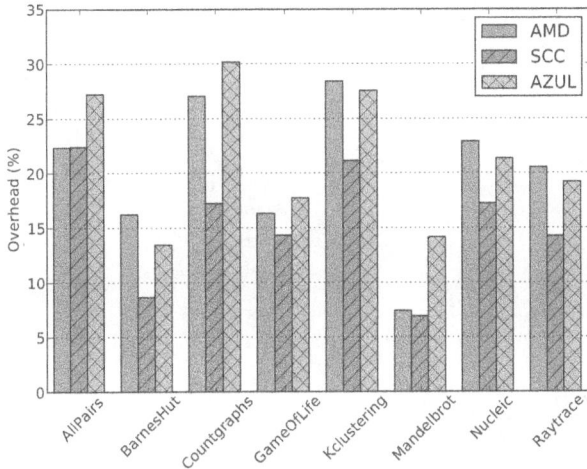

Figure 2: Read barrier overhead as a percentage of mutator time.

Benchmark	AllPairs	BarnesHut	Countgraphs	GameOfLife	Kclustering	Mandelbrot	Nucleic	Raytrace
Checks (X 10⁶)	9,753	2,864	2,584	4,858	3,780	2,980	2,887	2,217
Forwarded	123	52702	0	2143	101	23	328	0

Figure 3: Effectiveness of read barrier checks: Checks represents the number of read barrier invocations and forwarded represents the number of instances when the read barrier encountered a forwarded object.

ing non-pointer values. If such a type additionally happens to have value-carrying constructors that reference heap-allocated objects, the non-pointer value representing the empty constructor will be stored in the object pointer field. Hence, the read barrier must first check whether the presumed pointer does in fact point to a heap object. Otherwise, the original value is returned (line 2). If the given pointer points to a forwarded object, the current location of the object stored is returned. Otherwise, the original value is returned.

We evaluated a set of 8 benchmarks (described in Section 7.1) running on a 16 core AMD64, a 48 core Intel SCC and an 864 core Azul Vega 3 machine to measure read barrier overheads. Figure 2 shows these overheads as a percentage of mutator time. Our experiments reveal that, on average, the mutator spends 20.1%, 15.3% and 21.3% of time executing read barriers on the AMD64, SCC and Azul architectures, respectively, for our benchmarks.

Although a Brooks-style unconditional read barrier would have avoided the cost of the second branch in our read barrier implementation, it would necessitate having an additional address length field in the object header for an indirection pointer. Most objects in our system tend to be small. In our benchmarks, we observed that 95% of the objects allocated were less than 3 words in size, including a word-sized header. The addition of an extra word in the object header for an indirection pointer would lead to substantial memory overheads, which in turn leads to additional garbage collection costs. Hence, we choose to encode read barriers conditionally rather than unconditionally.

But, does the utility of the read barrier justify its cost? We measure the number of instances the read barrier is invoked and the number of instances the barrier finds a forwarded object (see Figure 3). We see that read barriers find forwarded objects in less than

one thousands of a percent of the number of instances they are invoked. Thus, in our system, the cost of read barriers is substantial, but only rarely do they have to perform the task of forwarding references. These results motivate our interest in a memory management design that eliminates read barriers altogether.

3. GC Design and Implementation

In this section, we describe the design and implementation of the runtime system and garbage collector.

3.1 Threading system

Our programming model separates program-level concurrency from the physical parallelism available in the underlying machine through the use of lightweight, user-level threads. These lightweight threads are multiplexed over system-level threads. One system-level thread is created for every core and is pinned to it. Thus, the runtime system effectively treats a system-level thread as a virtual processor. Load distribution is through work sharing, where threads are eagerly spawned on different cores in a round-robin fashion. Once created on a core, lightweight threads never migrate to another core.

Lightweight threads are preemptively scheduled on every core. On a timer interrupt, the threading system is informed that an interrupt has occurred by setting a flag at a known location. At every garbage collector safe-point, the current thread checks whether the timer interrupt flag has been set, and if it is, resets the flag and yields control to another thread.

3.2 Baseline collector (Stop-the-world)

The baseline heap design uses a single, contiguous heap, shared among all cores. In order to allow local allocation, each core requests a page-sized chunk from the heap. While a single lock protects the chunk allocation, objects are allocated within chunks by bumping a core-local heap frontier.

In order to perform garbage collection, all the cores synchronize on a barrier, with one core responsible for collecting the entire heap. The garbage collection algorithm is inspired from Sansom's [19] collector, which combines Cheney's two-space copying collector and Jonker's single-space sliding compaction collector. Cheney's copying collector walks the live objects in the heap just once per collection, while Jonker's mark-compact collector performs two walks. But Cheney's collector can only utilize half of memory allocated for the heap. Sansom's collector combines the best of both worlds. Copying collection is performed when heap requirements are less than half of the available memory. The runtime system dynamically switches to mark-compact collection if the heap utilization increases beyond half of the available space.

Since ML programs tend to have a high rate of allocation, and most objects are short-lived temporaries, it is beneficial to perform generational collection. The garbage collector supports Appel-style generational collection [2] for collecting temporaries. The generational collector has two generations, and all objects that survive a generational collection are copied to the older generation. Generational collection can work with both copying and mark-compact major collection schemes. The runtime system chooses to perform generational collection if the ratio of live objects to the total objects falls below a tunable threshold.

Our choice of a stop-the-world baseline collector was to enable better understanding of mutator overheads among various local collector designs, as opposed to illustrating absolute performance improvement of the local collectors over the baseline. Although a parallel collector would have improved overall baseline performance, we would expect poorer scalability due to frequent global synchronizations [10, 14, 20].

3.3 Local collector (Split-heap)

As mentioned earlier, the local collector operates over a single shared (global) heap and a local heap for each core. The allocation of the shared heap is performed similar to allocations in the stop-the-world collector, where each core allocates a page-sized chunk in the shared heap and performs object allocation by bumping its core-local shared heap frontier. Allocations in the local heaps do not require any synchronization. Garbage collection in the local heaps is similar to the baseline collector, except that it does not require global synchronization.

Objects are allocated in the shared heap only if they are to be shared between two or more cores. Objects are allocated in the shared heap because of exporting writes and remote spawns (Section 5.3). Apart from these, all globals are allocated in the shared heap, since globals are visible to all cores by definition. For a shared heap collection, all of the cores synchronize on a barrier and then a single core collects the heap. Moreover, along with globals, all the references from local heaps are considered to be roots for a shared heap collection. In order to eliminate roots from dead local heap objects, before a shared heap collection, local collections are performed on each core to eliminate such references.

The shared heap is also collected using Sansom's dual-mode garbage collector. However, we do not perform generational collection on the shared heap. This is because shared heap collection is expected to be relatively infrequent when compared to the frequency of local heap collections, and objects that are shared between cores, in general, live longer than a typical object collected during a generational collection.

3.3.1 Remembered stacks

In our system, threads can synchronously communicate with each other over first-class message-passing communication channels. If a receiver is not available, a sender thread can block on a channel. If the channel resides in the shared heap, the thread object, its associated stack and the transitive closure of all objects reachable from it on the heap would be lifted to the shared heap as part of the blocking action. Since channel communication is the primary mode of thread interaction in our system, we would quickly find that most local heap objects end up being lifted to the shared heap. This would be highly undesirable.

Hence, we choose never to move stacks to the shared heap. We add an exception to our heap invariants to allow thread → stack pointers, where the thread resides on the shared heap, and references a stack object found on the local heap. Whenever a thread object is lifted to the shared heap, a reference to the corresponding stack object is added to the set of remembered stacks. This remembered set is considered as a root for a local collection to enable tracing of remembered stacks.

Before a shared heap collection, the remembered set is cleared; only those stacks that are reachable from other GC roots survive the shared heap collection. After a shared heap collection, the remembered set of each core is recalculated such that it contains only those stacks, whose corresponding thread objects reside in the shared heap, and have survived the shared heap collection.

4. Cleanliness Analysis

In this section, we describe our cleanliness analysis. We first present auxiliary definitions that will be utilized by cleanliness checks.

4.1 Heap session

Objects are allocated in the local heap by bumping the local heap frontier. In addition, associated with each local heap is a pointer called `sessionStart` that always points to a location between the

```
1  Val writeBarrier (Ref r, Val v) {
2    if (isObjptr(v)) {
3      //Lift if clean or procrastinate
4      if (isInSharedHeap(r) &&
5          isInLocalHeap(v)) {
6        needsFixup = false;
7        if (isClean(v, &needsFixup))
8          v = lift(v, needsFixup);
9        else
10         v = suspendTillGCAndLift(v);
11     }
12     //Tracking cleanliness
13     if (isInLocalHeap (r) &&
14         isInLocalHeap(v)) {
15       n = getRefCount(v);
16       if (!isInCurrentSession (r))
17         setNumRefs(v, GLOBAL);
18       else if (n == ZERO)
19         setNumRefs(v, ONE);
20       else if (n < GLOBAL)
21         setNumRefs(v, LOCAL_MANY);
22     }
23   }
24   return v;
25 }
```

Figure 4: Write barrier implementation.

start of the heap and the frontier. We introduce the idea of a *heap session*, to capture the notion of recently allocated objects. Every local heap has exactly two sessions: a *current session* between the `sessionStart` and the heap frontier and a *previous session* between the start of the heap and `sessionStart`. Heap sessions are used by the cleanliness analysis to limit the range of heap locations that need to be scanned to test an object closure[1] for cleanliness. A new session can be started by setting the `sessionStart` to the current local heap frontier. We start a new session on a context switch, a local garbage collection and after an object has been lifted to the shared heap.

4.2 Reference count

We introduce a limited reference counting mechanism for local heap objects that counts the number of references from other local heap objects. Importantly, we do not consider references from ML thread stacks. The reference count is meaningful only for objects reachable in the current session. For such objects, the number of references to an object can be one of four values: `ZERO`, `ONE`, `LOCAL_MANY`, and `GLOBAL`. We steal 2 bits from the object header to record this information. A reference count of `ZERO` indicates that the object only has references from registers or stacks, while an object with a count of `ONE` has exactly one pointer from the current session. A count of `LOCAL_MANY` indicates that this object has more than one reference, but that all of these references originate from the current session. `GLOBAL` indicates that the object has at least one reference that originates from outside the current session.

The reference counting mechanism is implemented as a part of the write barrier. Lines 13–22 in Figure 4 illustrate the implementation of the reference counting mechanism, and Figure 5 illustrates the state transition diagram for the reference counting mechanism. Observe that reference counts are non-decreasing. Hence, the ref-

---

[1] In the following, we write *closure* (in the absence of any qualification) to mean the set of objects reachable from some root on the heap; to avoid confusion, we write *function closure* to mean the representation of an SML function as a pair of function code pointer and static environment.

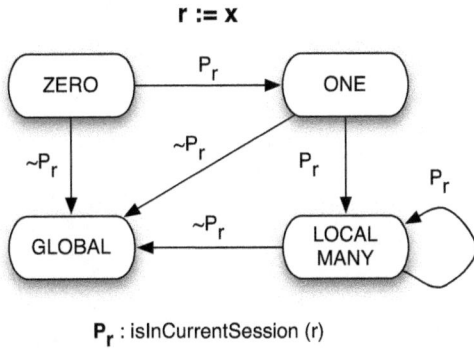

r := x

P_r : isInCurrentSession (r)

Figure 5: State transition diagram detailing the behavior of the reference counting mechanism with respect to object x involved in an assignment, r := x, where P $_r$ = isInCurrentSession(r).

```
1  bool isClean (Val v, bool* needsFixup) {
2    clean = true;
3    foreach o in reachable(v) {
4      if (!isMutable(o) || isInSharedHeap(o))
5        continue;
6      nv = getRefCount(o);
7      if (nv == ZERO)
8        clean &= true;
9      else if (nv == ONE)
10       clean &= (o != v);
11     else if (nv == LOCAL_MANY) {
12       clean &= (isInCurrentSession(o));
13       *needsFixup = true;
14     }
15     else
16       clean = false;
17   }
18   return clean;
19 }
```

Figure 6: Cleanliness check.

erence count of any object represents the maximum number of references that pointed to the object at any point in its lifetime.

4.3 Cleanliness

An object closure is said to be clean, if for each object reachable from the root of the closure,

- the object is immutable or in the shared heap. Or,
- the object is the root, and has ZERO references. Or,
- the object is not the root, and has ONE reference. Or,
- the object is not the root, has LOCAL_MANY references, and is in the current session.

Otherwise, the object closure is not clean. Figure 6 shows an implementation of an object closure cleanliness check.

If the source of an exporting assignment is immutable, we can make a copy of the immutable object in the shared heap, and avoid introducing references to forwarded objects. Unlike languages like Java or C#, Standard ML does not allow the programmer to test the referential equality of immutable objects. Equality of immutable objects is always computed by structure. Hence, it is safe to repli-

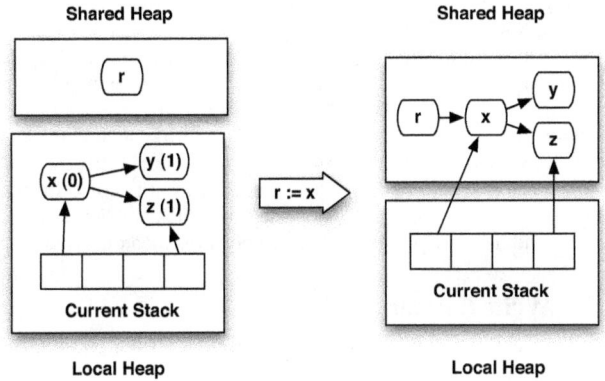

(a) Tree-structured object closure

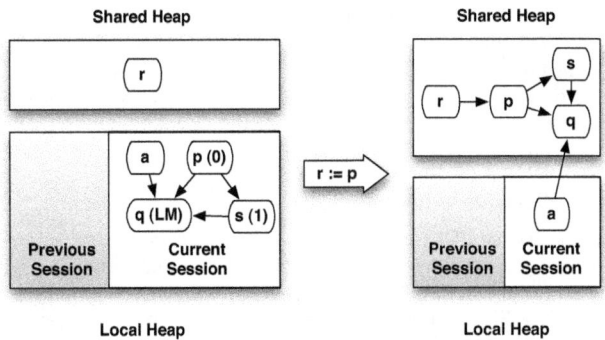

(b) Session-based cleanliness

Figure 7: Utilizing closure cleanliness information for exporting writes to avoid references to forwarded objects.

cate immutable objects. If the object is already in the shared heap, there is no need to move this object.

If the object closure of the source of a exporting write is clean, we can move the closure to the shared heap and quickly fix all of the forwarding pointers that might be generated. For example, consider an object that defines a tree structure; such an object is clean if the root has ZERO references and all of its internal nodes have ONE reference from their parent. A root having ZERO references means it is accessed only via the stack; if it had a count of ONE, the outstanding reference may emanate from the heap. Internal nodes having a reference count of ONE implies they are reachable only via other nodes in the object being traced. Figure 7a shows such a closure. In this example, we assume that all objects in the closure are mutable. The reference count of relevant nodes is given in the brackets. Both the root and internal nodes can have pointers from the current stack not tracked by the reference count. After lifting the closure, the references originating from the current stack are fixed by walking the stack.

But, object closures need not just be trees and can be arbitrary graphs, with multiple incoming edges to a particular object in the closure. How do we determine if the incoming edges to an object originate from the closure or from outside the closure (from the local heap)? We cannot answer this question without walking the local heap. Hence, we simplify the question to asking whether all the pointers to an object originate from the current session. This question is answered in the affirmative if an object has a reference count of LOCAL_MANY (lines 11–13 in Figure 6).

Figure 7b shows an example of a closure whose objects have at most LOCAL_MANY references. Again, we assume that all objects in the closure are mutable. In the transitive closure rooted at p, object q has locally many references. These references might originate from the closure itself (edges p → q and s → q) or from outside the closure (edge a → q). After lifting such closures to the shared heap, only the current session is walked to fix all of the references to forwarded objects created during the copy. In practice (Section 7.5), current session sizes are much smaller than heap sizes, and hence exporting writes can be performed quickly.

5. Write barrier

In this section, we present the modifications to the write barrier to eliminate the possibility of creating references from reachable objects in the local heap to a forwarded object. The implementation of our write barrier is presented in Figure 4. A write barrier is invoked prior to a write and returns a new value for the source of the write. The check isObjptr at line 2 returns true only for heap allocated objects, and is a compile time check. Hence, for primitive valued writes, there is no write barrier. Lines 4 and 5 check whether the write is exporting. If the source of the object is clean, we lift the transitive object closure to the shared heap and return the new location of the object in the shared heap.

5.1 Delaying writes

If the source of an exporting write is not clean, we suspend the current thread and switch to another thread in our scheduler. The source of the write is added to a queue of objects that are waiting to be lifted. Since the write is not performed, no forwarded pointers are created. If programs have ample amounts of concurrency, there will be other threads that are waiting to be run. However, if all threads on a given core are blocked on a write, we move all of the object closures that are waiting to be lifted to the shared heap. We then force a local garbage collection, which will, as a part of the collection, fix all of the references to point to the new (lifted) location on the shared heap. Thus, the mutator never encounters a reference to a forwarded object.

5.2 Lifting objects to the shared heap

Figure 8 shows the pseudo-C code for lifting object closures to the shared heap. The function lift takes as input the root of a clean object closure and a Boolean representing whether the closure has any object that has LOCAL_MANY references. For simplicity of presentation, we assume that the shared heap has enough space reserved for the transitive closure of the object being lifted. In practice, the lifting process requests additional shared heap chunks to be reserved for the current processor, or triggers a shared heap collection if there is no additional space in the shared heap.

Objects are transitively lifted to the shared heap, starting from the root, in the obvious way (Lines 22–24). As a part of lifting, mutable objects are lifted and a forwarding pointer is created in their original location, while immutable objects are copied and their location added to imSet (Lines 10–15). After lifting the transitive closure of the object to the shared heap, the shared heap frontier is updated to the new location.

After object lifting, the current stack is walked to fix any references to forwarding pointers (Line 27–28). Since we do not track references from the stack for reference counting, there might be references to forwarded objects from stacks other than the current stack. We fix such references lazily. Before a context switch, the target stack is walked to fix any references to forwarded objects. Since immutable objects are copied and mutable objects lifted, a copied immutable object might point to a forwarded object. We walk all the shared heap copies of immutable objects lifted from the local

```
1  Set imSet;
2  void liftHelper (pointer* op,
3                   pointer* frontierP) {
4    frontier = *frontierP;
5    o = *op;
6    if (isInSharedHeap(o)) return;
7    copyObject (o, frontier);
8    *op = frontier + headerSize(o);
9    *frontierP = frontier + objectSize(o);
10   if (isMutable(o)) {
11     setHeader(o, FORWARDED);
12     *o = *op;
13   }
14   else
15     imSet += o;
16 }
17
18 pointer lift (pointer op, bool needsFixup) {
19   start = frontier = getSharedHeapFrontier();
20   imSet = {};
21   //Lift transitive closure
22   liftHelper (&op, &frontier);
23   foreachObjptrInRange
24     (start, &frontier, liftHelper);
25   setSharedHeapFrontier(frontier);
26   //Fix forwarding pointers
27   foreachObjptrInObject
28     (getCurrentStack(), fixFwdPtr);
29   foreach o in imSet
30     foreachObjptrInObject(o, fixFwdPtr);
31   frontier = getLocalHeapFrontier();
32   if (needsFixup)
33     foreachObjptrInRange(getSessionStart(),
34                          &frontier, fixFwdPtr);
35   setSessionStart(frontier);
36   return op;
37 }
```

Figure 8: Lifting an object closure to the shared heap.

```
1  ThreadID spawn (pointer closure, int target) {
2    ThreadID tid = newThreadID();
3    Thread t = newThread(closure, tid);
4    needsFixup = false;
5    if (isClean(t, &needsFixup)) {
6      t = lift(t, needsFixup);
7      enqueThread(t, target);
8    }
9    else
10     liftAndReadyBeforeGC(t, target);
11   return tid;
12 }
```

Figure 9: Spawning a thread.

heap to fix any references to forwarded objects (Lines 29–30). If there were LOCAL_MANY references to any object in the lifted closure, the local session is walked to fix the references to forwarding pointers. Finally, session start is moved to the current frontier.

5.3 Remote spawns

Apart from exporting writes, function closures can also escape local heaps when threads are spawned on other cores. For spawning on other cores, the environment of the function closure is lifted to the shared heap and then, the function closure is added to the target core's scheduler. This might introduce references to forwarding pointers in the spawning core's heap. We utilize the techniques developed for exporting writes to handle remote spawns in a similar fashion.

Figure 9 shows the new implementation of thread spawn. If the function closure is clean, we lift the function closure to the shared heap, and enqueue the thread on the target scheduler. Otherwise, we add it to the list of threads that need to be lifted to the shared heap. Before the next garbage collection, these function closures are lifted to the shared heap, enqueued to target schedulers, and the references to forwarded objects are fixed as a part of the collection. When the target scheduler finds this new thread (as opposed to other preempted threads), it allocates a new stack in the local heap. Hence, except for the environment of the remotely spawned thread, all data allocated by the thread is placed in the local heap.

5.4 Barrier implementation

For our evaluation, we have implemented two local collector designs; one with read barriers (RB+ GC) and the other without read barriers incorporating the proposed techniques (RB- GC). Read barriers are generated as part of RSSA, one of the backend intermediate passes in our compiler. RSSA is similar to Static Single Assignment (SSA), but exposes data representations decisions. In RSSA, we are able to distinguish heap allocated objects from non-heap values such as constants, values on the stack and registers, globals, etc. This allows us to generate barriers only when necessary.

Although the code for tracking cleanliness is implemented as an RSSA pass (Lines 13–24 in Figure 4), the code for avoiding creation of references to forwarded objects (Lines 4–11 in Figure 4) is implemented in the primitive library, which has access to the lightweight thread scheduler. `suspendTillGCAndLift` (line 11 in Figure 4) is carefully implemented to not contain an exporting write, which would cause non-terminating recursive calls to the write barrier.

6. Target Architectures

We have implemented our GC design on three different architectures; a 16-core AMD64 running Linux (AMD), a 48-core Intel Single-chip Cloud Computer (SCC), and an 864-core Azul's Vega 3 machine. Our choice of architectures is primarily to study the robustness of our techniques across various architectures rather than exploiting the fine-grained architectural characteristics for our design.

The AMD machine has 8 dual core AMD Opteron processors, with each core running at 1.8 GHz. Each core has 64 KB of 2-way associative L1 data and instruction caches, and 1 MB of exclusive 16-way associative L2 cache with 32 GB of main memory. The peak memory bandwidth for serial access is 1.5 GB/s and 680 MB/s for all cores accessing the memory in parallel. These memory bandwidth numbers were measured using the STREAM [23] benchmark.

The Azul machine used in our experiments has 16 Vega 3 processors, each with 54-cores per chip; each core exhibits roughly 1/3 the performance of an Intel Core2-Duo. Out of the 864 cores, 846 are application usable while the rest of the cores are reserved for the kernel. The machine has 384 GB of cache coherent memory split across 192 memory modules. Uniform memory access is provided through a passive, non-blocking interconnect mesh. The machine has 205 GB/s aggregate memory bandwidth and 544 GB/s aggregate interconnect bandwidth. Each core has a 16KB, 4-way L1 data and instruction caches.

Intel's Single-chip Cloud Computer (SCC)[12] is an experimental platform from Intel labs with 48 P54C Pentium cores. The most interesting aspect of SCC is the complete lack of cache coherence

and a focus on inter-core interactions through a high speed mesh interconnect. The cores are grouped into 24 tiles, connected via a fast on-die mesh network. The tiles are split into 4 quadrants with each quadrant connected to a memory module. Each core has 16KB L1 data and instruction caches and 256KB L2 cache. Each core also has a small message passing buffer (MPB) of 8KB used for message passing between the cores.

Since the SCC does not provide cache coherence, coherence must be implemented in software if required. From the programmer's perspective, each core has a private memory that is cached and not visible to other cores. The cores also have access to a shared memory, which is by default not cached to avoid coherence issues. The cost of accessing data from the cached local memory is substantially less when compared to accessing shared memory. It takes 18 core cycles to read from the L2 cache; on the other hand, it takes 40 core cycles to request data from the memory controller, 4 mesh cycles for the mesh to forward the request and 46 memory cycles for the memory controller to complete the operation. Hence, in total, the delay between a core requesting data from the memory controller is $40\ k_{core}\ +\ 4*n\ k_{mesh}\ +\ 46\ k_{ram}$ cycles, where k_{core}, k_{mesh} and k_{ram} are the cycles of core, mesh network and memory respectively. In our experimental setup, where 6 tiles share a memory controller, the number of hops n to the memory controller could be $0 < n < 5$. Hence, shared heap accesses are much more expensive than local heap accesses.

6.1 Local collector on SCC

We briefly describe our runtime system design for the SCC. On the SCC, each core runs a Linux operating system and from the programmer's point-of-view, SCC is exposed as a cluster of machines. Thus, we believe that our local collector design is a must for circumventing coherence and segmentation restrictions, and making effective use of the memory hierarchy. Pointers to local memory are sensible only to the owning core. From the perspective of other cores, pointers might fall outside the segmentation boundary. If we were to utilize a single-shared heap design, where any object can point to any other object in the heap, the heap would have to be placed in the non-cached shared memory because of the lack of coherence.

Instead of spawning threads to represent virtual processors, we spawn one process on each core. Local heaps are placed in the cached private memory while the shared heap is placed in the non-cached shared memory. Since our local collector design only exports objects to the shared heap if they are to be shared between cores, most access are from the local heap and are cached. We modify the memory manager such that the shared heap is created at the same virtual address on each core. This avoids address translation overheads (and hence, read barriers) for shared heap reads.

Shared heap collection is *collective*; the collection proceeds in SPMD mode with each processor collecting roots from its local heap, followed by a single core collecting the shared heap. Finally, each core updates the references from its local heap to the shared heap with the new location of the shared heap object. The MPB is utilized by shared heap collection for synchronization and data exchange.

7. Results

7.1 Benchmarks

The benchmarks shown in Figure 10 were designed such that the input size and the number of threads are tunable; each of these benchmarks were derived from a sequential standard ML implementation, and parallelized using our lightweight thread system and CML-style [18] message-passing communication.

Benchmark	Allocation Rate (MB/s)			Bytes Allocated (GB)				# Threads		
	AMD	SCC	AZUL	AMD	SCC	AZUL	% Sh	AMD	SCC	AZUL
AllPairs	817	53	1505	16	16	54	11	256	512	32768
Barneshut	772	70	1382	20	20	876	2	512	1024	32768
Countgraphs	2594	144	4475	24	24	1176	1	128	256	16384
GameOfLife	2445	127	4266	21	21	953	13	256	1024	8192
Kclustering	3643	108	8927	32	32	1265	3	256	1024	8192
Mandelbrot	349	43	669	2	2	32	8	128	512	8192
Nucleic	1430	87	4761	13	14	609	1	64	384	16384
Raytrace	809	54	2133	11	12	663	4	128	256	2048

Figure 10: Benchmark characteristics. %Sh represents the average fraction of bytes allocated in the shared heap across all the architectures.

- **AllPairs**: an implementation of Floyd-Warshall algorithm for computing all pairs shortest path.

- **BarnesHut**: an n-body simulation using Barnes-Hut algorithm.

- **CountGraphs**: computes all symmetries (automorphisms) within a set of graphs.

- **GameOfLife**: Conway's Game of Life simulator

- **Kclustering**: a k-means clustering algorithm, where each stage is spawned as a server.

- **Mandelbrot**: a Mandelbrot set generator.

- **Nucleic**: Pseudoknot [11] benchmark applied on multiple inputs.

- **Raytrace**: a ray-tracing algorithm to render a scene.

Parameters are appropriately scaled for different architectures to ensure sufficient work for each of the cores. The benchmarks running on AMD and SCC were given the same input size. Hence, we see that the benchmarks allocate the same amount of memory during their lifetime. But, we increase the number of threads on the SCC when compared to AMD since there is more hardware parallelism available. For Azul, we scale both the input size and the number of threads, and as a result we see a large increase in bytes allocated when compared to the other platforms. Out of the total bytes allocated during the program execution, on average 5.4% is allocated in the shared heap. Thus, most of the objects allocated are collected locally, without the need for stalling all of the mutators.

We observe that the allocation rate is highly architecture dependent, and is the slowest on the SCC. Allocation rate is particularly dependent on memory bandwidth, processor speed and cache behavior. On the SCC, not only is the processor slow (533MHz) but the serial memory bandwidth for our experimental setup is only around 70 MB/s.

7.2 Performance

Next, we analyze the performance of the new local collector design. In order to establish a baseline for the results presented, we have ported our runtime system to utilize the Boehm-Demers-Weiser (BDW) conservative garbage collector [7]. We briefly describe the port of our runtime system utilizing BDW GC.

Although BDW GC is conservative, it can utilize tracing information when provided. Our compiler generates tracing information for all objects, including the stack. However, we provide the tracing information for all object allocations except the stack. Stack objects in our runtime system represent all of the reserved space for a stack, while only a part of the stack is actually used which can grow and shrink as frames are pushed and popped. Since the BDW GC does not allow tracing information of objects to be changed af-

ter allocation, we scan stack objects conservatively. BDW uses a mark-sweep algorithm, and we enable parallel marking and thread-local allocations.

Figure 11a illustrates space-time trade-offs critical for any garbage collector evaluation. STW GC is the baseline stop-the-world collector described in Section 3.2, while RB+ and RB- are local collectors. RB+ is a local collector with read barriers while RB- is our new local collector design without read barriers, exploiting procrastination and cleanliness. We compare the normalized running times of our benchmarks under different garbage collection schemes as we decrease the heap size. For each run of the experiment, we decrease the maximum heap size allowed and report the maximum size of the heap utilized. Thus, we leave it to the collectors to figure out the optimal heap size, within the allowed space. This is essential for the local collectors, since the allocation pattern of each core is usually very different and depends on the structure of the program.

The results presented here were collected on 16 cores. As we decrease overall heap sizes, we see programs under all of the different GC schemes taking longer to run. But RB- exhibits better performance characteristics than its counterparts. We observe that the minimum heap size under which the local collectors would run is greater than the STW and BDW GCs. In the local collectors, since the heap is split across all of the cores, there is more fragmentation. Also, under the current scheme, each local collector is greedy and will try to utilize as much heap as it can in order to reduce the running time (by choosing semi-space collection over mark-compact), without taking into account the heap requirements of other local collectors. Currently, when one of the local cores runs out of memory, we terminate the program. Since we are interested in throughput on scalable architectures where memory is not a bottleneck, we have not optimized the collectors for memory utilization. We believe we can modify our collector for memory constrained environments by allowing local heaps to shrink on demand and switch from semi-space to compacting collection, if other local heaps run out of memory.

The STW and BDW GCs are much slower than the two local collectors. In order to study the reason behind this slowdown, we separate the mutator time (Figure 11b) and garbage collection time (Figure 11c). We see that STW GC is actually faster than the local collectors in terms of mutator time, since it does not pay the overhead of executing read or write barriers. But, since every collection requires stopping all the mutators and a single collector performs the collection, it executes serially during a GC. Figure 11d shows that roughly 70% of the execution total time for our benchmarks under STW is spent performing GCs, negatively impacting scalability.

Interestingly, we see that programs running under the BDW GC are much slower when compared to other GCs. This is mainly due to allocation costs. Although we enabled thread-local allocations, on 16 cores, approximately 40% of the time was spent on object allocation. While the cost of object allocation for our other collectors only involves bumping the frontier, allocation in BDW GC is significantly more costly, involving scanning through a free list, incurring substantial overhead. Moreover, BDW GC is tuned for languages like C/C++ and Java, where the object lifetimes are longer and allocation rate is lower when compared to functional programming languages.

In Figure 11a, at 3X the minimum heap size, RB+, STW and BDW GCs are 32%, 106% and 584% slower than the RB- GC. We observe that there is very little difference between RB+ and RB-in terms of GC time but the mutator time for RB+ is consistently higher than RB- due to read barrier costs. The difference in mutator times is consistent since it is not adversely affected by the increased number of GCs incurred as a result of smaller heap sizes. This also

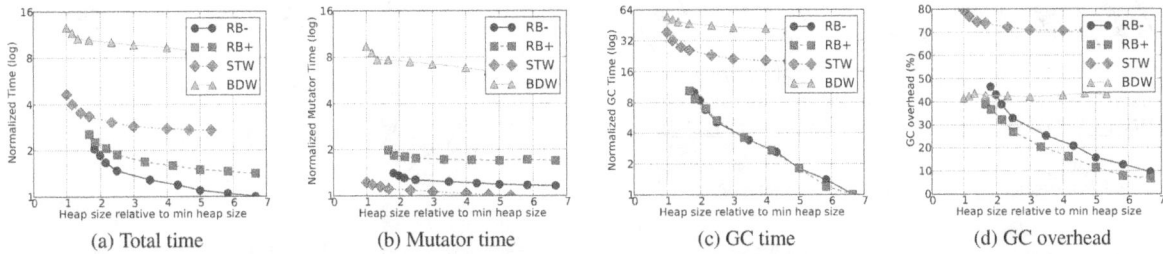

(a) Total time   (b) Mutator time   (c) GC time   (d) GC overhead

Figure 11: Performance comparison of Stop-the-world (STW), Boehm-Demers-Weiser conservative garbage collector (BDW), local collector with read barriers (RB+), and local collector without read barriers (RB-): Geometric mean for 8 benchmarks running on AMD64 with 16 cores.

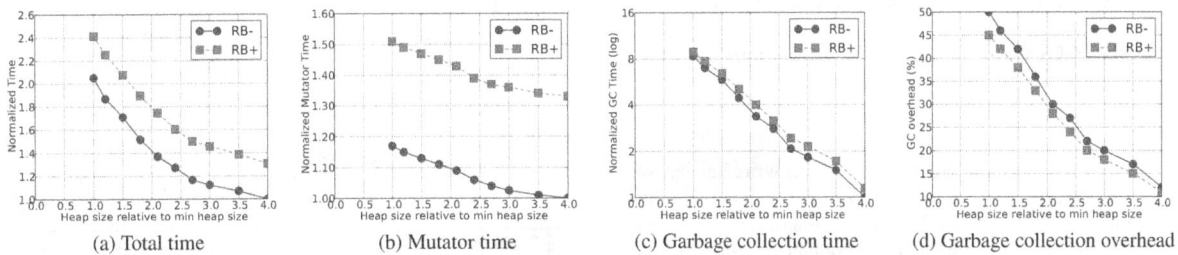

(a) Total time   (b) Mutator time   (c) Garbage collection time   (d) Garbage collection overhead

Figure 12: Performance comparison of local collector with read barriers (RB+) and local collector without read barriers (RB-): Geometric mean for 8 benchmarks running on Azul with 846 cores.

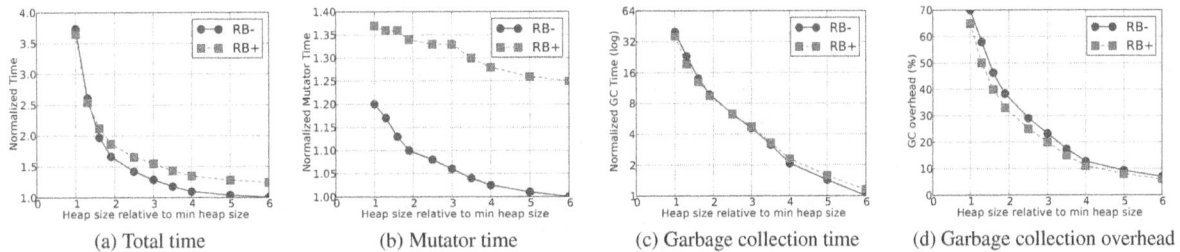

(a) Total time   (b) Mutator time   (c) Garbage collection time   (d) Garbage collection overhead

Figure 13: Performance comparison of local collector with read barriers (RB+) and local collector without read barriers (RB-): Geometric mean for 8 benchmarks running on SCC with 48 cores.

explains why the total running time of RB- approaches RB+ as the heap size is decreased in Figure 11a. With decreasing heap size, the programs spend a larger portion of the time performing GCs, while the mutator time remains consistent. Hence, there is diminishing returns from using RB- as heap size decreases.

Next, we analyze the performance on Azul (see Figure 12). We only consider performance of our local collectors since our AMD results show that the other collectors (STW and BDW) simply do not have favorable scalability characteristics. At 3X the minimum heap size, RB- is 30% faster than RB+.

SCC performance results are presented in Figure 13. At 3X the minimum heap size, RB- is 20% faster than RB+. From the total time graphs, we can see that the programs tend to run much slower as we decrease the heap sizes on SCC. Compared to the fastest running times, the slowest running time for RB- is 2.01X, 2.05X, and 3.74X slower on AMD, Azul, and SCC respectively. This is

due to the increased number of shared heap collections, which are more expensive than other architectures as a result of the absence of caching. This is noticeable by a more rapid increase in garbage collection overhead percentages (Figure 13d).

7.3 Impact of cleanliness

Cleanliness information allows the runtime system to avoid preempting threads on a write barrier when the source of an exporting write is clean. In order to study the impact of cleanliness, we removed the reference counting code and cleanliness check from the write barrier; thus, every exporting write results in a thread preemption and stall. The results presented here were taken on the AMD machine with programs running on 16 cores with the benchmark configurations given in Figure 10. The results will be similar on SCC and Azul.

57

Benchmark	AllPairs	BarnesHut	CountGraphs	GameOfLife	Kclustering	Mandelbrot	Nucleic	Raytrace
RB-	1831	46532	154	38621	25812	132	156	3523
RB- MU-	1831	4092312	192	735543	50323	209	433092	3743
RB- CL-	124232	67156821	50178	5867423	27023911	25491	912349	61198

Figure 14: Number of preemptions on write barrier.

Benchmark	AllPairs	BarnesHut	CountGraphs	GameOfLife	Kclustering	Mandelbrot	Nucleic	Raytrace
RB-	0.08	0.17	0	3.54	0	1.43	0	1.72
RB- MU-	0.08	19.2	0.03	9.47	0.02	2.86	9.37	1.72
RB- CL-	38.55	100	0.18	99.75	21.64	86.22	19.3	24.86

Figure 15: Forced GCs as a percentage of the total number of major GCs.

Figure 14 shows the number of preemptions on write barrier for different local collector configurations. RB- row represents the local collector designs with all of the features enabled; RB- MU- row shows a cleanliness optimization that does not take an object's mutability into consideration in determining cleanliness (using only recorded reference counts instead), and row RB- CL- row represents preemptions incurred when the collector does not use any cleanliness information at all. Without cleanliness, on average, the programs perform substantially more preemptions when encountering a write barrier.

Recall that if all of the threads belonging to a core get preempted on a write barrier, a local major GC is *forced*, which lifts all of the sources of exporting writes, fixes the references to forwarding pointers and unblocks the stalled threads. Hence, an increase in the number of preemptions leads to an increase in the number of local collections.

Figure 15 shows the percentage of local major GCs that were forced compared to the total number of local major GCs. Row RB-CL- shows the percentage of forced GCs if cleanliness information is not used. On average, 49% of local major collection performed is due to forced GCs if cleanliness information is not used, whereas it is less than 1% otherwise. On benchmarks like `BarnesHut`, `GameOfLife` and `Mandelbrot`, where all of the threads tend to operate on a shared global data structure, there are a large number of exporting writes. On such benchmarks almost all local GCs are forced in the absence of cleanliness. This adversely affects the running time of programs.

Figure 16 shows the running time of programs without using cleanliness. On average, programs tend to run 28.2% slower if cleanliness information is ignored. The results show that cleanliness analysis therefore plays a significant role in our GC design.

7.4 Impact of immutability

If the source of an exporting write is immutable, we can make a copy of the object in the shared heap and assign a reference to the new shared heap object to the target. Hence, we can ignore the reference count of such objects. Not all languages may have the ability to distinguish between mutable and immutable objects in the compiler or in the runtime system. Hence, we study the impact of our local collector design with mutability information in mind. To do this, we ignore the test for mutability in the cleanliness check

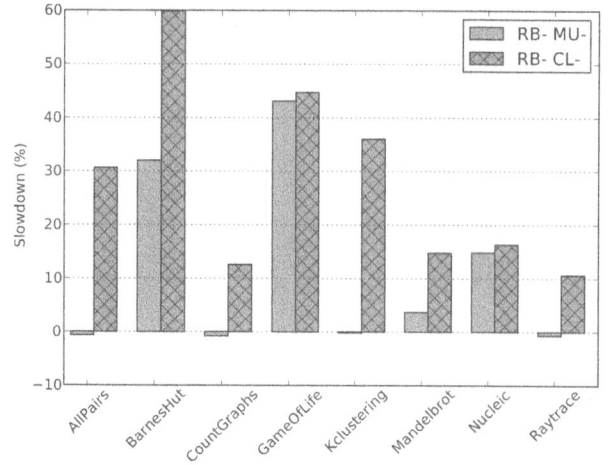

Figure 16: Impact of utilizing object mutability information and cleanliness analysis on the performance of RB- GC.

Benchmark	AllPairs	Barneshut	Countgraphs	GameOfLife	Kclustering	Mandelbrot	Nucleic	Raytrace
% LM clean	5.3	13.4	8.6	23.2	17.6	4.5	13.3	8.2
Avg. session size (bytes)	2908	1580	3612	1344	2318	8723	1264	1123

Figure 17: Impact of heap session: % LM clean represents the fraction of instances when a clean object closure has at least one object with `LOCAL_MANY` references.

(Line 4 in Figure 6) and modify the object lifting code in Figure 8 to treat all objects as mutable.

RB- MU- row in Figure 14 and Figure 15 show the number of write barrier preemptions and the percentage of forced GCs, respectively, if all objects were treated as mutable. For some programs such as `AllPairs`, `CountGraphs`, or `Kclustering`, object mutability does not play a significant factor. For benchmarks where it does, distinguishing between mutable and immutable objects helps avoid inducing preemptions on a write barrier since a copy of the immutable object can be created in the shared heap without the need to repair existing references to the local heap copy.

Figure 16 shows the performance impact of taking object mutability into account. `BarnesHut`, `GameOfLife` and `Nucleic` are slower due to the increased number of forced GCs. Interestingly, `AllPairs`, `CountGraphs`, `Kclustering` and `Raytrace` are marginally faster since they avoid manipulating the `imSet` (Line 14 in Figure 8) and walking immutable objects after the objects are lifted (Lines 25-27 in Figure 8). On average, we see a 11.4% performance impact if mutability information is not utilized for cleanliness.

7.5 Impact of heap session

In order to assess the effectiveness of using heap sessions, we measured the percentage of instances where the source of an exporting write is clean with at least one of the objects in the closure has a `LOCAL_MANY` reference. During such instances, we walk the current heap session to fix any references to forwarded objects. Without using heap sessions, we would have preempted the thread in the write barrier, reducing available concurrency. The results were obtained on the AMD with programs running on 16 cores with the configuration given in Figure 10. The results are presented in Figure 17.

The first row shows the percentage of instances when an object closure is clean and has at least one object with `LOCAL_MANY` references. On average, we see that 12% of clean closures have at least one object with `LOCAL_MANY` references. We also measured the average size of heap sessions when the session is traced as a part of lifting an object closure to the shared heap (Lines 29-31 in Figure 8). The average size of a heap session when it is traced is 2859 bytes, which is less than a page size. These results show that utilizing heap sessions significantly contributes to objects being tagged as clean, and heap sessions are small enough to not introduce significant overheads during tracing.

8. Related Work

Modern garbage collectors rely on read and write barriers for encapsulating operations to be performed when the mutator reads or writes a reference from or to some heap allocated object. The Baker read barrier [5] was the first to use protection and invariants for mutator accesses. While the Baker read barrier is a conditional read barrier, the Brooks read barrier [8] is an unconditional read barrier, where all loads unconditionally forward a pointer in the object header to get to the object. For objects that are not forwarded, this pointer points to the object itself. The Brooks read barrier eliminates branches but increases the size of objects. Trading branches with loads is not a clear optimization as modern processors allow speculation through multiple branches, especially ones that are infrequent.

Over the years, several local collector designs [1, 9, 21, 22] have been proposed for multithreaded programs. Recently, variations of local collector design have been adopted for multithreaded, functional language runtimes like GHC [14] and Manticore [3]. Doligez et al. [9] proposed a local collector design for ML with threads where all mutable objects are allocated directly on the shared heap, and immutable objects are allocated in the local heap. Similar to our technique, whenever local objects are shared between cores, a copy of the immutable object is made in the shared heap. Although this design avoids the need for read and write barriers, allocating all mutable objects, irrespective of their sharing characteristics can lead to poor performance due to increased number of shared collections, and memory access overhead due to NUMA effects and uncached shared memory as in the case of SCC. It is for this reason we do not treat the shared memory as the oldest generation for our local generation collector unlike other designs [9, 14].

Several designs utilize static analysis to determine objects that might potentially escape to other threads [13, 22]. Objects that do not escape are allocated locally, while all others are allocated in the shared heap. The usefulness of such techniques depends greatly on the precision of the analysis, as objects that might potentially be shared are allocated on the shared heap. This is undesirable for architectures like the SCC where shared memory accesses are very expensive compared to local accesses. Compared to these techniques, our design only exports objects that are definitely shared between two or more cores. Our technique is also agnostic to the source language, does not require static analysis, and hence can be implemented as a lightweight runtime technique.

Anderson [1] describes a local collector design (TGC) that triggers a local garbage collection on every exporting write of a mutable object, while immutable objects, that do not have any pointers, are copied to the shared heap. This scheme is a limited form of our cleanliness analysis. In our system, object cleanliness neither solely relies on mutability information, nor is it restricted to objects without pointer fields. Moreover, TGC does not exploit delaying exporting writes to avoid local collections. However, the paper proposes several interesting optimizations that are applicable to our system. In order to avoid frequent mutator pauses on exporting writes, TGC's local collection runs concurrently with the mutator. Though running compaction phase concurrently with the mutator would require read barriers, we can enable concurrent marking to minimize pause times. TGC also proposes watermarking scheme for minimizing stack scanning, which can be utilized in our system to reduce the stack scanning overheads during context switches and exporting writes of clean objects.

Marlow et al. [14] propose exporting only part of the transitive closure to the shared heap, with the idea of minimizing the objects that are globalized. The rest of the closure is exported essentially on demand during the next access from another core. This design mandates the need for a read barrier to test whether the object being accessed resides in the local heap of another core. However, since the target language is Haskell, there is an implicit read barrier on every load, to check whether the thunk has already been evaluated to a value. Since our goal is to eliminate read barriers, we choose to export the transitive closure on an exporting write.

9. Conclusions

The use of read barriers can impose non-trivial overheads in managed languages. In this paper, we consider a design of a runtime system for a thread-aware implementation of Standard ML that completely eliminates the need for read barriers. The design employs a split-heap to allow concurrent local collection, but exploits notions of procrastination and cleanliness to avoid creating forwarding pointers. Procrastination stalls threads about to perform an operation that would otherwise introduce a forwarding pointer, and thus can be used to eliminate read barriers for any exporting write. Cleanliness is an important optimization that helps avoid the cost of stalling by using runtime information to determine when it is safe to copy (rather than move) an object, deferring repair of pointers from the old (local) instance of the object to the new (shared) copy until a later collection. Experimental results on a range of benchmarks and architectural platforms indicate that read barrier elimination contributes to notable performance improvement without significantly complicating the runtime system.

Acknowledgments

We would like to thank our shepherd, Dave Detlefs, and the other anonymous reviewers for their detailed comments and suggestions. This work is supported by the National Science Foundation under grants CCF-0811631 and CNS-0958465, and by gifts from Intel and Samsung Corporation.

References

[1] T. A. Anderson. Optimizations in a Private Nursery-based Garbage Collector. In *ISMM*, pages 21–30, 2010.

[2] A. W. Appel. Simple Generational Garbage Collection and Fast Allocation. *Software Practice and Experience*, 19:171–183, February 1989.

[3] S. Auhagen, L. Bergstrom, M. Fluet, and J. Reppy. Garbage Collection for Multicore NUMA Machines. In *Workshop on Memory Systems Performance and Correctness*, pages 51–57, 2011.

[4] D. F. Bacon, P. Cheng, and V. T. Rajan. A Real-Time Garbage Collector with Low Overhead and Consistent Utilization. In *POPL*, pages 285–298, 2003.

[5] H. G. Baker, Jr. List Processing in Real Time on a Serial Computer. *Communication of the ACM*, 21:280–294, 1978.

[6] S. M. Blackburn and A. L. Hosking. Barriers: Friend or Foe? In *ISMM*, pages 143–151, 2004.

[7] H. Boehm. A Garbage Collector for C and C++, 2012. URL http://www.hpl.hp.com/personal/Hans_Boehm/gc.

[8] R. A. Brooks. Trading Data Space for Reduced Time and Code Space in Real-Time Garbage Collection on Stock Hardware. In *Lisp and Functional Programming*, pages 256–262, 1984.

[9] D. Doligez and X. Leroy. A Concurrent, Generational Garbage Collector for a Multithreaded Implementation of ML. In *POPL*, pages 113–123, 1993.

[10] L. Gidra, G. Thomas, J. Sopena, and M. Shapiro. Assessing the scalability of garbage collectors on many cores. *SIGOPS Operating Systems Review*, 45(3):15–19, 2012.

[11] P. Hartel, M. Feeley, M. Alt, and L. Augustsson. Benchmarking Implementations of Functional Languages with "Pseudoknot", a Float-Intensive Benchmark. *Journal of Functional Programming*, 6(4):621–655, 1996.

[12] Intel. SCC Platform Overview, 2012. URL `http://communities.intel.com/docs/DOC-5512`.

[13] R. Jones and A. C. King. A Fast Analysis for Thread-Local Garbage Collection with Dynamic Class Loading. In *International Workshop on Source Code Analysis and Manipulation*, pages 129–138, 2005.

[14] S. Marlow and S. Peyton Jones. Multicore Garbage Collection with Local Heaps. In *ISMM*, pages 21–32, 2011.

[15] R. Milner, M. Tofte, and D. Macqueen. *The Definition of Standard ML*. MIT Press, Cambridge, MA, USA, 1997.

[16] MLton. The MLton Compiler and Runtime System, 2012. URL `http://www.mlton.org`.

[17] MultiMLton. MLton for Scalable Multicore Architectures, 2012. URL `http://multimlton.cs.purdue.edu`.

[18] J. Reppy. *Concurrent Programming in ML*. Cambridge University Press, 2007.

[19] P. M. Sansom. Dual-Mode Garbage Collection. In *Proceedings of the Workshop on the Parallel Implementation of Functional Languages*, pages 283–310, 1991.

[20] F. Siebert. Limits of parallel marking garbage collection. In *ISMM*, pages 21–29, 2008.

[21] G. L. Steele, Jr. Multiprocessing Compactifying Garbage Collection. *Communcations of the ACM*, 18:495–508, September 1975.

[22] B. Steensgaard. Thread-Specific Heaps for Multi-Threaded Programs. In *ISMM*, pages 18–24, 2000.

[23] Streambench. The STREAM Benchmark: Computer Memory Bandwidth, 2012. URL `http://http://www.streambench.org/`.

[24] L. Ziarek, K. Sivaramakrishnan, and S. Jagannathan. Composable Asynchronous Events. In *PLDI*, pages 628–639, 2011.

Scalable Concurrent and Parallel Mark

Balaji Iyengar

Azul Systems Inc
balaji@azulsystems.com

Edward Gehringer

North Carolina State University
efg@ncsu.edu

Michael Wolf

Azul Systems Inc
wolf@azulsystems.com

Karthikeyan Manivannan

Azul Systems Inc
karthik@azulsystems.com

Abstract

Parallel marking algorithms use multiple threads to walk through the object heap graph and mark each reachable object as live. Parallel marker threads mark an object "live" by atomically setting a bit in a mark-bitmap or a bit in the object header. Most of these parallel algorithms strive to improve the marking throughput by using work-stealing algorithms for load-balancing and to ensure that all participating threads are kept busy. A purely "processor-centric" load-balancing approach in conjunction with a need to atomically set the mark bit, results in significant contention during parallel marking. This limits the scalability and throughput of parallel marking algorithms.

We describe a new non-blocking and lock-free, work-sharing algorithm, the primary goal being to reduce contention during atomic updates of the mark-bitmap by parallel task-threads. Our work-sharing mechanism uses the address of a word in the mark-bitmap as the key to stripe work among parallel task-threads, with only a subset of the task-threads working on each stripe. This filters out most of the contention during parallel marking with ~20% improvements in performance.

In case of concurrent and on-the-fly collector algorithms, mutator threads also generate marking-work for the marking task-threads. In these schemes, mutator threads are also provided with thread-local marking stacks where they collect references to potentially "gray" objects, i.e., objects that haven't been "marked-through" by the collector. We note that since this work is generated by mutators when they reference these objects, there is a high likelihood that these objects continue to be present in the processor cache. We describe and evaluate a scheme to distribute mutator generated marking work among the collector's task-threads that is cognizant of the processor and cache topology. We prototype both our algorithms within the C4 [28] collector that ships as part of an industrial strength JVM for the Linux-X86 platform.

Categories and Subject Descriptors D.3.3 [*Language Constructs and Features*]: Dynamic storage management; Concurrent programming structures; D.3.4 [*Processors*]: Memory management (garbage collection)

General Terms Algorithms, Design, Performance.

Keywords Parallel Marking, Work-stealing, Work-sharing, Scalable parallel algorithms, Compare-and-swap instruction, Concurrent marking, Processor and cache topology, Prefetching.

1. Introduction

Parallel garbage collection algorithms have been around for a while [21] and are best suited to take advantage of the modern multi-core architectures. Parallel marking algorithms[1] use multiple threads to mark through the live-set in the program heap. Each thread starts with a stack primed with references to root objects. Each object pointer in the marking-stack is popped, the object it points-to is marked and the references to its children are then pushed back onto the marking-stack. This is the typical tracing loop which proceeds until no new references to unmarked objects are found. In case of parallel marking schemes that use a mark-bitmap with a bit for every potential object address, the task-threads need to use atomic instructions such as the compare-and-swap(CAS) instruction to update the mark-bitmap. This is required in order to avoid losing simultaneous updates to the same word in the mark-bitmap by different task-threads. Byte-maps allow us to avoid the expense of atomic operations, with a byte in the marking byte-map for every potential object address, resulting in a 8-fold increase in memory usage. This is not very desirable, especially with the increasing heap sizes of current enterprise applications. Locating the mark bit in the object header allows us to avoid atomic updates in stop-the-world mark algorithms. However, concurrent marking implementations are generally required to atomically update the mark bit in the object header, since the header word is used for other purposes such as storing the object hash-codes. Mark bitmaps also have several other advantages compared to locating the marking bit in the object header. Marking bitmaps store marks much more densely. The collector does fewer writes to the object in a design using a mark-bitmap, resulting in fewer dirty cache-lines. Also, since objects live and die in clusters [22], mark-bits can be tested and cleared in groups. For these reasons, mark-bitmaps are prevalent in implementations of most commercial garbage collection algorithms [12, 13, 28].

At the outset, the parallel mark phase generally tries to distribute the work evenly among the task-threads. Most parallel marking implementations also rely on load-balancing algorithms [17–19, 26, 27, 30], where the primary focus is to ensure that there is enough work for every processor involved in marking. The initial work assignment and the subsequent work-sharing algorithms tend

---

[1] We only focus on GC algorithms that have a separate mark phase. We don't discuss mark-copy algorithms that tend to merge the two phases.

Task-Threads	1	2	4	6	8	10	12
% Duty-Cycle	55.911	57.694	58.913	61.226	63.784	64.609	65.096

Table 1. Mark-phase duty-cycle for the baseline C4 collector with increasing task-threads

to be oblivious of the memory location of the objects being processed by the respective task-threads and hence are classified as "processor-centric" algorithms [23]. The current work-sharing approaches achieve an improvement in marking throughput, however their scalability doesn't quite approach the ceilings of the available parallelism [7, 27].

The *mark phase* consumes the bulk of the time in a typical mark-compact GC cycle [9]. This is primarily attributable to the poor temporal and spatial locality properties of a pointer-chasing algorithm. Table 1, shows the variation in the percentage of GC-cycle time spent on marking with increasing number of task-threads for the C4 [28] algorithm. The numbers reflect average mark-phase duty-cycles for the Dacapo benchmark suite [8] for the new generation with the old generation displaying a similar pattern. While the absolute mark-times reduce with more marking task-threads, the marking duty-cycle continues to get worse with the number of threads. This is because the compaction-phase of a mark-compact algorithm scales much better with more task-threads compared to the mark-phase.

A purely processor-centric work-sharing scheme in the mark phase, along with the clustered nature of the mark-bitmap, results in multiple task-threads updating a single word in the mark-bitmap. In this paper, our premise is that contention caused by atomic updates to the mark-bitmap is one of the primary bottlenecks to the scalability of current work-sharing schemes in the mark phase. This results in increased cache traffic and cache pollution that adversely effects the marking throughput.

In order to study the performance characteristics of the CAS instruction, we wrote a micro-benchmark with three different scenarios: threads updating a thread-local/shared counter a million times via a store/atomic-CAS instruction(lock:cmpxchg on X86). Figure 1, plots the execution times in these scenarios normalized by the execution time of a single-thread updating the counter via a store(mov) instruction. Updating the shared counter using the store instruction, scales reasonably well. Cache line ping-ponging is the primary reason for slow-down in this case. As can be seen, the CAS update to thread-local counter has a constant overhead but also scales pretty well. We believe this constant overhead is the cost of locking the memory bus. The CAS update of the shared counter has the worst performance, with significant degradation in performance with increase in threads. We believe this is because of the multiplying effect of cache-line ping-ponging and serialization caused by memory bus locking. It is also clear that cache-line ping-ponging is the dominant reason for the performance degradation in this scenario, since CAS updates to the thread-local counter only suffer from a constant overhead of ~4X.

Figure 1, supports our premise in the scope of the micro-benchmark[2]. We discuss our evaluation methodology to derive similar conclusions for our baseline algorithm, in section 3.

We propose, implement and analyze a new work-sharing scheme that reduces contention among the task-threads during updates to the mark-bitmap in section 4. Our scheme makes a cache line in the mark-bitmap into the basic unit of work sharing. This ensures that

[2] All our experiments were done on a 2 socket, Intel Westmere-X5680 based system, running the 2.6.34 Linux kernel with 98GB of memory. Each socket has 6 hyper-threaded cores, making it a 24 "core" machine.

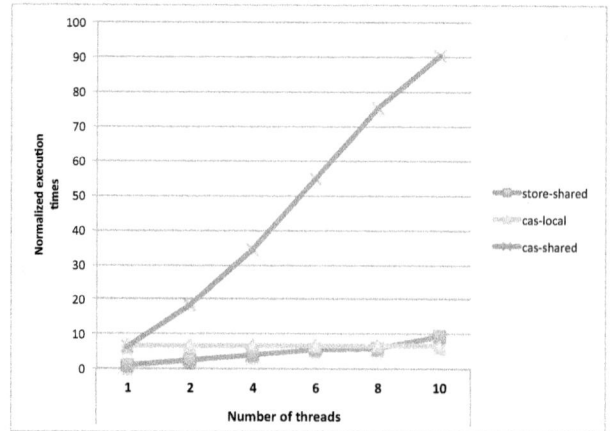

Figure 1. Scalability of the CAS/Store instructions.

only a smaller, tunable number of task-threads update addresses in the mark-bitmap that map to the same cache line. Our algorithm is non-blocking and lock-free. It is important to note that our scheme is orthogonal to load-balancing schemes such as work-stealing [18, 19], which can be easily overlaid on top of our proposed scheme. Similarly, our proposed scheme is also amenable to prefetching algorithms. The proposed scheme is a first of its kind "hybrid" work-sharing algorithm that tries to reduce cache traffic while keeping all involved processors busy.

Mutator threads are the other source of tracing work in concurrent [11, 28] as well as on-the-fly marking schemes [6, 15]. In these schemes, mutator threads are provided with thread-local marking stacks where they collect references to potentially "gray" [14] objects. The work accumulated in the mutator marking stacks is transferred to the collector's task-threads using different schemes. Domani et al. [15] use double ended queues for this purpose. Azatchi [6] uses soft handshakes to drain this work. The C4 collector [28] uses soft handshakes, referred to as checkpoints, to transfer this work to a global pool of marking stacks; the collector's task-threads then acquire these stacks from the global pool in a thread-safe manner and mark through the references in these stacks.

We note that since this work is generated by mutators when they reference these objects, there is a high likelihood that these objects continue to be present in the processor/core cache. In section 6, we describe and evaluate a scheme to distribute the mutator generated marking work among the collector's task-threads, that is cognizant of the system topology [2].

Our proposed algorithms have been prototyped within the C4 collector [28], that runs on a Linux based X86 machine. We would like to point out that the proposed algorithms are independent of the C4 collector algorithm and can be applied to other mark-sweep or mark-compact type GC algorithms. The contributions of this paper are:

- We describe a methodology to evaluate the scalability of a concurrent, parallel, marking algorithm and highlight a bottleneck therein.
- We identify the two primary sources of work for task-threads during the concurrent mark phase, i.e., work generated by the task-threads themselves and the work generated by mutator threads and propose separate algorithms to improve the parallel marking-throughput in each case.
- We describe and evaluate a new non-blocking and lock-free work-sharing algorithm for concurrent, parallel marking
- We finally describe a processor-and-cache-topology aware work-sharing scheme for mutator generated tracing work.

2. Related Work

There is a large body of work on improving the performance of the mark phase. There are two main approaches: techniques that focus on improving the single-threaded performance of a marker and those that aim to improve the overall "marking" throughput in a parallel environment with multiple marker threads.

Prefetching techniques [9, 10] focus on improving the single-threaded performance of a marker by trying to ensure that the object about to be marked-through is found in the processor cache. Prefetching-on-gray [9] fetches the first cache line of an object as that object is grayed, i.e., added to the marking stack. This technique relies on the timing of the prefetch and is susceptible to ineffective prefetches caused by the prefetch being either too early or too late. Cher et al. [10] add a FIFO stack in front of the traditional marking stack, prefetching an object when a reference to the object is first added to the FIFO stack. The fixed-size FIFO allows the timing of the prefetches to be tightly controlled, thereby increasing the chances of an effective prefetch. Garner et al. [20] restructure the tracing loop by enqueuing "edges" instead of "nodes". All non-null references to child objects are pushed onto the marking stack and the "test-and-mark" operation is performed when these references are popped from the stack. This sequence results in the marker performing back-to-back operations on the same object, increasing the benefits of having the object in cache via prefetching.

Parallel marking algorithms improve the tracing time by having multiple threads walk through disjoint sections of the object graph. Siebert [26] studies the amount of potential parallelism available to marker threads and points out that most applications have rich enough data structures to support a high level of parallelism. Several algorithms have tried to exploit this, most of which have been classified as processor-centric algorithms [23]. These algorithms rely on work-stealing [18, 19, 27] based load-balancing techniques to ensure that all participating threads are kept busy.

Endo et al. [18] use a per-thread marking stack and a steal-queue to implement their load-balancing algorithm. Each thread periodically allows up to half of its work to be stolen by transferring it from its private marking stack to the steal-queue. Once a thread is done draining the work in its marking stack, it attempts to obtain work from the steal queues of other task-threads. Steal-queues are protected by locks, with an optimization to avoid waiting on an already held lock. Flood et al. [19] use a per-thread fixed-size deque, in conjunction with a lock-free work-stealing algorithm based on Arora et al. [5] to achieve load-balancing. Their approach has very little synchronization overhead. Once a task-thread is done with the work in its marking stack, it steals a single piece of work from the marking stack of another task-thread. Siebert [27] also use a work-stealing mechanism in their implementation of a parallel and concurrent real-time garbage collector. In this case, the granularity of of work stolen is much larger, with a thief thread attempting to steal an entire marking stack. Each algorithm trades-off between the synchronization costs involved in work-stealing with the amount of work stolen. Wu et al. [30] use a scheme where each task-thread uses a single-writer, single-reader channel to push work out to other task-threads. In a system with M task-threads, each task-thread has an array of $M - 1$ circular buffers used for work-sharing. The single-writer, single-reader scheme allows them to avoid the expense of atomic operations during load balancing.

Parallel marking algorithms employing work-stealing have to implement a "termination" condition that ensures that all participating threads continue to stick around and assist their sibling threads even after they are done with their local work. Flood et al. [19] achieve this by having the task-threads spin on a non-zero status word that has a bit for each participating thread. Each thread sets its bit in the status word when it starts working. One can also use a counter based termination condition, where task-threads spin on an atomically updated counter that indicates the number of active task-threads. Wu et al. [30] use a dedicated thread to detect termination.

Currently, there aren't any "memory centric" [23] load-balancing algorithms used in parallel marking that we know of, although these are quite common in parallel copying algorithms. Our algorithm proposes a first of its kind, hybrid work-sharing scheme that attempts to reduce the contention during atomic updates of the mark-bitmap while keeping all participating threads busy.

3. Evaluating A Parallel Marking Algorithm

The primary goals of a parallel marking algorithm are:

1. To reduce the time it takes to mark the heap graph.
2. To make optimal use of the hardware resources assigned for marking. This generally implies the use of work-sharing schemes to ensure that all the involved processors/cores are ideally marking disjoint sections of the heap graph in parallel.
3. To keep the synchronization costs resulting from load balancing to a minimum.

We begin by describing our baseline concurrent, parallel marking algorithm. We then describe our measurement methodologies and highlight the bottlenecks in the algorithm.

3.1 Baseline Algorithm

The C4 collector is a concurrent, parallel, generational compacting collector with a tunable set of task-threads dedicated to collecting the garbage in each generation. The marking algorithm for both generations is identical. The C4 collector's use of the LVB-style read-barrier to support concurrent mark has been discussed in detail elsewhere [11, 28]. We won't focus on the read-barrier mechanism and the generational aspects of the collector from here on, since it is orthogonal to our current discussion.

Each task-thread has a LIFO style marking-stack used for the depth-first traversal of the heap graph. The mark phase starts with the marking stacks of the task-threads primed with references to root objects. Each task-thread first begins by draining its marking stack. For each reference in the stack, it enumerates the pointers to child objects, filters null references, marks the yet-unmarked child objects and pushes the references to these child objects back on to its marking stack. The marking stack can overflow during this process and when this happens, the marking stack is added to a global overflow-pool of marking stacks. The global overflow pool is maintained as a linked list of marking stacks. This is similar to the gray-packet approach used by Ossia et al. [25]. The global overflow pool of marking stacks is a non-blocking data structure; stacks are added-to and acquired-from the global pool using atomic instructions such as the compare-and-swap instruction(CAS). Empty marking stacks are maintained in a separate pool; hence our algorithm doesn't suffer from the "ABA" [5] problem. Each task-thread also gets a FIFO queue to enqueue prefetch requests [10].

Once a task-thread has drained its local marking stack, it tries to acquire a full marking stack from the overflow pool. If the overflow pool is found to be empty, the task-thread attempts to steal a single reference from another task-thread's marking stack. The work-stealing algorithm is a "steal-one" algorithm, the details of which we don't discuss here in the interest of space and since it is orthogonal to this paper's work. The overflow pool of marking stacks and the work-stealing algorithm are part of the processor-centric load-balancing algorithm used by the C4 collector. Since every GC algorithm uses a different processor-centric load-balancing scheme, our goal is to study the performance scalability of the common aspects of these GC algorithms. For this reason, we don't focus on the load-balancing aspects of the C4 collector in this paper.

The task-threads maintain a shared counter of the number of active threads, which is a single word in memory updated using the CAS instruction. This counter is used to calculate the termination condition [19]. The pseudo-code for the baseline algorithm is outlined in fig 2.

```
shared over_flow_pool
shared marking_stack[N]
shared task_thread_count = M // M task-threads
shared working_count
me = myThreadId
// acquire work from global overflow pool or steal from sibling thread
acquire_work() {
  if (!marking_stack[me].is_empty())
    return
  if acquire_from_overflow_pool(marking_stack[me])
    return
  i = 0
  while (i< task_thread_count) {
    if (ref = steal_one(marking_stack[i]))
      return
    i=i+1
  }
}
drain_marking_stack() {
  while (!marking_stack[me].is_empty()) {
    ref = pop(marking_stack[me]);
    mark_through(ref);
  }
}
mark_through(ref) {
  child_pointer_list = ref.child_pointer_list();
  for p in child_pointer_list {
    child = p.load()
    if (child != NULL)
      marking_stack[me].push(child)
  }
}
push(ref) {
  if (ref.test_and_mark())
    marking_stack[me].add(ref);
  if (marking_stack[me].is_full()) {
    add_to_overflow_pool(marking_stack[me])
  }
}
mark_task() {
  do {
    if(acquire_work()) {
      inc_working_count()
      drain_marking_stack()
      dec_working_count()
    }
  } while (working_count>0)
}
```

Figure 2. Baseline Marking Algorithm

3.2 Evaluation Methodology

A collector's task-thread performs a series of operations during the mark phase, such as atomically setting a bit in the mark-bitmap, pushing-to and popping-from the marking stack, and load balancing operations that vary depending on the algorithm being used. Testing whether an object is already marked and attempting to atomically update a word in the mark-bitmap is common to most parallel marking algorithms. We describe a methodology for measuring the performance of the test-and-mark operation in section 3.2.2. In section 3.2.3, we describe our approach for measuring the contention resulting from the collector's task-threads atomically updating the mark-bitmap. We first describe the benchmarks we use for our studies, the platform that we used for our runs and the heap-sizing policies in section 3.2.1.

3.2.1 Framework details

The size and the shape of the program live-set has a direct bearing on the performance of a marking algorithm. In order to study the performance of a marking algorithm, it is important to ensure that GC cycles are triggered during all program phases. This in turn guarantees that the marker has to deal with different shapes and sizes of the live-set. The maximum heap allocated(-Xmx) to

an application doesn't directly effect the time spent by the GC algorithm in marking. It can however, impact the GC heuristics that determine how often GC cycles are triggered. We avoid this by tweaking our GC heuristics to trigger periodic GC cycles. This ensures that the marker is forced to work during different program phases. The change in GC heuristic doesn't impact the size and the shape of the live-set kept live by "strong-references". We use a time based promotion policy, hence triggering frequent new generation cycles doesn't change the live-set in the old-generation.

Periodic garbage collection cycles can however end up frequently clearing soft/weak references that hold caches, which can result in changes in program behavior. In order to avoid this, we don't clear out soft/weak references and run with a generous enough heap size that allows the benchmarks to run to completion without running out of memory. Also, the C4 collector implementation differentiates between marking-through of strong-references versus weak/soft references. We use this feature of the C4 collector to measure performance only during the marking of strong-references. We note that strong-references" are the majority of the references in all the benchmarks, hence our measurement window covers bulk of the mark phase. However, we did run with different heap sizes and found no impact on the measurements, which is in line with the observation from Garner et al [20]. Similar to Garner et al [20], we run all our experiments with a generous heap size that allowed us to run to completion. We found that a heap-size of 1GB was enough to run all the benchmarks. We also use their approach to condense the huge amount of data produced by running a total of 22 benchmarks (14 from DaCapo [8] and 8 from SPECjvm-98 [3]) and report the geometric mean for each metric for the full set of benchmarks across both collector generations.

The C4 collector is a concurrent, generational collector and has a unique inter-generational concurrency property [28], i.e., both the new and the old generations can be collected concurrently. The C4 collector assigns a tunable set of task-threads for each generation. Since our experiments are done on a 24 core box, we don't allow the total number of task-threads across both generations to exceed that number. Also, for measuring the performance of our baseline algorithm and that of the proposed work-sharing algorithm during the mark phase, we have the C4 collector's marker operate in a stop-the-world mode. This ensures that all the processor cores in the system are available for the marker's task-threads and our numbers are not polluted by scheduler events.

We use the DaCapo (version 9.12-bach) [8] and the SPECjvm-98 [3] suite of benchmarks for our experiments.

3.2.2 Measuring the performance of "test-and-mark"

We chose the *average number of processor cycles* as the metric to measure the performance of test-and-mark for an object. On the X86 platform, we can obtain this by reading the time-stamp counter [1] prior to and after a test-and-mark operation for an object and recording the delta between the time-stamps. Other hardware platforms offer similar "tick" counters as well. While this approach gives us a high resolution measure of marking an object, it is also an expensive operation. The RDTSCP [1] instruction, used for reading the time-stamp counter on the X86 platform, is a serializing operation and waits for prior instructions to finish executing before reading the time-stamp counter. We would like to amortize this cost by measuring the test-and-mark cost in batches. However, in the traditional tracing loop outlined in Fig 2 there are several other operations between any two mark attempts, such as the "push", "pop", "null-check" and "enumerate pointer fields" operations. We tweak the tracing loop in order to tease out the test-and-mark operations and execute a batch of only these operations.

We place a fixed-size FIFO stack in front of the marking stack to hold references to unmarked objects. Non-null object references are first pushed onto this FIFO stack and a batch of test-and-mark operations is started when this buffer is full. As part of the batch operation, the task-thread executes a test-and-mark operation on each reference in the FIFO stack. The time-stamp counter is read prior to starting the batch operation and at the end of the batch operation. The delta in the time-stamp counter values and the number of references processed are accumulated in thread-local counters.

An object that was marked live by the task-thread as part of the batch needs to be marked-through, and hence a reference to that object needs to be pushed onto the main marking stack. The cost of this push should not be included in the cost of the batched test-and-mark operations. In order to exclude it, we use the highest bit in each stack slot of the FIFO buffer to indicate whether the particular object was marked as part of the batch operation. Since each stack slot is a single 64-bit memory word and the virtual address space is restricted to 48 bits on the X86 platform, we can safely use the highest bit of each slot for this purpose. At the end of the batch operation, we push the references that are in the slots with highest bit set, onto the main marking stack. This filtering out of references that were not marked live by the task-thread under consideration, reflects the original semantics of marking and doesn't pollute our measurements.

The pseudo-code is outlined in Fig 3. Using the time-stamp counter for measurements is susceptible to scheduling events that occur in the measurement window. This can result in large, undesirable spikes in the measurement. On a multi-core machine, this is exacerbated since the time-stamp counters are processor-local and not necessarily in sync. Using a small fixed-size FIFO allows us to tightly control the measurement window and avoid scheduling events in the middle of our measurement window for the most part. For our measurements, we use a FIFO stack with 10 entries. This approach filters out most of the scheduling events within the measurement window but not all. We discard measured values that exceed a static threshold that matches the scheduler time quantum on our platform(10ms). Such values occur extremely rarely. This gives us a pragmatic approach to obtaining high-resolution measurements.

```
marking_stack[]
batch_mark_stack[]
push(ref) {
  batch_mark_stack.add(ref);
  if (batch_mark_stack).is_full() {
    start_batch = time_stamp_counter();
    i = 0;
    while (i<batch_mark_stack.size()) {
      if (test_and_mark(batch_mark_stack[i]))
        set_marked_by_self(i)
      i++;
    }
    end_batch = time_stamp_counter();
    record (end_batch - start_batch);
    i=0;
    while (i<batch_mark_stack.size()) {
      if (marked_by_self(i))
        push_ref(marking_stack);
      i++;
    }
    reset_batch_mark_stack();
  }
}
```

Figure 3. Batch Marking

Fig 4 plots the processor-cycles to mark a reference against the number of task-threads for different heap sizes. The numbers are normalized by the cycles per reference for a single task-thread running in stop-the-world mode. As can be seen, the cycles-per-reference gradually increases and follows a trend that is independent of the heap size. Fig 5 plots the speedup in wall-clock mark times relative to the number of task-threads for different heap sizes. The metric is normalized by the mark time for a single task-thread

in stop-the-world mode. We continue to get a speedup by adding additional task-threads even though the mark-cycles-per-reference continues to creep up. This expected increased throughput is due to the increased parallelism although the single-threaded performance decreases. At some point in the graphs, the contention between the task-threads and the NUMA effects start to dominate, which results in the flattening of the speedup curve. On the Westmere-EP architecture there is a relatively big jump in mark-cycles-per-reference around 7 task-threads, which we think is because of NUMA effects on the 6 cores-per-socket machine.

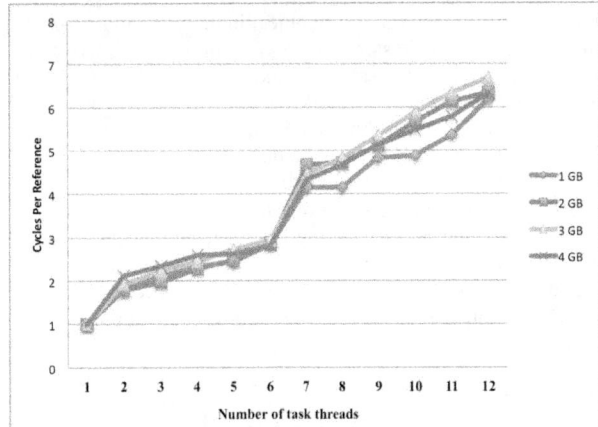

Figure 4. Cycles to mark a reference increases with the number of task-threads

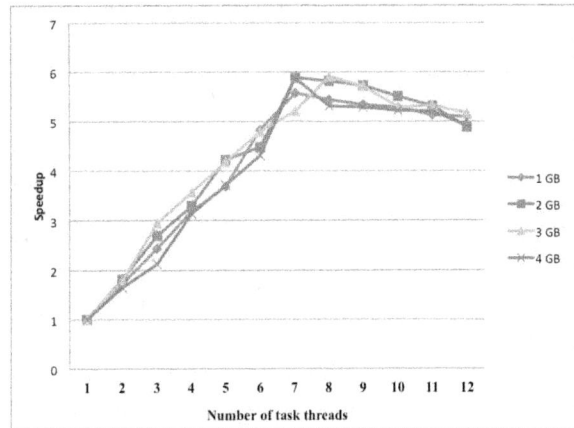

Figure 5. Speedup in parallel marking time flattens out as the number of task-threads crosses a threshold

3.2.3 Measuring contention during atomic updates to mark-bitmap

Atomic update instructions, such as CAS, implement the atomicity semantic by providing mutual-exclusion at the hardware level. On the X86 platform, the *lock* prefix, used in conjunction with the CAS instruction, results in a processor/core getting exclusive access to the system bus, thereby providing mutual-exclusion. Newer X86 processor architectures don't lock the system bus if the memory word being updated is present in the processor cache and is completely contained within a cache line [1]. In these cases, the cache coherency mechanism ensures atomicity. Other hardware platforms also benefit significantly from similar optimizations. Atomic updates of a memory word by different processors/cores can result in significant serialization of hardware resources and cache line ping-ponging.

In the case of parallel marking based on purely processor-centric work-sharing, our hypothesis is that a single word in the mark-bitmap is atomically updated by several task-threads resulting in contention that limits marking throughput. In order to verify this hypothesis, we track the number of unique task-threads that atomically update a set of words in the mark-bitmap that map to the same cache line. Our scheme assigns an unique thread-id to each task-thread and allocates a separate "mark-id" byte-map at the start. This byte-map is sized in a similar manner to the mark-bitmap and can store a byte value for every object in the heap. A task-thread that successfully marks an object live, stores its thread-id in the byte corresponding to the object in the mark-id byte-map. We don't need an atomic store for the write in the byte-map, since only one thread can successfully mark an object. At the end of marking, we walk through the mark-bitmap, a cache line at a time. For each bit that is set in the cache line of the mark-bitmap, we look up, in the mark-id byte-map the number of unique thread-id's that atomically updated the cache line.

Fig 6 plots the number of unique task-threads that write to a single cache line in the mark-bitmap. As suspected, in our baseline processor-centric work-sharing scheme, this number increases as the number of task-threads increase. On a multi-processor system with multiple cores per processor, this pattern will result in significant cache traffic, inhibiting throughput.

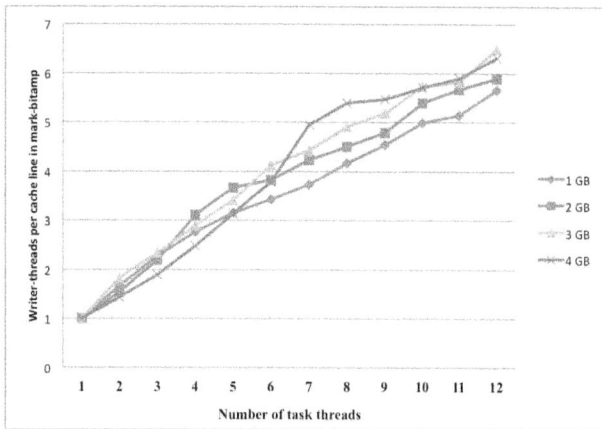

Figure 6. Number of task-threads writing to a cache line in the mark-bitmap relative to number of task-threads

4. Scalable Work Sharing At Cache Line Boundaries

Our core premise is that there is contention due to multiple GC threads attempting to atomically update words in the mark-bitmap that map to the same cache line. This contention is a limiting factor in the scalability of parallel marking and we aim to reduce this.

Our algorithm is based on distributing the marking work onto N stripes. Each object reference maps to a unique stripe. The stripe index for a reference is based on the address of the mark-bitmap word that corresponds to the reference. Similarly, each task-thread maps to a unique stripe, i.e., is responsible for draining work from a single stripe. However, we could have multiple task-threads mapping to the same stripe. In a system with a total of M task-threads, M/N task-threads are responsible for draining the work in each stripe. A task-thread's stripe index is determined by modulo arithmetic, i.e., *task-thread-id % N*. This scheme ensures that a maximum of M/N threads can update a single word in the mark-bitmap. In our baseline algorithm, $N = 1$, implying that all the task-threads could potentially update a single word in the mark-

bitmap. On the other hand, when $N = M$, only one task-thread can update a single word in the mark-bitmap.

4.1 Data Structures

In order to stripe the work N ways, every task-thread starts off with an array of N private, thread-local marking stacks. Of these, the stack corresponding to the task-thread's stripe-index is treated as its "current" marking stack. The task-thread uses its current marking stack in the usual manner for marking-through references that belong to its work-stripe. The other $N - 1$ work-sharing marking stacks, are used by the task-thread to generate marking work for other task-threads. Note that a task-thread both pushes-to and pops-from its current, marking stack, while it only pushes work onto the other $N - 1$ work-sharing stacks.

A task-thread's N marking stacks are private and invisible to the other threads, until they are "published". Each task-thread maintains a "published-pool" of marking stacks, striped N ways. A full marking-stack is pushed on to the task-thread's published-pool and at that point becomes eligible to be stolen by other task-threads. A full marking-stack is added to the same stripe-index in the published-pool corresponding to its original stripe-index. Each stripe in the published-pool is maintained as a singly linked-list of marking stacks. Pushing a marking-stack onto the published-pool is a lock-free operation and can be achieved via a CAS instruction. Each task-thread also maintains a thread-local pool of free marking stacks in order to avoid the "ABA" [5] problem. Fig 7, illustrates the data structures for each task-thread.

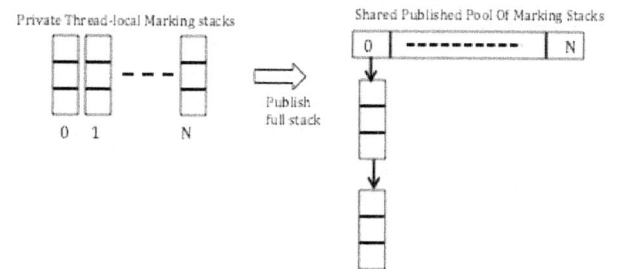

Figure 7. Marking Data Structures For A Task Thread

4.2 Algorithm

We describe our algorithm in a format used by the Jones et al. [23], focusing on the key sub-tasks of acquiring, performing and generating marking work.

Acquire work: A task-thread starts off by popping references from its current marking stack. As in the baseline algorithm, working on the current marking stack doesn't require any atomic operations. Once that is done, it attempts to acquire full marking stacks from its stripe in the published-pools. The task-thread starts off looking for work in its own published-pool and then moves on to the published-pool of other task-threads. Each time it only acquires work from the work-stripe it is responsible for. Acquiring work from a stripe is a lock-free operation done using CAS operations.

Perform work: For every reference that the task-thread acquires, it enumerates the pointers to its child objects. For each non-null reference to a child object, the task-thread has to decide whether it "falls" into its work-stripe. This check has to be made prior to testing whether the object is already marked, in order to avoid cache pollution in the case where the object doesn't fall into the task-thread's work-stripe. The task-thread performs the usual test-and-mark operation on a reference that maps to its work-stripe. References that map to other work-stripes are pushed onto the correct thread-local work-sharing marking stack; the task-thread doesn't read or update the corresponding word in the mark-bitmap for these references.

Generate work: A task-thread adds full marking stacks to the right stripes in its published-pool. Partially full marking stacks owned by a task-thread are not visible to other task-threads. This is necessary to avoid a race between the "owner" task-thread and the "stealer" thread, where the owner-thread could still be pushing references onto an already stolen stack resulting in stack corruption. However, this can result in work being kept away from potentially idle task-threads. We reduce the possibility of this happening by having the task-thread flush the partially full private marking stacks to its published-pool each time it finishes draining its current marking stack.

Termination condition: The task-threads spin on a single status word that is updated atomically. The bottom M bits of the status word, with a bit for each of the M participating task-threads, indicate availability of work for the corresponding task-thread. The top $\log_2 M$ bits of the status word are used to maintain a count of active task-threads. The two fields need to be part of a single word, since it is necessary to update them atomically.

During tracing, each task-thread can potentially push work onto any other work-stripe, including the work-stripes that it is not responsible for. A task-thread needs a mechanism to signal to the other task-threads that there is new work available on their stripes. This is critical, since task-threads only drain work from the stripes that they map to. The bit-mask in the status word is used for this purpose. However, the bit-mask by itself is not enough to ensure that the work generated by one task-thread for another task-thread is actually picked up by the responsible task-thread. There is a time window where a sibling task-thread can exit its main work loop before it sees the bit set in the status word. In order to close out this race, we need a count of active task-threads to be part of the same status word.

At the start, all the bits of the bit-mask in the status word are set. This ensures that all task-threads will enter the main work loop at least once. Before it enters the main work-loop, a task-thread clears its bit in the bit-mask and increments the active thread count with a single atomic operation. Incrementing the active thread count in the status word, ensures that even task-threads that don't currently have any work in their stripes continue to be in the work-loop. As part of the tracing loop, each task-thread generates a bit-mask with a bit corresponding to each of the sibling task-threads that now have new work available for them. The task-thread does this by setting a bit in a local bit-mask each time it pushes work on to a stripe in the published-pool. Once the task-thread exits its tracing loop, it atomically updates the status word with a new value. The new value of the status word has a decremented active thread count and a bit-mask that is obtained by or'ing the current bit-mask of the status word with the bit-mask generated by the task-thread. This ensures that task-threads will continue to drain newly generated work in their stripes even if the active thread count momentarily falls to zero. Note that while task-threads can set bits in the bit-mask for other task-threads, these bits can only be cleared by its owner task-thread.

Marking concludes when every task-thread has drained its current marking stack, doesn't find any work in its stripe in any of the published-pools and generates no new work. The pseudo code for the proposed algorithm is outlined in Fig 8

4.3 Discussion

We now discuss some of our design choices. Having presented our algorithm, this is also a good opportunity for us to discuss how our approach relates to a couple other algorithms that share certain properties with ours.

```
shared published_pool[M][N]     // M task-threads and N stripes
shared status_word
//work for other task-threads is pushed onto these
private marking_stack[N-1]
private current_marking_stack
me = myThreadId
my_stripe = me %
// walk through published_pools for all threads
// and attempt to acquire from my stripe
acquire_from_published_pool(current_marking_stack) {
    for (task_thread_id=0;task_thread_id < M; task_thread_id++) {
        for (stripe=0; stripe < N; stripe++) {
            if (stripe == my_stripe) {
                current_marking_stack=get(published_pool[task_thread_id][stripe])
            }
        }
    }
}
drain_marking_stack() {
    while (!current_marking_stack.is_empty()) {
        ref = pop(marking_stack[me])
        bitmask |= mark_through(ref)
    }
}
mark_through(ref) {
    child_pointer_list = ref.child_pointer_list();
    for p in child_pointer_list {
        child = p.load();
        if (child != NULL) {
            if (my_stripe == stripe_for_reference(child)) {
                if (child.test_and_mark())
                bitmask |= mcurrent_marking_stack.push(child)
            } else {
                bitmask |= marking_stack[child.stripe()].push(child)
            }
        }
    }
    return bitmask
}
stripe_for_reference(child)) {
    return (mark_word(child) % BytesPerCacheLine) % N
}
push(ref) {
    add(ref);
    if (self.is_full()) {
        bitmask = add_to_published_pool(self, stripe_for_reference(ref));
    }
}
add_to_published_pool(stack, stripe) {
    published_pool[me][stripe].add(stack)
    return (bitmask = (1 << stripe))
}
mark_task() {
    while (status_word>0) {
        inc_working_count_clear_bit(me);
        bitmask = drain_marking_stack();
        dec_working_count_set_bit_mask(bitmask);
    }
}
```

Figure 8. Work Sharing at Cache-Line Boundaries

Stack sizes: The size of the marking stacks plays an important role in the performance of the algorithm. Large work-sharing marking stacks can result in a task-thread generating work that remains unavailable to other threads, since this work is mainly published when these stacks get full. Work-sharing marking stacks with very few entries, can result in frequent pushes to the published pool, thereby causing contention. Also, a task-thread's current marking stack should be large enough for it to continue working without frequent overflows. We find that asymmetrical stack sizes with a large current marking stack and small work-sharing marking stacks perform best. This allows a task-thread to continue on its share of the work while frequently publishing work for other task-threads.

Number of work-stripes: Our primary goal is to reduce contention during updates to the mark-bitmap. A 1:1 mapping between the task-threads and the number of stripes performs best in this regard. A 1:1 mapping implies that each task-thread have $M - 1$ work-sharing marking stacks. In most architectures, this results in a situation where the marking stacks of an individual task-thread quickly occupy the L1 cache. Performance degrades in this case, since we have just traded contention misses for capacity misses. In practice we find that a 1:1 mapping is not necessary and a 1:4 mapping effectively filters out bulk of the contention.

Edge enqueuing: This is a property of a marker where all non-null object references are pushed onto a marking stack without a test-and-mark operation. Our algorithm shares this property with the algorithm proposed by Garner et al. [20]. However, while their primary motivation is to improve the single-threaded performance by increasing the effectiveness of prefetching, our goal is to increase scalability in a parallel framework by reducing contention. Garner et al. [20], show that edge-enqueuing benefits the most in a single-threaded environment when the mark-bit is located in the object header. Since our main premise is the use of a side mark-bitmap, we claim that our performance benefits are not purely because of edge-enqueuing but rather due to reduced contention during atomic updates to mark-bitmaps. As observed by Garner et al. [20], edge-enqueuing has the side-effect of pushing an increased number of object references onto the marking stacks. We concur with their observation that these extra, thread-local pushes/pops don't seem to affect performance negatively.

Single-writer, single-reader channels: The work-sharing algorithm proposed by Wu et al. [30] shares some similarities with our algorithm. In their scheme, each task-thread is required to have an array of $M - 1$ work-sharing queues, where M is the total number of task-threads. There is always a 1:1 mapping between the number of per-thread work-sharing queues and the number of threads, which allows them to avoid atomic operations during load-balancing. They avoid capacity misses by picking very small queues; they get their best performance with queue sizes of 1 or 2. Our algorithm is not restricted to a 1:1 mapping between task-threads and the number of per-thread work-sharing stacks and hence can support larger individual work-sharing stacks. Wu et al. [30] also indicate that the scalability of their algorithm suffers when they use atomic operations to update the mark-bit, which in their implementation, is located in the object header. Having the mark-bit in a side mark-bitmap would only make the situation worse. This gives further credence to our hypothesis that atomic updates to the mark-bitmap are a fundamental source of bottlenecks in parallel marking algorithms.

5. Results

We now evaluate the effectiveness of our work-sharing scheme using the same metrics as before. Our work-sharing algorithm relies on striping the work N ways with M/N threads mapping to each stripe, where M is the total number of task-threads. Each task-thread also starts off with $N - 1$ "work-sharing" marking stacks. As stated earlier, this mapping ratio effects the performance of our algorithm in a couple different ways. A smaller mapping ratio implies less contention between the task-threads during the mark-bitmap updates. However, it also implies a larger number of per-thread work-sharing marking stacks, which can result both in memory overhead as well as capacity misses. We vary this critical ratio to measure its effect on the performance of the proposed algorithm. We tweak the sizes of the marking stacks and the plots reflect the best sizes for the set of benchmarks. The marking stacks in our baseline algorithm have 2K entries each, we size our stacks to keep the memory overhead low. In our runs, a current marking stack with 1K entries and work-sharing stacks with 128 entries each gives us our best performance numbers. As seen in the performance numbers of our baseline algorithm, the heap-sizes don't have an effect on our metrics. We find this to be true for our proposed algorithm as well; the plots reflect numbers with a heap size of 1GB.

The proposed algorithm requires that the minimum number of task-threads be equal to that of the number of work-sharing stripes. This is because, threads drain work only from their assigned stripes, hence a lesser number of task-threads than the number of stripes would result in stripes that wouldn't be drained. Our plots reflect this property of the algorithm. In each of our plots, we also add the corresponding measurement for the baseline algorithm. All the metrics are normalized by the corresponding metric for the single-threaded stop-the-world mode.

Fig 9 plots the mark-cycles-per-reference relative to the number of task-threads for different number of work-sharing stripes. The metric creeps up as the number of task-threads increase but stays well below the baseline measurement. As would be expected, we see a reduction in the mark-cycles-per-reference as the M/N ratio decreases with an increasing number of work-sharing stripes. Fig 10 plots the speedup in wall-clock mark times for the proposed

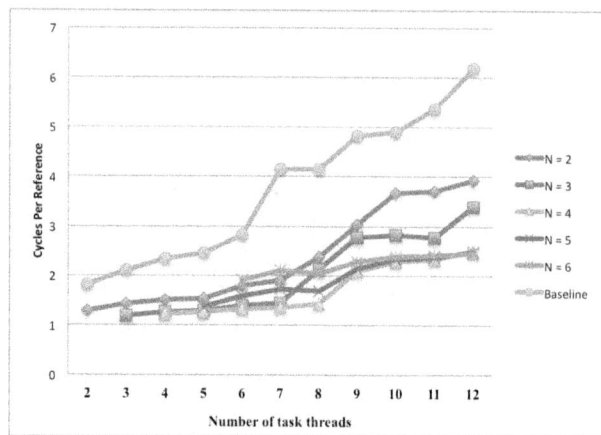

Figure 9. Cycles to mark a reference relative to number of task-threads scales much better compared to the baseline algorithm

algorithm. The baseline algorithm starts to flatten out and has a drop in performance beyond 7/8 task-threads; the proposed algorithm continues to scale albeit gradually. The proposed algorithm sees a 15-20% increase in speedup when the task-thread count goes over 4. For smaller counts of task-threads, the performance is very close to the baseline algorithm. This is because, with smaller counts of task-threads, the baseline algorithm suffers from less contention as expected, while the proposed algorithm continues to pay the additional work-sharing costs, i.e., that of enqueuing work into the work-sharing marking stacks and publishing these stacks. Note also that a cache line in the mark-bitmap is a good granularity for work-sharing.

Fig 11 demonstrates the effectiveness of our striping mechanism in reducing the number of task-threads that update a single cache line in the mark-bitmap. This metric stays well below the total number of task-threads per work-sharing stripe. This implies that our scheme is an effective means of reducing contention even without a 1:1 mapping between the task-threads and the work-sharing stripes.

6. System Topology Aware Work Distribution

Modern SMP systems generally have multiple, multi-core processors. The processor topology defines the number of physical packages, the number of cores in each package and the number of hyperthreads per core. Processor cores that are part of the same physical package are referred to as sibling cores. Hardware execution threads on a hyper-threaded core are referred to as sibling threads. The cache topology defines the number of caches per core, the type

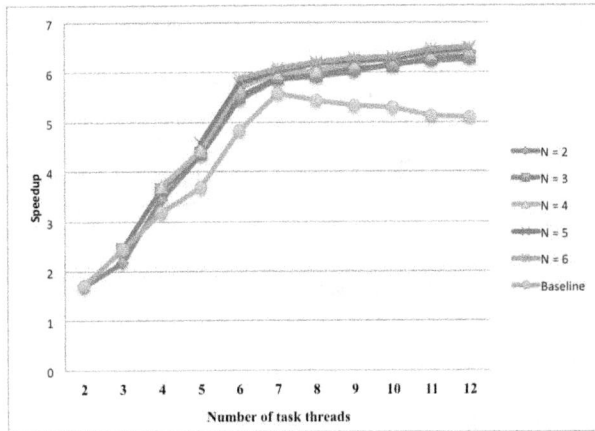

Figure 10. Speedup in parallel, marking time continues to scale with the number of task-threads

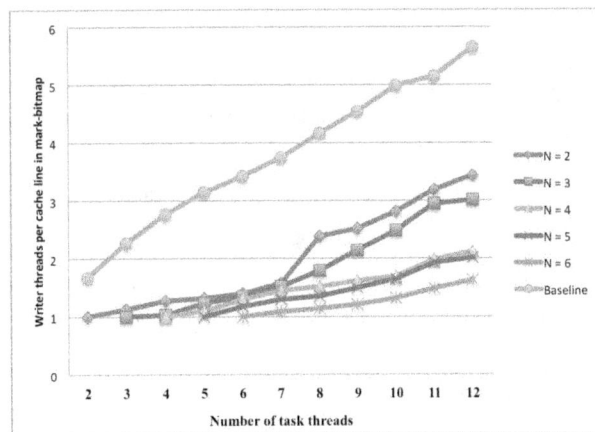

Figure 11. Number of task-threads writing to a cache line in the mark-bitmap relative to number of task-threads

of cache, e.g., instruction cache/data cache, the cache levels and the cache sharing among the sibling cores/threads. On Linux systems, this information can be obtained from the "sys" pseudo-filesystem (sysfs). As previously noted our Westmere-EP system has 2 sockets with 6 hyper-threaded cores per socket. Each of the 6 cores in the same socket have individual L1/L2 caches, but they do share the L3. The hyper-threads on each core share both the L1 and the L2 cache. The L2 is non-inclusive while the L3 is an inclusive cache. This is a fairly common cache topology on current systems.

Most modern multiprocessor systems, such as our Westmere-EP platform, are cc-NUMA, shared-memory platforms. On cc-NUMA machines, each node is assigned some amount of local memory. The cost of accessing remote memory is significantly higher than the cost of accessing local memory. On Linux systems, the "sys" pseudo file system also publishes the NUMA information for the system, i.e., the amount of memory per node, the memory layout, and the cost of memory accesses at each node[3]. We consider the processor and the cache topology along with the per-node NUMA information to be the "system topology". The system topology, along with the cost of accessing the different levels of caches and

the memory at different nodes, paints a full picture of its effect on the performance of a multi-threaded application.

Prior work on NUMA-aware garbage collection algorithms has primarily been in the domain of copying collectors, with the focus being on increasing mutator performance by copying objects to nodes that are most likely to access them [24, 29]. Our scheme is the first of its kind to make use of the system topology information to increase marking performance.

Concurrent and on-the-fly collectors [6, 15, 28], have to deal with mutators accessing references to potentially "white" objects and propagating these references into "black" objects while marking is still in progress. These algorithms generally have mutators collect these references in thread-local buffers using barrier mechanisms. These buffers are handed over to the marker to be marked-through via synchronization mechanisms such as checkpoints [6, 28] or at stop-the-world safepoints. A "trap-on-access" mechanism, along with general locality principles, would imply that there is a high likelihood of these objects continuing to be in the cache of the processor/core that executed the mutator trap code. A collector task-thread that is scheduled on a sibling core/thread of the core that executed the mutator trap code could then potentially benefit, if it were assigned the work of marking through these objects. This is similar to techniques that use hyper-threads as helper threads for prefetching purposes [16]

In our implementation of the baseline C4 algorithm, each mutator thread gets a thread-local marking stack. During the concurrent mark phase, mutators that trigger the "lvb" style read-barrier [28] on access to a potential "gray" reference, record it in their thread-local marking stack. These mutator marking stacks are pushed onto a global pool of mutator marking stacks at a checkpoint [28]. The collector's task-threads acquire these marking stacks from the mutator-marking-stack-pool and mark-through the references in these stacks.

In our topology-aware work-distribution scheme, we maintain the mutator-marking-stack-pool as an array of head pointers to linked-lists of mutator marking stacks. The "processor-id" serves as the index into this array. A mutator attempting to add its marking stack to this pool, looks up its current processor-id using the CPUID [1] instruction and uses that as the stripe-index. It is possible that the mutator queued most of the work in its marking stack while running on a different core. However, we find this to be rare, since the scheduler generally tends to schedule threads on the same core as before.

When a collector task-thread looks for work in the mutator-marking-stack-pool, it looks up its processor-id and prioritizes indexes in the pool that map to its sibling-threads and sibling-cores. We therefore refer to this scheme as "processor-affinity" based work-distribution. This is only an optimization, and all stripes in the mutator-marking-stack-pool are eventually drained. However, this does serve as a very effective filter. The processor topology map is read once at the beginning using the "sys" pseudo file system.

6.1 Evaluation

While working through the references in a mutator marking stack, the collector's task-threads would likely benefit from processor-affinity based policy by finding the objects being marked-through in the processor cache. In order to evaluate this algorithm, we turn off prefetching. We also turn off the mark-bitmap address based striping. We use the previously discussed evaluation method for batch marking to measure the average number of processor cycles to mark-through an object . We now include the 'enumeration'

---

[3] The processor and cache topology information can be obtained from: /sys/devices/system/cpu/cpu*/cache

The NUMA information can be obtained from: /sys/devices/system/node

of child pointers as part of the batch. We only collect our metrics when the task-threads work on the mutator marking stacks in the concurrent mark mode. We use the Volano 2.9.0 [4] benchmark, a highly multi-thread benchmark that measures the performance of the Volano chat server to evaluate this algorithm. A highly multi-threaded benchmark like Volano is more likely to have larger number of mutator threads that generate marking work and is likely an ideal benchmark for our proposed algorithm.

Fig 12 plots the relative speedup in the processor cycles for marking-through a reference, normalized by the single-threaded measurement in the concurrent mark mode. As expected, for smaller counts of task-threads we don't see much benefits since task-threads would be expected to drain work from all the "processor" stripes. We see the biggest jump in speedup when we go to 7 task-threads, which is likely because of NUMA effects on our 6 processor per socket Westmere-EP machine. We see a performance benefit of about 11% for the maximum alloted threads per generation. We restrict ourselves to a maximum of 12 task-threads per generation on our 24 core machine to account for the inter-generation concurrency of the C4 [28] collector that can result in both generations being garbage collected at the same time. We use the default scheduler mechanism and don't use any scheduler affinity calls to divide the task-threads among the 2 sockets.

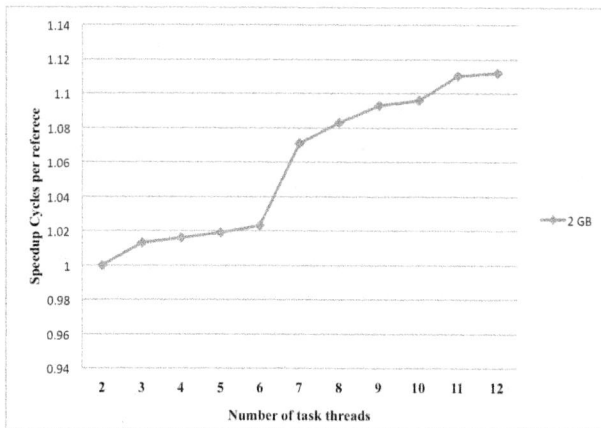

Figure 12. Cycles per reference marked-through relative to number of task-threads

7. Conclusion

We have studied the performance and scalability of a concurrent, parallel marking algorithm that uses a mark-bitmap to maintain object liveness information. Our evaluation methodology allows us to tease out the 'test-and-mark' operation and measure its performance and scalability. We also shed light on the contention between the collector's task-threads while atomically updating the mark-bitmap. We use these to make the case that in a modern SMP system a purely processor-centric work-sharing algorithm has inherent scalability limitations. We then describe our new non-blocking and lock-free work-sharing algorithm that distributes work based on the addresses in the mark-bitmap. It is a first of its kind, "hybrid" work-sharing algorithm that uses the memory address of a word in the mark-bitmap, to both reduce contention among the task-threads as well as keep them busy. We observe a ~20% improvement in parallel marking times with this scheme. We finally describe our processor and cache topology aware work-distribution algorithm for mutator generated marking work applicable to parallel, concurrent/on-the-fly markers. We believe that the topology aware algorithms should be a focus of the research community,

considering the fact that cc-NUMA architectures are quite common place in modern servers.

References

[1] Intel 64 and IA-32 architectures developer's manual: Combined volumes, . URL http://www.intel.com/content/dam/www/public/us/en/documents/manuals/64-ia-32-architectures-software-developer-manual-325462.pdf.

[2] Intel 64 architecture processor topology enumeration, . URL http://software.intel.com/en-us/articles/intel-64-architecture-processor-topology-enumeration/.

[3] Standard performance evaluation corporation. spec jvm98. URL http://www.spec.org/jvm98/.

[4] The volano benchmark. URL http://www.volano.com/benchmarks.html.

[5] N. S. Arora, R. D. Blumofe, and C. G. Plaxton. Thread scheduling for multiprogrammed multiprocessors. In SPAA, pages 119–129, 1998.

[6] H. Azatchi, Y. Levanoni, H. Paz, and E. Petrank. An on-the-fly mark and sweep garbage collector based on sliding views. pages 269–281. doi: 10.1145/949305.949329.

[7] K. Barabash, O. Ben-Yitzhak, I. Goft, E. K. Kolodner, V. Leikehman, Y. Ossia, A. Owshanko, and E. Petrank. A parallel, incremental, mostly concurrent garbage collector for servers. ACM Trans. Program. Lang. Syst., 27(6):1097–1146, 2005.

[8] S. M. Blackburn, R. Garner, C. Hoffman, A. M. Khan, K. S. McKinley, R. Bentzur, A. Diwan, D. Feinberg, D. Frampton, S. Z. Guyer, M. Hirzel, A. Hosking, M. Jump, H. Lee, J. E. B. Moss, A. Phansalkar, D. Stefanović, T. VanDrunen, D. von Dincklage, and B. Wiedermann. The DaCapo benchmarks: Java benchmarking development and analysis. In OOPSLA '06: Proceedings of the 21st annual ACM SIGPLAN conference on Object-Oriented Programing, Systems, Languages, and Applications, pages 169–190, New York, NY, USA, Oct. 2006. ACM Press. doi: http://doi.acm.org/10.1145/1167473.1167488.

[9] H.-J. Boehm. Reducing garbage collector cache misses. pages 59–64.

[10] C.-Y. Cher, A. L. Hosking, and T. Vijaykumar. Software prefetching for mark-sweep garbage collection: Hardware analysis and software redesign. pages 199–210. doi: 10.1145/1024393.1024417.

[11] C. Click, G. Tene, and M. Wolf. The pauseless gc algorithm. In Proceedings of the 1st ACM/USENIX international conference on Virtual execution environments, VEE '05, pages 46–56, New York, NY, USA, 2005. ACM. ISBN 1-59593-047-7. URL http://doi.acm.org/10.1145/1064979.1064988.

[12] D. Detlefs and T. Printezis. A Generational Mostly-concurrent Garbage Collector. Technical report, Mountain View, CA, USA, 2000.

[13] D. Detlefs, C. H. Flood, S. Heller, and T. Printezis. Garbage-first garbage collection. In ISMM, pages 37–48, 2004.

[14] E. W. Dijkstra, L. Lamport, A. J. Martin, C. S. Scholten, and E. F. M. Steffens. On-the-fly garbage collection: An exercise in cooperation. In Language Hierarchies and Interfaces: International Summer School, volume 46, pages 43–56. Marktoberdorf, Germany, 1976.

[15] T. Domani, E. K. Kolodner, and E. Petrank. A generational on-the-fly garbage collector for java. In PLDI, pages 274–284, 2000.

[16] U. Drepper. What every programmer should know about memory. URL http://www.akkadia.org/drepper/cpumemory.pdf.

[17] T. Endo and K. Taura. Reducing pause time of conservative collectors. In MSP/ISMM, pages 119–131, 2002.

[18] T. Endo, K. Taura, and A. Yonezawa. Predicting scalability of parallel garbage collectors on shared memory multiprocessors. In Proceedings of the 15th International Parallel & Distributed Processing Symposium, IPDPS '01, pages 43–, Washington, DC, USA, 2001. IEEE Computer Society. ISBN 0-7695-0990-8. URL http://dl.acm.org/citation.cfm?id=645609.662496.

[19] C. H. Flood, D. Detlefs, N. Shavit, and X. Zhang. Parallel garbage collection for shared memory multiprocessors. In Proceedings of the

2001 Symposium on JavaTM Virtual Machine Research and Technology Symposium - Volume 1, JVM'01, pages 21–21, Berkeley, CA, USA, 2001. USENIX Association. URL `http://dl.acm.org/citation.cfm?id=1267847.1267868`.

[20] R. Garner, S. M. Blackburn, and D. Frampton. Effective prefetch for mark-sweep garbage collection. In *ISMM*, pages 43–54, 2007.

[21] R. H. Halstead. Multilisp: A language for concurrent symbolic computation. *ACM Trans. Prog. Lang. Syst.*, 7(4):501–538, Oct. 1985. doi: 10.1145/4472.4478.

[22] R. Jones and C. Ryder. A study of Java object demographics. pages 121–130. doi: 10.1145/1375634.1375652.

[23] R. Jones, A. Hosking, and E. Moss. *The Garbage Collection Handbook: The Art of Automatic Memory Management*. CRC Applied Algorithms and Data Structures. Chapman & Hall, Aug. 2011. ISBN 978-1420082791.

[24] T. Ogasawara. Numa-aware memory manager with dominant-thread-based copying gc. In *Proceedings of the 24th ACM SIGPLAN conference on Object oriented programming systems languages and applications*, OOPSLA '09, pages 377–390, New York, NY, USA, 2009. ACM. ISBN 978-1-60558-766-0. URL `http://doi.acm.org/10.1145/1640089.1640117`.

[25] Y. Ossia, O. Ben-Yitzhak, I. Goft, E. K. Kolodner, V. Leikehman, and A. Owshanko. A parallel, incremental and concurrent GC for servers. pages 129–140. doi: 10.1145/512529.512546.

[26] F. Siebert. Limits of parallel marking garbage collection. In *Proceedings of the 7th international symposium on Memory management*, ISMM '08, pages 21–29, New York, NY, USA, 2008. ACM. ISBN 978-1-60558-134-7. doi: http://doi.acm.org/10.1145/1375634.1375638. URL `http://doi.acm.org/10.1145/1375634.1375638`.

[27] F. Siebert. Concurrent, parallel, real-time garbage-collection. In *Proceedings of the 2010 international symposium on Memory management*, ISMM '10, pages 11–20, New York, NY, USA, 2010. ACM. ISBN 978-1-4503-0054-4. doi: http://doi.acm.org/10.1145/1806651.1806654. URL `http://doi.acm.org/10.1145/1806651.1806654`.

[28] G. Tene, B. Iyengar, and M. Wolf. C4: the continuously concurrent compacting collector. In *Proceedings of the international symposium on Memory management*, ISMM '11, pages 79–88, New York, NY, USA, 2011. ACM. ISBN 978-1-4503-0263-0. URL `http://doi.acm.org/10.1145/1993478.1993491`.

[29] M. M. Tikir and J. K. Hollingsworth. Numa-aware java heaps for server applications. IPDPS '05, pages 108.2–. IEEE Computer Society. ISBN 0-7695-2312-9. URL `http://dx.doi.org/10.1109/IPDPS.2005.299`.

[30] M. Wu and X.-F. Li. Task-pushing: a scalable parallel gc marking algorithm without synchronization operations. In *IPDPS*, pages 1–10, 2007.

Down for the Count?
Getting Reference Counting Back in the Ring *

Rifat Shahriyar

Australian National University

Rifat.Shahriyar@anu.edu.au

Stephen M. Blackburn

Australian National University

Steve.Blackburn@anu.edu.au

Daniel Frampton

Australian National University

Daniel.Frampton@anu.edu.au

Abstract

Reference counting and tracing are the two fundamental approaches that have underpinned garbage collection since 1960. However, despite some compelling advantages, reference counting is almost completely ignored in implementations of high performance systems today. In this paper we take a detailed look at reference counting to understand its behavior and to improve its performance. We identify key design choices for reference counting and analyze how the behavior of a wide range of benchmarks might affect design decisions. As far as we are aware, this is the first such quantitative study of reference counting. We use insights gleaned from this analysis to introduce a number of optimizations that significantly improve the performance of reference counting.

We find that an existing modern implementation of reference counting has an average 30% overhead compared to tracing, and that in combination, our optimizations are able to completely eliminate that overhead. This brings the performance of reference counting on par with that of a well tuned mark-sweep collector. We keep our in-depth analysis of reference counting as general as possible so that it may be useful to other garbage collector implementers. Our finding that reference counting can be made directly competitive with well tuned mark-sweep should shake the community's prejudices about reference counting and perhaps open new opportunities for exploiting reference counting's strengths, such as localization and immediacy of reclamation.

Categories and Subject Descriptors D.3.4 [*Programming Languages*]: Processors—Memory management (garbage collection)

General Terms Design, Performance, Algorithms, Measurement

Keywords Reference Counting, Memory Management, Garbage Collection, Java

1. Introduction

In an interesting twist of fate, the two fundamental branches of the garbage collection family tree were born within months of each other in 1960, both in the Communications of the ACM [10, 20]. On the one hand, reference counting [10] *directly* identifies garbage by noticing when an object has no references to it, while on the other hand, tracing [20] identifies live objects and thus only *indirectly*

---

* This work supported by the Australian Research Council DP0666059.

identifies garbage (those objects that are not live). Reference counting offers a number of distinct advantages over tracing, namely that it: a) can reclaim objects as soon as they are no longer referenced, b) is inherently incremental, and c) uses object-local information rather than global computation. Nonetheless, for a variety of reasons, reference counting is rarely used in high performance settings and remains somewhat neglected within the garbage collection literature. The goal of this work is to revisit reference counting, understand its shortcomings, and address some of its limitations. We are not aware of any high performance system that relies on reference counting. However, reference counting is popular among new languages with relatively simple implementations. The latter is due to the ease with which naive reference counting can be implemented, while the former is due to reference counting's limitations. We hope to give new life to this much neglected branch of the garbage collection literature.

Reference counting works by keeping a count of incoming references to each object and collecting objects when their count falls to zero. Therefore in principle all that is required is a write barrier that notices each pointer change, decrementing the target object's count when a pointer to it is overwritten and incrementing the target object's count whenever a pointer to it is created. This algorithm is simple, inherently incremental, and requires no global computation. The simplicity of this naive implementation is particularly attractive and thus widely used, including in well-established systems such as PHP, Perl and Python. By contrast, tracing collectors must start with a set of *roots*, which requires the runtime to enumerate all pointers into the heap from global variables, the stacks, and registers. Root enumeration thus requires deep integration with the runtime and can be challenging to engineer [14].

Reference counting has two clear limitations. It is unable to collect cycles of garbage because a cycle of references will self-sustain non-zero reference counts. We do not address this limitation, which can be overcome with a backup demand-driven tracing mechanism. However, reference counting is also slow. Naive reference counting is extremely costly because of the overhead of intercepting every pointer mutation, including those to the registers and stacks. High performance reference counting overlooks changes to the stacks and registers [12] and may even elide many changes to heap references [16]. However, even high performance reference counting is slow. We compare high performance reference counting and mark-sweep implementations and find that reference counting is over 30% slower than its tracing counterpart.

We reconsider reference counting. We start by identifying key design parameters and evaluating the intrinsic behaviors of Java workloads with respect to those design points. For example, we study the distribution of maximum reference counts across Java benchmarks. Our analysis of benchmark intrinsics motivates three optimizations: 1) using just a few bits to maintain the reference count, 2) eliding reference count operations for newly allocated objects, and 3) allocating new objects as dead, avoiding a significant overhead in deallocating them. We then conduct an in-depth performance analysis of mark-sweep and reference counting, including combinations of each of these optimizations. We find that together these optimizations eliminate the reference counting overhead, leading to performance consistent with high performance mark-sweep.

This paper makes the following contributions: 1) we identify and evaluate key design choices for reference counting implementations, 2) we conduct an in-depth quantitative study of intrinsic benchmark behaviors with respect to reference counting, 3) guided by our analysis, we introduce optimizations that greatly improve reference counting performance, and 4) we conduct a detailed performance study of reference counting and mark-sweep, showing that our optimizations eliminate the overhead of reference counting.

We hope that the insights and optimizations brought to light in this paper may give new life to reference counting. Our detailed study of intrinsic behaviors will help other garbage collector implementers design more efficient reference counting algorithms. Our optimizations remove the performance barrier to using reference counting rather than mark-sweep, thereby making the incrementality, locality, and immediacy of reference counting compelling.

2. Background and Design Space

We now explore the design space for reference counting implementations. In particular, we explore strategies for: 1) storing the reference count, 2) maintaining an accurate count, and 3) dealing with cyclic data structures. We describe each of these and survey major design alternatives.

2.1 Storing the Count

Each object has a reference count associated with it. This section considers the choices for storing the count. This design choice is a trade-off between the space required to store the count, and the complexity of accurately managing counts when limited bits are available.

Use a dedicated word per object. By using a dedicated word we can guarantee that the reference count will never overflow. In a 32-bit address space, in the worst case, if every word of memory pointed to a single object, the count would only be 2^{30}. However, an additional header word has a significant cost, not only in terms of space, but also time, as allocation rate is also affected. For example, the addition of an extra 32-bit word to the object header incurs an overhead of 2.5% in total time and 6.2% in GC time, on average across our benchmark suite when using Jikes RVM's production garbage collector.

Use a field in each object's header. Object headers store information to support runtime operations such as virtual dispatching, dynamic type checking, synchronization, and object hashing. Although header bits are valuable, it may be possible to use a small number of bits to store the reference count. The use of a small number of bits means that the reference counter must handle *overflow*, where a count reaches a value too large for small number of bits. Two basic strategies to deal with overflow exist: 1) have an auxiliary data structure such as a hash table to store accurate counts, 2) have *sticky* counts (once they overflow future increments and decrements are ignored). In the latter case, one may depend on a backup tracing cycle collector to either restore count or directly collect the object [15].

2.2 Maintaining the Count

Simple, *immediate* reference counters count *all* references, both on the heap and in local variables. Whenever references are created,

copied, destroyed, or overwritten, increment and decrement operations are performed on the referents. Because such references are very frequently mutated, immediate reference counting has a high overhead. However, immediate reference counting needs very minimal runtime support, so is a popular implementation choice when performance is not the highest priority. The algorithm requires just barriers on every pointer mutation, and the capacity to identify all pointers within an object when the object dies. The former is easy to implement, for example through the use of *smart pointers* in C++, while the latter can be implemented through a destructor. In contrast, tracing collectors must be able to identify all pointers held in the runtime state, such as those in stacks, registers, and global variables. To identify all pointers from the stack into the heap, the runtime must implement *GC maps*, which are generally difficult to implement and maintain correctly.

Deferred Deutsch and Bobrow [12] introduced deferred reference counting. In contrast to the immediate reference counting described above, deferred reference counting ignores mutations to frequently modified variables such as those stored in registers and on the stack. Periodically, these references are enumerated into a root set, and any objects that are neither in the root set nor referenced by other objects in the heap may be collected. They achieve this directly by maintaining a zero count table that holds all objects known to have a reference count of zero. This zero count table is enumerated, and any object that does not have a corresponding entry in the root set is identified as garbage. Bacon et al. [3] avoid the need to maintain a zero count table by buffering decrements between collections. At collection time, elements in the root set are given a temporary increment while processing all of the buffered decrements. Deferred reference counting performs all increments and decrements during collection time. Although much faster than immediate reference counting, these schemes require *GC maps*, removing the implementation advantage over tracing.

Coalescing Heap references are mutated very frequently: even with stack mutations deferred, we measured millions of reference mutations per second. Levanoni and Petrank [16, 17] observed that all but the first and last in any chain of mutations to a given reference within a given window could be *coalesced*. Only the *initial* and *final* states of the reference are necessary to calculate correct reference counts: intervening mutations generate increments and decrements that cancel each other out. This observation can be exploited by remembering only the initial value of a reference field between periodic reference counting collections. At each of these collections, only the objects referred to by the initial (stored) and current values of the reference field need to be updated. Levanoni and Petrank implemented coalescing using *object remembering*. The first time an object has a reference modified since the last collection: a) the mutated object is marked dirty and all outgoing reference values are remembered; b) all future reference mutations for that (now dirty) object are ignored; c) during the next collection the remembered object is scanned, increments are performed on all outgoing pointers, decrements are performed on all remembered outgoing references, and the dirty flag is cleared. New objects are remembered and allocated dirty, ensuring that outgoing references are incremented at the next collection. No old values are recorded for new objects because all outgoing references start as *null*.

Generational Blackburn and McKinley [4] introduced *ulterior reference counting*, a hybrid collector that combines copying generational collection for the young objects and reference counting for the old objects. It restricts copying and reference counting to the object demographics for which they perform well and safely ignores mutations to select heap objects. It can achieve high performance with reduced pause time. Ulterior reference counting is not difficult to implement, but the implementation is a hybrid, and thus manifests the complexities of both a standard copying nursery and a reference counted heap.

Age-Oriented   Paz et al. [21] introduced *age oriented* collection, which aimed to exploit the generational hypothesis that most objects die young. Their age-oriented collector uses a reference counting collection for the old generation and a tracing collection for the young generation that establishes reference counts during tracing. This provides a significant benefit as it avoids performing expensive reference counting operations for the many young objects that die. Like ulterior reference counting, this collector is a hybrid, so manifests the complexities of two orthodox collectors.

2.3   Collecting Cyclic Objects

As discussed above, reference counting alone cannot collect all garbage. Objects can form a cycle, where a group of objects point to each other, maintaining non-zero reference counts. There exist two general approaches to deal with cyclic garbage: *backup tracing* [22] and *trial deletion* [2, 9, 18, 19]. Frampton [13] conducted a detailed study of cycle collection.

Backup Tracing   Backup tracing performs a mark-sweep style trace of the entire heap to eliminate cyclic garbage. The only key difference to a classical mark sweep is that during the sweep phase, decrements must be performed from objects found to be garbage for their descendants into the live part of the heap. To support backup tracing each object needs to be able to store a mark state during tracing. Backup tracing can also be used to restore *stuck* reference counts as described in Section 2.1.

Trial Deletion   Trial deletion collects cycles by identifying groups of self-sustaining objects using a partial trace of the heap in three phases. In the first phase, the sub-graph rooted from a selected candidate object is traversed, with reference counts for all outgoing pointers (temporarily) decremented. Once this process is complete, reference counts reflect only external references into the sub-graph. If any object's reference count is zero then that object is only reachable from within the sub-graph. In the second phase, the sub-graph is traversed again, and outgoing references are incremented from each object whose reference count did not drop to zero. Finally, the third phase traverses the sub-graph again, sweeping all objects that still have a reference count of zero. The original implementation was due to Christopher [9] and has been optimized over time [2, 18, 19].

Cycle collection is not the focus of this paper, however some form of cycle collection is essential for completeness. We use backup tracing, which performs substantially better than trial deletion and has more predictable performance characteristics [13]. Backup tracing also provides a solution to the problem of reference counts that become stuck due to limited bits.

3.   Analysis of Reference Counting Intrinsics

Recall that despite the implementation advantages of simple immediate reference counting, reference counting is rarely used because it is comprehensively outperformed by tracing collectors. To help understand the sources of overhead and identify opportunities for improvement, we now study the behavior of standard benchmarks with respect to operations that are *intrinsic* to reference counting. In particular, we focus on metrics that are neither user-controllable nor implementation-specific.

3.1   Methodology

We instrument Jikes RVM to identify, record, and report statistics for every object allocated. We control the effect of cycle collection by performing measurements with cycle collection policies at both

extremes (*always* collect cycles vs. *never* collect cycles) and report when this affects the analysis.

Jikes RVM   We use Jikes RVM and MMTk for all experiments. Jikes RVM [1] is a high performance research JVM with a well-tuned garbage collection infrastructure MMTk [7]. Jikes RVM is open source written almost entirely in a slightly extended Java. Jikes RVM does not have a bytecode interpreter. Instead, a fast template-driven baseline compiler produces machine code when the VM first encounters each Java method. To ensure performance and repeatability, all of our experiments were run using Jikes RVM's replay compilation feature. We use the most recent version, which executes one iteration of each benchmark using only the unoptimized baseline compiler, before using user-provided profile information to optimize hot methods all at once, prior to the second iteration. The second iteration of the benchmark then executes this optimized version of the code. This approach offers the performance of steady state in an adaptively optimized system, whilst avoiding the non-determinism of adaptive compilation.

MMTk   MMTk is Jikes RVM's memory management sub-system. It is a programmable memory management toolkit that implements a wide variety of collectors that reuse shared components [6]. To perform our analysis, we instrument the standard configuration of reference counting to gather information on different metrics while running the benchmarks. This instrumentation does not affect the garbage collection workload (the exact same set of objects is collected with or without the instrumentation). The instrumentation slows the collector down considerably, but since this part of our analysis is not concerned with collector performance, this slowdown is irrelevant. We do not use the instrumentation for our subsequent performance study. All of the collectors we evaluate are parallel, including the standard reference counting we use as our baseline. The optimizations we present here are correct with respect to parallel collection and the results we present here exploit parallel collection.

We use mark-sweep as our representative tracing collector and principal point of comparison because it utilizes the same heap organization and allocator as the reference counters. We compare our best reference counting system with the high performance Immix tracing collector [5], but this is not our main point of comparison because the principal advantage of the Immix collector is its unique heap organization which is orthogonal to our optimizations.

Benchmarks   We use 19 benchmarks from the DaCapo and SPEC benchmark suites in all the measurements and performance studies taken in this paper. SPEC provides both Java client and server side benchmarks. The DaCapo suite [8] is a suite of nontrivial real-world open source Java applications. We use the superset of all benchmarks from DaCapo 2006 and DaCapo 9.12 that can run successfully with Jikes RVM, using the more recent version of any given benchmark when the opportunity exists. We identified a nominal minimum heap size for each benchmark by finding the minimum heap size in which the benchmark could successfully complete using any of the three systems we evaluate (standard reference counting, our optimized reference counting, and mark-sweep). Unless otherwise stated we conduct all of our performance experiments while holding the heap size constant at $2\times$ the minimum heap size, which is a modest size.

Experimental Platform   The results we present here were measured on a modern Core i5 670 dual-core processor with two-way SMT, a clock rate of 3.4 GHz, 4 MB of last level cache, and 4 GB of RAM. We conducted our evaluation on a range of modern and older x86 processors and found that our analysis and optimizations are robust.

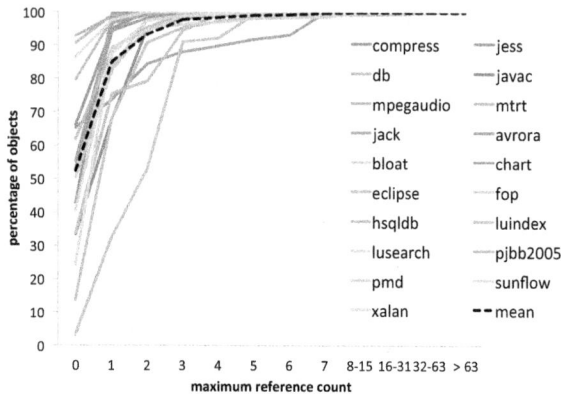

Figure 1. Most objects have very low maximum reference counts. This graph plots the cumulative frequency distribution of maximum reference counts among objects in each benchmark.

Figure 2. The number of objects which suffer overflowed reference counts drops off rapidly as the number of available bits grows from two to five.

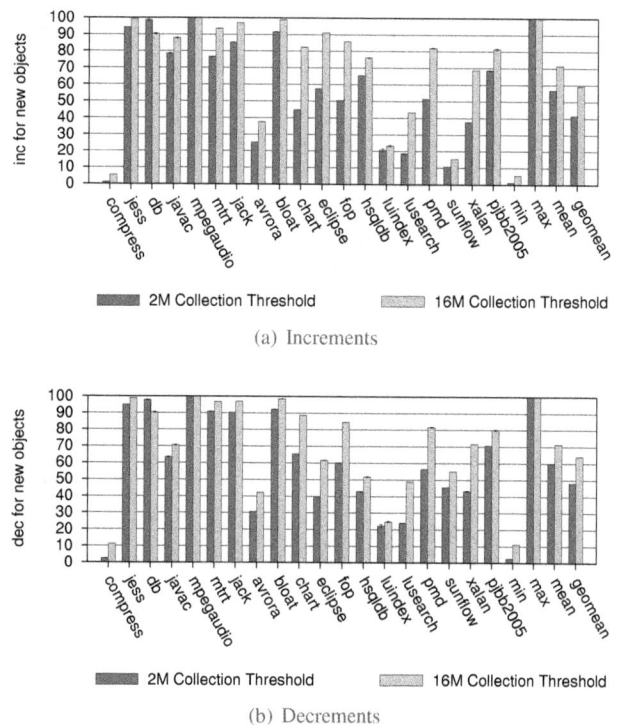

Note that the analysis of intrinsic properties we present in this Section *does not* depend on Jikes RVM or MMTk. The measurements we make here could have been made on any other JVM to which we had access to the source.

3.2 Distribution of Maximum Reference Counts

We start by measuring the distribution of *maximum reference counts*. For each object our instrumented JVM keeps track of its maximum reference count, and when the object dies we add the object's maximum reference count to a histogram. In Table 1 we show the cumulative maximum reference count distributions for each benchmark. For example, the table shows that for the benchmark eclipse, 68.2% of objects have a maximum reference count of just one, and 95.4% of all objects have a maximum reference count of three. On average, across all benchmarks, 99% of objects have a maximum reference count of six or less. The data in Table 1 is displayed pictorially in Figure 1.

3.3 Limited Reference Count Bits and Overflow

When the number of bits available for storing the reference count is restricted, the count may overflow. In Table 2 we show for different sized reference count fields, measurements of: a) the fraction of *objects* that would ever overflow, and b) the fraction of *reference counting operations* that act on overflowed objects. The first measure indicates how many objects at some time had their reference counts overflow. An overflowed reference count will either be stuck until a backup trace occurs, or will require an auxiliary data structure if counts are to be unaffected. The second measure shows how many operations occurred on objects that were already stuck, and is therefore indicative of how much overhead an auxiliary data structure may experience.

Results for reference count fields sized from one to five bits are shown in Table 2. For example, the table shows that when three bits are used, only 0.65% of objects experience overflow, and for compress and mpegaudio, none overflow. Although the percentage of overflowed objects is less than 1%, it is interesting to note that these overflowed objects attract nearly 23% of all increment and decrement operations, on average. Overflowed objects thus appear to be highly popular objects. The data in Table 2 is displayed pictorially in Figure 2.

3.4 Sources of Reference Counting Operations

Table 3 shows for each benchmark the origin of the increment and decrement operations. In each case we account for the operations

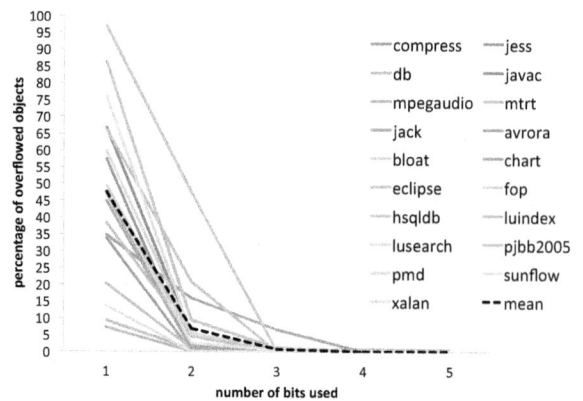

(a) Increments

(b) Decrements

Figure 3. New objects are responsible for the majority of reference counting operations. We show here the fraction of (a) increments and (b) decrements that are due to objects allocated within the most recent 2 MB and 16 MB of objects allocated.

as being due to: a) newly allocated objects (*new*), b) mutations to non-new *scalar* and *array* objects, and c) temporary operations due to root reachability when using deferred reference counting. For decrements, we also include a fifth category that represents decrements that occur during cycle collection. We performed this measurement with collections artificially triggered at a range of intervals from 2MB to 16MB, and report only 2MB and 16MB to show the significant differences. The definition of 'new' is anything allocated within the last interval, so as the interval becomes larger, a larger fraction the live objects are 'new'.

max count	mean	compress	jess	db	javac	mpegaudio	mtrt	jack	avrora	bloat	chart	eclipse	fop	hsqldb	luindex	lusearch	pjbb2005	pmd	sunflow	xalan
0	**52.4**	66.1	42.7	90.6	33.2	92.7	79.8	55.2	65.3	50.5	52.9	13.6	50.3	3.1	33.7	24.2	61.8	40.4	86.5	52.2
1	**85.1**	95.0	99.7	99.1	67.8	98.7	97.7	96.5	73.8	83.6	94.3	68.2	82.5	32.4	75.4	89.3	88.9	88.6	97.5	87.3
2	**93.2**	99.9	99.8	99.2	95.0	99.8	99.1	99.1	84.3	97.5	98.2	90.6	95.3	52.6	79.3	94.4	95.3	94.9	100	97.5
3	**97.7**	100	99.9	99.3	98.2	100	99.7	99.8	87.9	99.2	100	95.4	98.7	90.9	94.4	98.9	99.5	99.7	100	98.9
4	**98.5**	100	99.9	99.3	99.1	100	99.8	100	89.7	99.5	100	97.3	99.4	92.0	99.5	100	99.7	97.0	100	99.2
5	**99.2**	100	99.9	99.3	99.4	100	99.8	100	91.9	99.9	100	98.3	99.6	99.6	99.7	100	99.8	98.2	100	99.3
6	**99.3**	100	99.9	99.3	99.4	100	99.8	100	93.3	99.9	100	98.9	99.7	99.8	99.8	100	99.9	98.5	100	99.4
7	**99.7**	100	99.9	99.3	99.5	100	99.9	100	99.9	99.9	100	99.2	99.8	99.9	99.9	100	99.9	98.7	100	99.5
8-15	**99.9**	100	100	99.4	99.7	100	99.9	100	99.9	100	100	99.8	99.9	100	100	100	100	99.8	100	99.9
16-31	**99.9**	100	100	99.5	99.9	100	100	100	99.9	100	100	99.9	100	100	100	100	100	99.9	100	99.9
32-63	**100**	100	100	100	99.9	100	100	100	99.9	100	100	100	100	100	100	100	100	100	100	100
> 63	**100**	100	100	100	100	100	100	100	100	100	100	100	100	100	100	100	100	100	100	100

Table 1. Most objects have very low maximum reference counts. Here we show the cumulative frequency distribution of maximum reference counts among objects in each benchmark. For many benchmarks, 99% of objects have maximum counts of 2 or less.

bits used	mean	compress	jess	db	javac	mpegaudio	mtrt	jack	avrora	bloat	chart	eclipse	fop	hsqldb	luindex	lusearch	pjbb2005	pmd	sunflow	xalan
							percentage of overflowed objects													
1	47.65	33.93	57.31	9.37	66.77	7.29	20.23	44.76	34.74	49.54	47.08	86.36	49.68	96.89	66.31	75.83	38.23	59.62	13.54	47.83
2	6.75	0.08	0.16	0.80	4.96	0.16	0.95	0.95	15.74	2.54	1.83	9.38	4.73	47.38	20.75	5.57	4.67	5.15	0.01	2.47
3	0.65	0	0.08	0.68	0.59	0	0.16	0.01	6.69	0.10	0.02	1.15	0.31	0.21	0.16	0.01	0.14	1.53	0.01	0.59
4	0.11	0	0.06	0.68	0.28	0	0.08	0	0.06	0.05	0.01	0.24	0.10	0.01	0.01	0.01	0.02	0.26	0.01	0.17
5	0.06	0	0.03	0.49	0.12	0	0.03	0	0.06	0.03	0.01	0.07	0.05	0.01	0.01	0.01	0.01	0.14	0.01	0.06
							percentage of increments on overflowed objects													
1	100	100	100	100	100	100	100	100	100	100	100	100	100	100	100	100	100	100	100	100
2	41.2	8.2	77.5	96.9	19.9	2.5	35.2	3.6	28.6	71.7	17.2	25.5	20.0	39.7	63.8	16.3	68.4	61.8	84.7	41.9
3	22.7	0	76.8	83.6	12.2	0	29.9	0	17.1	51.3	14.1	10.9	8.9	5.0	0.9	8.0	35.3	14.5	35.0	27.3
4	17.8	0	75.6	55.1	9.7	0	25.8	0	14.8	36.2	13.1	7.0	7.0	4.9	0	7.4	18.9	10.1	34.3	18.2
5	13.4	0	73.6	16.7	7.5	0	22.2	0	11.1	20.5	11.2	5.0	5.5	4.8	0	6.5	14.2	8.6	33.0	14.5
							percentage of decrements on overflowed objects													
1	100	100	100	100	100	100	100	100	100	100	100	100	100	100	100	100	100	100	100	100
2	43.0	10.4	77.5	96.9	21.3	2.4	40.0	3.5	28.4	71.9	17.8	32.4	20.1	48.1	64.4	17.4	69.8	65.6	84.7	44.0
3	23.3	0	76.7	83.6	13.0	0	34.8	0	17.0	51.4	14.6	13.7	7.3	6.1	0.9	8.5	36.1	15.3	35.0	28.7
4	18.3	0	75.5	55.1	10.3	0	30.3	0	14.6	36.3	13.5	9.0	5.3	5.9	0	7.9	19.3	10.8	34.3	19.2
5	13.8	0	73.6	16.7	8.1	0	26.3	0	11.0	20.5	11.6	6.6	4.0	5.8	0	6.9	14.4	9.1	33.0	15.3

Table 2. Reference count overflow is infrequent when a modest number of bits are used. The top third of this table shows the number of objects which ever suffer overflow when 1, 2, 3, 4, or 5 bits are used for reference counts. The middle third shows how many increments are applied to overflowed objects. The bottom third shows how many decrements are applied to overflowed objects.

types	collection trigger	mean	compress	jess	db	javac	mpegaudio	mtrt	jack	avrora	bloat	chart	eclipse	fop	hsqldb	luindex	lusearch	pjbb2005	pmd	sunflow	xalan
								breakdown of increments													
new	2M	57	1.1	94.1	98.5	78.5	99.8	76.5	85.2	25.4	91.5	44.9	57.6	50.4	65.4	20.6	18.5	68.7	51.5	10.7	37.6
	16M	71	5.3	99.1	90.3	87.8	99.8	93.5	96.8	37.6	98.8	82.4	91.0	85.9	76.2	23.1	43.4	81.4	82.0	15.1	68.7
scalar	2M	16	0.8	0.1	0	9.0	0	2.7	2.6	69.3	0.1	5.9	0.5	6.5	14.2	64.8	20.7	12.2	18.2	57.3	11.3
	16M	18	0.8	0	0	8.0	0	3.0	1.1	61.5	0	6.2	0.5	4.4	14.0	69.7	40	14.1	12.6	79.3	18.3
array	2M	1	0	0	0.6	2.6	0	0	0.4	0	0.1	0	1.0	0	6.7	5.1	0.2	0.4	0.3	0	4.1
	16M	2	0.1	0	9.6	2.4	0	0	0.4	0	0	0.2	0.4	0	6.8	5.1	0.3	1.6	0.2	0	2.8
root	2M	27	98.1	5.8	0.9	9.9	0.2	20.7	11.7	5.3	8.3	49.1	41.0	43.0	13.7	9.5	60.6	18.7	29.9	32.0	47.0
	16M	9	93.8	0.8	0.1	1.8	0.2	3.5	1.7	0.8	1.1	11.2	8.2	9.7	3.0	2.2	16.3	3.0	5.2	5.6	10.1
								breakdown of decrements													
new	2M	60	2.4	95.0	97.7	63.5	99.8	90.8	90.4	30.7	92.1	65.3	39.7	60.1	42.9	22.2	24.0	70.5	56.4	45.5	43.2
	16M	71	11.3	98.9	90.3	70.5	99.8	96.7	97.0	42.2	98.6	88.7	61.5	84.4	51.7	24.8	48.8	80	81.6	54.9	71.5
scalar	2M	15	0.8	0.4	0.1	16.1	0	1.0	2.1	64.4	0.3	4.6	3.6	4.0	25.8	63.5	19.7	13.2	15.1	34.4	10.7
	16M	15	0.9	0.4	0	14.9	0	0.9	0.8	57.0	0.1	4.0	4.1	1.8	25.3	67.9	33.7	14.5	9.8	41.4	14.9
array	2M	1	0	0	0.5	2.5	0	0	0.3	0	0.2	0	0.9	0	6.2	5.1	0.8	0.3	0.3	0	3.7
	16M	2	0	0	9.4	2.4	0	0	0.4	0	0	0.3	0		6.2	5.2	1.3	1.1	0.2	0	2.2
root	2M	21	96.7	4.5	1.7	7.7	0.2	6.9	7.2	4.8	7.2	28.3	37.7	29.7	12.5	9.1	53.8	14.0	25.1	20.1	40
	16M	8	87.3	0.6	0.3	1.3	0.2	1.1	1.7	0.8	1.0	4.9	7.2	5.7	2.7	2.1	12.8	2.1	4.5	3.7	7.8
cycle	2M	3	0.1	0.1	0	10.3	0	1.3	0	0	0.1	1.8	18.1	6.2	12.7	0.1	1.8	2.0	3.1	0	2.3
	16M	4	0.6	0.1	0	10.9	0	1.4	0	0	0.2	2.4	26.9	8.1	14.1	0.1	3.3	2.3	4.0	0	3.6

Table 3. New objects account for a large fraction of increment and decrement operations. This table shows the sources of increment (top) and decrement (bottom) operations when collections are forced at 2 MB and 16 MB intervals. In all cases new objects dominate.

max count	mean	compress	jess	db	javac	mpegaudio	mtrt	jack	avrora	bloat	chart	eclipse	fop	hsqldb	luindex	lusearch	pjbb2005	pmd	sunflow	xalan
0	0	0	0	0	0	0	0	0	0	0	0	0	0	0	0	0	0	0	0	0
1	31	72.1	17.3	0.8	23.4	67.5	50.2	77.5	2.7	6.2	63.4	32.8	38.2	8.8	5.9	54.1	13.6	18.3	10.5	28.2
2	18	27.3	5.0	0.1	47.7	27.2	7.6	12.5	53.7	5.6	13.2	29.2	31.2	20.9	3.1	19.2	7.4	7.9	4.8	24.6
3	9	0.6	0.1	0.1	9.5	5.3	7.1	7.9	5.4	1.4	8.6	9.5	12.3	37.7	16.5	16.5	10.5	3.2	0	10.6
4	5	0	0	0	3.2	0	1.2	1.5	4.0	0.4	0.3	5.6	5.5	1.4	52.9	4.5	7.5	7.7	0	1.2
5	4	0	0	0	1.0	0	0.3	0.3	5.6	0.6	0.1	3.6	1.6	25.3	4.2	0	6.8	26.7	0	0.5
6	1	0	0	0	0.4	0	0.2	0.2	3.7	0.1	0	2.6	0.8	0.5	3.6	0	8.2	4.8	0	0.6
7	2	0	0	0	0.5	0	0.3	0.1	16.8	0.1	0	1.8	0.8	0.2	4.0	0	1.7	7.3	0	0.4
8-15	3	0	0.1	0.1	1.9	0	3.0	0.1	0	0.4	0	5.6	2.0	0.3	9.8	0	3.9	11.6	0	13.1
16-31	2	0	0.2	4.6	2.2	0	4.5	0	0	6.0	0.4	3.0	1.7	0	0	0	21.3	1.3	0	1.8
32-63	7	0	0.2	89.9	1.6	0	2.2	0	0.1	27.8	1.5	1.8	1.5	0	0	0.2	3.1	2.2	0	4.5
> 63	17	0	77.0	4.4	8.4	0	23.5	0	8.1	51.4	12.4	4.5	4.6	4.9	0.1	5.5	16.1	8.9	84.7	14.5

Table 4. 49% of increment and decrement operations occur on objects with maximum reference counts of just one or two. This table shows how increment operations are distributed as a function of the maximum reference count of the object the increment is applied to.

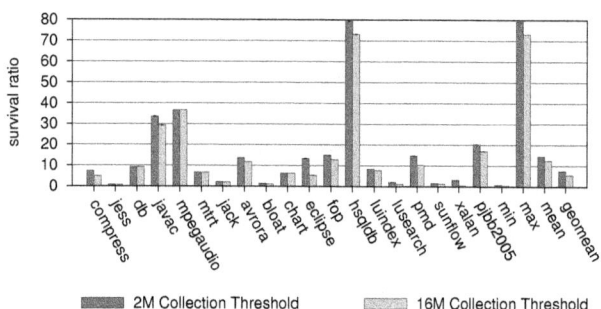

Figure 4. Most benchmarks have very low object survival ratios. This graph shows the percentage of objects that survive beyond 2 MB and 16 MB of allocation.

On average 71% of increments and 71% of decrements are performed upon newly allocated objects (over 90% for some benchmarks). For most benchmarks increments and decrements to non-new objects are low (around 9-10%), consistent with previous findings [4]. Around 10% of operations are due to root reachability. 4% of decrements are performed during cycle collection.

Figures 3(a) and 3(b) illustrate data from Table 3 graphically, showing the fraction of increments and decrements due to new objects, where *new* is defined in terms of both 2 MB and 16 MB allocation windows.

Conventionally, when using deferred reference counting, new objects are born 'live', with a temporary increment of one. A corresponding decrement is enqueued and applied at the next collection. Thus a highly allocating benchmark will incur a large number of increments and decrements simply due to the allocation of objects. Furthermore, newly allocated objects are relatively more frequently mutated, so contribute further to the total count of reference counting operations.

Table 4 shows the fraction of increments as a function of maximum reference count. For example, the table shows that on average 31% of increments are performed for objects having maximum reference count of one and 18% increments are performed for objects having maximum reference count of two. Interestingly, on average 17% of increments are due to objects with very high maximum reference counts (>63).

Figure 4 shows that most benchmarks have survival ratio of under 10%, indicating that over 90% of objects are unreachable by the time of the first garbage collection. This information and the data which shows that new objects attract a disproportionate fraction of increments and decrements confirms previous suggestions that new objects are likely to be a particularly fruitful focus for optimization of reference counting [4, 21].

3.5 Efficacy of Coalescing

Coalescing is most effective when individual reference fields are mutated many times, allowing the reference counter to avoid performing a significant number of reference count operations. To determine whether this expectation matches actual behavior, we compare the total number of reference mutation operations to the number of reference mutations observable by coalescing (i.e., where the final value of a reference field does not match the initial value). We control the window over which coalescing occurs by triggering collection after set volumes of application allocation (from 2 MB to 8 MB).

Table 5 shows, for example, that with a window of 8 MB, coalescing observes 50.5% and 92.2% of reference mutations for compress and jess respectively. For a few benchmarks, such as avrora, luindex, and sunflow, coalescing is extremely effective, eliding 90% or more of all reference mutations. However, for many benchmarks, coalescing is not particularly effective, eliding less than half of all mutations. In addition to measuring this for all objects, we separately measure operations over *new* objects — those allocated since the start of the current time window. This data shows that coalescing is significantly more effective with old objects. This is consistent with the idea that frequently mutated objects tend to be long lived, and is not inconsistent with the prior observation [4] that most mutations occur to young objects (since over the life of a program, young objects typically outnumber old objects by around 10:1).

Table 6 provides a different perspective by showing the breakdown of total reference mutations per unit time (millisecond).

3.6 Cyclic Garbage

Table 7 shows key statistics for each benchmark related to cyclic garbage. For each benchmark we show: 1) the fraction of objects that can be reclaimed by pure reference counting, and 2) the fraction of objects that are part of a cyclic graph when unreachable, so can only be reclaimed via cycle collection, and 3) the fraction of objects that are statically known to be acyclic (i.e., an object of that type can never transitively refer to itself). Note that 2) may not be directly participating in a cycle but may be referenced by a cycle. These results show that the importance of cycle collection varies significantly between benchmarks, with some benchmarks relying heavily on cycle collection (javac, mpegaudio, eclipse, hsqldb and pmd) while the cycle collector is responsible for reclaiming almost no memory (less than 1% for jess, db, jack, avrora, bloat and sunflow).

collection trigger	mean	compress	jess	db	javac	mpegaudio	mtrt	jack	avrora	bloat	chart	eclipse	fop	hsqldb	luindex	lusearch	pjbb2005	pmd	sunflow	xalan
percentage of pointer field changes seen (overall)																				
2M	36.4	48.0	92.2	26.9	54.7	0.1	47.9	53.3	10.0	12.1	71.9	54.8	60.6	43.8	3.9	27.7	23.9	32.3	8.9	19.2
4M	36.2	49.6	92.2	26.4	54.5	0.1	47.9	53.3	10.0	12.1	71.9	55.9	60.6	43.8	3.9	22.2	22.1	32.3	8.9	19.2
8M	36.2	50.5	92.2	26.1	54.1	0.1	47.9	53.3	10.0	11.8	71.9	55.9	60.6	43.8	3.8	22.1	23.4	32.3	8.9	19.1
percentage of pointer field changes seen (for new objects)																				
2M	48.5	53.3	92.4	28.6	61.1	0.1	48.8	56.4	31.3	12.0	79.1	58.3	67.4	67.7	25.5	74.8	45.9	41.3	48.3	28.6
4M	46.5	53.3	92.4	28.5	59.7	0.1	48.8	56.0	30.8	12.1	78.1	57.4	66.5	66.9	13.5	58.4	45.6	40.2	48.0	27.4
8M	45.8	53.2	92.4	28.2	59.1	0.1	48.8	55.2	30.8	11.7	76.4	57.0	66.4	65.5	9.4	56.2	45.2	40.0	48.3	26.7
percentage of pointer field changes seen (for old objects)																				
2M	10.3	12.8	45.3	13.7	29.0	20.0	4.0	1.2	0.1	21.0	18.1	9.6	10.5	2.7	1.0	0.2	2.7	1.8	0.8	0.3
4M	9.9	14.1	38.2	8.0	30.4	20.0	3.5	1.0	0.0	22.1	18.6	13.5	11.4	1.3	1.2	0.1	1.8	1.6	0.7	0.2
8M	9.7	14.5	32.7	4.9	29.2	21.1	2.6	1.1	0.0	28.6	19.0	12.9	11.5	0.7	0.9	0.1	1.4	1.5	0.7	0.1

Table 5. Coalescing elides around 64% of pointer field changes on average, and around 90% for old objects. This table shows the fraction of mutations that *are* seen by coalescing given three different collection windows. The top third shows the overall average. The middle third shows results for new objects. The bottom third shows old objects.

types	mean	compress	jess	db	javac	mpegaudio	mtrt	jack	avrora	bloat	chart	eclipse	fop	hsqldb	luindex	lusearch	pjbb2005	pmd	sunflow	xalan
Scalar	8027	2	3165	896	7689	3185	2319	9046	3305	36862	3234	2432	1872	11162	10051	10059	13080	11558	13894	8695
Array	1788	0	3026	7806	1010	1	3069	2099	15	551	106	3242	72	3080	937	280	2723	1320	62	4566
Bulk	114	0	2023	0	6	0	0	6	0	4	3	91	2	7	0	0	0	11	0	7
Total	9928	2	8214	8702	8705	3186	5389	11151	3320	37417	3343	5765	1945	14249	10989	10339	15804	12890	13955	13268

Table 6. References are mutated around 10 million times per second on average, on our 3.4 GHz Core i5. This graph shows the rate of mutations per millisecond for each benchmark, broken down by scalars, arrays and bulk copy operations.

types	mean	compress	jess	db	javac	mpegaudio	mtrt	jack	avrora	bloat	chart	eclipse	fop	hsqldb	luindex	lusearch	pjbb2005	pmd	sunflow	xalan
pure rc objects	84	91	99.7	100	77	64	93	99.9	99.8	99	94	47	82	27	91	84	87	80	99.99	90
cyclic objects	16	9	0.3	0	23	36	7	0.1	0.2	1	6	53	18	73	9	16	13	20	0.01	10
acyclic objects	38	55	18	4	34	44	3	38	16	49	49	54	46	35	49	28	35	21	97	44

Table 7. The importance of cycle collection. This table shows that on average 84% of objects can be collected by reference counting without a cycle collector, and that on average 38% of all objects are inherently acyclic. These results vary considerably among the benchmarks.

4. Improving Reference Counting

We now explore two areas for optimization that arise from our analysis of the intrinsic data presented in the previous section. We describe the insights, evaluate the designs, and evaluate the ideas in combination.

4.1 Storing the Reference Count

Because the vast majority of objects have low maximum reference counts, the use of just a few bits for the reference counting is appealing. The idea has been proposed before [15], but to our knowledge has not been systematically analyzed. Key insights that can be drawn from our intrinsic analysis are that most objects have maximum reference counts of seven or less, and that objects with high maximum reference counts account for a disproportionate fraction of reference counting operations. The former motivates using around three bits for storing the count, while the latter suggests that any strategy for dealing with overflow must not be too expensive since it is likely to be heavily invoked. We now describe three strategies for dealing with reference count overflow.

Hash table on overflow (**HashTable RC**)   When an object's reference count overflows, the reference count can be stored in a hash table. Increments and decrement are performed in the hash table until the reference count drops below the overflow threshold, at which point the hash table entry is released. Each entry in the hash table requires two words, one word for the object (key) and one word for the count (value). We measure the size of hash table across the benchmarks and find that 1 MB table is sufficient for all benchmarks.

Stuck and Ignored on Overflow (**StuckIgnore RC**)   When an object's count overflows, it may be left stuck at the overflow value and all future increments and decrements will be ignored. Reference counting is thus unable to collect these objects, so they must be recovered by the backup tracing cycle collector (note that a trial deletion cycle collector cannot collect such objects).

Stuck and Restored on Overflow (**StuckRestore RC**)   A refinement to the previous case has the backup trace *restore* reference counts within the heap during tracing, by incrementing the target object's count for each reference traversed. Although this approach imposes an additional role upon the backup trace, it has the benefit of freeing the backup trace from performing decrement operations for collected objects.

In Figure 5 we evaluate these strategies. In Jikes RVM we have up to one byte (8 bits) available in the object header for use by the garbage collector. We use two bits to support the dirty state for coalescing, one bit for the mark-state for backup tracing, and the remaining five bits to store the reference count. All results are normalized to MMTk's default reference counting configuration, *Standard RC*, a coalescing deferred collector using an additional header word and that uses backup tracing cycle collector.

For the majority of the benchmarks *HashTable RC* performs poorly, with *Standard RC* 1% better in total time (Figure 5(a)) and 13% better in collection time (Figure 5(b)) than *HashTable RC* on average. The performance of jess and db is much worse in *HashTable RC* compared to other benchmarks. This was predicted by our analysis, which showed that these benchmarks had

(a) Total Time

(b) GC Time

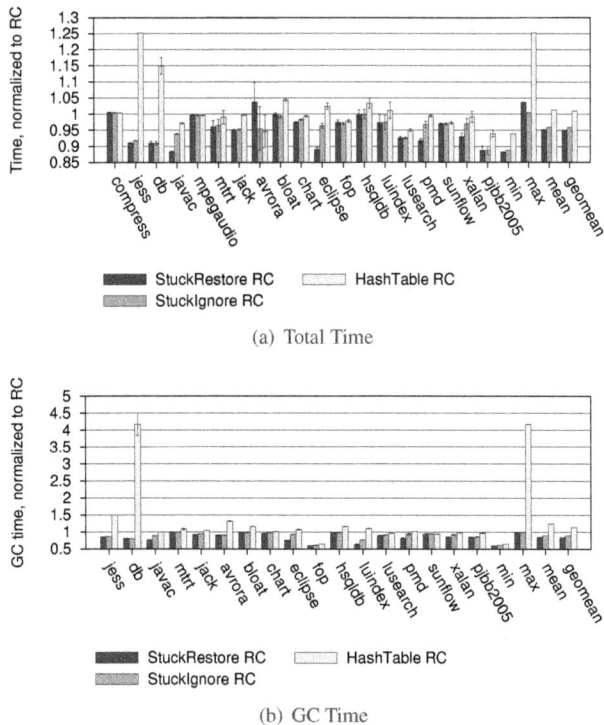

Figure 5. Using a hash table to account for reference count overflow is not a good solution. These graphs show three strategies for dealing with overflow. Results vary greatly among benchmarks.

(a) Increments

(b) Decrements

Figure 6. Lazy treatment of new objects greatly reduces the number of reference counting operations necessary compared to *Standard RC*. The effectiveness varies greatly among the benchmarks.

high rates of reference counting operations on overflowed objects. While *HashTable RC* benefits from not requiring an additional header word, this benefit is outweighed by the cost of performing increment and decrement operations in the hash table. In *HashTable RC*, the processing of increments and decrements are 30% and 17% slower than in *Standard RC*, respectively.

Given the poor performance of the hash table approach, we turn our attention to the systems that use backup tracing to collect objects with sticky reference counts, *StuckIgnore RC* and *StuckRestore RC*. Both *StuckIgnore RC* and *StuckRestore RC* outperform *Standard RC* (by 4% and 5% respectively). This is primarily due to no longer requiring an additional header word, although there is also some advantage from ignoring reference counting operations. Comparing the two sticky reference count systems, *StuckRestore RC* performs slightly better in both total time and collection time. Backup tracing in *StuckRestore RC* performs more work than *StuckIgnore RC* because it restores the count for the objects. But as mentioned earlier, during backup tracing if any object's reference count is zero then only the object is reclaimed and count of the descendants are not decremented, giving *StuckRestore RC* a potential advantage.

We also measured (but do not show here) the three overflow strategies with an additional header word, to factor out the source of difference with *Standard RC*. In this scenario, the extra word is not used to store the reference count but simply acts as a placeholder to evaluate the impact of the space overhead. In that case, *StuckIgnore RC* performs same as *Standard RC* and *StuckRestore RC* only marginally outperformed *Standard RC* (by 1% in total time), indicating that most of their advantage comes from the use of a small reference counting field.

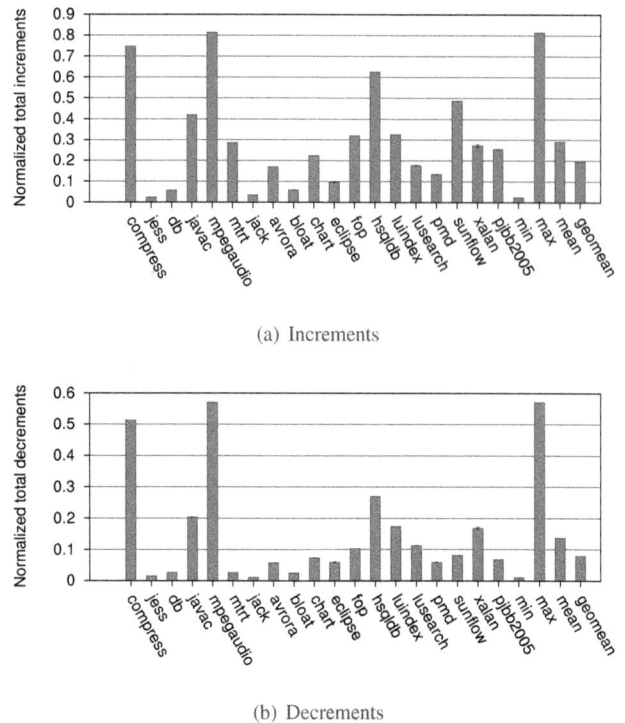

4.2 Lazy Treatment of New Objects

Our analysis shows that reference counting overheads are dominated by the behavior of new objects, and yet the vast majority of those objects do not survive a single collection. Two previous systems proposed hybrid collectors that successfully exploited this property. Blackburn and McKinley [4] combined copying generational collection and reference counting, using the copying collector to absorb the impact of the young objects. Paz et al. developed a similar scheme that combined mark-sweep collection with reference counting [21]. Like the previous work, we propose to avoid reference counting operations on new objects. However, our goal is to do so within the framework of reference counting, without creating a hybrid by introducing another collector.

We leverage two insights that allow us to ignore new objects until their first collection, at which point they can be processed lazily as they are discovered. First, coalescing reference counting uses a dirty bit in each object's header to ignore mutations to objects between their initial mutation and the bit being reset at collection time. A collector that ignores new objects could straightforwardly use this mechanism. Second, in a deferred reference counter any new object reachable from either the roots or old objects will be included in the set of increments. Furthermore, the set of increments will only include references to new objects that are live.

We further observe that if new objects are allocated dead, and only made live upon discovery, then a significant fraction of expensive freeing operations can be avoided, since the vast majority of objects do not survive the first collection.

We start by considering the treatment of new objects in a collector that uses deferred reference counting and coalescing, and we use this as our point of comparison. In such a collector, new objects are allocated dirty with a reference count of one. The object is added

80

(a) Total time

(b) GC time

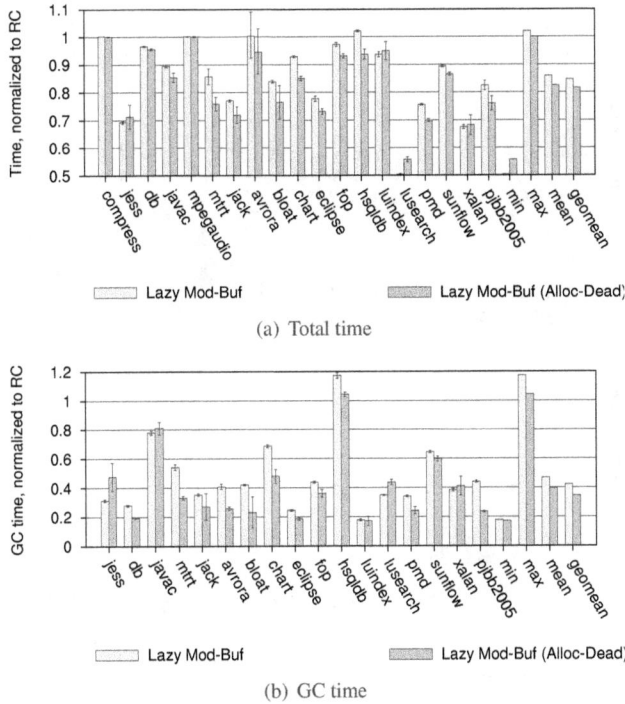

Figure 7. Lazy treatment of new objects reduces total time by around 20% compared to *Standard RC*. Most of this benefit comes from not eagerly adding new objects to the *mod-buf*.

(a) Total time

(b) GC time

Figure 8. The combined effect of our optimizations is a 24% improvement in total time compared to *Standard RC*. Both jess and lusearch see nearly two-fold improvements.

to the deque of decrements (*dec-buf*), and a decrement cancelling the reference count of one is applied once the *dec-buf* is processed at the next collection [12]. The object is also added to the deque of modified objects (*mod-buf*) used by the coalescing mechanism. At the next collection, the collector processes the *mod-buf* and applies an increment for each object that the processed object points to. Because all references are initially *null*, the coalescing mechanism does not need to explicitly generate decrements corresponding to outgoing pointers from the initial state of the object [16].

Lazy Mod-Buf Insertion Our first optimization is to not add new objects to the *mod-buf*. Instead, we add a 'new' bit to the object header, and add objects lazily to the *mod-buf* at collection time, only if they are encountered during the processing of increments. Whenever the subject of an increment is marked as new, the object's new bit is cleared, and the object is pushed onto the *mod-buf*. Because in a coalescing deferred reference counter, all references from roots and old objects will increment all objects they reach, our approach will retain all new objects directly reachable from old objects and the roots. Because each object processed on the *mod-buf* will increment each of its children, our scheme is transitive. Thus new objects are effectively traced. However, rather than combing reference counting and tracing to create a hybrid collector [4, 21], our scheme achieves a similar result via a very simple optimization to existing reference counting collector. This optimization required only very modest changes to MMTk's existing reference counting collector.[1] Figure 6(a) shows the massive reduction in the total number of increments.

Allocate As Dead As a simple extension of the above optimization, instead of allocating objects live, with a reference count of one and a compensating decrement enqueued to the *dec-buf*, our second

optimization allocates new objects as dead and does not enqueue a decrement. This inverts the presumption: the reference counter does not need to identify those new objects that are *dead*, but it must rather identify those that are reachable. This inversion means that work is done in the infrequent case of a new object being reachable, rather that the common case of it being dead. New objects are only made live when they receive their first increment while processing the *mod-buf* during collection time. Our optimization removes the need for creating compensating decrements and avoids explicitly freeing short lived objects. Figure 6(b) shows that decrements are reduced by over 80%.

We evaluate performance of both optimizations for lazy treatment of new objects. Figures 7(a) and 7(b) show the effect of the optimizations on total time and garbage collection time respectively relative to orthodox deferred reference counting with coalescing (*Standard RC*). The first optimization (*Lazy Mod-Buf*) improves over *Standard RC* by 16% in total time and 58% in collection time, on average, over the set of benchmarks. The two optimizations combined (*Lazy Mod-Buf (Alloc-Dead)*) are 19% faster in total time and 66% faster in collection time than *Standard RC* on average.

4.3 Bringing It All Together

Figure 8 presents an evaluation of the impact of the three most effective optimizations operating together: a) limited bits for the reference count and restore counts during backup trace, b) lazy *mod-buf* insertion, and c) allocate as dead. The combined effect of these optimizations is 24% faster in total time (Figure 8(a)) and 74% faster in collection time (Figure 8(b)) compared to our base case (*Standard RC*), on average over the benchmarks. This substantial improvement over an already optimized reference counting implementation should change perceptions about reference counting and its applicability to high performance contexts.

---

[1] We have contributed our code to Jikes RVM.

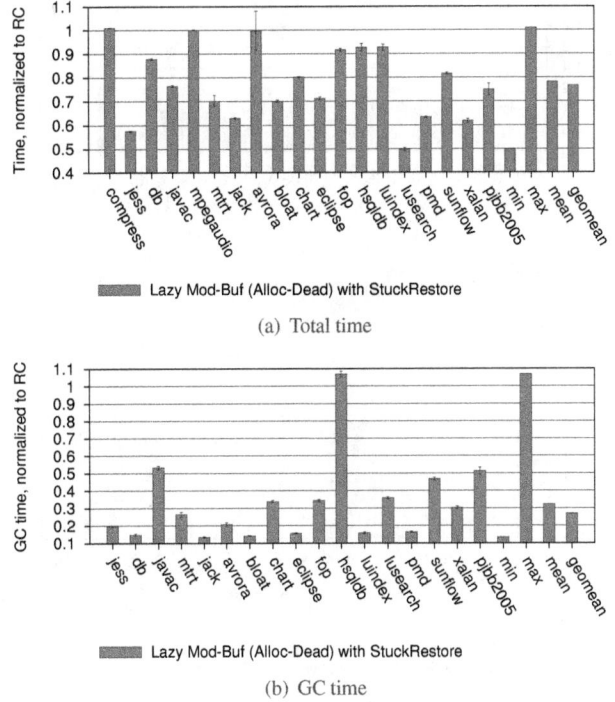

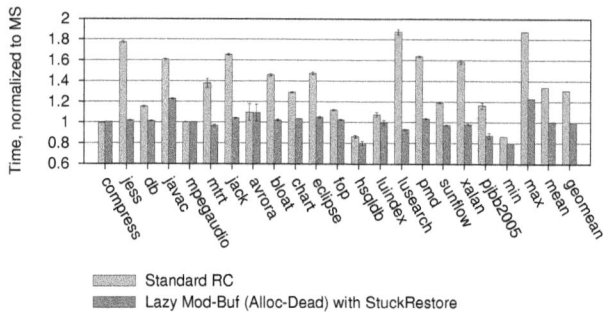

(a) Total time

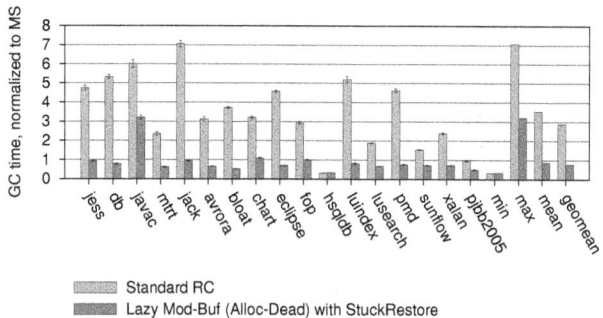

(a) Total time

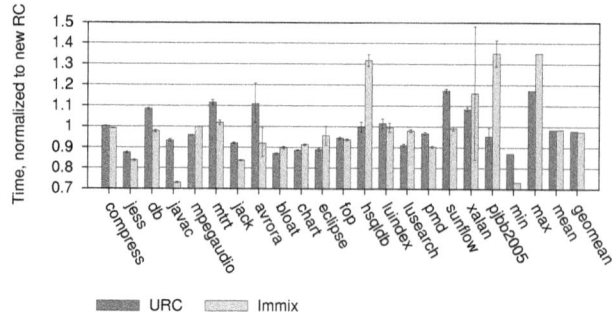

(b) GC time

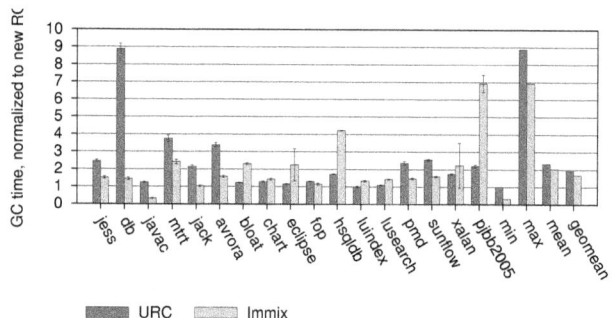

(b) GC time

Figure 9. Our optimized reference counting very closely matches mark-sweep, while standard reference counting performs 30% worse.

Figure 10. Our optimized reference counting collector also performs very well compared to ulterior reference counting and Immix. Our collector lags URC by 2% and Immix by 3% on average.

5. Back In The Ring

The conventional wisdom is that reference counting is totally uncompetitive compared to a modern mark-sweep collector [4]. Figure 9 shows the evaluation of *Standard RC* and *Lazy Mod-Buf (Alloc-Dead)* against a well tuned mark-sweep collector. Consistent with conventional wisdom, *Standard RC* performs substantially worse than mark-sweep, slowing down by 30%. However, our optimized reference counter, *Lazy Mod-Buf (Alloc-Dead)*, is able to entirely eliminate the overhead and perform marginally faster than mark-sweep on average, and is at worst 22% worse than mark-sweep (javac whose performance largely depends on the triggering of cycle collection) and at best 21% better than mark-sweep (hsqldb).

We compared our improved reference counting with ulterior reference counting [4] and Immix [5]. Ulterior reference counting combines copying generational collection for the young objects and reference counting for the old objects. Immix is a mark-region based tracing garbage collector with opportunistic defragmentation, which mixes copying and marking in a single pass. It achieves space efficiency, fast reclamation, and mutator performance. Much of its performance advantage over mark-sweep is due to its heap organization. Figure 10 shows that our improved reference counting is 2% slower than ulterior reference counting and 3% slower than Immix.

We also compare our improved reference counting with sticky mark bits collectors [5, 11]. These collectors are similar to ours in that they combine generational ideas in a non-moving context. However, they use tracing and they use a write barrier to avoid tracing the whole heap at every collection. Like our approach, they identify new objects using bits in the object header to treat them separately. Figure 11 shows that our improved reference counting collector performs the same as Sticky MS and 10% slower than

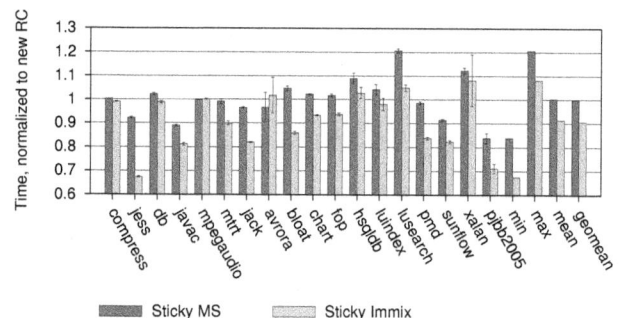

(a) Total time

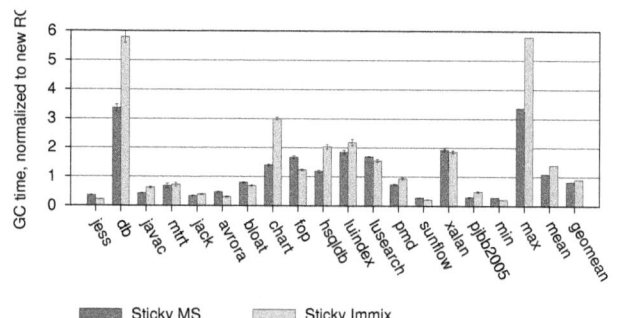

(b) GC time

Figure 11. Sticky Immix outperforms our optimized reference counting collector by 10%. The combination of the optimized reference counter and the Immix heap layout appears to be promising.

Sticky Immix. Sticky Immix should therefore be a good indicator of the performance of our improved reference counting projected onto the Immix heap organization. This is an exciting prospect because Sticky Immix is only 3% slower than Jikes RVM's production collector.

6. Conclusion

Of the two fundamental algorithms on which the garbage collection literature is built, reference counting has lived in the shadow of tracing. It has a niche among language developers for whom either performance or completeness is not essential, and is unused by mature high performance systems, despite a number of intrinsic advantages such as promptness of recovery and dependence on local rather than global state. The basis for its poor standing is that high performance reference counting significantly lags high performance tracing algorithms in performance.

We have conducted a comprehensive analysis of reference counting, confirmed that its performance lags mark-sweep by over 30%, and measured a number of reference counting intrinsics which give insight into its behavior and opportunities for improvement. We have identified two significant optimizations which together entirely eliminate the performance gap with mark-sweep. Unlike prior work, our optimizations are not hybrids, but modest changes to orthodox reference counting that significantly improve its performance.

Our hope is that our optimizations and our analysis of reference counting behavior will give new life to reference counting garbage collection.

References

[1] B. Alpern, C. R. Attanasio, J. J. Barton, M. G. Burke, P. Cheng, J.-D. Choi, A. Cocchi, S. J. Fink, D. Grove, M. Hind, S. F. Hummel, D. Lieber, V. Litvinov, M. Mergen, T. Ngo, J. R. Russell, V. Sarkar, M. J. Serrano, J. Shepherd, S. Smith, V. C. Sreedhar, H. Srinivasan, and J. Whaley. The Jalapeño virtual machine. *IBM Systems Journal*, 39(1):211–238, February 2000. doi: 10.1147/sj.391.0211.

[2] D. F. Bacon and V. T. Rajan. Concurrent cycle collection in reference counted systems. In *European Conference on Object-Oriented Programming*, pages 207–235, Budapest, Hungary, 2001. doi: 10.1007/3-540-45337-7_12.

[3] D. F. Bacon, C. R. Attanasio, H. B. Lee, V. T. Rajan, and S. Smith. Java without the coffee breaks: A nonintrusive multiprocessor garbage collector. In *ACM Conference on Programming Language Design and Implementation*, pages 92–103, Snowbird, UT, USA, 2001. doi: 10.1145/378795.378819.

[4] S. M. Blackburn and K. S. McKinley. Ulterior reference counting: Fast garbage collection without a long wait. In *ACM Conference on Object-Oriented Programming Systems, Languages, and Applications*, pages 344–358, Anaheim, CA, USA, 2003. doi: 10.1145/949305.949336.

[5] S. M. Blackburn and K. S. McKinley. Immix: A mark-region garbage collector with space efficiency, fast collection, and mutator locality. In *ACM Conference on Programming Language Design and Implementation*, pages 22–32, Tucson, AZ, USA, 2008. doi: 10.1145/1379022.1375586.

[6] S. M. Blackburn, P. Cheng, and K. S. McKinley. Oil and water? High performance garbage collection in Java with MMTk. In *Proceedings of the 26th International Conference on Software Engineering*, pages 137–146, Edinburgh, Scotland, UK, 2004. doi: 10.1109/ICSE.2004.1317436.

[7] S. M. Blackburn, P. Cheng, and K. S. McKinley. Myths and realities: The performance impact of garbage collection. In *Proceedings of the ACM Conference on Measurement & Modeling Computer Systems*, pages 25–36, New York, NY, USA, 2004. doi: 10.1145/1005686.1005693.

[8] S. M. Blackburn, R. Garner, C. Hoffmann, A. M. Khang, K. S. McKinley, R. Bentzur, A. Diwan, D. Feinberg, D. Frampton, S. Z. Guyer, M. Hirzel, A. Hosking, M. Jump, H. Lee, J. E. B. Moss, A. Phansalkar, D. Stefanović, T. VanDrunen, D. von Dincklage, and B. Wiedermann. The DaCapo benchmarks: Java benchmarking development and analysis. In *ACM Conference on Object-Oriented Programming Systems, Languages, and Applications*, pages 169–190, Portland, OR, USA, 2006. doi: 10.1145/1167473.1167488.

[9] T. W. Christopher. Reference count garbage collection. *Software: Practice and Experience*, 14(6):503–507, June 1984. doi: 10.1002/spe.4380140602.

[10] G. E. Collins. A method for overlapping and erasure of lists. *Communications of the ACM*, 3(12):655–657, December 1960. doi: 10.1145/367487.367501.

[11] A. Demers, M. Weiser, B. Hayes, H. Boehm, D. Bobrow, and S. Shenker. Combining generational and conservative garbage collection: Framework and implementations. In *Proceedings of the Seventeenth Annual ACM Symposium on the Principles of Programming Languages*, pages 261–269, San Francisco, CA, USA, 1990. doi: 10.1145/96709.96735.

[12] L. P. Deutsch and D. G. Bobrow. An efficient, incremental, automatic garbage collector. *Communications of the ACM*, 19(9):522–526, September 1976. doi: 10.1145/360336.360345.

[13] D. Frampton. *Garbage Collection and the Case for High-level Low-level Programming*. PhD thesis, Australian National University, June 2010. URL http://cs.anu.edu.au/~Daniel.Frampton/DanielFrampton_Thesis_Jun2010.pdf.

[14] I. Jibaja, S. M. Blackburn, M. R. Haghighat, and K. S. McKinley. Deferred gratification: Engineering for high performance garbage collection from the get go. In *ACM SIGPLAN Workshop on Memory Systems Performance and Correctness*, pages 58–65, San Jose, CA, USA, 2011. doi: 10.1145/1988915.1988930.

[15] R. E. Jones, A. Hosking, and J. E. B. Moss. *The Garbage Collection Handbook: The Art of Automatic Memory Management*. Chapman and Hall/CRC Applied Algorithms and Data Structures Series, USA, 2011.

[16] Y. Levanoni and E. Petrank. An on-the-fly reference counting garbage collector for Java. In *ACM Conference on Object-Oriented Programming Systems, Languages, and Applications*, pages 367–380, Tampa, FL, USA, 2001. doi: 10.1145/504282.504309.

[17] Y. Levanoni and E. Petrank. An on-the-fly reference-counting garbage collector for Java. *ACM Transactions on Programming Languages and Systems*, 28(1):1–69, January 2006. doi: 10.1145/1111596.1111597.

[18] R. D. Lins. Cyclic reference counting with lazy mark-scan. *Information Processing Letters*, 44(4):215–220, December 1992. doi: 10.1016/0020-0190(92)90088-D.

[19] A. D. Martinez, R. Wachenchauzer, and R. D. Lins. Cyclic reference counting with local mark-scan. *Information Processing Letters*, 34(1):31–35, February 1990. doi: 10.1016/0020-0190(90)90226-N.

[20] J. McCarthy. Recursive functions of symbolic expressions and their computation by machine, part I. *Communications of the ACM*, 3(4):184–195, April 1960. doi: 10.1145/367177.367199.

[21] H. Paz, E. Petrank, and S. M. Blackburn. Age-oriented concurrent garbage collection. In *International Conference on Compiler Construction*, Edinburgh, Scotland, UK, 2005. doi: 10.1007/978-3-540-31985-6_9.

[22] J. Weizenbaum. Recovery of reentrant list structures in Lisp. *Communications of the ACM*, 12(7):370–372, July 1969. doi: 10.1145/363156.363159.

The Collie: A Wait-Free Compacting Collector

Balaji Iyengar

Azul Systems Inc
balaji@azulsystems.com

Gil Tene

Azul Systems Inc
gil@azulsystems.com

Michael Wolf

Azul Systems Inc
wolf@azulsystems.com

Edward Gehringer

North Carolina State University
efg@ncsu.edu

Abstract

We describe the Collie collector, a fully concurrent compacting collector that uses transactional memory techniques to achieve wait-free compaction. The collector uses compaction as the primary means of reclaiming unused memory, and performs "individual object transplantations" as transactions. We introduce new terms and requirements useful for analyzing concurrent relocating collectors, including definitions of referrer sets, object transplantation and the notion of individually transplantable objects. The Collie collector builds on these terms and on a detailed analysis of an object's legal states during compaction.

Collie uses a combination of read barriers, write barriers and transactional memory operations. Its read-barrier supports fast, direct object referencing while using a bound, constant time, wait-free triggering path. Collie thereby avoids the constant indirection cost of Brooks [9] style barriers or handle-based heaps [25]. Collie is demonstrated using speculative multi-address atomicity [11], a form of hardware transactional memory supported by the Azul Vega architecture [2].

We evaluate the Collie collector on the Azul platform, on which previous concurrent collectors such as the Pauseless Collector [12] and its generational variant [30] have been commercially available for several years. We discuss Collie's performance while running sustained workloads, and compare it to the Pauseless collector on the same platform. The Collie collector provides significant MMU [5] improvements even in the 1-msec time windows compared to the Pauseless collector. At the same time, it matches Pauseless in throughput and in the ability to scale to large heap sizes.

We believe that the Collie collector is the first garbage collector to leverage hardware-assisted transactional memory. While Collie directly leverages Vega's speculative multi-address atomicity feature (SMA) [11], its design can be easily adapted to other hardware-assisted transactional memory systems. Specifically, the upcoming Intel TSX instruction set extensions [21] include capabilities similar to SMA. We expect Collie to be easily implementable on future

commodity servers based on Intel Haswell processors and following processor generations.

Categories and Subject Descriptors D.3.3 [*Language Constructs and Features*]: Dynamic storage management; Concurrent programming structures; D.3.4 [*Processors*]: Memory management (garbage collection); Run-time environments; D.4.2 [*Storage Management*]: Garbage collection; Virtual memory

General Terms Algorithms, Design, Performance.

Keywords Transactional memory, Atomicity primitives, Concurrent garbage collection, Read barrier, Virtual memory, Runtime systems, Memory management, Compaction, Minimum mutator utilization.

1. Introduction

Managed runtime environments, such as Java, have been grappling with an abundance of cheap compute and memory capacity for some time now. With enterprise application responsiveness expectations that are often in the 10s of milliseconds or lower, scaling runtime instance memory to levels readily available in server platforms has been a challenge. In systems where guarantees or bounds on response time behavior is expected, such as soft or hard real time environments, the challenge is even more pronounced. Along with limitations in practical instance memory size, other scale metrics such as object allocation and access throughput rates are limited when response time requirements are imposed.

The use of stop-the-world garbage collection presents a fundamental fault line in the design of managed runtimes. Garbage collection algorithms in which application threads are stopped for significant periods of time while memory is being reclaimed are clearly in direct conflict with the dual goals of maintaining application responsiveness and scaling application memory instance sizes. As heap sizes grow to 10s and 100s of gigabytes, such stop-the-world techniques become untenable for online processing application. Historically, server growth trends have motivated the design and implementation of several concurrent garbage collection algorithms [3, 12, 23, 26, 30] that all strive to recycle memory without stopping the application, as well as hybrid implementations where at least some of the collection work is concurrent [14].

Controlling fragmentation is an essential part of any garbage collection algorithm meant for sustainable, long running environments. Early concurrent collector implementations [14] delayed compaction, and provided fragmentation control through fallbacks to monolithic stop-the-world compaction modes. Incremental stop-the-world algorithms that attempt to break the monolithic nature of

ISMM'12, June 15–16, 2012, Beijing, China.
Copyright © 2012 ACM 978-1-4503-1350-6/12/06...$10.00

full heap compaction by identifying and compacting parts of the heap in a sequence of incremental pauses [15] have also evolved. However, as heap sizes, live set sizes and allocation throughput all continue to grow, and required response time bounds continue to shrink, implications of such stop-the-world pauses will become unacceptable for most application domains.

Techniques for maintaining responsiveness by allowing concurrent application execution while combating fragmentation span a wide range. Most fall into one of two key categories: completely eliminating the need for compaction, or using concurrent compaction. Eliminating the need for compaction is most often achieved by capping the size of individual memory-contiguous objects, and breaking up objects that require larger sizes into non-contiguous sub-parts (arraylets, objectlets, spines, etc.) [4, 28]. Such no-compaction techniques are often used in real time environments, and are effective at eliminating external fragmentation, but often involve a significant mutator performance overhead due to common access into potentially non-contiguous structures. Concurrent compaction techniques relocate objects in the heap while the application executes concurrently. This introduces synchronization issues between the application threads and the garbage collector, such as the need to ensure correct mutator access through object references that may refer to objects that have been, are being, or are about to be relocated in memory. Concurrent compaction techniques use varying means to grapple with these synchronization issues.

Concurrent compacting collectors [4, 12, 20, 23, 30] often introduce artifacts that impact mutator utilization [5] and performance. These include potentially high barrier [20] or other fast-path costs, such as in the case of Brooks style barriers [4] and handelized-heaps [25]. Other performance limiters include frequent barrier triggering during collector phase shifts [12, 30], and a variable [12, 30] and sometimes unbound [23, 26] amount of time spent in the triggered barrier handling code, for example when the mutator may be required to perform cooperative relocation of object contents in order to handle a triggered barrier. These mutator utilization impacts can have an adverse effect on application throughput and increase jitters in application response times. Supporting ever higher application throughput and ever improving consistent response times while concurrently compacting the heap continues to be the holy grail of garbage collection. We expect that concurrent compactors will see challenges in maintaining expected mutator utilization levels during compaction if they remain prone to high barrier triggering rates and large or potentially unbounded work required for triggered barrier handling.

We believe that advancements in synchronization techniques, such as the use transactional memory, can be used to alleviate some of the limitations that we expect concurrent compactors to run into. In the past couple of decades, transactional memory [18] has emerged as an alternative, potentially scalable synchronization technique on modern hardware systems. Transactional memory typically provides multi-address atomicity semantics, spanning the spectrum from pure hardware implementations [11] to pure software implementations [27], with various hybrid variations [13]. Commercially available hardware assisted transactional memory systems have been available from Azul Systems since 2005 [11]. More recently IBM has been shipping Power cores with hardware transactional memory capabilities in the BlueGene/Q system [16]. While such hardware capabilities have not been available in mainstream servers until now, this has recently changed with Intel's recent anouncement that the upcoming Haswell processors will include transactional memory [21]. It is now expected that hardware transactional memory will become a mainstream feature in commodity servers in the 2013-2014 timeframe.

Our goal in this paper is to take a fresh look at concurrent compaction issues while keeping in sight the ever-increasing responsiveness and scale objectives mentioned above. We describe the Collie collector, a new approach to concurrent compaction that focuses on individual object relocation and leverages transactional memory techniques to provide a bounded cost to triggered barrier operations. In building to the Collie design, we take a general look at concurrent compaction in section 2, and discuss the object transplantation abstraction and its associated correctness requirements. We introduce the concept of individual object transplantation in section 3, and lay out the requirements for maintaining the individual object transplantation quality. In section 4 we build a theoretical, though not quite practical, barrier free algorithm based on this new concept. In section 5, we evolve to the full blown Collie collector– a practical, wait-free implementation of a concurrent compacting garbage collector based on the individual object transplantation concept that leverages read/write barriers and transactional memory.

The contributions of this paper are:

1. We introduce the concept of an "individual object transplantation", the state associated with it, and a set of constraints based on the linearizability [19] framework that are necessary for correct concurrent transplantation.

2. We introduce the first (theoretical, though not practical) barrier-free compacting algorithm.

3. We introduce the first wait-free read barrier with a bounded, constant-time triggering path. The read barrier is self-healing [12] and avoids the constant indirection cost of Brooks [9] style barriers in the fast path.

4. We present an evaluation of our implementation on the Azul Vega platform, and compare Collie with the Pauseless Collector [12] running on the same platform.

We implemented Collie within a fully functional Azul JVM running on an Azul Vega-3 model 7340 appliance containing 432 cores and 384GB in a symmetric memory configuration [2]. Previous collectors such as Pauseless Collector [12] and its generational variant [30] have been shipping commercially on the same platform for several years now. While Collie directly leverages Vega's speculative multi-address atomicity feature [11], its design can be easily adapted to other hardware-assisted transactional memory systems. Specifically, the upcoming Intel TSX instruction set extensions [21] include capabilities similar to the Azul Vega SMA feature. We expect Collie to be easily implementable on future commodity servers based on Intel Haswell processors and following processor generations.

2. A General Look at Concurrent Compaction

Compaction of objects involves copying the reachable objects from a from-space into mostly contiguous memory locations in a to-space, replacing all pointers to from-space locations with corresponding pointers to to-space locations and reclaiming from-space memory for re-use. While the "from" and the "to" spaces could technically overlap in some collectors (such as the case in in-place compactors), this paper is mostly concerned with compactors that use non-overlapping from-space and to-space address ranges.

Stop-the-world compaction is fairly straightforward, with the full set of compaction operations appearing to occur atomically from the mutator's perspective. However, concurrent compacting collectors[1] must deal with concurrent mutator activity. Concurrent compaction inevitably involves periods during object relocation, where multiple copies of the same object may exist at different addresses [30]. In this case, the collector must make sure that all threads see the same consistent state of the object, as specified by the memory model. Concurrent compacting collectors impose a set of constraints on the mutators to achieve the required consistency and usually enforce these constraints using different barrier mechanisms.

There are two main options for maintaining consistency of object state during concurrent compaction. The first, which this paper is mostly focused on, is to ensure that mutators can only observe one version of the object at any given time. For example, some collectors [6, 12, 23, 30] enforce a *to-space invariant*, where the mutator can only observe the to-space version of the object. The second option is to allow multiple copies to be visible to the mutators, with the collector guaranteeing that all reads from and writes to the contents of the logical object (which may interact with different copies) remain consistent as specified by the memory model[2]. For example, concurrent copying collectors such as the Sapphire collector [20] take this approach.

The *to-space invariant* is often enforced using a read barrier. When the barrier encounters a from-space reference, it will look up the corresponding to-space location and use it instead, copying the object to its to-space location if necessary. This ensures that all concurrent accesses to the object are performed to the to-space version of the object's contents. In some variations, the first thread to access a reference to a from-space object claims the rights to copy the object's contents to the to-space, while other concurrent accessors of the object wait on the copy to finish to obtain the object's to-space pointer. In wait-free copying variations, concurrent accessors may race and concurrently attempt to copy the same object's contents without waiting, where a "winning" copy is decided via an atomic operation. Collectors that use the Brooks style indirection barrier [7, 9] always traverse a forwarding pointer that always points to the current (to-space) version of the object. Such indirection barriers are generally coupled with a write barrier to avoid propagation of from-space pointers. In contrast to indirection barriers, direct-access barriers enforce the *to-space invariant* on loaded reference values, e.g. Baker style [6] and LVB-style [12, 30] barriers. Varying implementations of direct-access barrier implementation exist including, hardware read barrier instructions [12], inlined code that checks for invariants [30] and virtual memory protection techniques [12, 23].

Having garnered an intuitive feel for the requirements of compaction in general and for the consistency requirements specific to correct concurrent compaction, we now attempt to crystallize these into a set of constraints. We use concepts from *linearizability* [19] to highlight the requirements for correct concurrent relocation of an object. Within the linearizability framework, each operation appears to "take effect" instantaneously and the order of non-concurrent operations is preserved. Objects should go from a well-defined and consistent pre-operation state to a well-defined and consistent post-operation state. Intermediate states are not defined and should not be visible. The linearizability framework maintains a history of operations on the object under consideration and defines a *legal sequential history*. A *sequential specification* for an object is a prefix-closed set of sequential histories for that object. A sequential history is *legal* if each object subhistory belongs to the *legal sequential specification* for that object. A *linearizable* object is one whose concurrent histories are linearizable with respect to the *legal sequential specification*. The *legal sequential specification* is obviously different for each concurrent data structure.

2.1 Referrer Sets and Object Transplantation

We introduce the notion of "Object Transplantation": from the point of view of an individual object, *any* relocating collector effectively "transplants" the object from one location to another. The transplantation of a single object includes the consistent moving of the object's contents to its to-space location (often referred to as relocation), as well as the replacement of all references to the object's from-space location with correct to-space references (often referred to as fixup). Transplantation of a given object is "complete" when both the contents move and all required reference replacement are complete.

Next, we define two terms for an individual object:

1. Referrer set: identifies the precise set of all object references (in the heap or in thread stacks/registers) that point to the object's location.

2. Conservative Referrer Set: identifies a set of object references (in the heap or in thread stacks/registers) that includes all references in the object's actual referrer set, but may also include other references that do not point to the object.

All relocating collectors transplant objects. Since each object transplantation must reliably correct all references in the object's referrer set before it is complete, the typical relocating collector achieves this reliability by using an extremely conservative global referrer set: a full from-roots traversal of all references in the object space being compacted, usually performed once in order to assure the completion of all object transplantations (e.g. copying collectors [20], or relocate + remap collectors [23, 30]). As a result such collectors only ensure that each object's transplantation is complete at the completion of a full from-roots traversal.

2.2 Constraints for General Concurrent Transplantation

It is useful to consider the key requirements that must be met for correct concurrent transplantation. We start with a general set of constraints that all concurrently transplanting collectors must adhere to. Section 3 will add further constraints to these, needed to support individual object transplantation capabilities. We define the notion of an "object's transplantation state" as:

1. The contents of the object itself.

2. The object's referrer set.

On a timeline, an object's transplantation state encompasses its state from the time it is marked for transplantation until transplantation is complete. In linearizability framework terms, a legal sequential specification for general concurrent transplantation is:

1. Until transplantation is complete, all observable copies of the object contents should remain consistent as specified by the platform's memory model.

2. Once transplantation is complete, no references pointing to the object's from-space location can exist in the object's referrer set.

A sequence of operations that violates this set of rules would result in an incorrect concurrent transplantation algorithm. We believe that all known relocating collectors (concurrent or not) adhere to these two rules. Baker [6] style algorithms, for example, meet all the linearizability requirements by assuring that threads always obtain the to-space pointer to the object and copying the object to the to-space if necessary, as object transplantation is assured to be complete at the end of the copy phase. Since copying is done by the first

---

[1] This includes mostly concurrent compacting collectors such as the Baker collector [6] as well as fully concurrent compacting collectors such as the C4 collector [30].

[2] According to the Java language spec [20], it is not necessary that the writes to different versions of the objects be visible in the same order except in the case of volatile fields. However, ordering of reads and writes to non-volatile fields must still follow the memory model's ordering rules with regards to ordering operations such as crossing synchronization events and volatile access [22].

thread to claim rights to the object while other threads that try to access the object concurrently wait for the copy to complete, the object's observable contents remain consistent. The complete traversal of the reachable references resulting during the copy phase ensures that no object transplantation set will include any from-space references. Another example is the Sapphire collector [20], which allows mutators to observe from-space references, and propagates writes to both versions of the object to make sure that they meet the consistency requirement, and will ensure that no references pointing to from-space locations exist at the end of a compaction phase thereby meeting the second requirement.

3. Individual Transplantation

We introduce the distinction between individually transplantable and non-individually transplantable objects. In contrast to existing relocating collectors, the collector algorithms we introduce in section 5 use individual-object conservative referrer sets, which are significantly less conservative than a complete from-roots traversal. Where such individual conservative referrer sets can be established and maintained, we use them to perform individually complete object transplantations, which can be identified as complete well before the completion of a GC cycle. For the purposes of the new algorithms we describe in this paper, we introduce two additional sets of progressively restrictive requirements:

Heap-stable referrer set limitations: Per-object referrer sets can be established through tracing, so long as they meet and maintain certain requirements. We define a set that includes all heap locations containing references to an individual object and one that remains stable after tracing is complete, as a *heap-stable* set. Such sets, together with the global set of references in all thread stacks and registers, form conservative heap-stable referrer sets. Objects with valid heap-stable referrer sets after the end of the tracing pass are ones which, in addition to general concurrent transplantation limitations (above), adhere to an additional limitation on the legal sequential specification:

1. Once tracing begins, no references to the object may be written to the heap.

For objects that adhere to these limitations, the heap-stable referrer set will remain correctly conservative until the object's transplantation is complete. Objects that fail to adhere to these limitations at any point, from the beginning of tracing to the successful completion of their transplantation, are "hard" to establish a stable per-object conservative referrer set for, and are deemed to be non-individually transplantable.

Stable referrer set limitations: Individual object transplantation can be safely performed on objects that have a stable referrer set for the duration of their transplantation. Objects with a *stable* referrer set are ones which, in addition to heap-stable referrer set limitations, adhere to two additional limitations on the legal sequential specification:

1. At the beginning of transplantation, no thread stack/register references exist in the object's referrer set.

2. Once transplantation of an object begins, no new references may be added to the object's transplantation state until the transplantation completes.

Objects that adhere to these limitations exhibit a stable referrer set and can be individually transplanted in a single, object-specific "transplantation transaction". Since these limitations assure that no mutator can observe or modify the object contents during the transplantation operation, the transplantation state will appear to transition atomically from a pre-transplantation to a post-transplantation state. Objects that fail to adhere to these limitations at any point,

from the beginning of tracing to the successful completion of their transplantation, are deemed to be non-individually transplantable. We discuss this further in section 5.

In order to examine the implication of the legal sequential specification for an individually transplantable object, it is useful to discuss possible sequences of operations to which these rules apply: the operations that affect an object's transplantation state, as well as the operations used to establish "heap-stable referrer sets" (primarily a trace operation). The set of possible operations on are:

1. Trace() : GC thread begins a trace to establish conservative heap-stable referrer sets.

2. Copy(ObjRefFrom, ObjRefTo) : GC thread begins copying object contents from its from space location to its to-space location.

3. UpdateRefs(ObjectFrom, ObjectTo) : GC thread begins to update all references to the object's from-space location to point to the object's to-space location.

4. Transplant(ObjRef) : GC thread begins the transplantation of the object (which consists of Copy() and UpdateRefs() operations).

5. Read/Write(ObjRef) : Java thread begins to read/write contents of an object through a reference to the object.

6. ObjRef=ReadRef(Object) : Java thread begins to read a reference to the object from a heap location.

7. WriteRef(ObjRef) : Java thread begins to write a copy of a reference into a heap location.

8. OK(Operation) : Acknowledgement of successful completion of any of the above operations.

It is important to note that the ReadRef() and the WriteRef() operations both add to the transplantation state of the object, since they create additional references (in the stack or the heap) that point to the object. We now consider a sample heap graph, and will follow with some examples of operation sequences that violate our legal sequential specification. In figure 1, object A is being transplanted to a new location A'. The graph on the left hand side illustrates the object graph prior to transplanting object A. Object B and C have references to object A, while object A has a reference to object D. The pre-transplantation state associated with object A is represented as: $\{A, B_A, C_A\}$. The letter 'A' represents the contents of the object A, while a letter with a sub-script indicates a reference to the object. The post-transplantation state is illustrated on the right

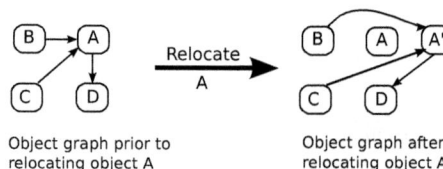

Object graph prior to relocating object A

Relocate A

Object graph after relocating object A

Figure 1. Object Graph Illustrating Object Relocation

hand side of figure 1, The post-transplantation state is represented as: $\{A', B_{A'}, C_{A'}\}$, '). The pre and the post-transplantation states are the only legally observable states according to the sequential specification and all other states are invalid. Note: In our representation, A' indicates a consistent object contents, and inconsistent object contents should not be visible to the mutator threads. Examples of sequences that violate the legal sequential specification for an individually transportable object: Consider a partial sequence of operations: $[..., Transplant(A), Copy(A, A'), stackRefA1 =$

$ReadRef(A), OK(Copy(A, A')), OK(ReadRef(stackRef-$
$A1)),...]$. This sequence violates the legal sequential specification since ReadRef(A) creates an additional reference, $stackRefA1$, to the object A after transplantation begins, thereby violating the stable referrer set limitations above, and rendering object A non-individually transplantable. Similarly the partial sequence listed below, where there is a write to the object being copied (via $stackRefA1$) can result in inconsistent from- and to-copies of the object contents, thereby violating the first condition listed above: $[..., stackRefA1 = ReadRef(A), OK(ReadRef(stackRef-$
$A1)), Transplant(A), Copy(A, A'), Write(stackRefA1),$
$OK(Copy(A, A')), OK(Write(A)), ...]$. Consider this sequence: $[..., stackRefA1 = ReadRef(A), OK(ReadRef(stackRef-$
$A1)), Transplant(A), Copy(A, A'), OK(Copy(A, A')), Up-$
$dateRefs(A, A'), OK(Transplant(A)), Read(stackRefA1),$
$OK(Read(stackRefA1)), ...]$; this is an illegal sequence because the lifetime of stack-reference, $stackRefA1$, spans the transplantation operation, and a reference to the object's from-space location exists after transplantation. On the other hand, the following elaborate sequence involving reads and writes of both object contents and references meets all the limitations for object A to be individually transplantable: $[Trace(), stackRefA1 =$
$ReadRef(A), OK(stackRefA1 = ReadRef(A)), Read(st-$
$ackRefA1), Write(stackRefA1), OK(Read(stackRefA1)),$
$OK(Write(stackRefA1)), OK(Trace()), ReadRef(stack-$
$RefA2), OK(ReadRef(stackRefA2)), Write(stackRef-$
$A2), OK(Write(stackRefA2), Transplant(A), Copy(A, A'),$
$OK(Copy(A, A')), UpdateRefs(A, A'), OK(Transplant(A)),$
$stackRefA1 = ReadRef(A'), OK(ReadRef(stackRefA1)),$
$Read(stackRefA1), Write(stackRefA1), WriteRef(stack-$
$RefA1), ...]$

4. Barrier-Free Compaction

We focus our discussion here primarily on concurrent compaction, since concurrent marking is widely discussed [12, 14, 15, 30], and we believe that a highly performant, wait-free, and precise wavefront concurrent marker is essentially a solved problem with the C4's single-pass marker [30]. We now propose a completely barrier-free algorithm to individually transplant a specific object using a transplantation transaction. This barrier-free algorithm is not meant to be practical in cost or implementation. Instead, we will build on it by adding appropriate barriers and other mechanisms to describe the full Collie collector algorithm in later sections. We build on the notion of the transplantation state of the object. For the sake of discussion, we assume that the current and precise transplantation state of the object is available to the barrier-free collector when it starts to relocate the object. This implies that at that point in time, the version of the object reflects the consistent application state of the object contents, as per the runtime's memory model, and that the referrer set has precise information about all references to the object. We also assume that the referrer set includes only references that reside in the heap, and that no references to the object exist in any mutator thread stacks/registers. For now, we have:

- a current and consistent version of the object contents.

- a precise referrer set to the object, that includes addresses of all the heap pointers to the object.

The collector starts the transplantation transaction, copies the object contents to its to-space location and updates all references in the referrer set to point to the to-space location of the object. Committing the transaction at this point would publish the pointers to the to-space version of the object and transplantation would be "complete". In order for this "commit" to be correct, the following must remain true:

- ReadRef() operations should not occur concurrently with a committed transplantation transaction.

- Write() and WriteRef() operations should not occur concurrently with the transplantation transaction if the writes could result in an inconsistent copy being created by the transaction.

These transaction rules could obviously be enforced by a simple (but expensive) lock scheme, where the transplantation transaction, mutator ReadRef() operations, and mutator Write() and WriteRef() operations all use a lock on the object's from-space copy to synchronize their operations, but such locking would constitute barriers on these mutator operations. We base our algorithm on the use of an Azul style implicit transactional-memory implementation [11], where all memory accesses are implicitly considered transactional once the transaction is started with a transaction-start operation and are committed atomically using a transaction-commit operation. The transaction fails on potentially inconsistent concurrent writes to the transaction data set and vectors to a transaction failure-handler routine. Concurrent reads of a transaction's "read" data set do not terminate the transaction. Inconsistent concurrent reads of memory locations that are written to inside the transaction will result in a transaction failure.

Using these implicit transactional-memory semantics, the collector starts a memory transaction, "protects" the referrer set by writing to each of its references within the transaction, copies the object to its new location and updates the elements in the referrer set to point to the new location of the object. Committing the transaction at this point will publish both the to-space object contents and the reference values that point to the to-space location of the object, completing the transplantation.

However, there is a window between the time the object is marked for transplantation and the point in the transaction where each member of the referrer set has been protected by being written to within the transaction. Within this time window, the referrer set is not protected and ReadRef() operations can expand the referrer set without failing the transaction. To avoid this, we start the transaction inside a global safepoint, and establish protection of the referrer set before allowing threads to continue past the safepoint.

Once allowed to run past the safepoint, mutator ReadRef() operations that happen concurrently with the transaction will abort the transaction, since the read is of one of the elements of the referrer set which belongs to the transaction's already-established write set. Since the mutator cannot obtain a reference to the object before the transaction completes without failing the transaction, concurrent reads or writes of the object's contents will also implicitly fail the transaction.

In essence, this algorithm requires a stop-the-world phase that builds a precise referrer set for the object and protects it within the starting transaction. Once the referrer set is established and protected, the remaining parts of the transplantation transaction can be executed and committed concurrently since the implicit transaction semantics protect the transaction data set, including the referrer set. In the barrier-free compactor, such a safepoint would be for every object we wish to relocate, making it quite impractical. Figure 2 reflects the pseudo-code for relocating a single object in the barrier-free algorithm.

```
Start Safepoint.
Build Precise Referrer Set For Object.
Start Transaction
Protect Referrer set by writing to it.
End Safepoint
Relocate Object: Copy & Update Referrer Set
End Transaction
```

Figure 2. Barrier-Free Compaction

There are some key takeaways from this version of the algorithm:

- Barriers are not necessary during concurrent transplantation as long as the update of the referrer set and the object copy of the object contents are performed within a transaction.

- ReadRef() operations can pollute the referrer set outside of the transaction and need to be tracked or prevented. This can be done using either safepoints or barrier mechanisms.

5. The Collie Collector Algorithm

We introduce the Collie Collector: a wait-free compacting collector that uses bounded cost read and write barriers combined with transactional operation to achieve concurrent, individual object transplantation. The Collie collector builds on the barrier-free compacting collector described in the previous section. It uses a concurrent wait-free tracer (performed as part of a C4-style [30] concurrent mark phase) along with a transactional transplantation phase to establish conservative, stable referrer sets. The collector develops conservative referrer sets for the vast majority of objects in the heap in a single tracing pass, relegating other objects to be transplanted into a newly introduced non-compacted *mirrored-to-space* using *zero-copy transplantation*. Collie replaces the requirement for a global safepoint in the barrier-free compacting collector with a combination of an enhanced LVB-style read barrier [30], a write barrier, a checkpoint operation [12], a copy operation, and a transactional transplantation operation.

5.1 Mirrored-to-space and Zero-copy Transplantation

Before we identify the various mechanisms listed above as a replacement for the global safepoint, we introduce the notion of the "mirrored-to-space". The mirrored-to-space is a virtual address space that is identical in size to the from-space. Each from-space page is mapped or aliased to the same physical address as a corresponding mirrored-to-space page. A simple form of a mirrored-to-space is one where a single high order bit differs between addresses in each mirrored-to-space page and its corresponding from-space page and where mirrored-to-space pages differ in this bit setting from all non-mirrored parts of the to-space. This form makes it easy to identify mirrored-to-space pages, and allows for easy "flipping" of roles between from-space and mirrored-to-space at the end of each GC cycle. The mirrored-to-space is logically considered part of to-space for mutator invariant and barrier test purposes, but is easily distinguished from "regular" to-space by operations that need to make such distinctions.

The purpose of the mirrored-to-space is to facilitate the *zero-copy, non-compacting transplantation* of objects from from-space to to-space. Since the object contents is inherently consistent across from-space object locations and their corresponding mirrored-to-space locations, such transplantation only requires the correcting of references pointing to the from-space location such that they point to the mirrored-to-space. This can be done in a straight forward manner using wait-free, bounded, and relatively cheap read barrier operations that easily fold into the LVB-style read barrier used by the Collie collector.

The Collie will attempt to individually transplant the vast majority of objects in the heap, compacting pages from which all objects were individually transplanted. However, the Collie is an aborting relocating collector and will abort the individual transplantation of objects that fail to meet the legal sequential specification limitations for stable referrer sets. Leaving such aborted objects in the from-space will break the to-space invariant, unnecessarily complicate the self-healing LVB-style read barrier, and increase its cost both statically and dynamically. Instead, the Collie performs a global (as opposed to individual) transplantation of all objects that fail to be individually transplanted, to their corresponding mirrored-to-space virtual addresses. Unlike typical global transplantation, no object copying operations are required for mirrored-to-space transplantation, making the transplantation no more costly for the mutator than concurrent mark.

5.2 Mutator Protocol

The mutator protocol includes a write-barrier and a read-barrier, as well as the implicit ability of each thread to individually come to a safepoint where the stack and registers can be scanned.

Write-Barrier: The Collie write-barrier intercepts all stores of references to the heap, identifying any object to which such references point as "non-individually transplantable" by setting a "not relocatable" bit associated with the object's location. *The Collie write barrier directly satisfies the limitation required by heap-stable referrer sets*, thereby allowing the collector to reliably identify and use heap-stable referrer sets in a wait-free manner, without requiring a global safepoint[3].

Read-Barrier: The Collie collector uses an LVB-style read barrier which intercepts all reference loads from the heap. The LVB-style barrier is used to support both the concurrent tracer (in a manner similar to the C4 [30] concurrent mark phase, not discussed here), as well as Collie's concurrent compaction. Once the transplantation phase starts, the Collie read barrier ensures that any load of a heap reference that observes a from-space reference will attempt to atomically replace the from-space reference value in the heap with a mirrored-to-space reference value and then reload the reference from the heap location. Figure 3 shows the pseudo-code for the read-barrier trap handler. If the barrier succeeds in replacing the reference value in the heap, it has effectively atomically identified the object as "non-individually transplantable"[4]. *The Collie read barrier directly satisfies the second limitation required by stable referrer sets as per section 3*. Combined with the write barrier and the pre-compaction checkpoint this quality allows the Collie to reliably establish and use stable referrer sets in both a cheap and wait-free manner, without requiring a global safepoint.

```
triggered_read_barrier_handler(address, oldValue) {
    mirror = mirror(oldValue)
    AtomicCompareAndSwap(address, oldValue, mirror);
    return *address
}
```

Figure 3. Pseudo-code for read-barrier trap code

6. The Collector Protocol

The Collie collector operates in two phases: *the mark-record* phase and the *transplantation* phase. There is no separate "fixup" phase and there is also no need to store forwarding pointers. The referrer set is essentially a per-object remembered set and is constructed during the mark phase which already involves walking through the entire heap graph.

---

[3] While the write barrier will identify the object that the reference being written is pointing to as non-individually transplantable, it does not do so for the object that the overwritten reference was pointing to. As a result, a reference write may shrink a precise referrer set without recording the shrinking, making the previously established members of the referrer set conservative (they may be pointing to other objects). The conservative set remains correct, as it is inclusive of the precise set.

[4] If the replacement failed and the value had changed from the originally observed from-space reference, the newly loaded reference value is guaranteed to be a valid to-space reference, installed by a racing mutator or by a collector transplantation.

6.1 Mark-Record Phase:

The mark-record phase traces through all live objects in the heap, and serves the dual purpose of identifying the live objects as well as constructing per-object *heap-stable referrer sets*. The marking part of the algorithm is identical to that of the C4 collector [30]; we don't reiterate it here, focusing instead on the changes necessary for building the per-object heap-stable referrer sets.

The mark routine is overloaded to build the per-object heap-stable referrer set; when the mark routine reaches a "live" object as part of the heap graph walk, it already has the address of the referrer's reference field pointing to the object. Referrer set sizes can be capped at a static size, with objects that have more references than can fit in a referrer set being deemed "non-individually transplantable". The first time a referrer to an object is found, a referrer set is allocated and associated with the object. Objects that have more references pointing to them than can fit in a size-capped referrer set, or fail to allocate a referrer set, are deemed as "popular" objects and are identified as "non-individually transplantable" by setting a "not-relocatable" state associated with the object's location. Similar state can also be stored in the object header, and can be separately tracked to affect per-page relocation decisions[5].

At the end of marking, the heap-stable referrer set for each object includes, in addition to the per-object referrer set, the set of all mutator stacks and registers. A stack-scanning operation would still be required in order to qualify a heap-stable referrer set as a stable referrer set that includes only heap references.

This straightforward tracking of referrer sets has obvious memory overheads. Since the referrer set is nothing more than a per-object remembered set, one can think of various compact representations of the referrer set that would allow convenient access at transplantation time. From empirical studies we know that most objects have only one or two references pointing to them, and as a result, we expect size-capping to be very effective in containing memory overhead. Similarly to other aborting relocators such as Staccato collector [7] and the Chicken collector [26], avoiding transplantation of popular objects could potentially prevent some significant portion of the heap from being compacted. Empirically, popular objects make up a very small percentage of the live set for most applications. Not relocating popular objects could have some benefits as well, as noted in [15]. We discuss a workaround for the degenerate cases where the popular objects form a significant percentage of the live set.

6.2 The Transplantation Phase:

The concurrent transplantation phase copies live objects to the to-space and eliminates references to from-space, allowing the from-space to be reclaimed. The collector compacts at a page granularity and uses the quick release technique [30] that allows it to free the physical memory backing each from-space page before references to it are eliminated, assuming it was able to copy all the live objects from the source page to the target page.

At the start of the transplantation phase the collector knows of a set of pages that are currently relocatable as well as a set of the per-object currently heap-stable referrer sets. The transplantation phase will individually transplant objects for which it can successfully

maintain stable referrer sets. Objects that fail to be individually transplanted will be transplanted to the mirrored-to-space by the end of the GC cycle.

Collie's flavor of LVB-style read barrier serves two simultaneous functions: it assures that completed transplantation transactions are done using qualified stable referrer sets and supports the concurrent relocation of non-individually-transplantable into mirrored-to-space.

6.2.1 Pre-Compaction Checkpoint

In order to perform individual object transplantation, the transplantation phase needs to establish and maintain a stable referrer set for each individually transplanted object. The already established heap-stable referrer sets include all references in the thread stacks and registers. The pre-compaction checkpoint establishes these stable referrer sets by scanning the roots and designating any object that they directly refer to as "non-individually transplantable". The scanning of individual thread stacks is done in a checkpoint [12] without requiring a global safepoint. The pre-compaction checkpoint also arms the LVB-style read barrier, so that it will trigger on any load of a reference to a page that was currently relocatable at the start of the checkpoint.

At the end of the checkpoint, all objects that remain individually transplantable now have currently stable referrer sets. Any attempt to add references to such an object's transplantation state will render it non-individually transplantable. Thus, the pre-compaction checkpoint, combined with the read barrier's behavior directly satisfy the first limitation of *stable referrer sets*.

6.2.2 Concurrent Compaction

Once the collector establishes stable referrer sets and a set of individually transplantable objects using the concurrent tracer and the pre-compaction checkpoint, the Collie collector uses transactional operations to complete individual object transplantations. Each individual object transplantation starts by copying the object's contents of an individually transplantable object to a to-space location. The copying of object contents does not need to occur within a transaction because no mutator access to individually transplantable object contents can occur after the pre-compaction checkpoint without rendering the object "non-individually transplantable". The collector uses transactional memory to update the referrer set:

1. A memory transaction is started. All memory accesses from this point until the transaction completes are done atomically with respect to other threads in the system.

2. Each reference in the currently stable referrer set is checked to verify that the reference does not currently point to the mirror virtual address of the object being transplanted. If any of the references fail this test, the transaction is aborted.

3. Each reference in the currently stable referrer set which points to the object's from-space location is replaced with a reference to the object's to-space location.

4. The memory transaction is committed.

The object transplantation is successful and complete when transaction commit succeeds. If the transaction fails or aborts for any reason, the object is rendered non-individually transplantable.

Upon a successful individual transplantation the collector updates the stable referrer sets of any individually transplantable objects pointed to from the newly relocated object. This maintains the integrity of referrer sets that include references from this object. These referrer-set updates only need to be synchronized against collector activity, and not against the mutator.

---

[5] Compaction is performed at page granularity. While we are able to individually transplant the rest of the objects from a heap page that has a single "non-individually transplantable" object, the from-space page's physical resources cannot be freed if there are any objects in its corresponding mirrored-to-space page. For this reason and as an optimization, tracing can mark pages with "popular" objects in them as "not-relocatable" such that no compaction would be attempted on them in the compaction phase. In some cases, it may be desirable to still allow other objects to be individually transplanted away from some popular pages in order to increase the likelihood of the page being fully compacted in the future

Through a combination of constraints applied by the LVB-style read barrier, the pre-compaction checkpoint, and the transplantation transaction, successful transactional transplantation operations are known to have satisfied all required limitations of stable and heap-stable referrer sets. They therefore result in correct, safe, and wait-free individual object transplantation.

Individually transplanted objects do not require a fixup phase, as each successful transplantation transaction has, by definition, already fixed all references to these objects. However, in order to complete the zero-copying transplantation of non-individually transplantable objects (to the mirrored to-space), the collector still needs to perform a full from-roots fixup traversal. Read-barriers are self-healing, no copying operations are involved, and all read barriers encountered by the mutator on not-yet-corrected references are both bound and "cheap". There is therefore no hurry to perform this traversal. Much like C4 [30], Collie simply rolls this fixup traversal into the next mark phase.

The collector invariant at the end of attempting to relocate an object is: *"all referrers to that object switch to using either the mirrored-to-space reference to the object or the to-space reference to the object".*

7. Discussion and Implementation

The Collie collector is a concurrent compacting collector based on the notion of an individual object's transplantation state. While an object's transplantation state includes the object's contents as well as all references to it, the collector requires only the atomic update of each individual object referrer set when relocating the object to a new location, and allows object contents to be copied non-atomically. Collie relies on transactional memory techniques to implement the atomic state transitions across multiple heap addresses. The transactional memory use is very constrained since only an individual object's referrer set gets updated inside each transaction, and the common individual object referrer set has few elements in it. This results in a high percentage of successful transactions and makes the algorithm amenable even for restricted capacity implementations of multi-address atomicity such as multi-word-CAS [1, 17].

The use of transactional memory on the collector side simplifies the mutator's triggered read-barrier handling code to a single atomic CAS followed by an unconditional read, thereby bounding the read barrier cost. The algorithm does not require any stop-the-world pauses; only checkpoints are needed to ensure coordination with the mutator.

The aborting read-barrier can potentially cause GC-induced fragmentation. This happens when a read-barrier aborts the copy of an object in a page that has been partially compacted by the collector. The collector can't reclaim the original source page or the target page. This however tends to be a rare event since the working-set of an application is a small fraction of the live-set, and the working-set generally correlates fairly closely with the root-set, which the collector doesn't attempt to relocate. This is similar to the issue faced by the Staccato collector [7] and their suggested solution of increasing page density of these pages will work for us as well.

As described, the Collie algorithm is a full-heap collector. However, it can easily be extended to be generational along the lines of C4 [30], which shares its key barrier and synchronization techniques. While generational collection is an almost absolute requirement for a production quality garbage collector on modern hardware, incorporating one into the Collie is orthogonal to our work.

The algorithm is i,mplemented in the production quality Azul JVM [12]. While the algorithm is truly concurrent and does not require any global safepoints, our current implementation does rely on safepoints due to practical runtime concerns, e.g. system-dictionary scanning, class unloading, monitor deflation etc.

8. Evaluation

The Collie algorithm aims to be a high throughput collector that maintains consistent response times. The wait-free, constant time, aborting read-barrier is one of the key elements of the collector that allows the application to maintain response times that are within the SLA requirements. The collector also avoids relocating the working-set of the application, thereby reducing the application exposure to jitter inducing barrier triggers. We intend to evaluate and confirm that the collector is able to provide high responsiveness while at the same time being able to sustain high throughput.

The collector has some unique facets such as the individual object referrer set and the property of not relocating the root-set and the popular-set. It also shares the aborting nature of the read-barrier with other collectors such as Staccato [7] and Chicken [26]. We evaluate the effect of these design choices to ensure that they do not adversely affect the collector's ability to perform its primary function, which is to recycle memory. We use a set of standard benchmarks for our experiments: the SPECjvm98 [29] suite, the Dacapo [8] suite, and the SPECjbb2000 benchmark [29]. We run all our tests on an Azul Systems Vega-3 model 7340 appliance– an 8-socket (432-core) appliance with 384GB of physical memory [2]. We compare all our results to a modified version of Pauseless collector [12], a full heap collector running in a single-threaded mode. This allows us to make an apples-to-apples comparison, since both collectors were implemented inside the same JVM, are single-threaded, are full heap collectors, use the same LVB style read barrier (although the triggered barrier code differs), have identical heuristics that determine when GC cycles are triggered and run on the same hardware. This gives us a unique opportunity to shed light on the performance differential resulting from features that are unique to the Collie collector as compared to the Pauseless Collector. We evaluate the behavior of Collie collector's unique properties in section 8.1, and follow that with an evaluation of Collie's latency 8.2 and throughput 8.3 behaviors.

8.1 Evaluating The Collector Properties

The Collie collector builds a per-object referrer set which is then atomically updated during object transplantation. Objects that are referred to by more references than can be tracked by the referrer set allotted for the object are deemed "popular". Pages containing popular objects are deemed popular-pages and are not compacted. The space allotted for object referrer sets directly affects the percentage of popular objects, thereby affecting the percentage of objects transplanted by the Collie collector. The space allotted for object referrer sets also has an effect on the percentage of aborted transplantations, as more popular objects are more likely to experience transplantation aborting accesses. Larger per-object referrer sets allow the collector to compact more of the heap, thereby exposing it to more aborts as well.

The aggregate effective space overhead needed for referrer set storage will depend on the specific mechanisms chosen to implement per-object referrer sets. Efficient mechanisms are possible, in which storage requirements would be approximated by the number of actual non-null references in the heap that do not point to popular objects. Similarly, the global space allotted can be easily capped. We do not explore specific referrer set storage mechanisms in this paper. Instead, we study the effects of capping individual object referrer set sizes on the % of garbage collected, popular pages, and pages aborted; independent of how the referrer set itself is implemented. Our implementation allows us to place an arbitrary cap on individual object referrer set size. We vary the size of this cap in our experiments and measure the effects on the collector properties we present.

Figure 4 plots the amount of garbage reclaimed by the collector at varying referrer set cap sizes. The amount of garbage reclaimed is represented as a percentage of the garbage found. As expected, the result show that increasing the size of the referrer set allows the collector to reclaim more garbage. The percentage of memory reclaimed seems to top off for a referrer set size of 4 words. For most of the benchmarks run, the largest improvement in the amount of garbage reclaimed occurs when varying the cap size from 1 to 2 tracked references. A referrer set size of 2 tracked references allows Collie to reclaim over 80% of the garbage found in most cases.

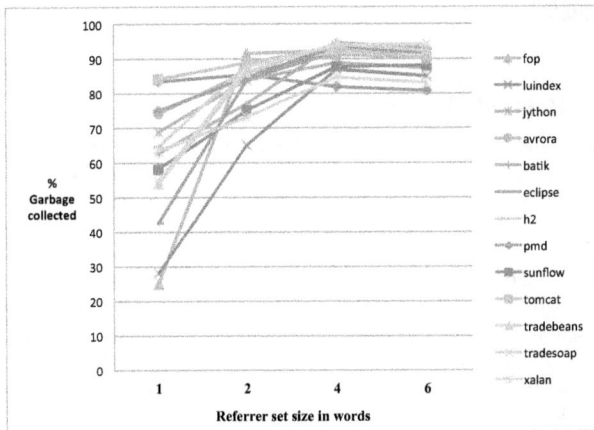

Figure 4. % of Garbage collected versus referrer set size

Figure 5 plots the percentage of popular pages at varying referrer set cap sizes. The percentage of popular pages is computed from the ratio between the number of popular pages and the size of the set of all pages that contain live object. This ratio is not dependent on heap size. As expected, the percentage of popular pages drops as the referrer set cap size increases. The largest reduction in popular page percentage occurs when varying the cap size from 1 to 2 tracked references.

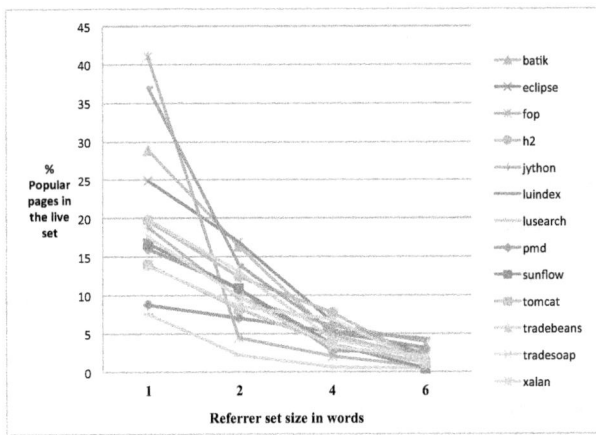

Figure 5. % of Popular pages versus referrer set size

It is interesting to correlate figures 4 and 5. For the smaller referrer set cap sizes of 1 or 2 tracked references, Collie shows a high percentage of popular pages but at the same time is able to reclaim a high percentage of the garbage found. This implies that popular pages are relatively dense in the tests performed, and the live set mostly resides in these pages. Thus the collector would not benefit as much from relocating these pages.

The Collie collector's use of an aborting read barrier has the side effect of creating GC induced fragmentation in non compacted pages. It is important to measure the percentage of pages that had have their compaction aborted. Figure 6 plots the percentage of pages that had their compaction aborted due to mutator interference at varying cap sizes. The percentage of pages aborted is computed from the ratio between the number of aborted pages and the number of pages selected for compaction by the collector. The results indicates a steady, slow growth in the percentage of aborted page-compactions as the per-object referrer size cap increases. This is expected since larger referrer sets imply a higher chance for collision with mutator activity. The percentage of pages aborted still remains a small percentage even at referrer set size cap of 6, allowing the collector to successfully reclaim most of the garbage found.

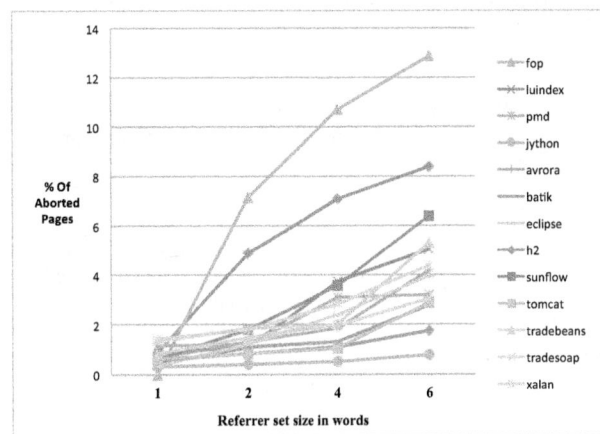

Figure 6. % of Aborted pages versus referrer set size

All runs were performed with a 512MB heap and the GC heuristic set to run continuous, back-to-back GC cycles. The back-to-back collections make our results relatively insensitive to heap size. We experienced variance of less than +/- 3% across a wide range of heap sizes and runs.

8.2 Latency Evaluation

Collie's main goal is to provide high mutator responsiveness during compaction. We measure the minimum mutator utilization (MMU) metric [5] to demonstrate application responsiveness. We compare Collie to the Pauseless [12] collector. Since the implementations of both collectors use a similar marking algorithm and identical phase transitions, we focus our measurements on the MMU achieved specifically during the concurrent compaction phase, as MMU effects during other collection phases are identical for the two collectors. MMU for the Pauseless collector has been studied elsewhere [12, 30].

Table 1 indicates the MMU percentages for compaction phases of the Collie and Pauseless collectors over various time windows ranging from 1ms to 200ms. Each column contain two values, the first reflects the MMU for the Collie collector for the given time window while the second number reflects the same metric for the Pauseless collector. The SPECjvm98 benchmarks were all run with 128M heap, while DaCapo benchmarks were run with a 512M heap size. As expected, the Collie collector shows improved MMU across the entire range of time window sizes, with improvements becoming more significant as the MMU time window size

Benchmark	at 1ms	at 5ms	at 20ms	at 50ms	at 100ms	at 200ms
compress	94/21	96/66	98/87	98/95	99/96	98/98
jess	85/35	95/56	98/68	99/77	99/85	99/92
raytrace	88/45	92/65	96/87	99/82	99/93	99/95
db	91/21	94/41	96/47	98/50	99/57	97/69
javac	87/24	93/56	98/71	99/79	99/86	99/88
mtrt	89/44	92/64	96/86	99/92	99/95	99/99
mpegaudio	87/45	90/66	92/87	99/92	99/95	99/97
batik	73/32	84/49	89/77	92/86	97/92	99/96
fop	78/21	85/31	88/62	92/79	96/82	99/84
luindex	84/39	92/80	96/94	98/97	99/98	99/99
sunflow	82/26	88/54	95/74	96/88	97/94	98/97
tomcat	80/0	86/29	93/73	98/83	92/92	99/95
lusearch	81/26	83/52	86/77	91/87	96/94	99/97
xalan	80/22	86/39	89/64	94/72	97/82	99/87
pmd	78/32	81/45	83/59	87/69	92/72	93/88
eclipse	70/16	82/43	84/49	87/58	89/75	92/82
h2	76/23	83/47	81/52	88/69	90/78	93/83
tradebeans	79/29	87/43	86/74	91/83	96/94	99/97
tradesoap	81/23	86/48	86/69	93/79	97/92	98/96

Table 1. MMU % at different time windows for the Collie/Pauseless collector

Collection Algorithm	SPECjbb2000	SPECjvm98	DaCapo
Pauseless collector	1.0x	1.0x	1.0x
Collie collector	1.15x	1.12x	1.09x

Table 2. Aggregate throughput comparison

Benchmark	at 1ms	at 5ms	at 20ms	at 50ms	at 100ms	at 200ms
SPECJbb2000	81/22	86/45	89/64	91/80	95/81	96/83
SPECjvm98	88/33	93/59	96/76	98/81	99/86	98/91
DaCapo	78/24	85/46	88/68	92/80	94/87	97/91

Table 3. Aggregate MMU % at different time windows for the Collie/Pauseless collector

decreases. We believe that these improvements are primarily attributable to the aborting read barrier and the Collie collector's tendency to not transplant the "working-set" of the application.

8.3 Throughput Evaluation

The focus of this paper is on compaction, and specifically on wait-free compaction behavior. As such the latency behavior and MMU metrics of the new algorithm's compaction phase, described in section 8.2, are the main focus of our evaluation. The purpose of the throughput comparison in this section is to provide a sanity check for application throughout during compaction. While our measurements show that Collie improved the overall throughput during compaction when compared to Pauseless [12], it is important to note that our focus with Collie was not on improving the throughput of either the collector or the mutator through wait-free compaction. Such improvements are simply an interesting but expected side effect of the lower read barrier triggering rates and the reduced mutator work on triggered barriers.

We use SPECJbb2000 [29], DaCapo [8], and SPECjvm98 [29] benchmarks to specifically compare application throughput during the compaction phases of the Collie and the Pauseless [12] collectors. In order to do this, we modified the heuristics for both the collectors so that we trigger continuous, back-to-back GC cycles, and changed both collectors to use stop-the-world mark phases. With these changes, we ensure that productive benchmark work is only performed during concurrent compaction, and is unaffected by marking, thus allowing us to make a normalized comparison of the application throughput during compaction.

The back-to-back collections and stop-the-world marker, measurement techniques make both throughput and MMU results relatively insensitive to heap size. We experienced variance of less than +/- 3% across a wide range of heap sizes and runs. The results presented for SPECjbb2000 runs used 32 warehouses and a 30G heap. The results presented for the DaCapo and SPECjvm98 benchmarks were obtained with a 512MB heap.

Table 2 shows the relative application throughput during compaction phase of the Collie collector when compared to the Pauseless collector. As we would expect with lower read barrier triggering rates and cheaper triggered-barrier work, the Collie collector improves on this metric. For reference, Table 3 shows the MMU for different time windows for the two collectors during concurrent compaction. As with the results detailed in section 8.2, the Collie collector shows consistently better MMU than the Pauseless collector for these runs.

9. Related Work

Cheng and Blelloch [10], designed and implemented a concurrent copying garbage collection with a bounded response time for a modern platform and also formalized the notion of minimum mutator utilization(MMU). The Staccato collector [7] is the closest to our work in that it uses an aborting read-barrier to obtain a lock-free mutator behavior. However, Staccato is strongly tied to a Brooks' style barrier, an indirection barrier that suffers from the cost of an extra indirection in the mutator fast-path and requires an extra word in the object header. The Collie algorithm is technically agnostic to the flavor of the read barrier and could be used with a Brooks style barrier; however, the benefits of direct object access in the mutator fast-path with a LVB-style healing barrier are hard to overlook. Compressor [23] is a concurrent compacting collector that uses page protection techniques to achieve concurrent compaction but can suffer from significant trap storms and operating system overheads. Variations of the Azul collectors [12, 30], have been shipping in commercial systems for several years, and have focused on addressing the issue of scaling to modern memory and compute capacities while maintaining consistent response times through the use of concurrent compaction. Collie's improvement in MMU behavior compared to Pauseless shows promise in bringing concurrent collection into lower latency and even more latency-sensitive domains. The use of transactional memory in GC algorithms is relatively new; [24] is a modified version of the Sapphire collector that relies on software transactional memory to make sure that concurrent updates to the object being relocated are not lost. We believe that Collie is the first garbage collector to leverage hardware assisted transactional memory.

10. Conclusion & Future Work

The Collie collector is a concurrent compacting collector that leverages transactional memory and uses a wait-free aborting read barrier. This work breaks new ground in several ways itemized in section 1, but most importantly it represents the first collector to directly leverage hardware-assisted transactional memory, and to achieve wait-free mutator behavior during concurrent compaction by doing so. With hardware assisted transactional memory poised to become a commodity feature and widely available in servers within a year or two, Collie demonstrates that core issues in managed runtime scalability and responsiveness can be addressed using this new capability. We believe that Collie only scratches the surface of the potential for using transactional memory for systemic managed runtime benefits. Future work includes applying Collie in a generational collection environment and applying Collie to commodity server environments as they become available. The newly introduced concepts of individual object referrer sets and individually transplantable objects can be studied in further detail, and additional uses may be found in other garbage collection algorithms and even in areas outside of garbage collection.

References

[1] AMD Corp. Advanced Synchronization Facility. http://developer.amd.com/tools/ASF/Pages/default.aspx, 2009.

[2] Azul Systems Inc. Vega 3 Processor. http://www.azulsystems.com/products/vega/processor, 2005.

[3] D. F. Bacon, P. Cheng, and V. T. Rajan. A real-time garbage collector with low overhead and consistent utilization. In *Proceedings of the 30th ACM SIGPLAN-SIGACT Symposium on Principles of Programming Languages*, POPL '03, New York, NY, USA, 2003. ACM. ISBN 1-58113-628-5. URL http://doi.acm.org/10.1145/604131.604155.

[4] D. F. Bacon, P. Cheng, and V. T. Rajan. A real-time garbage collector with low overhead and consistent utilization. In *Proceedings of the 30th ACM SIGPLAN-SIGACT symposium on Principles of programming languages*, POPL '03, pages 285–298, New York, NY, USA, 2003. ACM. URL http://doi.acm.org/10.1145/604131.604155.

[5] D. F. Bacon, P. Cheng, and V. T. Rajan. A real-time garbage collector with low overhead and consistent utilization. In *Proceedings of the 30th ACM SIGPLAN-SIGACT symposium on Principles of programming languages*, POPL '03, pages 285–298, New York, NY, USA, 2003. ACM. URL http://doi.acm.org/10.1145/604131.604155.

[6] H. G. Baker, Jr. List processing in real time on a serial computer. *Commun. ACM*, 21:280–294, April 1978. ISSN 0001-0782. URL http://doi.acm.org/10.1145/359460.359470.

[7] P. C. Bill McCloskey, David F. Bacon and D. Grove. Staccato: A parallel and concurrent real-time compacting garbage collector for multiprocessors. In *IBM Research Report RC24505*, pages 285–298. IBM Research, 2008.

[8] S. M. Blackburn, R. Garner, C. Hoffman, A. M. Khan, K. S. McKinley, R. Bentzur, A. Diwan, D. Feinberg, D. Frampton, S. Z. Guyer, M. Hirzel, A. Hosking, M. Jump, H. Lee, J. E. B. Moss, A. Phansalkar, D. Stefanović, T. VanDrunen, D. von Dincklage, and B. Wiedermann. The DaCapo benchmarks: Java benchmarking development and analysis. In *OOPSLA '06: Proceedings of the 21st annual ACM SIGPLAN conference on Object-Oriented Programing, Systems, Languages, and Applications*, pages 169–190, New York, NY, USA, Oct. 2006. ACM Press.

[9] R. A. Brooks. Trading data space for reduced time and code space in real-time garbage collection on stock hardware. In *Proceedings of the 1984 ACM Symposium on LISP and functional programming*, LFP '84, pages 256–262, New York, NY, USA, 1984. ACM. ISBN 0-89791-142-3. URL http://doi.acm.org/10.1145/800055.802042.

[10] P. Cheng and G. E. Blelloch. A parallel, real-time garbage collector. In *Proceedings of the ACM SIGPLAN 2001 conference on Programming language design and implementation*, PLDI '01, pages 125–136, New York, NY, USA, 2001. ACM. ISBN 1-58113-414-2. doi: 10.1145/378795.378823. URL http://doi.acm.org/10.1145/378795.378823.

[11] J. Choquette, G. Tene, and K. Normoyle. Speculative multiaddress atomicity, 2006. US Patent 7,376,800.

[12] C. Click, G. Tene, and M. Wolf. The Pauseless GC algorithm. In *Proceedings of the 1st ACM/USENIX International Conference on Virtual Execution Environments*, VEE '05, pages 46–56, New York, NY, USA, 2005. ACM. ISBN 1-59593-047-7. URL http://doi.acm.org/10.1145/1064979.1064988.

[13] P. Damron, A. Fedorova, Y. Lev, V. Luchangco, M. Moir, and D. Nussbaum. Hybrid transactional memory. In *Proceedings of the 12th international conference on Architectural support for programming languages and operating systems*, ASPLOS-XII, pages 336–346, New York, NY, USA, 2006. ACM.

[14] D. Detlefs and T. Printezis. A Generational Mostly-concurrent Garbage Collector. Technical report, Mountain View, CA, USA, 2000.

[15] D. Detlefs, C. Flood, S. Heller, and T. Printezis. Garbage-first garbage collection. In *Proceedings of the 4th International Symposium on Memory Management*, ISMM '04, pages 37–48, New York, NY, USA, 2004. ACM. ISBN 1-58113-945-4. URL http://doi.acm.org/10.1145/1029873.1029879.

[16] R. H. et al. The ibm blue gene/q compute chip. *Micro, EEE*, 32(2):48 –60, march-april 2012. ISSN 0272-1732. doi: 10.1109/MM.2011.108.

[17] T. L. Harris, K. Fraser, and I. A. Pratt. A practical multi-word compare-and-swap operation. In *In Proceedings of the 16th International Symposium on Distributed Computing*, pages 265–279. Springer-Verlag, 2002.

[18] M. Herlihy and J. E. B. Moss. Transactional memory: architectural support for lock-free data structures. In *Proceedings of the 20th annual international symposium on computer architecture*, ISCA '93, pages 289–300, New York, NY, USA, 1993. ACM. URL http://doi.acm.org/10.1145/165123.165164.

[19] M. P. Herlihy and J. M. Wing. Linearizability: a correctness condition for concurrent objects. *ACM Trans. Program. Lang. Syst.*, 12:463–492, July 1990. ISSN 0164-0925. URL http://doi.acm.org/10.1145/78969.78972.

[20] R. L. Hudson and J. E. B. Moss. Sapphire: copying gc without stopping the world. In *Proceedings of the 2001 joint ACM-ISCOPE conference on Java Grande*, JGI '01, pages 48–57, New York, NY, USA, 2001. ACM. URL http://doi.acm.org/10.1145/376656.376810.

[21] Intel Inc. Intel Architecture Instruction Set Extensions Programming Reference. http://software.intel.com/file/41604, 2012.

[22] JCP. JSR 166: Concurrency Utilities. http://jcp.org/en/jsr/detail?id=166, 2010.

[23] H. Kermany and E. Petrank. The Compressor: concurrent, incremental, and parallel compaction. In *Proceedings of the 2006 ACM SIGPLAN conference on Programming Language Design and Implementation*, PLDI '06, pages 354–363, New York, NY, USA, 2006. ACM. ISBN 1-59593-320-4. URL http://doi.acm.org/10.1145/1133981.1134023.

[24] P. McGachey, A.-R. Adl-Tabatabai, R. L. Hudson, V. Menon, B. Saha, and T. Shpeisman. Concurrent gc leveraging transactional memory. In *Proceedings of the 13th ACM SIGPLAN Symposium on Principles and practice of parallel programming*, PPoPP '08, pages 217–226, New York, NY, USA, 2008. ACM. URL http://doi.acm.org/10.1145/1345206.1345238.

[25] S. C. North and J. H. Reppy. Concurrent garbage collection on stock hardware. In *Proc. of a conference on Functional programming languages and computer architecture*, pages 113–133, London, UK, UK, 1987. Springer-Verlag. ISBN 0-387-18317-5. URL http://dl.acm.org/citation.cfm?id=36583.36591.

[26] F. Pizlo, E. Petrank, and B. Steensgaard. A study of concurrent real-time garbage collectors. In *Proceedings of the 2008 ACM SIGPLAN conference on Programming Language Design and Implementation*, PLDI '08, pages 33–44, New York, NY, USA, 2008. ACM. ISBN 978-1-59593-860-2. URL http://doi.acm.org/10.1145/1375581.1375587.

[27] N. Shavit and D. Touitou. Software transactional memory. In *Proceedings of the 14th ACM Symposium on Principles of Distributed Computing*, pages 204–213. Aug 1995.

[28] F. Siebert. Realtime garbage collection in the jamaicavm 3.0. In *Proceedings of the 5th international workshop on Java technologies for real-time and embedded systems*, JTRES '07, pages 94–103, New York, NY, USA, 2007. ACM. ISBN 978-1-59593-813-8. doi: 10.1145/1288940.1288954. URL http://doi.acm.org/10.1145/1288940.1288954.

[29] SPEC. Spec: The Standard Performance Evaluation Corporation. http://www.spec.org/, 2010.

[30] G. Tene, B. Iyengar, and M. Wolf. C4: the continuously concurrent compacting collector. In *Proceedings of the international symposium on Memory management*, ISMM '11, pages 79–88, New York, NY, USA, 2011. ACM. URL http://doi.acm.org/10.1145/1993478.1993491.

new Scala() instanceof Java

A Comparison of the Memory Behaviour of Java and Scala Programs

Andreas Sewe   Mira Mezini

Technische Universität Darmstadt

{andreas.sewe,
mira.mezini}@cs.tu-darmstadt.de

Aibek Sarimbekov
Danilo Ansaloni   Walter Binder

University of Lugano

{aibek.sarimbekov, danilo.ansaloni,
walter.binder}@usi.ch

Nathan Ricci
Samuel Z. Guyer

Tufts University

{nricci01, sguyer}@eecs.tufts.edu

Abstract

While often designed with a single language in mind, managed runtimes like the Java virtual machine (JVM) have become the target of not one but many languages, all of which benefit from the runtime's services. One of these services is automatic memory management. In this paper, we compare and contrast the memory behaviour of programs written in Java and Scala, respectively, two languages which both target the same platform: the JVM. We both analyze core object demographics like object lifetimes as well as secondary properties of objects like their associated monitors and identity hash-codes. We find that objects in Scala programs have lower survival rates and higher rates of immutability, which is only partly explained by the memory behaviour of objects representing closures or boxed primitives. Other metrics vary more by benchmark than language.

Categories and Subject Descriptors   C.4 [*Performance of Systems*]: Performance attributes;   D.2.8 [*Metrics*]: Performance measures;   D.3.4 [*Processors*]: Memory management (garbage collection)

General Terms   Languages, Measurement, Performance

Keywords   Object demographics, Java, Scala

1. Introduction

The Java virtual machine (JVM) [18] has become an attractive target for literally dozens of programming languages. Some of these languages, like Ceylon, sport features that are close to Java while others, like Clojure, exhibit characteristics that are not very Java-like at all, e.g., dynamic typing, first-class functions, or continuations. All these languages' implementations, however, benefit from the maturity of the Java platform in general and from the availability of robust, high-performance garbage collectors in particular.

Now, the golden rule of performance optimization is to "make the common case fast." What is common for Java, however, may be rather uncommon for some of these other languages. In this paper, we therefore present a comprehensive analysis of the memory behaviour of Scala programs on the Java virtual machine. In

terms of its characteristics, Scala [20], a statically-typed language with strong influences from both functional and object-oriented languages, resides somewhere between Ceylon and Clojure. How close the memory behaviour of Scala programs is to that of Java programs is another question we will answer in this paper. While some prior evidence exists that Scala code suffers from some pathologies like excessive boxing of primitives [27], to our knowledge this is the first analysis of Scala programs focusing exclusively on issues of memory-management.

The major scientific contributions of this paper thus revolve around the experiments performed and properties measured:

Garbage Collector Workload. We show that objects in Scala programs are even more likely to die "young" and that closures and boxed primitives contribute significantly to this.

Object Churn. Despite the above, we show that objects in Scala do not necessarily die "close" to their allocation site.

Object Sizes. We show that very small objects play a significantly larger role in Scala than in Java.

Immutability. We show that immutable fields and objects play an even larger role in Scala programs than in Java programs.

Zeroing. We show that the implicit zeroing of fields during allocation is mostly unnecessary, in particular for Scala programs.

Synchronization. We ascertain that Scala code does not negatively affect common lock implementations optimized for Java code.

Identity Hash-Codes. We show that the identity hash-code associated with objects is rarely used by Scala and Java programs.

Outline   Section 2 describes our experimental setup, in particular the two profiling tools used: Elephant Tracks and DiSL. Section 3 describes the results obtained by our experiments, which are then discussed in Section 4. Section 5 comments on related work, before Section 6 concludes with suggestions for future work.

2. Experimental Setup

In the following we describe our experimental setup, i.e., the choice of benchmarks and profilers, and the threats to validity these choices entail.

2.1 Benchmarks

The Java programs[1] for our study stem from the DaCapo benchmark suite [4], version 9.12 (nicknamed "Bach"), while the Scala

---

[1] We are aware that the DaCapo benchmark suite includes one non-Java benchmark (jython), but for the sake of brevity we use the terms "Java program" and "DaCapo benchmark" interchangeably.

programs stem from the 0.1 release snapshot of the DaCapo-based Scala benchmark suite developed by several of the authors [27].[2] We chose the DaCapo benchmark suite over the SPECjvm2008 suite[3] simply because the available Scala benchmark suite is based on the former and re-uses the DaCapo harness; this ensures that the measurements can be easily compared without being disturbed by the use of a different harness (cf. Section 2.3).

2.2 Profilers

All profilers used in this study are completely independent from any particular JVM; in particular, they require no modifications to the JVM itself, which allowed us to conduct all measurements on standard Java-6 production JVMs.

Elephant Tracks To collect garbage collection traces, we use Elephant Tracks [25],[4] a profiler developed by some of the authors. This profiler uses a combination of bytecode instrumentation and JVMTI (JVM Tool Interface) callbacks to maintain a shadow heap. It then applies the Merlin algorithm [14], which produces exact garbage collection traces. Bytecode instrumentation is done in a separate JVM process; thus, the instrumentation activity does not disturb the execution of the base program under analysis. We developed a Garbage Collection simulation framework (GC Simulator) to analyze the traces produced by Elephant Tracks offline. The GC simulator allows us to test the theoretical garbage collector workload of a particular program run, independently of any implementation decisions that might be made in an actual garbage collector. Use of Elephant Tracks is quite heavy-weight; for some benchmarks, the resulting traces occupy hundreds of gigabytes, even in compressed form.

DiSL For more light-weight, tailored analyses we use DiSL [19],[5] a domain-specific language for bytecode instrumentation. DiSL allows rapid development of efficient dynamic program analysis tools with complete code-coverage, i.e., all executed bytecodes can be instrumented, including those from the Java runtime library. Like Elephant Tracks, DiSL's implementation performs bytecode instrumentation in a separate JVM. Unlike Elephant Tracks, however, the custom analyses we developed maintain their data structures in the JVM process under evaluation. This approach requires that the so-called reference-handler thread, which the JVM uses to process weak references (including those part of the analyses' data structures), is exempt from the analysis. The code of all our tailored analyses is available online for study: http://www.disl.scalabench.org/.

2.3 Threats to Validity

Choice of Benchmarks The benchmarks from the DaCapo benchmark suite [4], which represent our real-world "Java programs," have been widely accepted by researchers in diverse communities, from the memory-management community to the static analysis community. The benchmarks from the Scala benchmark suite [27] are much newer than their Java counterparts; they have been presented at the OOPSLA 2011 conference and were only publicly released earlier that year. Consequently, they have not yet gained the same degree of acceptance as the DaCapo benchmark suite. Nevertheless, it has been shown [27] that the benchmarks of the Scala benchmark suite indeed exhibit diverse behaviour and may thus justly be taken to represent a variety of real-world "Scala programs."

As both Elephant Tracks and the custom profilers written in DiSL incur massive overhead, a few benchmarks from either suite that contain hard-coded timeouts had to be excluded from our measurements (tradebeans, tradesoap, actors). Moreover, the tomcat and scalatest benchmarks from the DaCapo and Scala benchmark suite, respectively, had to be excluded as they fail when used in conjunction with instrumentation-based analyses like the ones written in DiSL. The former exhibits a "controlled" stack overflow which interferes with the instrumentation (DaCapo bug ID 2934521) and the latter requires that line number information is preserved during instrumentation, which DiSL does not do yet. Despite these exclusions we still cover eleven DaCapo benchmarks and ten Scala benchmarks, making this study the most comprehensive comparison of their memory behaviour to date.

Choice of Scala Version There is one further threat to validity concerning the Scala benchmarks: All of them are written in Scala 2.8.x. As both the Scala library and the Scala compiler are subject to much faster evolution than their Java counterparts, it is unclear whether all of our findings carry over to newer versions of Scala.[6]

Startup/Shutdown In performance evaluations, it is typically undesirable to include the start-up and shutdown activity of both the JVM and the benchmark harness in the actual measurements. The DaCapo benchmark suite thus offers a callback mechanism which allows one to limit the measurements to the benchmark iteration itself. This mechanism, however, was designed with performance measurements in mind; it is not very suitable for characterizing the memory behaviour of benchmarks. Objects which are used during the benchmark iteration, e.g., may have been allocated well in advance, i.e., during start-up. Our measurements are thus based on the overall execution of the JVM process for a single benchmark run.

We furthermore present results for a dummy benchmark, which performs no work of its own. This allows one to compare the results for a complete benchmark run, i.e., start-up, iteration, and shutdown, with a run consisting of start-up and shutdown only. This methodology, which is similar to the use of an "empty" program by Dufour et al. [8], is not perfect, however, as it may exaggerate the effect of benchmark start-up.

Imprecision In the present paper, we exclusively resort to dynamic metrics. On the upside, our results are therefore not subject to *static imprecision* [10], as any static analysis is by nature pessimistic. The results are not disturbed by the intricacies of a particular static analysis but directly mirror each benchmark's behaviour. On the downside, some metrics may optimistically hint at optimization opportunities which only an omniscient compiler or collector would be able to exploit. Any real-world compiler or collector itself needs to resort to static analysis and hence tends towards pessimism rather than optimism, although techniques like dynamic de-optimization may alleviate this. When a particular metric is subject to *dynamic imprecision* [10], i.e., when the profiler cannot deliver entirely accurate results, this is mentioned for the metric in question.

3. Experimental Results

In the following, we present several experiments which all measure properties linked to optimizations performed by modern JVMs.

3.1 Garbage Collector Workload

How does the garbage collector workload differ between Java and Scala programs? We have answered this question by using Elephant Tracks [25] to produce an exact trace containing object allocations and deaths as well as field updates. We then ran the resulting

---

[2] See http://www.scalabench.org/.

[3] See http://www.spec.org/jvm2008/.

[4] See http://www.cs.tufts.edu/research/redline/elephantTracks/.

[5] See http://dag.inf.usi.ch/projects/disl/.

[6] As of this writing, Scala 2.9.1 is the latest stable version.

Benchmark	Cons	Marks	Mark/Cons	Survival
avrora	2075466	59684	0.03	2.88 %
batik	1088785	327505	0.30	30.08 %
eclipse	66569509	171766557	2.58	30.82 %
fop	2982888	486253	0.16	16.30 %
h2	100265924	1948804662	19.44	46.00 %
jython	43752983	10654369	0.24	24.35 %
luindex	404186	50616	0.13	12.52 %
lusearch	13323025	29544022	2.22	19.86 %
pmd	9110278	2671559	0.29	29.32 %
sunflow	61883982	3577022	0.06	5.78 %
xalan	10250705	747468	0.07	7.29 %
apparat^{small}	8953723	338633	0.04	3.78 %
factorie	1505398186	6475518895	4.30	1.24 %
kiama	12891237	205002	0.02	1.59 %
scalac	19875421	433046	0.02	2.18 %
scaladoc	18077250	395418	0.02	2.19 %
scalap	1948053	64735	0.03	3.32 %
scalariform	10077808	325769	0.03	3.23 %
scalaxb	4343541	42037	0.01	0.97 %
specs	12684716	248027	0.02	1.96 %
tmt^{small}	395247346	59516039	0.15	0.01 %

Table 1. Garbage collection marks and cons (object allocations) used, together with the survival rates in a 4 MiB nursery. (To keep the traces produced by Elephant Tracks manageable, two benchmarks had to be run with a reduced input size.)

trace through our GC simulator, which was configured to simulate a generational collection scheme: New objects are allocated in a 4 MiB nursery, a nursery size that was also used by Blackburn et al. in their analysis of the initial version of the DaCapo benchmarks [4]. When full, the nursery is collected, and any survivors are promoted to the older generation. This older generation was set to 4 GiB. When this older generation is full as well, a full-heap collection is performed. While this setup is far simpler than the generational collectors found in production JVMs, it nevertheless gives a good initial intuition of the garbage collector workload posed by the different benchmarks. Moreover, our setup is similar enough to that of Blackburn et al. [4] to allow for comparisons with the older version of the DaCapo benchmark suite.

Table 1 shows the results of our simulation. In this table, cons is the total number of objects allocated by the benchmark, marks refers to the total number of times those objects are marked as live, and the nursery survival rate denotes the fraction of allocated objects which survive a minor garbage collection, i.e., which are promoted to the older generation. As can be seen, the nursery survival rate of the Scala programs in the benchmark suite is considerably lower than that of the Java programs from the DaCapo 9.12 suite. Aside from avrora, the entirety of the DaCapo suite has a higher nursery survival rate than the Scala benchmark suite, whose apparat benchmark sports the highest nursery survival rate therein with a mere 3.78 %.

The low nursery survival rate observed in the simulation suggests that, at least for most Scala benchmarks, objects die younger than for the Java benchmarks. Figures 1a and 1b confirm this. For half of the Java benchmarks at least 10 % of objects survive for 20 MiB, whereas few objects allocated by the Scala benchmarks survive for more than a few MiB of allocation.

The question arises whether the sharp drop of the Scala benchmarks' survival rates can be explained by the fact that the Scala compiler generates many short-lived objects under the hood, e.g., to represent closures. For the purpose of this study, we have identified four classes of such "under-the-hood" objects: objects representing closures, objects representing variables captured by a

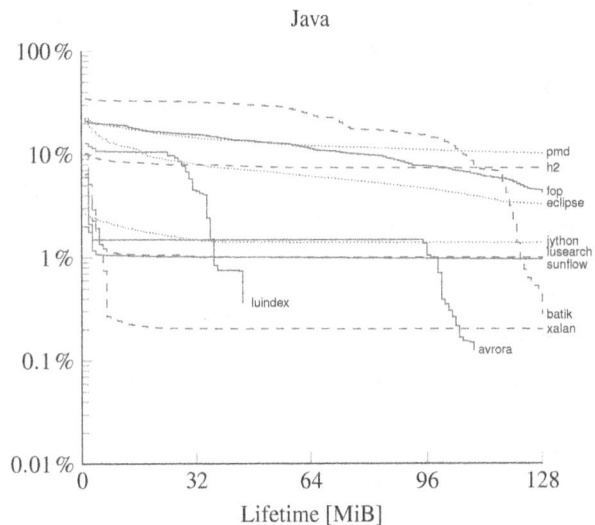

Figure 1a. Fraction of objects surviving more than a given amount of allocation for the Java benchmarks

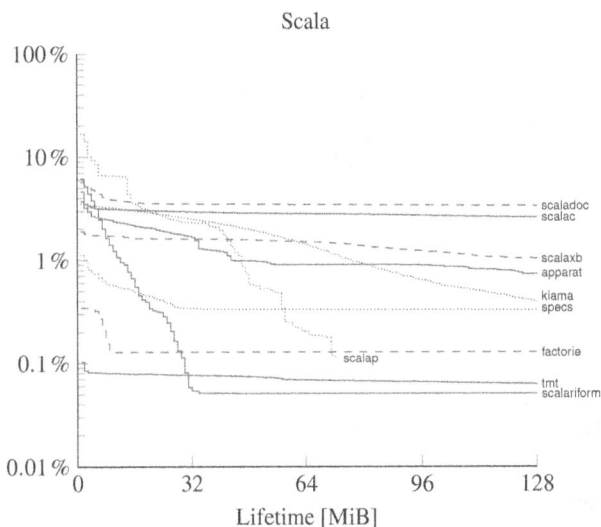

Figure 1b. Fraction of objects surviving more than a given amount of allocation for the Scala benchmarks

closure (e.g., `scala.runtime.IntRef`), boxed primitives (e.g., `java.lang.Integer`), and rich primitives (e.g., `scala.runtime.RichInt`). Like boxed primitives, the latter wrap a single primitive value, albeit for a different purpose, namely to seemingly add extra methods to a primitive type through an implicit conversion [20, Chapter 16].

To answer the aforementioned question, Table 2 tabulates both the likelihood of a new object belonging to one of the four classes of "under-the-hood" objects or to the class of other objects together with the likelihood of these objects surviving just 1 MiB of allocation. As can be seen, for all Scala benchmarks a significant portion of allocations is due to what we termed "under-the-hood" objects; only 68.62 % of allocations are due to "regular" objects. Closures in particular contribute significantly to overall allocations. 19.19 % of objects allocated by the scalac benchmark, e.g., represent closures. However, only 0.10 % of those objects exhibit a lifetime of 1 MiB or more; for this benchmark, most closures are extremely short-lived.

Benchmark	Closures Allocations	Survival	Captured Variables Allocations	Survival	Boxed Primitives Allocations	Survival	Rich Primitives Allocations	Survival	Other Objects Allocations	Survival
apparat	3.45 %	1.31 %	1.35 %	0.07 %	0.41 %	21.28 %	0.64 %	0.00 %	94.15 %	5.82 %
factorie	20.48 %	0.00 %	1.22 %	0.00 %	19.15 %	0.76 %	0.00 %	0.00 %	59.15 %	0.34 %
kiama	8.53 %	0.44 %	1.14 %	0.20 %	2.34 %	0.13 %	4.48 %	0.00 %	83.51 %	4.21 %
scalac	19.19 %	0.10 %	4.40 %	0.04 %	2.25 %	1.49 %	4.52 %	0.00 %	69.64 %	5.28 %
scaladoc	12.40 %	0.73 %	3.16 %	0.01 %	1.14 %	1.08 %	17.35 %	0.00 %	65.95 %	8.54 %
scalap	29.67 %	19.78 %	1.84 %	60.53 %	1.78 %	32.13 %	0.13 %	0.00 %	66.58 %	13.74 %
scalariform	11.89 %	0.21 %	1.41 %	0.17 %	4.90 %	0.13 %	0.20 %	0.00 %	81.61 %	7.49 %
scalaxb	22.79 %	0.00 %	0.95 %	0.01 %	10.67 %	0.14 %	0.92 %	0.00 %	64.66 %	2.88 %
specs	3.16 %	1.44 %	0.20 %	0.05 %	0.49 %	1.56 %	0.32 %	0.00 %	95.83 %	1.09 %
tmt^{small}	1.38 %	0.16 %	0.00 %	0.04 %	92.99 %	0.04 %	0.47 %	0.00 %	5.16 %	1.29 %
Arith. mean	13.29 %	2.42 %	1.57 %	6.11 %	13.61 %	5.87 %	2.90 %	0.00 %	68.62 %	5.07 %

Table 2. Distribution of allocations for the Scala benchmarks, together with the 1 MiB survival rate for each of the five classes

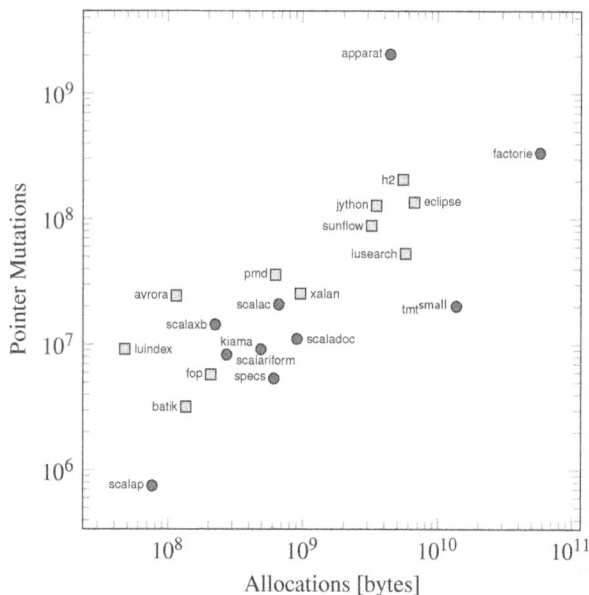

Figure 2. The complexity of the Java (□) and Scala (●) benchmarks

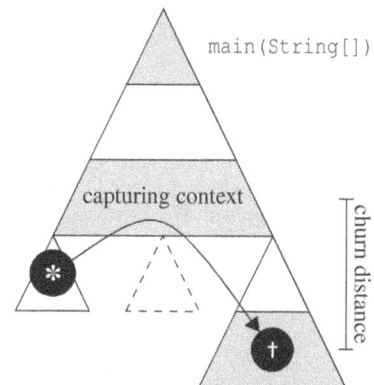

Figure 3. The churn distance of an object is computed as the largest distance between its allocation (✱) respectively death (†) context and its closest capturing context.

What Table 2 also shows is that boxed primitives play a noticeable role for almost all benchmarks, with only apparat and specs spending less than 1 % of their respective allocations on boxed primitives. As noted elsewhere [27], the tmt benchmark is an outlier in this respect; almost all objects allocated by this numerical-intensive benchmark are boxed floating-point numbers, which happen to be extremely short-lived.

However, while Table 2 shows that short-lived "under-the-hood" objects indeed significantly contribute to the low survival rates observed for the Scala benchmarks (cf. Figure 1b), on average they account for only one third of allocations. The remaining two thirds are regular objects allocated directly on behalf of the program. They too exhibit low survival rates.

Lifetimes and survival rates are one important component of a garbage collector's workload, but the sheer amount of allocations and pointer mutations, if some write barrier is employed, are another. Figure 2 thus visualizes the size of the different benchmarks, both in terms of allocation volume and pointer mutations. This figure not only gives a good impression of the size of traces the GC simulator had to process, but also shows that the Java benchmarks from the DaCapo benchmark suite are more likely to favour mutation over allocation than their counterparts from the Scala benchmark suite, with the sole exception of apparat. Also, the two Scala

benchmarks factorie and tmt are far more allocation-intensive than any other benchmarks in either suite—in particular, since Figure 2 shows only the small input size for the latter benchmark.

3.2 Object Churn

Object churn, i.e., the creation of many temporary objects, is an important source of overhead which badly hurts framework-intensive Java programs [10]. But as we have shown in the previous section, Scala programs suffer at least as much from short-lived objects as Java programs. The fact that temporary objects are often not only used within a single method but either passed on or returned to others makes intra-procedural escape analysis ineffective in identifying such temporaries. Their identification thus requires either an expensive inter-procedural analysis [10] or careful use of method inlining [28] to expose multiple methods to an inexpensive intra-procedural analysis. In particular in the latter case, it is not so much of interest how long an object lives but how closely it is captured by a calling context."under-the-hood" Ideally, the object dies in the calling context it was allocated in.

To study object churn, we define the metric of dynamic churn distance, illustrated by Figure 3. For each object, we determine both its allocation and death context. From these two, we derive the closest capturing context; intermediate contexts are ignored. The dynamic churn distance is then either the distance from the capturing context to the object's allocation context or the distance from the capturing context to the object's death context, whichever is larger. Note that the object's death context is defined with respect to the object's allocating thread, which may or may not have been the thread which relinquished the last reference to the object in ques-

Benchmark	Closures	Captured Variables	Boxed Primitives	Rich	Other Objects
apparat	3↓	1↓	13↑	1↓	4
factorie	2	4↑	3↑	1↓	1↓
kiama	4↑	5↑	3	1↓	3
scalac	3	1↓	3	1↓	3
scaladoc	3↑	1↓	6↑	1↓	3↑
scalap	6↑	26↑	18↑	1↓	4
scalariform	3↓	0↓	3↓	1↓	4
scalaxb	3	1↓	4↑	1↓	3
specs	7↑	1	7↑	1	1
tmt	2↓	0↓	3	1↓	1↓

Table 3. Median churn distances for the Scala benchmarks for each of the five classes, together with an indication whether the class's median churn distance is lower (↓) or higher (↑) than the overall median (cf. Figure 4)

tion. We believe that this simple definition is sufficient, however, as objects that escape their allocating thread are not only hard to optimize away but typically also quite rare.

Figure 4 depicts the distribution of churn distances for both the Java and Scala benchmarks, as derived from the traces produced by Elephant Tracks. As can be seen, the distribution is remarkably benchmark-dependent, with the most uneven histograms belonging to number-crunching benchmarks: avrora (processor simulation), sunflow (raytracing), and tmt (machine learning). Here, a small kernel dominates the pattern of object allocations and deaths. What is furthermore remarkable is that for most benchmarks a churn distance of zero is very rare, with a maximum of 12.83 % (sunflow) and an average of only 2.64 % and 1.27 % for the Java and Scala benchmarks, respectively (excluding dummy). Nevertheless, large churn distances are also relatively uncommon; the median churn distance is never larger than 4, with that for the Scala programs generally being higher than for their Java counterparts.

Re-using the classification of Table 2, Table 3 tabulates the median churn distances observed for different classes of objects. What is noteworthy is that rich primitives not only exhibit a median churn distance of one for all benchmarks, but that their churn distance is *always* one. This is a direct consequence of their typical usage pattern, which creates a rich primitive in an implicit conversion method, invokes a method on the returned object, and then discards it. In contrast to rich primitives, boxed primitives predominately exhibit median churn distances higher than the overall median. This indicates that these objects are kept for longer, e.g., to be passed around in a collection. Unlike for rich and boxed primitives, the churn distances of "under-the-hood" objects that represent closures and their captured variables exhibit no such pattern; their churn distances vary widely from benchmark to benchmark.

3.3 Object Sizes

If a program allocates not only many, but many small objects the ratio of payload to header overhead gets worse. It is thus of interest to examine the distribution of object sizes depicted in Figure 5 for the different Java and Scala benchmarks. This figure focuses on objects of small size (less than 88 bytes) and shows that Scala programs on average allocated significantly smaller objects than Java programs: For most Scala benchmarks the median is either just 8 bytes or 16 bytes, the size of one or two pointers, respectively. Thus, the overhead introduced by the object header, on whose properties we will focus later (cf. Sections 3.7 and 3.8), becomes more pronounced.

3.4 Immutability

While favouring immutable data structures is considered a best practice in Java [5, 11], it is even more so in Scala [20]; in particular, Scala's collection library offers a large selection of basic, immutable data structures in the scala.collection.immutable package. But not only does immutable data make it easier for the programmer to reason about a program, it also allows for various optimizations [21].

We thus assess to what extent Java and Scala programs make use of immutable data structures. In our analysis, we distinguish between class and object immutability [13] as well as between per-class and per-object field immutability: A class is considered immutable if all of its instances are immutable objects.[7] Likewise, an object is considered immutable if all of its instance fields are immutable. If a field proves to be immutable not just for a single instance, but for all objects of a class, we consider it to be per-class immutable.

While the above definitions are straight-forward, the question when exactly a field is considered immutable is a tricky one, as even otherwise immutable fields are commonly initialized to some value. We therefore adopt the following definition: An object's field is immutable if it is never written to outside of the dynamic extent of that object's constructor. Note, however, that not all initialization needs to happen inside the constructor. In particular, cyclic data structure or Java beans are frequently initialized outside the constructor [13]. Also, arrays, by their very nature, do not have a constructor; thus, arrays were not considered in this analysis. Note furthermore that the above definition differs from definitions of immutability found elsewhere [11, 12]. In particular, a field may be immutable in a particular program run only.

We implemented a tailored analysis using DiSL to measure immutability. Figure 6a depicts the fraction of instance fields that are never mutated during the course of the respective benchmark, except, of course, during construction. Figure 6b contrasts this with the fraction of fields that are per-class immutable. In other words, Figure 6b provides a static view, whereas the view of Figure 6a is dynamic. As can be seen, these two views differ significantly. Nevertheless, the Scala benchmarks in general exhibit a higher fraction of immutable fields than their Java counterparts—both per-object and per-class.

Figures 6a and 6b considered each field individually. However, an object may contain both mutable and immutable fields, rendering the entire object mutable if it contains just a single mutable field. Figures 7a and 7b thus consider object and class immutability, respectively. The Scala benchmarks exhibit a consistently larger fraction of immutable classes than the Java benchmarks: 79.67 % and 52.06 %, respectively. What is furthermore interesting to observe is that the numbers from Figure 7b (immutable classes) for the Scala benchmarks (excluding dummmy) almost exactly mirror those from Figure 6b (per-class immutable fields); a mixture of mutable and immutable fields within the same class is extremely rare in the Scala programs—but not in Java programs.

3.5 Zero Initialization

Related to object allocation is zero initialization, which is mandated by the JVM specification [18]; depending on its type, every field is guaranteed to be initialized to a "zero value" of 0, false, or null, respectively. However, this zeroing has a surprisingly large impact on performance [29]. Now, if the constructor initializes a field explicitly by assigning it a value (including a zero value), the implicit initialization to a zero value is unnecessary.

We use a tailored dynamic analysis written in DiSL to measure to what extent such unnecessary zeroing occurs in practice, which

---

[7] Static fields are not considered in this analysis.

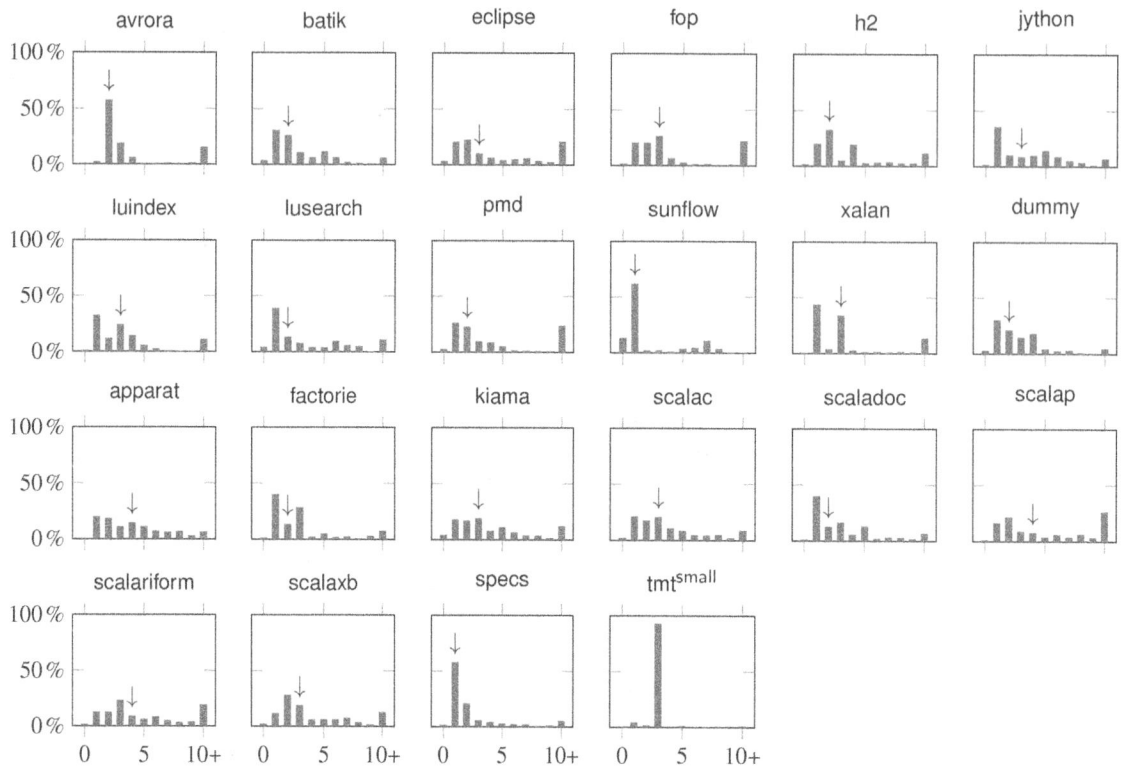

Figure 4. The distribution of churn distances with median marked (↓)

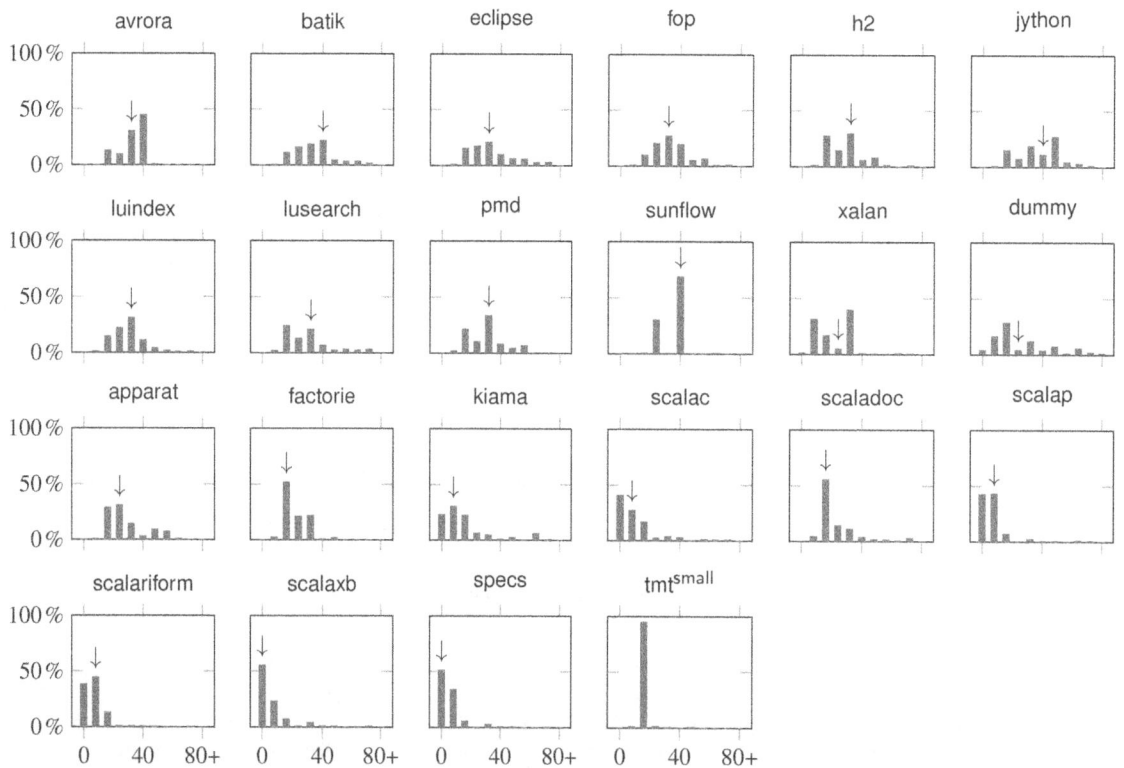

Figure 5. The distribution of object sizes (excluding the header) with median marked (↓). Each bin is 8 bytes wide, the size of a pointer.

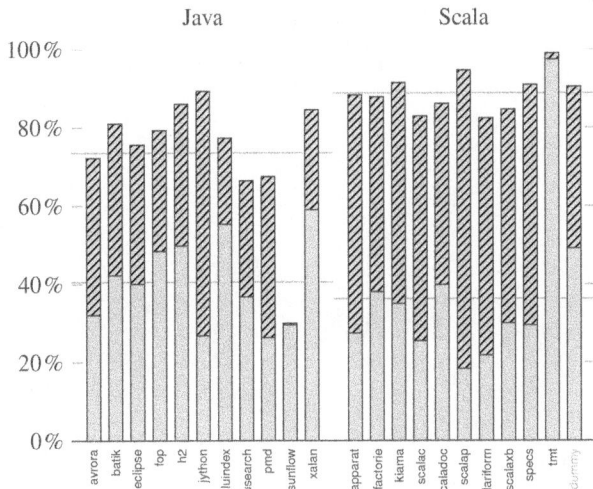

Figure 6a. Fraction of primitive (☐) and reference (▨) *instance* fields that are per-object immutable (including averages without dummy)

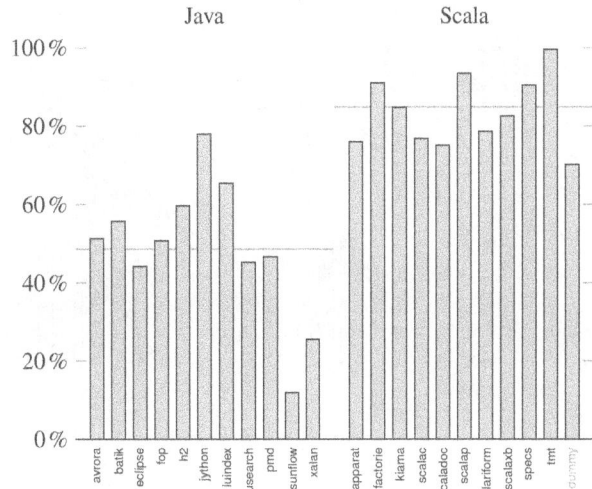

Figure 7a. Fraction of immutable objects (including averages without dummy)

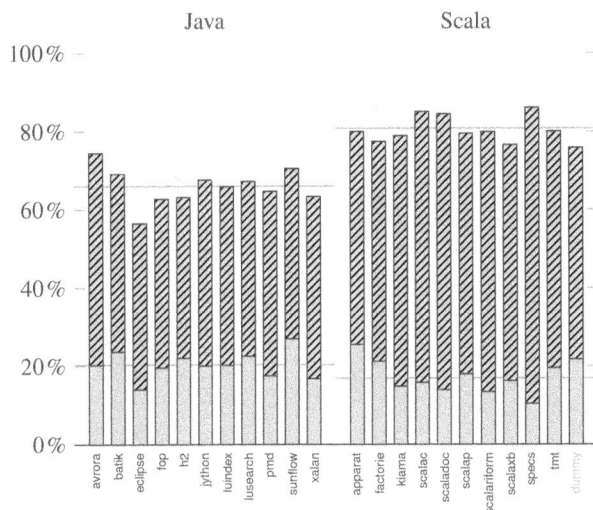

Figure 6b. Fraction of primitive (☐) and reference (▨) fields that are per-class immutable (including averages without dummy)

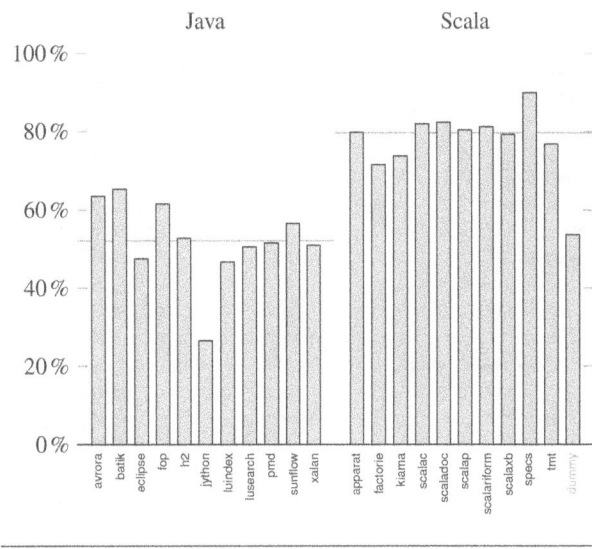

Figure 7b. Fraction of immutable classes (including averages without dummy)

hints at an optimization opportunity. This analysis considers zeroing of an instance field unnecessary if the following condition is met: The field is assigned in the dynamic extent of the constructor without being read before. In particular, zeroing of a field that is neither read nor written to in the dynamic extent of the constructor is *not* considered unnecessary.

Note that the above condition does not take into account the fact that the JVM, in order to elide unnecessary zeroing, has not only to ensure that the program does not observe the uninitialized field, but also that the garbage collector remains unaware of the field's uninitialized state.[8] But this source of imprecision is inevitable if the metric should be VM-independent.

Figure 8 depicts the extent to which zeroing of instance fields is unnecessary, distinguishing between fields of primitive (`int`, `double`, etc.) and reference type. In general, zeroing of reference fields is necessary less often than zeroing of primitive fields; the initial value is `null` less often than `0` or `false`. Furthermore, for the Scala benchmarks, reference fields play a larger role than for the Java benchmarks. The sole exception is the tmt benchmark, which suffers from excessive boxing of primitive values [27]; almost all `Double` instances (accounting for 97.87 % of the objects allocated) have their `value` field explicitly set in the constructor.

3.6 Sharing

Many of the Java benchmarks and some of the Scala benchmarks are at least to some extent multi-threaded. It is thus of interest to what extent objects are shared between different threads. Consistent with our custom immutability analysis, we analyze sharing at

---

[8] The Oracle HotSpot VM implements this intricate optimization.

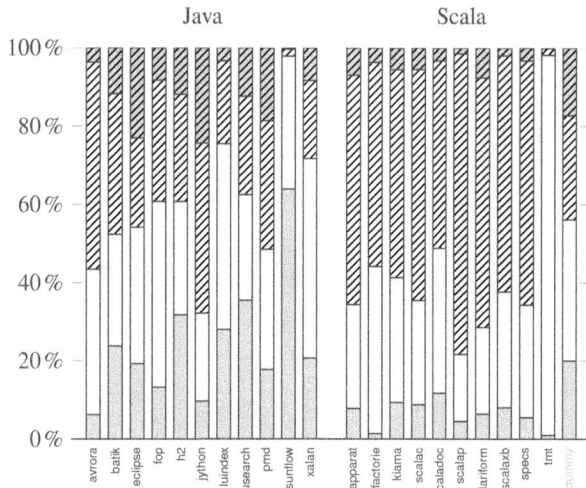

Figure 8. Necessary (□) and unnecessary (□) zeroing of primitive (□) and reference (☒) instance fields, respectively

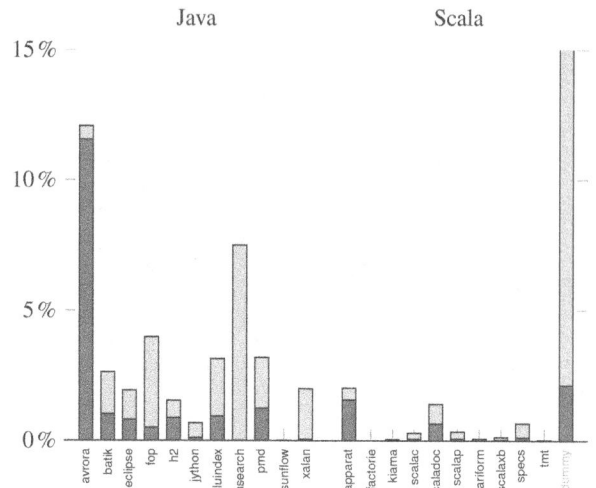

Figure 9a. Partially (□) and fully (■) shared objects with respect to read accesses, i.e., with fields read by multiple threads

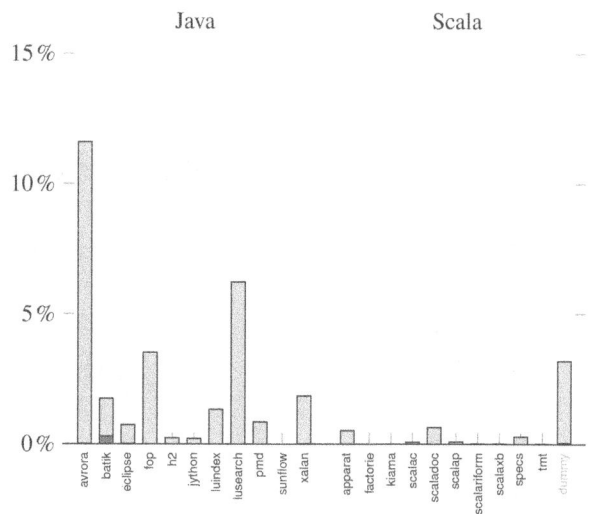

Figure 9b. Partially (□) and fully (■) shared objects with respect to write accesses, i.e., with fields written to by multiple threads

the level of individual fields. This makes it possible to recognize situations where only parts of an object are accessed by different threads.

We use a tailored dynamic analysis written in DiSL to track read and write accesses by the different threads, distinguishing between the thread that allocated the object in question and all other threads. For the purpose of this analysis, arrays are treated as objects with two pseudo-fields: one keeping the array's length and one keeping its components (treated as a single field). Static fields, however, are not taken into account.

One minor source of imprecision is that the DiSL instrumentation is not yet active while the JVM is bootstrapping. For the few objects allocated during that time, the dynamic analysis is obviously unable to determine the allocating thread; the object and its fields may be incorrectly flagged as shared.

The results of our analysis are depicted in Figures 9a and 9b. Only a small fraction of objects allocated during a benchmark invocation is shared among threads, the big exceptions being avrora and lusearch, two Java benchmarks from the DaCapo suite.[9] These two benchmarks are again quite different as there is just one type predominantly shared among threads in avrora (`RippleSynchronizer.WaitLink`) whereas there are several in lusearch (`FSIndexInput`, `CSIndexInput`, `char[]`, `Token`, etc.). Figures 9a and 9b illustrate the fraction of individual instances shared among threads, which on average is quite low. But as Figure 9c illustrates, the number of classes for which at least one instance is shared is surprisingly high: 28.94 % (Java) and 11.56 % (Scala); thus, all these classes potentially require some synchronization.

Such synchronization, however, is superfluous if the object in question is of an immutable class (cf. Section 3.4). Of those (non-array) objects whose fields are read but not written by multiple threads, more than 53.57 % belong to a (potentially) immutable class in the case of the Java programs. In the case of the Scala programs, this fraction is even higher; more than 87.06 % of objects belong to a class whose fields are not mutated after construction.

---

[9] The dummy benchmark also exhibits a high fraction of shared objects, but allocates very few objects overall, namely 7300.

3.7 Synchronization

Conceptually, on the Java virtual machine every object has an associated monitor. A thread acquires such a monitor either explicitly by entering a **synchronized** block (executing a **monitorenter** instruction) or implicitly by entering a **synchronized** method and releases it again after exiting the block (**monitorexit**) or method, respectively. This locking facility, alas, comes at a cost.

To avoid both the runtime and memory cost of multi-word "fat locks" kept in a data structure separate from their associated objects, researchers have developed "thin locks" [1, 3], which require only a handful of bits in the header of the object itself. These lock compression techniques exploit the fact that most locks are never subject to contention by multiple threads. If they are, however, the affected locks must be decompressed again. Biased locks [22, 26] go one step further than thin locks by exploiting the fact that most locks are not only never contented for, but are also only ever owned

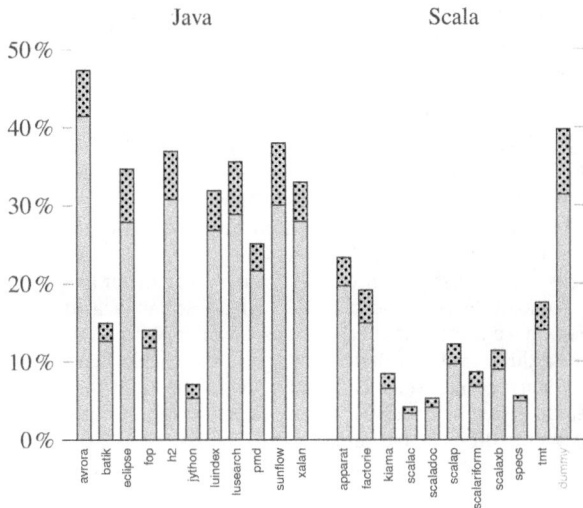

Figure 9c. Fraction of scalar (☐) and array (▨) types that are shared, i.e., for which at least one instance is shared

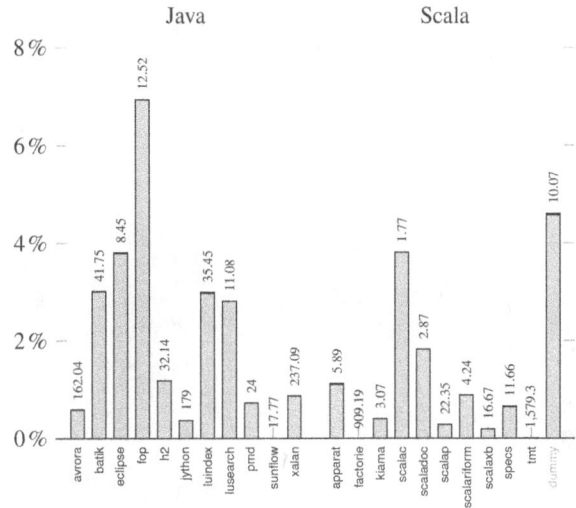

Figure 10. Fraction of objects synchronized on by one (☐) or more threads (▨), together with the average number of lock operations per object

by one thread. The resulting lock further improves the runtime cost of lock acquisition and release, if not the lock's memory cost.

To be effective, both thin locks and biased locks rely on some assumptions, which we have validated using a tailored dynamic analysis written in DiSL: Most locks are only acquired by a single thread and nested locking is shallow. The former assumption is fundamental to biased locking whereas the latter affects all compression techniques that reserve only a few bits in the object header for the lock's recursion count.[10] Especially in light of the deeply recursive calls common in Scala programs [27], the latter metric is of interest. Like Bacon et al. [3] we furthermore record the total number of objects, total number of synchronized objects, and total number of synchronization operations, as depicted in Figure 10.[11]

As can be seen, the vast majority of objects are only ever synchronized on by a single thread; on average only 0.49 % (Java) respectively 1.75 % (Scala) of all locks are owned by more than one thread. This makes thin locks in general and biased locks in particular effective for both Java and Scala programs. However, in both benchmark suites there exist notable outliers: 3.37 % (sunflow, Java) and 13.68 % (tmt, Scala), respectively. This is countered, however, by the very small fraction of objects these two benchmarks synchronize on at all; it is virtually zero in both cases.

Figure 11 confirms the findings of Bacon et al. [3] that nested locking does not prevent the use of thin locks; all locking operations are relatively shallow. In fact, only four benchmarks (avrora, eclipse, h2, and xalan) exhibit more than ten levels of recursive synchronization on the same object. The fact that these are all Java benchmarks also shows that Scala programs, despite their tendency towards deeply recursive calls, only exhibit shallow locking.

We finally assess to what extent code from different sources[12] employs synchronization. Of the lock operations performed by the Java benchmarks, on average 68.8 % target objects from the Java Runtime and 31.2 % target objects from the (Java) application and its libraries. For the Scala benchmarks, an even higher fraction of operations targets Java Runtime objects (77.4 %). Naturally, Java libraries play only a small role (1.1 %), whereas objects from both

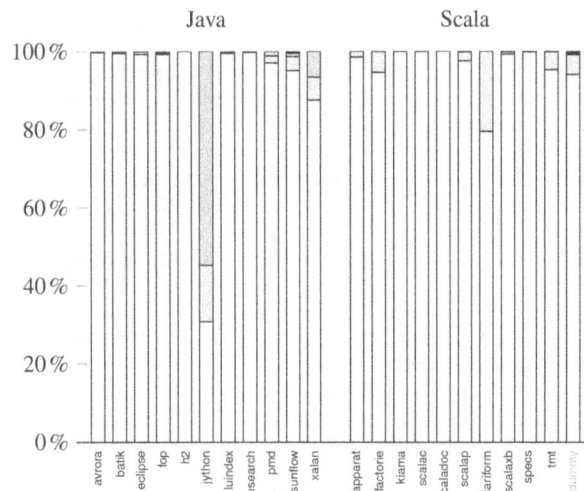

Figure 11. The maximum nesting depth reached per lock, ranging from 0 (☐) to 10 or more (■)

the Scala Runtime (8.5) and the Scala application (13.0 %) are targeted by a fair number of lock operations. The small part of the Scala Runtime written in Java plays no role at all (0.0 %).

3.8 Identity Hash-Codes

On the Java virtual machine, it is possible to compute a hash code of every object (including arrays) by invoking its `hashCode` method. However, not every class overrides this method. It is thus up to the virtual machine to provide some implementation of `Object.hashCode()`.[13] As the return value of this method, its so-called identity hash-code must not change across invocations, it is tempting to simply store it in an extra slot in the object's header.

---

[10] Techniques exists to store the recursion count outside the thin lock [26].

[11] Explicit locks from `java.util.concurrent.locks` we not considered.

[12] We follow the classification of Sewe et al. [27, Section 3.3].

---

[13] Even if a class overrides `Object.hashCode()`, its implementation is always accessible as `System.identityHashCode(Object)` as well.

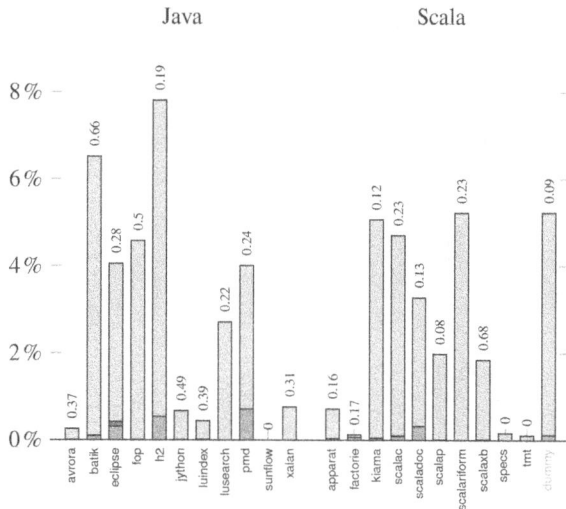

Figure 12. Fraction of objects hashed using the identity hashCode method (▨), an overriding implementation thereof (□), or both (■) together with the average number of hash operations per object

This, however, wastes space, in particular since the identity hash-codes of many objects are never queried.

This observation led to research on header compression techniques that do not store the identity hash-code but rather turn the object's address into its hash-code [2]. This address-based hashing eliminates the overhead completely, but does not work as-is for copying collectors, which must add the extra header slot upon moving any object whose identity hash-code has already been computed.

To assess the usage of hash-codes we use a tailored dynamic analysis written in DiSL. But as DiSL relies on bytecode instrumentation, only calls to System.identityHashCode(Object) and Object.hashCode() made from methods with a bytecode representation are covered; calls made from native code are not. We believe this to be a negligible source of dynamic imprecision.

Our analysis results are depicted in Figure 12. Here, we distinguish between objects whose identity hash-code was taken and objects whose hash-code was provided by their own, overriding implementation of hashCode(). Only the former objects require, if hashed and then moved by the garbage collector [2], additional space in the object header to permanently keep their identity hash-code. Note that virtually no objects have both their identity and custom hash-code taken. But if this is the case, this is almost exclusively due to a overriding hashCode() implementation performing a super-call to Object.hashCode(). The only notable exception to this rule are objects of class String, where the same object is kept in hashtables using Object.hashCode() and System.identityHashCode(Object), respectively.

That being said, at most 0.70% of objects (pmd) have their identity hash-code taken, with an average of 0.16% and 0.06% for the Java and Scala benchmarks, respectively. Address-based hashing is thus expected to work as good if not better for Scala than it does for Java programs.

4. Discussion

The results in Section 3 indicate that the memory behaviour of Scala programs is in some aspects similar to that of programs written in functional languages: Objects are more likely to be small, immutable, and to die "young" than the objects found in a purely

object-oriented Java program. However, this behaviour is not necessarily easy to exploit by a virtual machine. The larger churn distances found in Scala programs (cf. Section 3.2) in particular make it difficult for the VM to seize the opportunity to stack-allocate some objects, if the VM's just-in-time compiler is not willing to inline more aggressively than it does for Java code; the cost-benefit trade-off is different. This is all the more an issue if the Scala compiler resorts to boxing of primitives [27].

The Scala compiler has thus itself acquired the capability to perform some of these optimizations (-Yinline, -Yclosure-elim options; @specialize annotation) [7]. However, to our knowledge only some of the Scala benchmarks, namely scalac, scaladoc, and scalap, make use of these capabilities. Even so, these three benchmarks exhibit patterns quite similar to other Scala benchmarks, e.g., when it comes to the creation of "under-the-hood" objects (cf. Table 2). A detailed study of the effects of the aforementioned options on the different benchmarks that also takes into account improvements made since Scala 2.8.1 is subject to future work (cf. Section 6).

In general, it can be said that Scala programs benefit more than their Java counterparts from low per-object overhead, since the average object is small. Boxed primitives are only the most pronounced example of this.

5. Related Work

To our knowledge, Dieckmann and Hölzle [6] performed the first extensive study on the memory behaviour of Java programs. Similar to our use of Elephant Tracks, their experimental setup uses traces together with a heap simulator to measure heap composition and the age distribution of objects. In their experiments, Dieckmann and Hölzle found that both arrays and non-reference fields contribute to a large extent to a Java program's memory consumption. Furthermore, by comparison to other studies the authors found that Java objects are less likely to die at a young age than in ML or Lisp programs. With respect to the present paper, this puts Scala's memory behaviour firmly in the camp of functional languages like ML or Lisp.

Kim et al. [17] analyzed the performance impact of garbage collection and heap size along with the effect of object lifetime on cache performance. They collected traces using an exception-based tracing tool called JTRACE that allowed them to avoid any bytecode instrumentation and therefore avoid potential interfering with the observed application, although we believe the disturbances by Elephant Tracks and DiSL to be low as well. Their study of the SPECjvm98 benchmarks has shown that Java programs generate a substantial amount of short-lived objects and that both heap size and cache effects significantly affects garbage collection.

Since the SPECjvm98 benchmark suite, which the works of Dieckmann and Hölzle and Kim et al. are based on, doesn't reflect the reality of large-scale Java programs anymore, Blackburn et al. [4] developed the DaCapo benchmark suite. They furthermore compared and contrasted their new suite with the older SPECjvm98 suite chiefly with respect to the benchmark's memory behaviour. In contrast to the present paper, whose study also utilizes (the latest version of) the DaCapo suite, the experimental setup of Blackburn et al. relies heavily on an instrumented virtual machine, namely the Jikes RVM. This makes it harder to carry over their setup to modern benchmark suites, which are incompatible with the now outdated Jikes RVM 2.4.x. Our reliance on portable tools like Elephant Tracks and DiSL avoids this problem; they work with any standard-compliant JVM.

This paper builds on the Scala benchmark suite we introduced in previous work [27]. In it, we compared the behaviour of Scala and Java programs but concentrated on properties more relevant to the JVM's interpreter and JIT compiler than to its garbage collector.

Two metrics, however, are indeed of interest to the developers of memory managers: the usage of reflection to allocate objects [27, Section 4.6] and the usage of boxed types [27, Section 4.7]. The latter in particular shows a marked difference between Scala and Java programs: Boxing of primitives is very common in the former but rarely requested in the latter.

Dufour et al. [8] describe and measure metrics in five different categories, two of which, dynamic memory use and concurrency, are also the subject of this paper. In particular with respect to concurrency, the metrics used in our experiments differ significantly; we are interested in the sharing of data between threads rather than in the number of threads running overall. Moreover, we refrain from measuring fickle properties like lock contention and rather measure more stable properties that impact the effectiveness of current lock implementations, like bias and nesting.

Jones and Ryder [16] conducted a detailed study of Java object demographics and found that the Java programs require lifetime classifications more complex than "short-lived," "long-lived," and "immortal." That being said, they also found that only a small number of lifetime distribution patterns dominates. These distributions are mostly determined by just two levels of allocation context (allocation site and one level of stack context). Their study operated on object traces at 64 KB granularity produced by the GCSpy framework [24].

To illustrate the importance of modern garbage collectors, a recent study by Jibaja et al. [15] contrasted the memory management schemes used by PHP and Java; while programs written in the two languages exhibit remarkably similar characteristics, PHP's use of a simple reference counting GC puts the language at a performance disadvantage. In contrast to their study, ours compares two languages that already use the same underlying platform. It thus focuses more on potential differences rather than similarities.

Porat et al. [23] introduced a static analysis algorithm for identifying immutable classes and objects. In contrast, our work is build on a tailored dynamic analysis which sidesteps certain limitations that hinder the static analysis. Therefore, our definition of immutability differs somewhat from that used by Porat et al. (cf. Section 3.4).

Pechtchanski and Sarkar [21] presented a framework for processing and verifying immutability annotations that could lead later on to potential code optimizations, e.g., global value numbering, load elimination, loop-invariant code motion. The authors developed a formal definition for describing immutability and applied it using Java assertions; thus, checking for violations becomes automatic. According to their results on several Java benchmarks a significant number of read accesses can potentially be classified as immutable. Moreover, the use of immutability annotations in optimization can significantly reduce the number of field accesses.

To motivate their work on thin locks, Bacon et all. [3] performed a study on synchronization for a large albeit ad-hoc set of Java benchmarks. While the study performed in this paper (cf. Section 3.7) is similar in nature and scope, it uses and compares two state-of-the-art benchmarks suites for Java and Scala, respectively.

In motivation of some of their further work on header compression techniques, Bacon et al. [2] observed that most Java programs (taken from the SPECjvm98 and SPECjbb2000 suite) compute the identity hash-code of just a small percentage of objects (at most 1.3%). This paper replicates the measurements of Bacon et al. for both a more recent Java benchmark suite and an all-new Scala benchmark suite (cf. Section 3.8).

6. Conclusions and Future Work

In this paper, we have provided the first detailed comparison of the memory behaviour of real-world Java and Scala programs. As we interpret memory behaviour to not only encompass object demographics but also properties like immutability and sharing, we were able to pinpoint those areas where Scala programs behave Java-like and those where their behaviour differs, the key differences being that objects in Scala programs are both more likely to die young and more likely to be immutable than objects in Java programs. Our analysis thus helps implementers of virtual machines to make informed decisions when designing a garbage collector or object model that plays well not just with Java but also with a language like Scala, which also targets the JVM.

Future work is needed to assess the effect of Scala programs on the garbage collectors of real-world virtual machines. Temporary objects like the ones for closures and implicit wrappers, in particular, may be either stack-allocated or optimized away entirely by modern just-in-time compilers. But whether the complex translation from Scala source to Java bytecode produces something that is feasible for the JVM to analyze is an open question.

A complementary strain of future work would assess the effectiveness of the optimizations performed by the Scala compiler [7] rather than the JVM. This would require variants of all the Scala benchmarks, built with different compiler options or even different versions of the Scala compiler. Such a study might also benefit from some compiler support for tagging "under-the-hood" objects with the cause of their allocation. Similar tagging support has been used by Dufour et al. in measuring the dynamic behaviour of AspectJ programs [9].

Acknowledgments

We are grateful to the anonymous reviewers for the thoughtful suggestions on how to improve the various metrics presented here.

This work is supported by the Center for Advanced Security Research Darmstadt (www.cased.de) and by the Swiss National Science Foundation (project CRSII2_136225/1). This work is supported in part by the National Science Foundation under grant CCF 1018038.

References

[1] O. Agesen, D. Detlefs, A. Garthwaite, R. Knippel, Y. Ramakrishna, and D. White. An efficient meta-lock for implementing ubiquitous synchronization. Technical report, Sun Microsystems, Inc., 1999.

[2] D. Bacon, S. Fink, and D. Grove. Space- and time-efficient implementation of the Java object model. In *Proceedings of the European Conference on Object-Oriented Programming (ECOOP)*, 2006.

[3] D. F. Bacon, R. Konuru, C. Murthy, and M. Serrano. Thin locks: featherweight synchronization for Java. In *Proceedings of the Conference on Programming Language Design and Implementation (PLDI)*, 1998.

[4] S. M. Blackburn, R. Garner, C. Hoffmann, A. M. Khang, K. S. McKinley, R. Bentzur, A. Diwan, D. Feinberg, D. Frampton, S. Z. Guyer, M. Hirzel, A. Hosking, M. Jump, H. Lee, J. E. B. Moss, B. Moss, A. Phansalkar, D. Stefanović, T. VanDrunen, D. von Dincklage, and B. Wiedermann. The DaCapo benchmarks: Java benchmarking development and analysis. In *Proceedings of the 21st Conference on Object-Oriented Programming, Systems, Languages, and Applications (OOPSLA)*, 2006.

[5] J. Bloch. *Effective Java*. Sun Microsystems, Inc., 2nd edition, 2008.

[6] S. Dieckmann and U. Hölzle. A study of the allocation behavior of the SPECjvm98 Java benchmarks. In *Proceedings of the European Conference on Object-Oriented Programming (ECCOP)*, 1999.

[7] I. Dragos. *Compiling Scala for performance*. PhD thesis, École polytechnique fédérale de Lausanne, 2010.

[8] B. Dufour, K. Driesen, L. Hendren, and C. Verbrugge. Dynamic metrics for Java. In *Proceedings of the 18th Conference on Object-Oriented Programming, Systems, Languages, and Applications (OOPSLA)*, 2003.

[9] B. Dufour, C. Goard, L. Hendren, O. de Moor, G. Sittampalam, and C. Verbrugge. Measuring the dynamic behaviour of AspectJ programs. In *Proceedings of the 19th Conference on Object-Oriented Programming, Systems, Languages, and Applications (OOPSLA)*, 2004.

[10] B. Dufour, B. G. Ryder, and G. Sevitsky. A scalable technique for characterizing the usage of temporaries in framework-intensive Java applications. In *Proceedings of the 16th International Symposium on Foundations of Software Engineering (FSE)*, 2008.

[11] B. Goetz, T. Peierls, J. Bloch, J. Bowbeer, D. Holmes, and D. Lea. *Java Concurrency in Practice*. Addison-Wesley Longman Publishing Co., Inc., 2006.

[12] J. Gosling, B. Joy, G. Steele, and G. Bracha. *Java Language Specification*. Addison-Wesley Longman Publishing Co., Inc., 3rd edition, 2005.

[13] C. Haack and E. Poll. Type-based object immutability with flexible initialization. In *Proceedings of the European Conference on Object-Oriented Programming (ECCOP)*, 2009.

[14] M. Hertz, S. M. Blackburn, J. E. B. Moss, K. S. McKinley, and D. Stefanović. Generating object lifetime traces with Merlin. *ACM Transactions on Programming Languages and Systems*, 28(3):476–516, 2006.

[15] I. Jibaja, S. Blackburn, M. Haghighat, and K. McKinley. Deferred gratification: Engineering for high performance garbage collection from the get go. In *Proceedings of the Workshop on Memory Systems Performance and Correctness (MSPC)*, 2011.

[16] R. E. Jones and C. Ryder. A study of Java object demographics. In *Proceedings of the 7th International Symposium on Memory management (ISMM)*, 2008.

[17] J.-S. Kim and Y. Hsu. Memory system behavior of Java programs: methodology and analysis. In *Proceedings of the 2000 ACM SIGMETRICS Conference on Measurement and Modeling of Computer Systems (SIGMETRICS)*, 2000.

[18] T. Lindholm and F. Yellin. *Java Virtual Machine Specification*. Addison-Wesley Longman Publishing Co., Inc., 2nd edition, 1999.

[19] L. Marek, A. Villazón, Y. Zheng, D. Ansaloni, W. Binder, and Z. Qi. DiSL: a domain-specific language for bytecode instrumentation. In *Proceedings of the 11th International Conference on Aspect-Oriented Software Development (AOSD)*, 2012.

[20] M. Odersky, L. Spoon, and B. Venners. *Programming in Scala*. Artima Press, 2nd edition, 2010.

[21] I. Pechtchanski and V. Sarkar. Immutability specification and its applications. In *Proceedings of the 2002 joint ACM-ISCOPE Conference on Java Grande*, 2002.

[22] F. Pizlo, D. Frampton, and A. L. Hosking. Fine-grained adaptive biased locking. In *Proceedings of the 9th International Conference on Principles and Practice of Programming in Java (PPPJ)*, 2011.

[23] S. Porat, M. Biberstein, L. Koved, and B. Mendelson. Automatic detection of immutable fields in Java. In *Proceedings of the 2000 Conference of the Centre for Advanced Studies on Collaborative Research (CASCON)*, 2000.

[24] T. Printezis and R. Jones. GCspy: an adaptable heap visualisation framework. In *Proceedings of the 17th Conference on Object-Oriented Programming, Systems, Languages, and Applications (OOPSLA)*, 2002.

[25] N. P. Ricci, S. Z. Guyer, and J. E. B. Moss. Elephant Tracks: generating program traces with object death records. In *Proceedings of the 9th International Conference on Principles and Practice of Programming in Java (PPPJ)*, 2011.

[26] K. Russell and D. Detlefs. Eliminating synchronization-related atomic operations with biased locking and bulk rebiasing. In *Proceedings of the 21st Conference on Object-Oriented Programming, Systems, Languages, and Applications (OOPSLA)*, 2006.

[27] A. Sewe, M. Mezini, A. Sarimbekov, and W. Binder. Da Capo con Scala: Design and analysis of a Scala benchmark suite for the Java Virtual Machine. In *Proceedings of the 26th Conference on Object-Oriented Programming, Systems, Languages, and Applications (OOPSLA)*, 2011.

[28] A. Shankar, M. Arnold, and R. Bodik. Jolt: lightweight dynamic analysis and removal of object churn. In *Proceedings of the 23rd Conference on Object-Oriented Programming, Systems, Languages, and Applications (OOPLSA)*, 2008.

[29] X. Yang, S. M. Blackburn, D. Frampton, J. B. Sartor, and K. S. McKinley. Why nothing matters: the impact of zeroing. In *Proceedings of the 26th Conference on Object-Oriented Programming, Systems, Languages, and Applications (OOPSLA)*, 2011.

A Generalized Theory of Collaborative Caching

Xiaoming Gu   Chen Ding

Department of Computer Science
University of Rochester
Rochester, New York, USA
{xiaoming, cding}@cs.rochester.edu

Abstract

Collaborative caching allows software to use hints to influence cache management in hardware. Previous theories have shown that such hints observe the inclusion property and can obtain optimal caching if the access sequence and the cache size are known ahead of time. Previously, the interface of a cache hint is limited, e.g., a binary choice between LRU and MRU.

In this paper, we generalize the hint interface, where a hint is a number encoding a priority. We show the generality in a hierarchical relation where collaborative caching subsumes non-collaborative caching, and within collaborative caching, the priority hint subsumes the previous binary hint. We show two theoretical results for the general hint. The first is a new cache replacement policy, priority LRU, which permits the complete range of choices between MRU and LRU. We prove a new type of inclusion property—non-uniform inclusion—and give a one-pass algorithm to compute the miss rate for all cache sizes. Second, we show that priority hints can enable the use of the same hints to obtain optimal caching for all cache sizes, without having to know the cache size beforehand.

Categories and Subject Descriptors B.3.2 [*MEMORY STRUCTURES*]: Design Styles - Cache memories; D.3.4 [*PROGRAMMING LANGUAGES*]: Processors - Compilers, Optimization

General Terms Algorithms, Performance, Theory

Keywords collaborative caching, cache replacement policy, priority cache hint, priority LRU, optimal size-oblivious hint

1. Introduction

The performance of modern chips is largely determined by cache management. A program has a high performance if the working set can be cached. When the size of the working set is too large, replacement decisions have to be made. LRU replacement policy, the most commonly used one in practice, is rigid in that it caches program data in the same way whether the data is part of the program's working set or not. This may lead to serious under-utilization of cache. An alternative solution is for a program to influence the cache management by providing hints distinguishing the type of data it uses.

A number of hardware systems have been built or proposed to provide an interface for software to influence cache management. Examples include cache hints on Intel Itanium [4], bypassing access on IBM Power series [25], and evict-me bit [29]. Wang et al. called a combined software-hardware solution *collaborative caching* [29].

In this paper, we study collaborative caching in the framework shown in Figure 1. Given an execution trace, hints are added by annotating each memory access with a numerical priority. Data accessed with a higher priority (smaller numerical value) takes precedence than data accessed with a lower priority (larger value). We number the priority this way to match the numbering of memory hierarchy, where the layers of caches are numbered top down starting with L1 cache at the highest level.

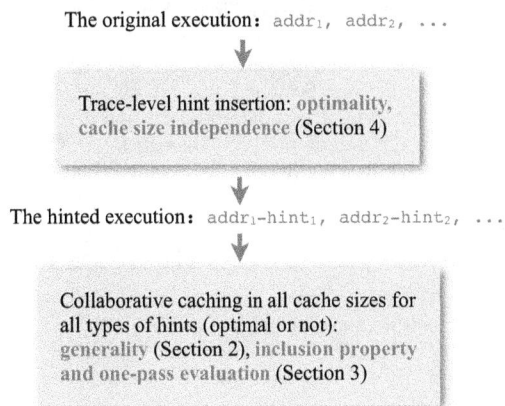

The original execution: addr$_1$, addr$_2$, ...

Trace-level hint insertion: optimality, cache size independence (Section 4)

The hinted execution: addr$_1$-hint$_1$, addr$_2$-hint$_2$, ...

Collaborative caching in all cache sizes for all types of hints (optimal or not): generality (Section 2), inclusion property and one-pass evaluation (Section 3)

Figure 1. The framework of collaborative caching. Hints are added in software to influence hardware cache management. The interaction raises questions concerning the benefit of software intervention and the stability of the hardware cache under such intervention. We answer the questions in this paper for the generalized priority hints.

In traditional caching methods such as LRU, the hardware infers the "importance" of data and manages cache based on the inferred priority. Collaborative cache enables software intervention, which specifies the "importance" of data and changes the priority in which the hardware manages the data. In previous types of hints including evict-me [29], cache bypass [1, 25], and LRU-MRU hints [11, 12], they all have a single bit and exert a binary effect—it gives a data block either the highest or the lowest priority. Priority hints generalizes the interface and allows software to choose any priority.

In this paper, we address mainly three issues concerning this generalization:

- We categorize the effect of priority hints on cache management. The complete effect includes four cases at a cache hit and two cases at a cache miss. The many cases make it difficult to analyze caching properties such as cache inclusiveness. We go through a lengthy but thorough proof to consider all these cases.

- We show a unique phenomenon of non-uniform inclusion, caused by the conflicts between the hinted priority and the inferred priority (by the cache) from the past accesses. One cannot simulate such cache using a priority list, as has been done for all other types of inclusive cache including LRU, OPT, and collaborative LRU-MRU. We describe a more general representation called span and give a new, one-pass simulation algorithm based on spans.

- Previous single-bit hints for optimal performance are cache-size dependent. A consequence is that the inability to optimize a memory hierarchy with multiple layers of cache. We show how to obtain size-oblivious optimal hints using priority hints.

The results in this paper are mostly theoretical (except for the cost of stack simulation). There are significant obstacles preventing a practical use. First, for a clean theory we consider fully associative cache. The same idea may be applied to each set of set associative cache. It improves efficiency since the number of priorities will be limited by the set associativity rather than the cache size. Second, we assume unit size cache blocks.[1] Third, we insert hints at the trace level. A program-level method may be devised as done for LRU-MRU hints [12]. Despite of the limitations, the theoretical results are valuable. Previous schemes of LRU, MRU and collaborative LRU-MRU are all but a few special cases of priority hints. The range of choices is far greater in this general case. It exposes and solves a fundamental problem in collaborative caching—the conflict between the priorities stated in the hints and those implied in the access sequence.

The rest of the paper is organized as follows. Section 2 introduces the basic concepts. Section 3 categorizes the six cases of cache accesses, proves the inclusion property and gives the algorithm for calculating the priority LRU stack distance. Cache hints for optimal performance for all cache sizes are discussed in Section 4 followed by the related work in Section 5 and a summary.

2. Basic Concepts and Generalized Caching

Inclusive cache   The inclusion property is first characterized by Mattson et al. in their seminal paper in 1970 [19]. The property states that a larger cache always contain the content of a smaller cache. The property is fundamental for three reasons.

i) In inclusive caches, the miss ratio is a monotone function of the cache size. Belady anomaly does not occur [2].

ii) The miss ratio of an execution can be simulated in one pass for all cache sizes. Mattson's algorithms used a stack and hence are called stack algorithms [19].

iii) Stack simulation provides a metric called stack distance. Stack distance is useful for program analysis because it is independent of specific cache sizes. In particular, the reuse distance, which is the LRU stack distance, has been extensively used in improving program and system locality [37].

Stack algorithms   An inclusive cache can be viewed as a stack—data elements at the top c stack positions are the ones in a cache of size c. The stack position defines the priority of the stored data. Stack simulation is to simulate cache of an infinite size. All accessed data are ordered by their priority in a *priority list*. The

---

[1] Petrank and Rawitz showed that optimal data placement (in non-unit size cache blocks) cannot be solved or well approximated in polynomial time unless P=NP [21].

stack distance gives the minimal cache size to make an access a cache hit [19]. A stack distance is defined for each type of inclusive cache and computed by simulating that type of cache of an infinite size.

The following are examples of inclusive but non-collaborative cache.

- *LRU*   The data in an LRU cache is prioritized by the most recent access time. The data element with the least recent access time has the lowest priority (highest position number) and is evicted when a replacement happens. Most hardware implements pseudo-LRU for efficiency [27]. The LRU stack distance is called reuse distance in short. It measures the amount of data accessed between two consecutive uses of the same data element. Reuse distance is measured in near constant time by organizing the priority list as a dynamically compressed tree [37].

- *MRU*   The data in an MRU cache is also prioritized by the most recent access time. Unlike LRU, the lowest priority is the data element with the most recent access time.

- *OPT*   The data in an OPT cache is prioritized by the next access time. The data element with the furthest reuse has the lowest priority. OPT is impractical because it requires future knowledge. It is used as the upper bound of cache performance. The fastest method for calculating the OPT stack distance is the one-pass algorithm by Sugumar and Abraham [28].

We are the first to formalize the inclusion property in collaborative cache [12]:

- *LRU-MRU*   A hint indicates whether an access is LRU or MRU. The inclusion property holds even when LRU and MRU accesses are mixed arbitrarily. To calculate the LRU-MRU stack distance, the following priority scheme is used. An LRU access is assigned the current access time as the priority, while an MRU access is assigned the negation of the current access time as the priority. A stack algorithm can compute the LRU-MRU stack distance [12].

The inclusive cache management hierarchy   We organize the commonly used inclusive caching methods into the following three categories. They form a hierarchy based on the "implemented-by" relation, as explained below and shown pictorially in Figure 2.

- *Level 1, non-collaborative caching*, including LRU, MRU and OPT. The priority is entirely inferred from the access sequence.

- *Level 2, limited collaborative caching*, including cache bypass, evict-me bit, and LRU-MRU. The priority is specified by a hint. The specified priority is either the highest or the lowest. It is easy to see that LRU-MRU subsumes LRU and MRU. It also subsumes OPT as we have shown that LRU-MRU hints can obtain optimal caching [11].

- *Level 3, generalized collaborative caching*. The priority hint is the only member of this category. A priority hint is a number encoding a priority. Since it allows a hint to specify any priority, it subsumes the limited collaborative schemes in Level 2.

Being general, the priority hint not only can implement other cache hints but also can create cache management scenarios not possible with any prior method of inclusive caching. We will show such an example and describe proofs and solutions for this general scheme.

3. The Priority LRU Cache Replacement Policy

For this study, the cache is fully associative and organized as a stack. The default scheme is LRU, where the data element is placed

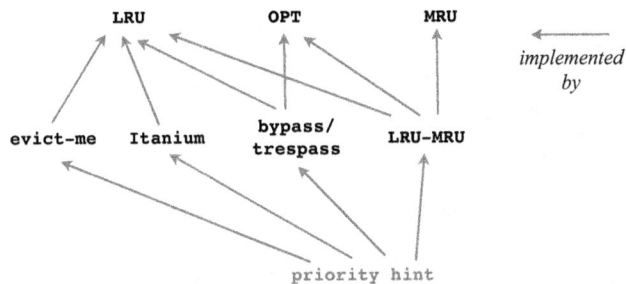

Figure 2. Common inclusive caching methods organized in a hierarchy based on the "implemented-by" relation. Limited collaborative caching of LRU-MRU [12] subsumes non-collaborative schemes of LRU, MRU and OPT [19]. Priority hint subsumes LRU-MRU and other prior collaborative methods.

at the top of the stack at position 1 and displaced at the bottom of the stack at position c, which is the cache size. Priority hint changes the default scheme. In this section, the priority value directly specifies the stack position to insert the associated data element. The phrase "a data element has a priority p" is used interchangeably with "a data element is at position p in the cache stack".

In priority LRU, an access is a pair (d, p), which means that the accessed data element d is to be inserted at position p in the cache stack. The priority p can be any positive integer. If p is always 1, priority LRU becomes LRU. If p is the cache size, priority LRU is the same as MRU. If p is greater than the cache size, the access is a cache bypass. If p can be either 1 or the cache size, priority LRU is the same as the collaborative LRU-MRU cache [12].

As an interface, priority hints may be used in arbitrary ways, sometimes optimal but probably suboptimal most times and even counter productive. In this section, we derive the properties for collaborative caching under all possible priority hints. The problem of optimal hint insertion will be discussed in Section 4.

We categorize priority LRU accesses into six classes, illustrated in Figure 3 and 4. Consider an access to w with the priority i, i.e. (w, i), arriving in the size-m cache. If w is in cache, the access is a hit. Otherwise, the access is a miss. Let the current stack position be j. A priority LRU access falls into one of the six classes, which is determined by the relations between i, j, m. The hit has four cases and the miss has two cases. To describe the change in priority, we use the terms up move, no move, and down move. We should note that the move is conceptual and may not be physical. The change in "position" requires only an update on the associated position bits.

i) A hit up move ($1 \leq i < j \leq m$)—Figure 3(a) shows that w is moved up to the position i, and the data elements between S_i and S_{j-1} are moved one position lower.

ii) A hit no move ($1 \leq j = i \leq m$)—Figure 3(c) shows that all data elements including w do not change their positions.

iii) A hit down move ($1 \leq j < i \leq m$)—Figure 3(b) shows that w is moved down to the position i in the cache, and the data elements between S_{j+1} and S_i are moved one position higher.

iv) A hit bypass ($1 \leq j \leq m < i$)—Figure 3(d) shows that w is moved out of the cache, and the data elements between S_{j+1} and S_m are moved one position higher. We also refer to this case as a voluntary eviction.

v) A miss insertion ($j = \infty$ and $1 \leq i \leq m$)—We take $j = \infty$ when the accessed data element w is not in the cache. Figure 4(a) shows that w is moved into the cache at the position

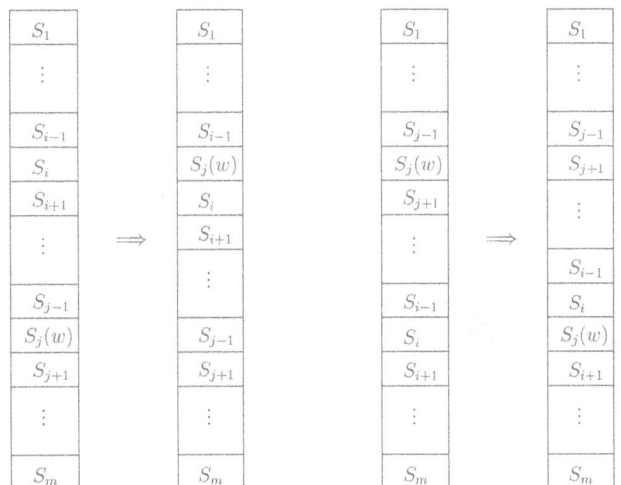

(a) Priority i is higher than initial position j (numerically $i < j$): w is moved up to position i

(b) Priority i is lower than j ($i > j$): w is moved down to position i

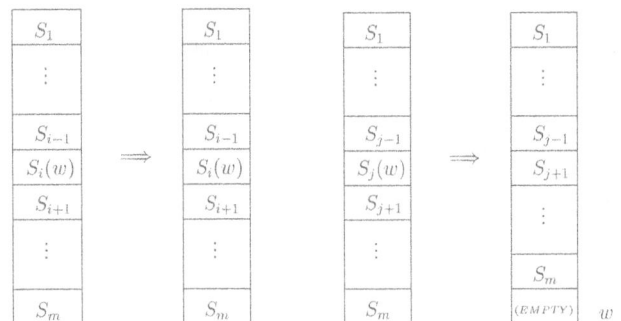

(c) $i == j$: no move

(d) Priority i is lower than the cache size m ($i > m$): w is moved out of the cache

Figure 3. Four cases of data hit in the priority cache when the data block w, at position j in cache, is accessed with a priority i.

i. The data elements between S_i and S_{m-1} are moved one position lower. The lowest priority element S_m is evicted.

vi) A miss bypass ($j = \infty$ and $i > m$)—We assume that the accessed data elements can be accessed without being stored in the cache. Figure 4(b) shows that w bypasses the cache. The data elements in the cache are unaffected.

We make a few observations of the above operations of priority LRU:

i) A cache bypass can happen either for a hit or for a miss. In the hit bypass, the accessed data element voluntarily vacates its space in the cache. Neither case of bypass happens in LRU or LRU-MRU.

ii) A forced eviction only happens in a miss insertion. The victim is the data element with the lowest priority at LRU position before the insertion. This is the same as LRU and LRU-MRU. If the LRU position is unoccupied, the eviction does not happen.

iii) Only a hit bypass or a miss insertion can change the content of the cache. No data element is moved into or out of cache in the other four cases.

111

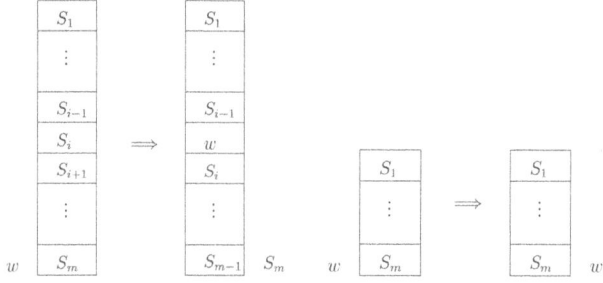

(a) Priority i is higher than the cache size m ($i \leq m$): w is moved into the cache at position i

(b) Priority i is lower than m ($i > m$): w bypasses the cache

Figure 4. Two cases of data miss in the priority cache when the data block w, not in cache before the access, is accessed with priority i.

iv) No data position is changed at the hit no-move case or the miss bypass case. The cache stack stays unchanged.

3.1 The Inclusion Property

THEOREM 1. *Let the access trace be executed on two priority LRU caches C_1 and C_2 ($|C_1| < |C_2|$). At each access, every data element in C_1 locates at the same or a lower position compared with the position of the corresponding element in C_2.*

Proof Let the access trace be $P = (x_1, x_2, ..., x_n)$. Let $C_i(t)$ be the collection of data in cache C_i after x_t. A function $loc()$ returns the location of a data element in the cache stack—$loc_i^t(d) = p$ ($1 \leq p \leq |C_i|$) means that the data element d is at the position p of C_i after x_t. In other words, $loc()$ returns the priority of a data element. We let $loc_i^t(d) = \infty$ if d is not in C_i after x_t. The initial situation is $C_1(0) = C_2(0) = \emptyset$, in which the theorem holds. Now we prove the theorem by induction on t.

Assume any $d, d \in C_1(t) \rightarrow loc_1^t(d) \geq loc_2^t(d)$. Suppose there is a data element d satisfying $d \in C_1(t)$ and $d \notin C_2(t)$. Then we have $loc_1^t(d) < loc_2^t(d) = \infty$—a contradiction of the assumption. So we have 9 possible cases for the next access $x_{t+1}(d', p')$ shown in Table 1. We prove for any d, $d \in C_1(t+1) \rightarrow loc_1^{t+1}(d) \geq loc_2^{t+1}(d)$ for each case. We do not have to check all data elements in $C_1(t+1)$ but only the ones moved up in C_1 or moved down in C_2.

	x_{t+1} hits in C_1 and C_2	x_{t+1} misses in C_1 but hits in C_2	x_{t+1} misses in C_1 and C_2
$1 \leq p' \leq |C_1|$	I	II	III
$|C_1| < p' \leq |C_2|$	IV	V	VI
$p' > |C_2|$	VII	VIII	IX

Table 1. The 9 cases for the next access x_{t+1} to d' with a priority p'.

I. From the assumption, we know that $loc_1^t(d') \geq loc_2^t(d')$. There are six sub-cases of x_{t+1} as shown in Table 2.

i) x_{t+1} is a hit up move in both C_1 and C_2, which means $p' < loc_2^t(d') \leq loc_1^t(d')$. The only data element moved up in C_1 is d', which goes to the same position p' in C_2. A data element d moved down in C_2 satisfies $p' \leq loc_2^t(d) < loc_2^t(d')$: ① if $p' \leq loc_1^t(d) < loc_1^t(d')$, given $loc_1^t(d) \geq loc_2^t(d)$, we have $loc_1^{t+1}(d) \geq loc_2^{t+1}(d)$ because $loc_1^{t+1}(d) = loc_1^t(d) + 1$ and $loc_2^{t+1}(d) = loc_2^t(d) + 1$; ② if $loc_1^t(d) > loc_1^t(d')$, given $loc_1^t(d) \geq$

	up move in C_2	no move in C_2	down move in C_2
up move in C_1	i	ii	iii
no move in C_1	IMPOSSIBLE	iv	v
down move in C_1	IMPOSSIBLE	IMPOSSIBLE	vi

Table 2. The 6 sub-cases of Case I in Table 1: the access x_{t+1} is a hit in both C_1 and C_2. A hit can be one of the cases shown in Figure 3 except the bypass case.

$loc_2^t(d)$, we have $loc_1^{t+1}(d) \geq loc_2^{t+1}(d)$ because $loc_2^{t+1}(d) \leq loc_2^t(d') \leq loc_1^t(d') < loc_1^t(d) = loc_1^{t+1}(d)$. The induction holds in this case.

ii) x_{t+1} is a hit up move in C_1 but a hit no move in C_2. The only data element moved up in C_1 is d', which goes to the same position p' in C_2. No other data location is changed in C_2. The induction holds.

iii) x_{t+1} is a hit up move in C_1 but a hit down move in C_2. d' is the only data element moved up in C_1 or the only one moved down in C_2, which goes to the same position p' in C_2. The induction holds.

iv) x_{t+1} is a hit no move in both C_1 and C_2. No data location is changed in either C_1 or C_2. The induction holds.

v) x_{t+1} is a hit no move in C_1 but a hit down move in C_2. No data location is changed in C_1. The only data element moved down in C_2 is d', which goes to the same position p' in C_1. The induction holds.

vi) x_{t+1} causes a down move in both C_1 and C_2, which means $loc_2^t(d') \leq loc_1^t(d') < p'$. A data element d moved up in C_1 satisfies $loc_1^t(d') < loc_1^t(d) \leq p'$: ① if $loc_2^t(d') < loc_2^t(d) \leq p'$, given $loc_1^t(d) \geq loc_2^t(d)$, we have $loc_1^{t+1}(d) \geq loc_2^{t+1}(d)$ because $loc_1^{t+1}(d) = loc_1^t(d) - 1$ and $loc_2^{t+1}(d) = loc_2^t(d) - 1$; ② if $loc_2^t(d) < loc_2^t(d')$, given $loc_1^t(d) \geq loc_2^t(d)$, we have $loc_1^{t+1}(d) \geq loc_2^{t+1}(d)$ because $loc_2^{t+1}(d) = loc_2^t(d) < loc_2^t(d') \leq loc_1^t(d') \leq loc_1^{t+1}(d)$. The only data element moved down in C_2 is d', which goes to the same position p' in C_1. The induction holds again as in all previous five cases.

II. There are three sub-cases about x_{t+1} as shown in Table 3.

	up move in C_2	no move in C_2	down move in C_2
a miss insertion in C_1	i	ii	iii

Table 3. The 3 sub-cases of case II in Table 1: the access x_{t+1} misses in C_1 but hits in C_2. The hit and miss cases are shown in Figures 3 and 4.

i) x_{t+1} is a miss insertion in C_1 but a hit up move in C_2. No data element is moved up in C_1 except that d' is moved into C_1, which goes to the same position p' in C_2. A data element d moved down in C_2 satisfies $p' \leq loc_2^t(d) < loc_2^t(d')$: ① if $d \in C_1(t)$ and $p' \leq loc_1^t(d) < |C_1|$, given $loc_1^t(d) \geq loc_2^t(d)$, we have $loc_1^{t+1}(d) \geq loc_2^{t+1}(d)$ because $loc_1^{t+1}(d) = loc_1^t(d) + 1$ and $loc_2^{t+1}(d) = loc_2^t(d) + 1$; ② if $loc_1^t(d) = |C_1|$, we do not have to worry about this case because d is evicted and not in $C_1(t+1)$; ③ if $d \notin C_1(t)$, we do not have to worry about this case either because d is not in $C_1(t+1)$. The induction holds.

ii) x_{t+1} is a miss insertion in C_1 but a hit no move in C_2. No data element is moved up in C_1 except that d' is moved

time	1	2	3	4	5	6	7	8	9
access & hint	A-2	B-2	C-5	D-1	B-6	D-6	A-4	C-1	A-4
stack: 1				D	D			C	C
2	A	B	B			A			
3		A	A	B	A				
4				A			A		A
5			C					Ⓐ	

(a) Cache size is 5. A is in position 5 after time 8.

time	1	2	3	4	5	6	7	8	9
access & hint	A-2	B-2	C-5	D-1	B-6	D-6	A-4	C-1	A-4
stack: 1				D	D			C	C
2	A	B	B			A			
3		A	A	B	A		C		
4				A		C	A	Ⓐ	A
5			C		C	B	B	B	B
6				C	B	D	D	D	D

(b) Cache size is 6. A is in position 4 after time 8.

Figure 5. An example of non-uniform inclusion. The priority LRU observes the inclusion principle but permits data to reside in different positions in the smaller cache than in the larger cache. In this example, after time 8, A locates at a lower position in the size-5 cache than in the size-6 cache.

into C_1, which goes to the same position p' in C_2. No data element changes location in C_2. The induction holds.

iii) x_{t+1} is a miss insertion in C_1 but a hit down move in C_2. No data element is moved up in C_1 except that d' is moved into C_1, which goes to the same position p' in C_2. And d' is the only data element moved down in C_2. The induction holds.

III. x_{t+1} is a miss insertion in both C_1 and C_2. No data element is moved up in C_1 except that d' is moved into C_1, which goes to the same position p' as in C_2. A data element d moved down in C_2 satisfies $loc_2^t(d) \geq p'$: ① if $d \in C_1(t)$ and $p' \leq loc_1^t(d) < |C_1|$, given $loc_1^t(d) \geq loc_2^t(d)$, we have $loc_1^{t+1}(d) \geq loc_2^{t+1}(d)$ because $loc_1^{t+1}(d) = loc_1^t(d)+1$ and $loc_2^{t+1}(d) = loc_2^t(d)+1$; ② if $loc_1^t(d) = |C_1|$, we do not have to worry about this case because d is evicted and not in $C_1(t+1)$; ③ if $d \notin C_1(t)$, we do not have to worry about this case either because d is not in $C_1(t+1)$. The induction holds.

IV. From the assumption, we know that $loc_1^t(d') \geq loc_2^t(d')$. So x_{t+1} is a hit bypass in C_1 but a hit down move in C_2, in which we have $loc_2^t(d') \leq loc_1^t(d') < p'$. A data element d moved up in C_1 satisfies $loc_1^t(d) > loc_1^t(d')$: ① if $loc_2^t(d') < loc_2^t(d) \leq p'$, given $loc_1^t(d) \geq loc_2^t(d)$, we have $loc_1^{t+1}(d) \geq loc_2^{t+1}(d)$ because $loc_1^{t+1}(d) = loc_1^t(d)-1$ and $loc_2^{t+1}(d) = loc_2^t(d)-1$; ② if $loc_2^t(d) < loc_2^t(d')$, given $loc_1^t(d) \geq loc_2^t(d)$, we have $loc_1^{t+1}(d) \geq loc_2^{t+1}(d)$ because $loc_2^{t+1}(d) = loc_2^t(d) < loc_2^t(d') \leq loc_1^t(d') \leq loc_1^{t+1}(d)$. The only data element moved down in C_2 is d', which is moved out of C_1. The induction holds.

V. There are three sub-cases about x_{t+1} as shown in Table 4.

	a hit up move in C_2	a hit no-move in C_2	a hit down move in C_2
a miss bypass in C_1	i	ii	iii

Table 4. The 3 sub-cases of x_{t+1} of case V

i) x_{t+1} is a miss bypass in C_1 but a hit up move in C_2. No data location is changed in C_1. A data element d moved down in C_2 satisfies $p' \leq loc_2^t(d) < loc_2^t(d')$: we do not have to worry about this case because $d \notin C_1(t+1)$. Otherwise, $d \in C_1(t+1)$ implies $d \in C_1(t)$ because x_{t+1} is a miss bypass in C_1, from which we get $loc_2^t(d) \leq loc_1^t(d) \leq |C_1| < p'$—a contradiction of the assumption $loc_2^t(d) \geq p'$. The induction holds.

ii) x_{t+1} is a miss bypass in C_1 but a hit no move in C_2. No data element changes location in either C_1 or C_2. The induction trivially holds.

iii) x_{t+1} is a miss bypass in C_1 but a hit down move in C_2. No data element changes location in C_1. The only data element moved down in C_2 is d', which is not in $C_1(t+1)$. The induction again holds.

VI. x_{t+1} is a miss bypass in C_1 but a miss insertion in C_2. No data element changes location in C_1. A data element d moved down in C_2 satisfies $loc_2^t(d) \geq p'$: we do not have to worry about this case because d is not in $C_1(t+1)$. Otherwise, $d \in C_1(t+1)$ implies $d \in C_1(t)$ because x_{t+1} is a miss bypass in C_1, from which we get $loc_2^t(d) \leq loc_1^t(d) \leq |C_1| < p'$—a contradiction of the assumption $loc_2^t(d) \geq p'$. The induction holds.

VII. x_{t+1} is a hit bypass in both C_1 and C_2. A data element d moved up in C_1 satisfies $loc_1^t(d) \geq loc_1^t(d')$: ① if $loc_2^t(d) > loc_2^t(d')$, given $loc_1^t(d) \geq loc_2^t(d)$, we have $loc_1^{t+1}(d) \geq loc_2^{t+1}(d)$ because $loc_1^{t+1}(d) = loc_2^t(d)-1$ and $loc_2^{t+1}(d) = loc_2^t(d)-1$; ② if $loc_2^t(d) < loc_2^t(d')$, given $loc_1^t(d) \geq loc_2^t(d)$, we have $loc_1^{t+1}(d) \geq loc_2^{t+1}(d)$ because $loc_2^{t+1}(d) = loc_2^t(d) < loc_2^t(d') \leq loc_1^t(d') \leq loc_1^{t+1}(d)$. No data element is moved down in C_2 except that d' is moved out in both C_1 and C_2. The induction therefore holds.

VIII. x_{t+1} is a miss bypass in C_1 and a hit bypass in C_2. No data element changes location in C_1. No data element is moved down in C_2 except that d' is moved out. The induction is preserved.

IX. x_{t+1} is a miss bypass in both C_1 and C_2. No data changes location in either C_1 or C_2. The induction trivially holds.

With the above long list, we have covered all possible cases. The theorem is proved. ∎

The inclusion property is shown in the following corollary.

COROLLARY 1. *An access trace is executed on two priority LRU caches—C_1 and C_2 ($|C_1| < |C_2|$). At any access, the content of cache C_1 is always a subset of the content of cache C_2.*

Proof Suppose a data element d is in $C_1(t)$ but not in $C_2(t)$. Then we have $loc_1^t(d) < loc_2^t(d) = \infty$—a contradiction of Theorem 1. The supposed situation is impossible. Priority LRU preserves the inclusion property. ∎

3.2 Uniform vs Non-uniform Inclusion

The generality of priority LRU can create cache management scenarios not possible in the past. In particular, the stack layout may differ based on cache size—the same data element may reside in a lower position in the smaller cache than in the larger cache. We call this case *non-uniform inclusion*. In comparison, all previous inclusive caching schemes, e.g. LRU and LRU-MRU, have *uniform inclusion*, in which the same data element has the same position regardless of the cache size.

Figure 5 shows an example of non-uniform inclusion. The stack layout at each access is shown in Figure 5(a) for cache size 5 and Figure 5(b) for cache size 6. The non-uniformity happens after the access at time 8—the data element A locates at the position 5 in the smaller cache but at the position 4 in the larger cache. The reason has to do with the data element C. Before time 8, C is out of the size-5 cache but in the size-6 cache. When C is accessed again at time 8, the element A is moved down by one position in the size-5 cache but stays in situ in the size-6 cache, creating different stack layouts. The example shows that the difference is allowed by priority LRU but does not violate the inclusion property.

The non-uniform inclusion is shown formally by Theorem 1, which allows for the data to locate in a lower position in a smaller cache. Previous inclusive caching schemes have the stronger property that the data has to be in the same position in caches of different sizes.

Non-uniform inclusion uncovers a subtle distinction between the inclusion property and the stack layout, which is that the inclusion principle does not have to imply identical placement. The inclusion property can hold without requiring different caches to have the same stack layout. Priority LRU represents this new category of non-uniform inclusive caching. For this new type of caching, computing the stack distance becomes problematic, as we discuss next.

3.3 The Priority LRU Stack Distance

For an access trace running on a priority LRU cache, for each access, a minimal cache size exists to make the access a hit because of the inclusion property. This critical minimal cache size is called *stack distance* [19]. With a one-pass stack distance analyzer, we can compute miss ratios for all cache sizes without doing cache simulations repeatedly for each cache size.

time	1	2	3	4	5	6	7	8	9
trace	A-2	B-2	C-5	D-1	B-6	D-6	A-4	C-1	A-4
stack 1				D	D			C	C
2	A	B	B			A			
3		A	A	B	A				
4				A			A		Ⓐ

Figure 6. For the same trace in Figure 5, the access at time 9 is a miss in the size-4 cache.

3.3.1 Priority List ... No Longer Works

A priority list is the core data structure in the original stack algorithms [19]. Different stack algorithms are identical in construction and maintenance of the priority list. The only difference is the priority used. For example, the priority used for LRU is the most recent access time but the one for OPT is the next access time. While Mattson et al. considered only non-collaborative caches, this solution extends to the case of limited collaboration in particular the LRU-MRU cache. Indeed, an important finding by us is a way to assign a "dual" priority based on the LRU-MRU hint to maintain a single priority list [12].

Because of non-uniform inclusion, a single priority list no longer works for priority LRU. Since the stack position changes depending on the cache size, so does the priority. We cannot maintain a single priority list to represent the layout for all cache sizes.

Still, can we solve the problem by simulating an infinitely large cache and use the lowest position as the stack distance? We can show a counter example as follows. Take the example trace in Figure 5(b). It is the same as a simulation of infinite cache size. The lowest position of A before the access at time 9 is 4 in the infinitely large cache. However, this access is a miss in the size-4 cache, as shown in Figure 6. The lowest stack position, 4, is not the right stack distance.

3.3.2 Span

We generalize the classic stack algorithms by replacing the priority list with the notion of span. The purpose is to track the position of a data element in all cache sizes (not just the infinite size). A span is denoted as (d, c_1, c_2, loc), which means the data element d is at position loc when cache size is between c_1 and c_2. An inherent constraint for a span is that $loc \leq c_1 \leq c_2$ when $loc \neq \infty$. If $loc = \infty$, d is not in the cache with the specific cache sizes. The span leverages the fact that a data element usually locates at the same position in multiple cache sizes.

In the following paragraphs, several cases of span update are discussed in details with an example. Figure 7 shows how spans work on an example trace with 9 accesses. Each step is a table showing spans for all data elements. Unlike previous stack algorithms that use an infinite cache size, the spans in these tables shows data positions in all cache sizes. The first column of the table lists all data. The first row shows all cache sizes. We show the sizes from 1 to 6 separately and the rest are compacted into a single "size" with ellipses. Each of the following rows with several spans is for a data element. For example, there are two spans $(A, 1, 1, \infty)$ and $(A, 2, \infty, 2)$ in Figure 7(a)—the former means that A is not in cache with a size-1 cache and the latter means that A is at the position 2 for all cache sizes no less than 2. In this way, the locations of the same data element for all cache sizes are represented. From the column view, each column for a cache size indicates how data elements locate in the cache with this specific cache size. Based on these spans, we are able to simulate all size caches at the same time. Because the spans accurately represent all stack layouts, the correctness is ensured.

At the beginning, all caches are empty. The access at time 1 is about creating spans for itself—$(A, 1, 1, \infty)$ and $(A, 2, \infty, 2)$ shown in Figure 7(a). For the first access to a data element, the stack distance is infinity since it is a compulsory miss [13]. The first access has an infinite stack distance. For the access at time 2, it is a miss bypass with a cache size 1 but a miss insertion for larger caches. So the span $(A, 1, 1, \infty)$ is unchanged because A stays outside the size-1 cache. The other span $(A, 2, \infty, 2)$ is first changed to $(A, 2, \infty, 3)$ because moving B to the position 2 makes A one position lower. Then the new $(A, 2, \infty, 3)$ is split into $(A, 2, 2, 3)$ and $(A, 3, \infty, 3)$—the former is updated to $(A, 2, 2, \infty)$ to indicate A is out of the size-2 cache. The two adjacent spans with the same

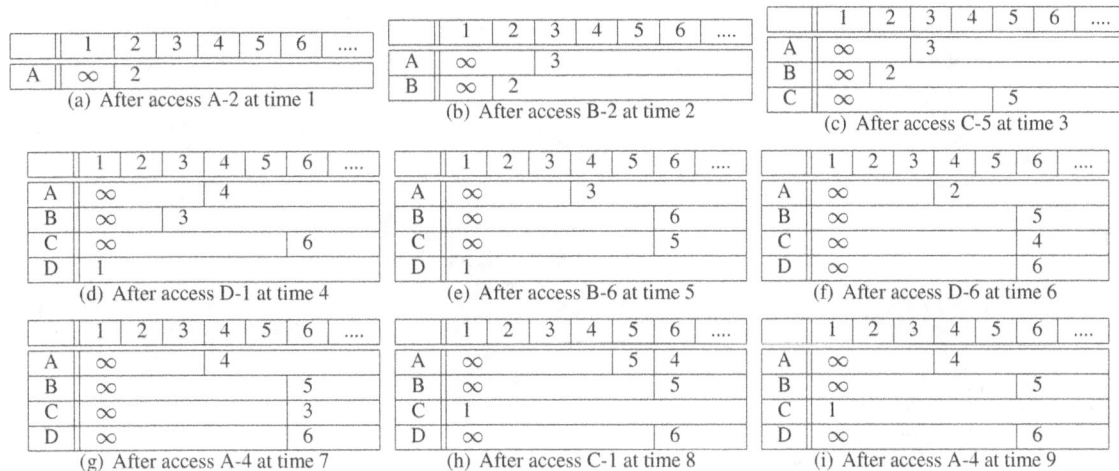

(a) After access A-2 at time 1

		1	2	3	4	5	6	....
A	∞		2					

(b) After access B-2 at time 2

		1	2	3	4	5	6	....
A	∞			3				
B	∞		2					

(c) After access C-5 at time 3

		1	2	3	4	5	6	....
A	∞			3				
B	∞		2					
C	∞					5		

(d) After access D-1 at time 4

		1	2	3	4	5	6	....
A	∞				4			
B	∞			3				
C	∞						6	
D	1							

(e) After access B-6 at time 5

		1	2	3	4	5	6	....
A	∞			3				
B	∞						6	
C	∞					5		
D	1							

(f) After access D-6 at time 6

		1	2	3	4	5	6	....
A	∞				2			
B	∞					5		
C	∞					4		
D	∞						6	

(g) After access A-4 at time 7

		1	2	3	4	5	6	....
A	∞				4			
B	∞					5		
C	∞			3				
D	∞						6	

(h) After access C-1 at time 8

		1	2	3	4	5	6	....
A	∞					5	4	
B	∞					5		
C	1							
D	∞						6	

(i) After access A-4 at time 9

		1	2	3	4	5	6	....
A	∞				4			
B	∞					5		
C	1							
D	∞						6	

Figure 7. An example of priority LRU stack simulation. The trace has 9 accesses to 4 data elements. A data element may locate at different stack positions depending on cache sizes. All possible positions for each data element are tracked by its *span* list, shown in each row. Cache sizes are shown by the header row.

loc, $(A,1,1,\infty)$ and $(A,2,2,\infty)$, are merged into a single span $(A,1,2,\infty)$. At last, we create the spans for B: $(B,1,1,\infty)$ and $(B,2,\infty,2)$. The updated all-size cache snapshot is in Figure 7(b). The second access is also a compulsory miss and has an infinite stack distance.

At time 5, the all-size cache snapshot is in Figure 7(d). First we update the spans for other data elements except for B. There are two spans for A—$(A,1,3,\infty)$ and $(A,4,\infty,4)$: the former stays the same, and the latter is updated to $(A,4,\infty,3)$ because moving B to the position 6 makes A one position higher. We update the spans of C and D in the same way and obtain the new all-size cache snapshot in Figure 7(e). When a data element is accessed again, the stack distance equals to the c_1 of the leftmost span with a finite loc, which is the minimal cache size to keep the accessed data element in cache. For this access, B is accessed again and its leftmost span with a finite loc is $(B,3,\infty,3)$. So the stack distance is 3. At last, we update the spans of B to $(B,1,5,\infty)$ and $(B,6,\infty,6)$.

At time 9 with the lower position exception, we have to look back into the access at time 8. In the cache snapshot in Figure 7(g), A has two spans $(A,1,3,\infty)$ and $(A,4,\infty,4)$. Moving C to the position 1 has a different impact on A for different cache sizes. The span $(A,1,3,\infty)$ stays the same. For the other span $(A,4,\infty,4)$, A is moved one position lower when the cache size is 4 or 5 but stays the same when the cache size is 6 or greater. This span is updated into two spans: $(A,4,5,5)$ and $(A,6,\infty,4)$. The new span $(A,4,5,5)$ is then split and merged with $(A,1,3,\infty)$ in the same way as in the case at time 2. Finally, A has three spans after the access at time 8: $(A,1,4,\infty)$, $(A,5,5,5)$, and $(A,6,\infty,4)$. When the access at time 9 to A happens, the left most span with a finite loc of A is $(A,5,5,5)$. The stack distance is 5.

3.3.3 The One-pass Simulation Algorithm

In the algorithm, each data element has a list of spans once it is accessed. A node in the list is a span but only with two fields for c_1 and loc. The c_2 equals to the c_1 of the next span minus one. For the last span, the c_2 equals to ∞. Only the spans with a finite value for loc show up in a span list, which implies the corresponding data element could not be contained in cache when the cache size is less than the c_1 of the first span node.

Function `process_one_access()` in Algorithm 1 is the top-level function to compute a stack distance. It mainly consists of

---

Algorithm 1: `process_one_access()`: compute the priority LRU stack distance for an access

Input: d is accessed with a priority p.
Output: returns the priority LRU stack distance of this access.

```
1  process_one_access(d,p)
2  begin
3  |   if There is no span list for d then
4  |   |   for Each current span list (list_iter) do
5  |   |   |   Update the span list by calling
   |   |   |   update_one_list(list_iter, NULL, p)
6  |   |   end
7  |   |   Create a new list for d
8  |   |   Create a new span for the current access with
   |   |   c1 = loc = p and insert it into the new list
9  |   |   Return an infinite stack distance
10 |   else
11 |   |   Set the_list to the span list for d
12 |   |   for Each current span list (list_iter) do
13 |   |   |   if list_iter ≠ the_list then
14 |   |   |   |   Update the span list by calling
   |   |   |   |   update_one_list(list_iter, the_list, p)
15 |   |   |   end
16 |   |   end
17 |   |   Save the c1 value of the first span in the_list to a
   |   |   temporary
18 |   |   Delete all the current spans in the_list
19 |   |   Create a new span for the current access with
   |   |   c1 = loc = p and insert it into the_list
20 |   |   Return the saved temporary as the stack distance
21 |   end
22 end
```

two cases: one for first-time accesses (compulsory misses) and the other for the other accesses. Both cases follow a similar procedure: update all the spans except the ones for the accessed data element; update the spans for the accessed data element; and return the stack distance. The first step is done by calling Function `update_one_list()` in Algorithm 2.

Function `update_one_list()` has three arguments providing sufficient information for span updates. The `while` loop traverses

---

Algorithm 2: `update_one_list`(): update the span list for a data element for all cache sizes

> **Input**: *updated_list* is the span list for a data element to be updated; *accessed_list* is the span list for the accessed data element, which has not been updated yet; *new_priority* is the new priority for the accessed data element.

1 `update_one_list`(*updated_list*,*accessed_list*,*new_priority*)
2 **begin**
3   Set *updated_span* to the last span of *updated_list*
4   **if** *accessed_list* $\neq$ *NULL* **then**
5   Set *accessed_span* to the last span of *accessed_list*
6   **else**
7   Set *accessed_span* to *NULL*
8   **end**
9   **while** *updated_span* $\neq$ *NULL* **do**
10   **if** *accessed_span* = *NULL* **then**
11   Do updates for *updated_span* including changing c_1 and *loc* values and merging unnecessary adjacent spans
12   Set *updated_span* to its predecessor
13   **else**
14   **if** *The c_1 of updated_span is no less than the c_1 of accessed_span* **then**
15   Do updates for *updated_span* including changing c_1 and *loc* values and merging unnecessary adjacent spans
16   **if** *The c_1 of accessed_span equals to the c_1 of updated_span* **then**
17   Set *accessed_span* to its predecessor
18   **end**
19   Set *updated_span* to its predecessor
20   **else**
21   Create a new span and set its c_1 to c_1 of *accessed_span* and *loc* to *loc* of *updated_span*
22   Insert the new span as the successor of the *updated_span*
23   Set *updated_span* to this new span
24   Do updates for *updated_span* including changing c_1 and *loc* values and merging unnecessary adjacent spans
25   Set *accessed_span* to its predecessor
26   Set *updated_span* to its predecessor
27   **end**
28   **end**
29   **end**
30 **end**

---

and updates the spans of a data element. The traversal is associated with another traversal through the span list of the accessed data element to make sure that span updates are done for the same cache sizes. The two correlated traversals both are done in the reverse order, from the last to the first, to make it easier to merge adjacent spans. The span updates, done in line 11, 15, and 24, have been demonstrated in the example in Figure 7.

In line 21 and 22, a span is split into two if neither the condition in line 10 nor the one in line 14 is satisfied. An example is the access at time 7 in Figure 7 when the span (A, 4, ∞, 4) is first split into (A, 4, 5, 4) and (A, 6, ∞, 4). The span splitting aligns the spans to be updated with the spans of the accessed data element. The updating operation becomes simpler since the current access has the same impact for all cache sizes within the being updated span. In this example, (A, 4, 5, 4) is updated to (A, 4, 5, 5) and (A, 6, ∞, 4) remains unchanged.

The span splitting is not always necessary. However, an unnecessary span can be merged with its successor shortly. For example, suppose we have only two spans (A, 5, ∞, 5) and (B, 8, ∞, 8), and the next access is B-1. The span (A, 5, ∞, 5) is first split into (A, 5, 7, 5) and (A, 8, ∞, 5). Then the new spans are updated to (A, 5, 7, 6) and (A, 8, ∞, 6). The span (A, 5, 7, 6) is split into (A, 5, 5, ∞) and (A, 6, 7, 6). The former span (A, 5, 5, ∞) is abandoned since we do not store a span with an infinite *loc*. The latter span (A, 6, 7, 6) is merged with its successor (A, 8, ∞, 6) into (A, 6, ∞, 6). It is possible to remove unnecessary span splittings with a more complex algorithm.

3.3.4 The Space and Time Overhead

The space cost per data element is proportional to the number of spans, which is bounded by the maximal priority M in a hint and the data set size D. The number of spans for a data item equals to the number of different priorities in all cache sizes. Because the possibly maximal priority for a data item is $M + D$, the possibly maximal number of spans is also $M + D$. The overall space cost is $\mathcal{O}(D \cdot (M+D))$. The bound is high in theory but not as formidable in practice. In the following empirical evaluation, the number of spans for a data element is only a few and much less than $M + D$.

The time cost consists primarily the operations involved in the span updates at line 11, 15, and 24 in Algorithm 2. The number of operations is proportional to the total number of spans of the datum being updated. If the number of spans is bounded by $M+D$, the time bound for each access is $\mathcal{O}(D \cdot (M + D))$. For LRU cache, there is only one span for each data element, so the time cost is $\mathcal{O}(D)$ per access and matches the cost of the original stack algorithm [19].

An Experiment To give a sense of the number of spans in practice, we have implemented the stack distance algorithm for priority LRU and tested it on a random trace with randomly generated accesses and priorities. The data size is set to 1024 and the trace length is 10 million. For the number of priorities, we choose to vary from 1 to 1 million in numbers that are powers of two. Instead of measuring the physical time and space, we use two logical metrics. The space is measured by the number of spans being stored. The time is measured by the number of span updates.

The columns in Table 5 shows 13 out of the 20 results on different priority ranges. We omit the cost results of other priority ranges because their measured costs are nearly equal to the computed numbers obtained by interpolating using the costs of the neighboring ranges shown in the table.

When the priority number is always 1, priority LRU degenerates into LRU. A priority list is enough to obtain the stack distance. Each data element has only one span. The space overhead for all data is 1024. For each access, the worst time cost is 2046, because the algorithm needs to do 2 updates on the span list for each of the remaining 1023 data elements. [2] The average is 1534.

In the other extreme when the maximal priority is 10 million, much greater than the data size, the overall cost is on average 1026 for space and 1537 for time, nearly identical to the cost of LRU. The highest average overall cost is 4317 for space and 6556 for time, incurred when the range of the priority is up to 1024, the size of data set. The costs in all other cases are at most half of the highest costs. If the priority is up to 512, the average overall space and time costs are 1024 and 1535, near identical to LRU.

From the results of the random access trace, we can make the following observations on the number of spans in practice. First, the number is mostly constant, close to the single span in LRU, in most cases. Second, in the worst case, the maximal number of

---

[2] Two updates are needed for a single-span list because of an unnecessary span splitting.

max priority		1 (i.e. LRU)	16	64	256	512	1K	2K	4K	8K	16K	64K	256K	1M
space overhead	avg overall	1024	1024	1024	1024	1024	4317	2015	1472	1239	1129	1050	1030	1026
	avg per data element	1.0	1.0	1.0	1.0	1.0	4.2	2.0	1.4	1.2	1.1	1.0	1.0	1.0
	max overall	1024	1025	1026	1035	1058	11731	5391	2859	2038	1500	1145	1057	1040
	max per data element	1	2	2	3	5	37	23	16	12	8	6	4	3
time overhead	overall avg	1534	1534	1534	1534	1535	6556	3014	2203	1856	1692	1573	1544	1537
	overall max	2046	2046	2046	2050	2072	33660	18361	12155	9961	6640	5257	4256	3667

Table 5. The measured overhead of Algorithm 1 when computing the priority LRU stack distance over a random-access trace with 10 million accesses to 1024 data elements with random priorities. The maximal priority number ranges from 1 to 1 million. The space is measured by the number of being stored spans. The time is measured by the number of calls to a span update. In most columns, the time and space costs are close to LRU stack simulation. The highest cost is incurred when the priority is up to 1024, but this worst cost is still far smaller than the theoretical upperbound.

spans per data item is far smaller than the theoretical upperbound, 37 vs. 2048.

4. Optimal Size-oblivious Hint Insertion

4.1 Cache Size-dependent Hint Insertion

We previously proposed an optimal collaborative caching scheme called Program-assisted Optimal Caching (P-OPT) for LRU-MRU cache, in which an OPT cache simulation is used to decide the access type, LRU or MRU, for each access [11]. The process is the same as shown in the introduction in Figure 1. By default, all accesses are initialized as LRU. During the OPT simulation, an access is changed to MRU if the next access to the same data element is a cache miss. In other words, an access is selected as MRU if it does not lead to a data reuse in the OPT cache with the given cache size. The new trace tagged with the single-bit cache hints has the same minimal number of misses as OPT.

The details to obtain the optimal cache hints is shown in Figure 8. We run an offline OPT simulation on a trace from a_1 to a_n with a given cache size. At a_j, we find out that the data element X is evicted. Then a_i, the most recent access to X, is selected to use MRU.

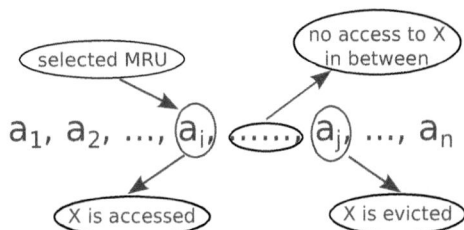

Figure 8. a_i is selected to use MRU for a given cache size during an OPT cache simulation

Compared with OPT, P-OPT encodes the future information by passing hints to the collaborative LRU-MRU cache. From the point view of hardware implementation, an LRU-MRU cache is much simpler than an OPT cache. In P-OPT, the access type for an access may change for different cache sizes in order to stay optimal. The hint insertion requires running another OPT cache simulation when the cache size is changed.

4.2 The Size-oblivious Hint Insertion

In P-OPT, cache hints may change with the cache size. However, the change is single directional similar to the inclusion property, as stated in the following Lemma 1.

LEMMA 1. *In P-OPT, an access is selected to use MRU in a smaller cache if it is selected to use MRU in a larger cache.*

Proof Assume we have two caches C_1 and C_2 ($|C_1| > |C_2|$) and an access trace. An access a_i to the data element X is selected to use MRU in C_1 in P-OPT, which means that the next access to X is a miss in an OPT cache with size $|C_1|$. Because of the inclusion property of OPT, the next access to X is also a miss in $|C_2|$. So a_i is selected as an MRU access in C_2 since a_i does not bring a cache reuse in OPT with size $|C_2|$. The lemma is proved. ∎

Lemma 1 indicates that a minimal cache size C exists for every access, which makes an access be selected to use MRU with the cache size no greater than C. Theorem 2 shows that the critical cache size is tightly correlated with the forward OPT stack distance, which is the minimal cache size to make the next reuse a cache hit in OPT.

THEOREM 2. *In P-OPT, an access is selected to use MRU if and only if the given cache size is less than its forward OPT stack distance.*

Proof Given an access a_i to a data element X, assume a_i has forward OPT stack distance d and the next access to X is a_j. From the definition of forward OPT stack distance, X is evicted between a_i and a_j if and only if the OPT cache size is less than d. Hence a_i is selected as MRU if and only if the cache size is less than d. The theorem is proved. ∎

A special case for Theorem 2 is the last accesses to data, which have infinite forward OPT stack distances. We use infinity as the critical cache size to select MRU for these last data accesses since none of them brings a cache reuse in any cache size.

The critical cache size serves well for all cache sizes to achieve optimal caching. We may encode forward OPT stack distances into priority hints for a dynamic cache control scheme, as shown in Figure 9. Like priority LRU, each access is associated with a priority hint. The cache logic in hardware dynamically compares the priority with the cache size and then chooses either the LRU or the MRU position for placing the accessed data element. As a result, a program is optimized for all cache sizes instead of a specific one. We need not know the cache size beforehand and the optimal hints are oblivious to the cache size.

5. Related Work

Cache hints and replacement policies The ISA of Intel Itanium extends the interface of the memory instruction to provide source and target hints [1]. The source hint suggests where data is expected, and the target hint suggests which level cache the data

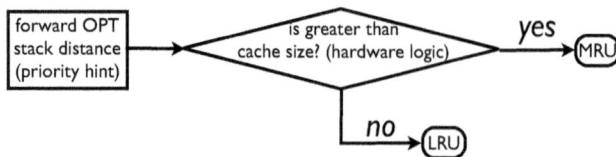

Figure 9. The dynamic cache control applies the optimal priority hint for a specific cache size.

should be kept. The target hint changes the cache replacement decisions in hardware. IBM Power processors support bypass memory access that do not keep the accessed data in cache [25]. Wang et al. proposed an interface to tag cache data with evict-me bits [29]. Our previous LRU-MRU studies considered single-bit hints for LRU and MRU [11, 12]. Recently, Ding et al. developed ULCC which uses page coloring to partition cache to separately store high locality and low locality data [8]. It may be used to approximate LRU-MRU cache management in software on existing machines. In this paper, a priority hint may place the accessed data element at an arbitrary position in cache, which is more general.

Mattson et al. established the property of inclusion and the metrics of stack distance [19]. The miss ratio of inclusive cache is monotonically non-increasing as the cache gets larger (whereas the Belady anomaly, more misses in larger cache, is impossible) [2]. Stack distance can be used to compute the miss ratio for cache of all sizes. They presented a collection of algorithms based on a priority list. The LRU stack distance, i.e. reuse distance in short, can be computed asymptotically faster (in near linear time for a guaranteed precision) using a (compression) tree [37]. The cost can be further reduced by sampling [36]. Recent work has developed multicore reuse distance to model the locality of multi-threaded programs [24] and the LRU-MRU stack distance to measure the performance of collaborative caching [12].

In this paper, we generalize the concept of inclusive cache and establish the new category of non-uniform inclusion. Previous algorithms cannot handle non-uniform inclusion. We give a new algorithm based on the notion of spans instead of the priority list or tree.

Collaborative caching Collaborative caching was pioneered by Wang et al. [29] and Beyls and D'Hollander [3, 4]. The studies were based on a common idea, which is to evict data whose forward reuse distance is larger than the cache size. Wang et al. used compiler analysis to identify self and group reuse in loops [20, 29, 30] and select array references to tag with the evict-me bit. They showed that collaborative caching can be combined with prefetching to further improve performance.

Beyls and D'Hollander used profiling analysis to measure the reuse distance distribution for each program reference. They added cache hint specifiers on Intel Itanium and improved average performance by 10% for scientific code and 4% for integer code [3]. Profiling analysis is input specific. Fang et al. showed a technique that accurately predicts how the reuse distances of a memory reference change across inputs [9]. Beyls and D'Hollander later developed a static analysis called reuse-distance equations and obtained similar improvements without profiling [4]. Compiler analysis of reuse distance was also studied by Cascaval and Padua for scientific code [5] and Chauhan and Shei for Matlab programs [6].

The prior methods used heuristics to identify data in small-size working sets for caching. It is unclear whether cache utilization could be further improved. We showed the theoretical potential of LRU-MRU collaborative caching to achieve optimal cache performance [12]. Our approach used the OPT replacement policy to gain insights into program behavior, as shown in Figure 8. The advan-

tage is that we can partition a large working set and partially cache it to fully utilize the available cache space.

Two recent papers show the benefits of collaborative caching on current x86 processors. Yang et al. used non-temporal writes for zero initialization in JVM to reduce cache pollution [33]. Rus et al. used non-temporal prefetches and writes to specialize string operations like memcpy(), based on the data reuse information in certain static program contexts [23].

Virtual machine, operating system and hardware memory management Garbage collectors may benefit from the knowledge of application working set size and the affinity between memory objects. For LRU cache, reuse distance has been used by virtual machine systems to estimate the working set size [32] and to group simultaneously used objects [35]. There have been much research in operating systems to improve beyond LRU. A number of techniques used last reuse distance instead of last access time in virtual memory management [14, 26, 38] and file caching [15]. The idea of evicting dead data or least reused data early has been extensively studied in hardware cache design, including deadblock predictor [18], forward time distance predictor [10], adaptive cache insertion [22], less reuse filter [31], virtual victim cache [17], and globalized placement [34].

These techniques do not require program changes but they could only collect program information by passive observation. They were evaluated for specific cache sizes. Our work complements them in two ways. First in theory, we show the conditions for these techniques to maintain the inclusion property, for either LRU-MRU [12] or the general priority in this work. Second in practice, we show that program information can be used to obtain optimal caching for caches of all sizes.

Optimal caching Optimal caching is difficult purely at the program level. Kennedy and McKinley [16] and Ding and Kennedy [7] showed that optimal loop fusion is NP hard. Petrank and Rawitz showed that given the order of data access and cache management, the problem of optimal data layout is intractable unless P=NP [21]. We showed that collaborative caching, in particular, bypass LRU and trespass LRU [11], LRU-MRU [12], and now priority LRU can be used to obtain optimal cache management. Sugumar and Abraham gave an efficient algorithm for simulating OPT [28]. We used their algorithm in off-line training to select optimal LRU-MRU hints [12]. With priority LRU, we can now encode optimal hints for caches of all sizes.

6. Summary

In this paper, we have presented priority LRU and generalized the theory of collaborative caching. We proved the inclusion property by a careful consideration of all possible effects of priorities on cache management. More interestingly, through the theorem (and an example), we show non-uniform inclusion, which is a new category of inclusive cache that has not been explored in the previous literature. We give an algorithm to compute the priority LRU stack distance. The algorithm is radically different from previous solutions and can solve the problem of non-uniform inclusion. Finally, we show that the same priority hints can obtain optimal caching for all cache sizes, without having to know the cache size beforehand. This removes a limitation in the previous work and provides new ways for dealing with the remaining difficulties in practice.

Acknowledgments

The idea of priority hints was suggested by Kathryn McKinley, which was the starting point of this entire work. We also wish to thank Michael Scott, Engin Ipek, Tongxin Bai, and anonymous reviewers for their helpful comments.

References

[1] *IA-64 Application Developer's Architecture Guide*. May 1999.

[2] L. A. Belady, R. A. Nelson, and G. S. Shedler. An anomaly in space-time characteristics of certain programs running in a paging machine. *Communications of ACM*, 12(6):349–353, 1969.

[3] K. Beyls and E. D'Hollander. Reuse distance-based cache hint selection. In *Proceedings of the 8th International Euro-Par Conference*, Paderborn, Germany, Aug. 2002.

[4] K. Beyls and E. D'Hollander. Generating cache hints for improved program efficiency. *Journal of Systems Architecture*, 51(4):223–250, 2005.

[5] C. Cascaval and D. A. Padua. Estimating cache misses and locality using stack distances. In *Proceedings of the International Conference on Supercomputing*, pages 150–159, 2003.

[6] A. Chauhan and C.-Y. Shei. Static reuse distances for locality-based optimizations in MATLAB. In *Proceedings of the International Conference on Supercomputing*, pages 295–304, 2010.

[7] C. Ding and K. Kennedy. Improving effective bandwidth through compiler enhancement of global cache reuse. *Journal of Parallel and Distributed Computing*, 64(1):108–134, 2004.

[8] X. Ding, K. Wang, and X. Zhang. ULCC: a user-level facility for optimizing shared cache performance on multicores. In *Proceedings of the ACM SIGPLAN Symposium on Principles and Practice of Parallel Programming*, pages 103–112, 2011.

[9] C. Fang, S. Carr, S. Önder, and Z. Wang. Instruction based memory distance analysis and its application. In *Proceedings of the International Conference on Parallel Architecture and Compilation Techniques*, pages 27–37, 2005.

[10] M. Feng, C. Tian, C. Lin, and R. Gupta. Dynamic access distance driven cache replacement. *ACM Transactions on Architecture and Code Optimization*, 8(3):14, 2011.

[11] X. Gu, T. Bai, Y. Gao, C. Zhang, R. Archambault, and C. Ding. P-OPT: Program-directed optimal cache management. In *Proceedings of the Workshop on Languages and Compilers for Parallel Computing*, pages 217–231, 2008.

[12] X. Gu and C. Ding. On the theory and potential of LRU-MRU collaborative cache management. In *Proceedings of the International Symposium on Memory Management*, pages 43–54, 2011.

[13] M. D. Hill. *Aspects of cache memory and instruction buffer performance*. PhD thesis, University of California, Berkeley, Nov. 1987.

[14] S. Jiang, F. Chen, and X. Zhang. CLOCK-Pro: An effective improvement of the clock replacement. In *USENIX Annual Technical Conference, General Track*, pages 323–336, 2005.

[15] S. Jiang and X. Zhang. LIRS: an efficient low inter-reference recency set replacement to improve buffer cache performance. In *Proceedings of the International Conference on Measurement and Modeling of Computer Systems*, Marina Del Rey, California, June 2002.

[16] K. Kennedy and K. S. McKinley. Typed fusion with applications to parallel and sequential code generation. Technical Report TR93-208, Dept. of Computer Science, Rice University, Aug. 1993. (also available as CRPC-TR94370).

[17] S. M. Khan, D. A. Jiménez, D. Burger, and B. Falsafi. Using dead blocks as a virtual victim cache. In *Proceedings of the 19th international conference on Parallel architectures and compilation techniques*, PACT '10, pages 489–500, New York, NY, USA, 2010. ACM.

[18] A.-C. Lai, C. Fide, and B. Falsafi. Dead-block prediction & dead-block correlating prefetchers. In *ISCA*, pages 144–154, 2001.

[19] R. L. Mattson, J. Gecsei, D. Slutz, and I. L. Traiger. Evaluation techniques for storage hierarchies. *IBM System Journal*, 9(2):78–117, 1970.

[20] K. S. McKinley, S. Carr, and C.-W. Tseng. Improving data locality with loop transformations. *ACM Transactions on Programming Languages and Systems*, 18(4):424–453, July 1996.

[21] E. Petrank and D. Rawitz. The hardness of cache conscious data placement. In *Proceedings of the ACM SIGPLAN-SIGACT Symposium on Principles of Programming Languages*, Portland, Oregon, Jan. 2002.

[22] M. K. Qureshi, A. Jaleel, Y. N. Patt, S. C. S. Jr., and J. S. Emer. Adaptive insertion policies for high performance caching. In *Proceedings of the International Symposium on Computer Architecture*, pages 381–391, San Diego, California, USA, June 2007.

[23] S. Rus, R. Ashok, and D. X. Li. Automated locality optimization based on the reuse distance of string operations. In *Proceedings of the International Symposium on Code Generation and Optimization*, pages 181–190, 2011.

[24] D. L. Schuff, M. Kulkarni, and V. S. Pai. Accelerating multicore reuse distance analysis with sampling and parallelization. In *Proceedings of the International Conference on Parallel Architecture and Compilation Techniques*, pages 53–64, 2010.

[25] B. Sinharoy, R. N. Kalla, J. M. Tendler, R. J. Eickemeyer, and J. B. Joyner. Power5 system microarchitecture. *IBM J. Res. Dev.*, 49:505–521, July 2005.

[26] Y. Smaragdakis, S. Kaplan, and P. Wilson. The EELRU adaptive replacement algorithm. *Perform. Eval.*, 53(2):93–123, 2003.

[27] K. So and R. N. Rechtschaffen. Cache operations by MRU change. *IEEE Transactions on Computers*, 37(6):700–709, 1988.

[28] R. A. Sugumar and S. G. Abraham. Efficient simulation of caches under optimal replacement with applications to miss characterization. In *Proceedings of the International Conference on Measurement and Modeling of Computer Systems*, Santa Clara, CA, May 1993.

[29] Z. Wang, K. S. McKinley, A. L.Rosenberg, and C. C. Weems. Using the compiler to improve cache replacement decisions. In *Proceedings of the International Conference on Parallel Architecture and Compilation Techniques*, Charlottesville, Virginia, 2002.

[30] M. E. Wolf and M. Lam. A data locality optimizing algorithm. In *Proceedings of the SIGPLAN '91 Conference on Programming Language Design and Implementation*, Toronto, Canada, June 1991.

[31] L. Xiang, T. Chen, Q. Shi, and W. Hu. Less reused filter: improving L2 cache performance via filtering less reused lines. In *Proceedings of the 23rd international conference on Supercomputing*, ICS '09, pages 68–79, New York, NY, USA, 2009. ACM.

[32] T. Yang, E. D. Berger, S. F. Kaplan, and J. E. B. Moss. CRAMM: Virtual memory support for garbage-collected applications. In *Proceedings of the Symposium on Operating Systems Design and Implementation*, pages 103–116, 2006.

[33] X. Yang, S. M. Blackburn, D. Frampton, J. B. Sartor, and K. S. McKinley. Why nothing matters: the impact of zeroing. In *OOPSLA*, pages 307–324, 2011.

[34] M. Zahran and S. A. McKee. Global management of cache hierarchies. In *Proceedings of the 7th ACM international conference on Computing frontiers*, CF '10, pages 131–140, New York, NY, USA, 2010. ACM.

[35] C. Zhang and M. Hirzel. Online phase-adaptive data layout selection. In *Proceedings of the European Conference on Object-Oriented Programming*, pages 309–334, 2008.

[36] Y. Zhong and W. Chang. Sampling-based program locality approximation. In *Proceedings of the International Symposium on Memory Management*, pages 91–100, 2008.

[37] Y. Zhong, X. Shen, and C. Ding. Program locality analysis using reuse distance. *ACM Transactions on Programming Languages and Systems*, 31(6):1–39, Aug. 2009.

[38] P. Zhou, V. Pandey, J. Sundaresan, A. Raghuraman, Y. Zhou, and S. Kumar. Dynamic tracking of page miss ratio curve for memory management. In *Proceedings of the International Conference on Architectural Support for Programming Languages and Operating Systems*, pages 177–188, 2004.

Exploiting the Structure of the Constraint Graph for Efficient Points-to Analysis

Rupesh Nasre

Indian Institute of Science, Bangalore, India
and
The University of Texas, Austin, USA
nasre@acm.org

Abstract

Points-to analysis is a key compiler analysis. Several memory related optimizations use points-to information to improve their effectiveness. Points-to analysis is performed by building a constraint graph of pointer variables and dynamically updating it to propagate more and more points-to information across its subset edges. So far, the structure of the constraint graph has been only trivially exploited for efficient propagation of information, e.g., in identifying cyclic components or to propagate information in topological order. We perform a careful study of its structure and propose a new inclusion-based flow-insensitive context-sensitive points-to analysis algorithm based on the notion of dominant pointers. We also propose a new kind of pointer-equivalence based on dominant pointers which provides significantly more opportunities for reducing the number of pointers tracked during the analysis. Based on this hitherto unexplored form of pointer-equivalence, we develop a new context-sensitive flow-insensitive points-to analysis algorithm which uses incremental dominator update to efficiently compute points-to information. Using a large suite of programs consisting of SPEC 2000 benchmarks and five large open source programs we show that our points-to analysis is 88% faster than BDD-based Lazy Cycle Detection and $2\times$ faster than Deep Propagation. We argue that our approach of detecting dominator-based pointer-equivalence is a key to improve points-to analysis efficiency.

Categories and Subject Descriptors D.3.4 [*Programming Languages*]: Processors-Optimization

General Terms Algorithms, Languages

Keywords constraint graph, dominators, points-to analysis, context-sensitivity

1. Introduction

Points-to analysis is a method of statically determining whether two pointers in a program may point to the same location at runtime. The two pointers are then said to be aliases of each other.

Points-to analysis enables several compiler optimizations and remains an important static analysis technique. With the advent of multi-core hardware and parallel computing, points-to analysis enjoys enormous importance as a key technique in code parallelization. Enormous growth of the code bases in proprietary and open source software systems demands scalability of heap analyses over millions of lines of code. A large number of points-to analysis algorithms have been proposed in literature that make this research area rich in content [2, 3, 6, 15, 31, 33].

For analyzing a general purpose C program in a flow-insensitive manner, it is sufficient to consider all pointer statements of the following forms: address-of assignment (p = &q), copy assignment (p = q), load assignment (p = *q) and store assignment (*p = q) [25]. Load and store assignments are also referred to as complex assignments. A heap allocation is represented using an address-of assignment. We deal with context-sensitive (which takes into account the calling context of a function), flow-insensitive (which ignores control-flow), field-insensitive (which assumes that access to a field of an aggregate is to the whole aggregate) inclusion-based (Andersen-style) points-to analysis in this work.

A flow-insensitive analysis iterates over a set of points-to constraints until a fixed-point is obtained. Typically, the flow of points-to information is represented using a constraint graph G, in which a node denotes a pointer variable and a directed edge from node n_1 to node n_2 represents propagation of points-to information from n_1 to n_2. Each node is initialized with the points-to information computed by evaluating the *address-of* constraints. Edges are added to G initially by *copy* constraints and then by *complex* (*load* and *store*) constraints as the analysis progresses. This is because the edges introduced by *complex* constraints depend upon the availability of points-to information at nodes which, in turn, depends upon the propagation. Thus, as the analysis performs an iterative progression of the points-to information propagation, new edges get introduced in G due to the evaluation of the *complex* constraints, resulting in the computation of more and more points-to information at its nodes. When no more edges can be added and no more points-to information can be computed, G gets stabilized and a fixed-point (points-to information at the nodes) is reached. The information can then be used by various clients (e.g., slicing, array-bounds checking, etc.). An outline of this analysis is given in Algorithm 1.

Techniques have been developed for efficient propagation of the points-to information across the edges of a constraint graph. Online cycle elimination [8] detects cycles in G on-the-fly and collapses all the nodes in a cycle into a representative node. Cycle collapsing is possible because all the nodes in a cycle eventually contain the same points-to information. This significantly reduces the number of pointers tracked and speeds up the overall analysis. Wave and Deep Propagation [25] techniques perform a topological ordering of the edges and propagate only the difference in the points-to information in breadth-first or depth-first manner respec-

ISMM'12 June 15–16, 2012, Beijing, China.
Copyright © 2012 ACM 978-1-4503-1350-6/12/06. . . $10.00

Algorithm 1 Points-to Analysis using Constraint Graph

Require: set C of points-to constraints
1: Process address-of constraints
2: Add edges to constraint graph G using copy constraints
3: **repeat**
4:   Propagate points-to information in G
5:   Add edges to G using load and store constraints
6: **until** fixed-point

---

tively. These propagation orders significantly improve the points-to analysis time. In yet another method, various heuristics like Greatest Input Rise, Greatest Output Rise, and Least Recently Fired [16] work on the amount and recency of information computed at various nodes in the constraint graph to achieve a quicker fixed-point.

We propose a structure-driven approach that complements the existing techniques. Our approach is based on the notion of dominators in a directed graph. A node d dominates a node n if all the paths that reach n from a designated start node go through d. Specifically, we observe that if two nodes have the same dominator in the constraint graph, then their points-to information would be equal. In other words, the two nodes are pointer-equivalent. Also, the points-to information of the dominated node is precisely the same as the points-to information of the dominator. This makes the dominator and the dominated node exhibit pointer-equivalence. Further, since the dominator relationship is transitive, i.e., d_1 dominates n and d_2 dominates d_1 implies that d_2 dominates n, the whole dominator tree can be collapsed into a single node. In other words, a dominator can act as a representative for all its (transitively) dominated nodes and we can greatly reduce the number of pointers tracked during the analysis.

Unfortunately, however, the constraint graph G is not static; new edges keep getting added to it (Line 5 of Algorithm 1). Therefore, the dominator of a node in G may dynamically change as the analysis progresses. We use efficient algorithm to incrementally update the dominator tree of a graph. Further, we reduce points-to information propagation based on a key insight related to *dominance containment* to address this issue. Briefly, when the dominator of a node n changes from d_1 to d_2, dominance containment makes sure that the information from d_1 continues to reach n, which is true for a flow-insensitive inclusion-based points-to analysis. Using these techniques and making several engineering choices, we develop a highly efficient context-sensitive flow-insensitive points-to analysis based on dominators.

Our contributions are summarized below.

- The study of the structure of constraint graph to understand potential optimization opportunities. We devise the notion of dynamic pointer-equivalence and use dominators to compute it. We also theoretically prove several properties of constraint graph that have been un-explored so far.

- An efficient context-sensitive flow-insensitive points-to analysis exploiting the structure of the constraint graph. We also prove that our analysis is sound and as precise as an inclusion-based points-to analysis.

- Detailed experimental evaluation of the points-to analysis algorithm using a suite of programs including SPEC 2000 benchmarks and five large open source programs (namely, *httpd, sendmail, ghostscript, gdb* and *wine-server*. Our context-sensitive points-to analysis is 88% faster than BDD-based Lazy Cycle Detection [12] and 39% faster than Andersen's analysis [2]. Our context-insensitive version is 2× faster than Deep Propagation [25].

- Detailed study of the effect of pointer-equivalence to conclude that dominator-based pointer-equivalence is critical to detect non-trivial pointer-equivalent variables in the program.

The paper is organized as below. We briefly explain constraint graph and dominators in Section 2. In the same section, we also introduce the notion of pointer-equivalence via dominance relation. Using this pointer-equivalence, we present our context-insensitive points-to analysis algorithm in Section 3. We extend the algorithm for context-sensitivity in Section 4. We evaluate the effectiveness of our approach in Section 5 by running it on 21 benchmarks and comparing against the-state-of-the-art methods. We contrast our work with the relevant related work in Section 6 before concluding in Section 7.

2. Exploiting The Structure of Constraint Graph

We first explain the dynamic nature of a constraint graph using an example. Next, we formally define and informally discuss the notion of dominance in a general directed graph. Then, we study dominators in the context of points-to analysis to devise the concept of dynamic pointer equivalence.

2.1 Running Example

Consider the following set of points-to constraints derived from a C/C++ program.

$$a = \&x; a = \&y; e = \&z; p = \&d; q = \&c; q = \&x;$$
$$b = a; *q = a; *p = c; d = b; e = c; *e = q; x = *p;$$

When Algorithm 1 is run on the example above, the computation of points-to information in each iteration is shown in Figure 1.

Algorithm 1 takes three iterations to compute fixed-point for this example. In each iteration, new points-to information is computed at the nodes and new edges are added to the constraint graph.

In a directed graph, a node d dominates node n if all the paths from a start node s to n go through d. The node d is called a *dominator* and the node n is called a *dominee*. At the end of the analysis of our example in Figure 1, we observe that node a dominates nodes b, c, d when a is the start node. Note that the points-to information of nodes a, b, c, d is the same {x, y}. Thus, the analysis can make all these nodes as pointer-equivalent, so that, only one of them can be tracked during the analysis. Identifying pointer-equivalent variables is a key optimization technique for scaling points-to analysis. It avoids propagation of points-to information across the edges between pointer-equivalent variables, improving analysis efficiency. Thus, identifying dominator information in the constraint graph helps identify more pointer-equivalent variables resulting in faster analysis.

Note that at the end of Iteration 1, node a dominates node x when a is the start node. However, addition of the edge from node q to node x in Iteration 2 breaks this dominator-dominee relationship. Therefore, the dominator information is dynamic and it should be computed on-the-fly to achieve analysis soundness. However, exhaustively re-computing dominator information can be quite time-consuming. Therefore, we use incremental dominance computation, along with a few novel heuristics, to improve the analysis efficiency. For instance, note that although the dominator-dominee relationship between nodes a and x is broken, at the end of the analysis, points-to information of x is a superset of that of a, since no edges are removed from the graph. This helps us keep only a difference in the information between x and a.

We also observe in Figure 1 that node a dominates node e, but the two nodes have different points-to information. This happens because of the address-of constraint $e = \&z$, which adds a different points-to information to node e. Thus, a naive way of computing dominators in the constraint graph does not yield a sound result.

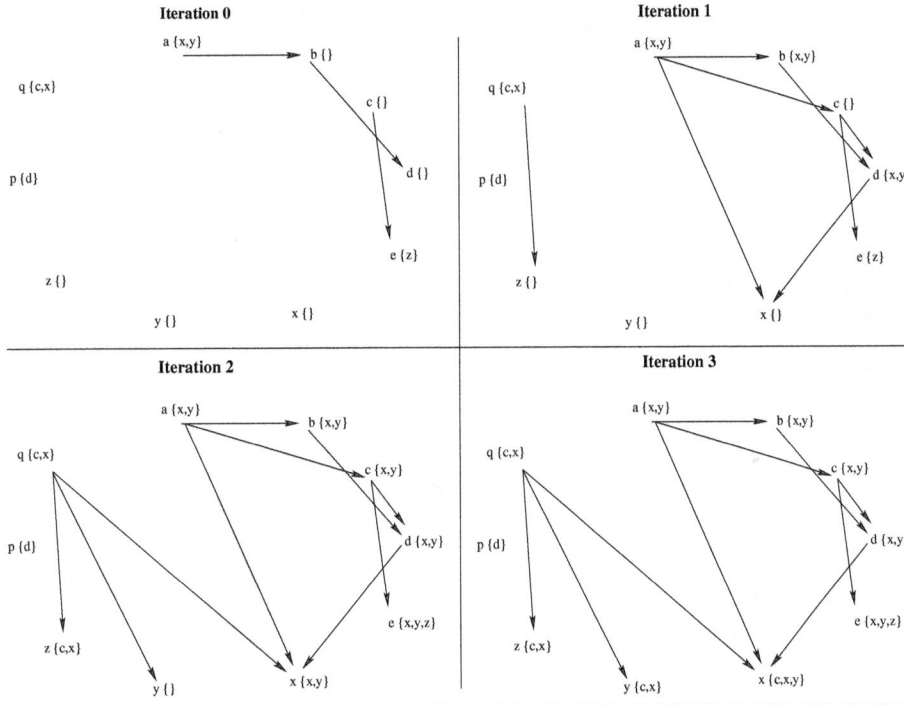

Figure 1. The state of the constraint graph in various iterations for the running example.

We modify the notion of constraint graph in the next subsection to seamlessly deal with such special cases.

2.2 Modified Constraint Graph

In our formulation, for ease of understanding and implementation, we slightly modify the constraint graph without affecting its characteristics. In the following discussion, we refer to a constraint graph by G and the modified constraint graph by G'. G = (V, E) where a vertex $v \in V$ represents a pointer node and a directed edge $(u, v) \in E$ represents a subset relationship between the points-to sets of pointers represented using nodes u and v, i.e., `pointsto(u)` $\subseteq$ `pointsto(v)`. We call u as the source node and v as the target node. We are now ready to modify the constraint graph G to G', which we use throughout our analysis.

First, G' = (V', E') contains a single unique node for each address-taken variable. Thus, V' = V $\cup$ {&v | v is an address-taken variable}. In the above example, the address-taken variables &d, &c, &x, &y, &z are represented using additional nodes as shown at the top in Figure 2. Note that in the original constraint graph G, the address-taken variables, which occur due to address-of constraints (p = &q), are directly added to the points-to set of the left-hand side pointer. In effect, G does not contain any node corresponding to the address-taken variables, and, in fact, it contains nodes corresponding to only the pointer variables. It should be noted that G' would contain one address-taken node and a separate pointer node for each address-taken variable (e.g., nodes x and &x).

Second, a directed edge is added for an address-of constraint p = &q from the node corresponding to &q to pointer node p. Thus, E' = E $\cup$ {(&u, v)|v = &u is an input constraint}.

In effect, while any node may act as a start node (node without any incoming edges) in G, in G', only those nodes that correspond to the address-taken variables can act as start nodes. If a pointer node n in the modified constraint graph G' does not contain any incoming edge, it can be proven that n has an empty points-to set.

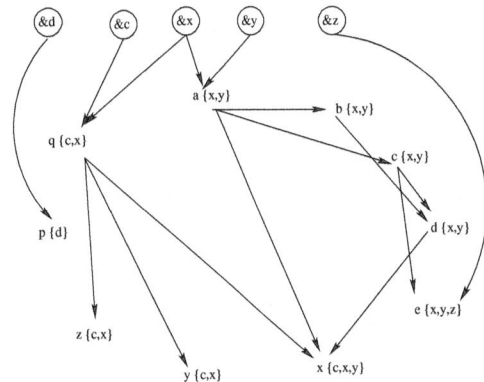

Figure 2. Modified constraint graph for the running example.

This formulation allows us to cast points-to analysis problem as a reachability problem in the constraint graph.

Theorem 1. *The points-to set of a pointer p is the set of start nodes from which the node p is reachable.*

The above claim can be easily verified from Figure 2. For instance, node x is reachable from start nodes &c, &x and &y and its points-to information is also {c, x, y}.

Corollary 2. *Two pointers reachable from the same set of start nodes are pointer equivalent.*

One may get tempted to conclude that a reachability formulation would allow us to discard any points-to information explicitly stored at the nodes, because of the availability of the same information in the form of paths (from address-of nodes to pointer nodes). In theory, this is true. However, it should be remembered that the constraint graph is dynamic, i.e., edges get added to G' in each iteration of the analysis. More succinctly, points-to analysis is essentially a dynamic reachability formulation over the modified constraint graph. The set of newly added edges depends upon the current points-to sets of pointers. Without storing the points-to sets explicitly at the nodes, the analysis would be compelled to re-compute the reachability in each iteration for adding edges. To avoid this inefficiency, points-to sets for pointers are maintained at the pointer nodes throughout the analysis.

2.3 Dominators

In traditional data-flow analysis, dominators are defined as below. A node d dominates node n if all the paths from a start node s to n go through d. When multiple start nodes $s_1, s_2, ..., s_i, ...$ exist, a usual trick is to create an extra start node s and add edges from s to all s_i. This trick allows us to take into account only a single start node without affecting the existing dominance relations. By definition, the dominance relation is reflexive, i.e., each node dominates itself.

In our analysis, we use a variant of the above definition which gets rid of the reflexivity property of the dominance relation. The modified definition not only makes our algorithm simpler, but is also more natural to understand and crucial to avoid special cases.

Definition 3 (Strict Dominator). *A node d strictly dominates another node n if all paths from all the start nodes s_i to n go through d. A node does not strictly dominate itself.*

A strict dominator is also called as proper dominator in literature [27]. A node may have zero, one or more strict dominators. Strict dominance is an irreflexive, asymmetric, but transitive relation. Efficient algorithms exist to compute dominators in a directed graph [5, 18].

Now onwards, unless mentioned otherwise, whenever we use the term dominator, it means a strict dominator.

2.4 Pointer Equivalence via Dominators

Computing dominators in a constraint graph is useful to identify pointer-equivalent variables. Two variables are pointer equivalent if they have the same points-to information. The above definition implicitly assumes that the points-to information of the two variables is considered at the fixed-point. However, in our case, since the dominator relationship across variables changes dynamically, pointer-equivalence is a dynamic relationship between pointer variables. In effect, two pointer-equivalent variables in an iteration may eventually cease to be pointer-equivalent. To the extent we know, ours is the first work that accounts for dynamic pointer equivalence and thus explores more opportunities to merge variables, resulting in a significantly improved analysis time.

We prove the following important claim which is a key to the efficiency of our points-to analysis.

Theorem 4. *A dominator and its dominee exhibit the same points-to information.*

Proof. The proof relies on the observation that `pointsto(dominator)` $\subseteq$ `pointsto(dominee)` and that by definition of dominance, no other points-to information flows into the dominee. □

Theorem 4 enables our analysis to collapse dominator and dominee into a single node, reducing the number of variables tracked during the analysis, greatly improving the analysis efficiency.

We would like to emphasize that most of the earlier work has focused on must pointer equivalence, i.e., once two pointers are identified as pointer equivalent, they continue to be so throughout the analysis. In a sense, the must pointer equivalence is a static property of two pointers. In our analysis, since the dominator information dynamically changes, the pointer equivalence between two pointers also changes as the analysis progresses. As we illustrate

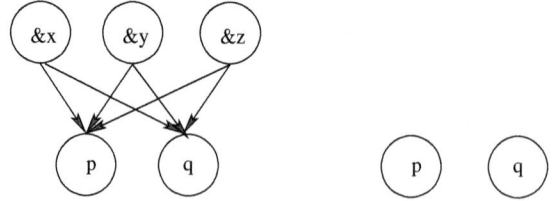

Figure 3. Example to illustrate that dominance relation does not cover all the pointer equivalence (a) Constraint graph (b) Dominance forest.

using an example below and experimentally in Section 5, dynamic pointer equivalence provides us with more opportunities to identify pointer equivalent variables.

2.5 Dominator Chain

The (strict) dominance relation can be pictorially depicted by a directed dominance edge from dominator d to node n Since dominance is a transitive relation, we can easily build a chain of dominators for each node ($d_k \rightarrow d_{k-1} \rightarrow ...d_2 \rightarrow d_1 \rightarrow n$). However, since two nodes may have the same dominator, the dominance relation exhibits a dominance tree. In general, the (strict) dominance graph is a forest.

Theorem 4 deals with a node and its dominator node. However, the theorem can also be applied to the dominator. Thus, Theorem 4, combined with the transitivity of dominance relation, provides us with the following important result.

Theorem 5. *All the pointers in a dominator tree are pointer-equivalent.*

Thus, an algorithm can represent a complete dominator tree using a single node and still compute the same fixed-point. Thus, the number of pointers tracked at any point during the points-to analysis is equal to the number of connected components (trees) in the dominance forest.

It is natural to ask whether the dominance relation *covers* all the pointer equivalence in the program, i.e., whether different connected components in the dominance forest can be pointer equivalent. It can be easily seen that two nodes in different dominance trees may have the same points-to information. An example is shown in Figure 3, wherein nodes p and q do not have a common dominator but they are pointer-equivalent.

Definition 6 (Immediate Dominator). *A node d is the immediate dominator of node n, if there exists no node d_2 such that d dominates d_2 and d_2 dominates n.*

The immediate dominator, when exists, is unique for a node. But several nodes may share the same immediate dominator. When a node has indegree = 1, i.e., it has a single incoming edge, then its parent is its immediate dominator.

Definition 7 (Farthest Dominator). *A dominator d is the farthest dominator of node n, if there exists no node d_2 such that d_2 dominates d.*

The farthest dominator, when exists, is unique for a node. But several nodes may share the same farthest dominator. The immediate and the farthest dominators for a node need not be distinct.

Dominance computation is a backward analysis, which starts from a node and traverses the graph backwards (from target to source of a directed edge) to reach its dominator. Such an analysis would first encounter the immediate dominator of a node and the farthest dominator in the end. Typically, one maintains only the immediate dominator information with each node which can then be transitively used to reach the farthest dominator. However, it

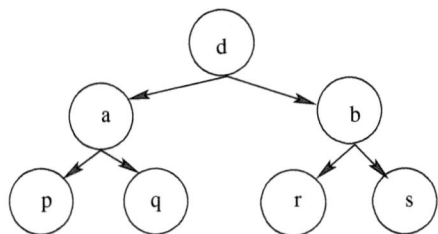

Figure 4. Example to illustrate the usefulness of maintaining the farthest dominator.

is easy to see that maintaining the farthest dominator information with each node would allow us more opportunities for identifying pointer equivalent variables. An example is shown in Figure 4. Nodes `p`, `q`, `r`, `s`, `a`, `b` all have the same farthest dominator d. However, their immediate dominators are not all same.

Maintaining the farthest dominator with each node, although more opportunistic, also poses a challenge. Recall that the constraint graph is dynamic and the dominance relations change in each iteration. We would like these relations to change as infrequently as possible, to reduce the cost of (incrementally) recomputing the new dominators. If each node maintains its farthest dominator, then addition of a random edge to the graph is more likely to change the farthest dominator, compared to the case when each node maintains its immediate dominator. Thus, there exists a tension between the cost of updating dominance relations and the opportunities for identifying pointer equivalent variables.

We address this dilemma using a mixed approach. In the initial iterations, when the constraint graph changes rapidly, our analysis maintains only the immediate dominator with each node. After a certain threshold number of iterations (calculated based on the size of the input program), the analysis starts moving the dominators up the dominator chain. Thus, each node's dominator information is updated as follows:

`dominator(n) := dominator(dominator(n))`, if exists.

Further, we also prioritize the constraint evaluation [22] so that edges are added near to the start nodes in the initial iterations, in order to reduce the number of changes to the dominator information in the later iterations.

3. Points-to Analysis using Dominators

In this section we present our points-to analysis algorithm using (strict) dominance relation. Since dominator information is dynamic (changes once per analysis iteration), incrementally recomputing dominators is essential for an efficient points-to analysis. We first explain incremental update of dominators and then present our points-to analysis algorithm. We prove that our approach is sound and the algorithm computes the same information as an inclusion-based points-to analysis.

3.1 Incremental Update of Dominators

Our constraint graph is essentially a directed acyclic graph; the cycles are collapsed by online cycle detection [24] in each iteration, before the dominators are incrementally updated. This enables us to use the incremental dominator update algorithm by Ramalingam and Reps [28] for reducible graphs. Since edges only get added and are never deleted from the constraint graph, we only need the relevant algorithm (Figure 3.4 from [28]). We only briefly mention the important steps of the algorithm below. The algorithm incrementally updates the dominator tree of the constraint graph for addition of an edge (u, v).

i. Compute the cut between two subgraphs of the constraint graph, one which contains node u and is reachable from the start nodes, and another which contains node v and is reachable from v. When v is already reachable from u, then it becomes a special case and can be solved efficiently.

ii. Compute the possibly affected set of nodes for each edge in the cut. The possibly-affected set is guaranteed to contain all the nodes for which a dominator update is required.

iii. Find the least common ancestor of all the predecessors of the nodes in the subgraph induced by forward edges, i.e., edges whose target nodes do not dominate their source nodes.

iv. Link the new dominator in the dominator tree.

We maintain the dominator tree using the same set of nodes in the constraint graph, but with an additional field pointing to its parent (when it exists) in the dominator tree. In addition, we maintain the following information.

- Whether an edge (u, v) is a back edge, i.e., whether v dominates u.

- An equivalence-class representative for each node, required for identifying pointer equivalent variables.

- Reachability information of each node from each of the start vertices. Note that this need not be separately maintained, as this is the same as the points-to information.

- A mapping from a dominator tree to its nodes, for easy enumeration of all the nodes of the tree when one is given as input. This mapping helps in updating the representatives of nodes when they are no longer in the same dominator tree.

The original algorithm for incremental update of dominator tree requires priorities assigned to the nodes for topological ordering. We do not explicitly maintain them since we maintain the incoming and outgoing edges with each node for traversing forward and backward in the constraint graph.

3.2 Points-to Analysis Algorithm

In this section we present our dominator-based points-to analysis. For better understanding, we first provide its outline in Algorithm 2 and then present the detailed steps in Algorithm 3.

Algorithm 2 takes a set of points-to constraints and a set of pointer variables and for each pointer variable, computes a set of values indicating its points-to information. The algorithm first processes the address-of constraints (Line 1) and creates a modified constraint graph G' as discussed in the previous section. It then processes the copy constraints and adds directed edges corresponding to them in G' (Line 2). At this stage, at Line 3 the algorithm computes an immediate dominator for each node in G'. This, in effect, creates a dominator tree (actually, a forest) over the nodes. Using the newly added edges in G', points-to information (generated due to the address-of constraints) is propagated to all the reachable nodes (Line 5). Various techniques like Wave/Deep Propagation [25] or Least Recently Fired [16] can be used to optimize the propagation. After the graph saturates, i.e., no more points-to information can be propagated, the algorithm adds more edges to G' using load/store constraints (Line 6). In Line 7, immediate dominators of the affected nodes are incrementally computed to obtain the modified dominator tree. Finally, in Line 8, the representatives of the dominator tree nodes are identified, which represent a complete dominator tree of pointer-equivalent variables. Steps in Lines 5–8 are repeated until there is no change in the points-to information of or until no more edges are added to the constraint graph, which suggests the algorithm has reached a fixed-point.

125

Algorithm 2 Outline of dominator-based points-to analysis.

Require: set C of points-to constraints, set V of variables
Ensure: each variable in V has a set of values indicating its points-to set
1: Process address-of constraints
2: Add edges to modified constraint graph G' using copy constraints
3: Build dominator tree DT for G'
4: **repeat**
5:     Propagate points-to information in G'
6:     Add edges to G' using load and store constraints
7:     Incrementally update dominator tree DT for the newly added edges
8:     Update the representatives of the dominator tree nodes.
9: **until** fixed-point

Iteration 1		Iteration 2		Iteration 3	
Node	Dominator	Node	Dominator	Node	Dominator
p	&d	p	&d	p	&d
b	a	b	a	b	a
d	b	d	a	d	a
		x	a	y	q
		z	q	z	q

Table 1. Immediate dominators in various iterations for the running example.

`for` loops at Lines 48–55 incrementally update the dominator trees for each newly added edge in `newedges`. The new dominator tree is computed by calculating the new immediate dominator of each affected node by the addition of an edge.

3.3 Example

When Algorithm 3 is executed on our running example from Section 2, the immediate dominators in various iterations are given in Table 1. The example reaches a fixed-point in Iteration 4 (which contains the same state of the dominator tree as in Iteration 3).

Note that the immediate dominator of d changes from b in Iteration 1 to a in Iteration 2, which illustrates the effect of immediate dominator moving up the dominator chain. Also note that the dominator-dominee relationship between (p, &d) and (b, a) remains fixed throughout the analysis and can be used to reduce the number of variables tracked. Further, the newly formed dominator-dominee relationships between (z, q) and (y, q) continue to hold until fixed-point and can also be used to reduce the number of variables tracked. Thus, for instance, all the instances of y can be replaced by q or vice versa, without affecting the final fixed-point. We emphasize that such dynamic relationships cannot be detected by any of the existing techniques and ours is the first approach which exploits the constraint graph structure to identify dominator-based pointer equivalence.

3.4 Soundness and Precision

We first prove that our dominator-based analysis is sound, i.e., it computes an over-approximation of the points-to information computed by an inclusion-based points-to analysis. We then prove that it is precise, i.e., it does not compute any additional information than that computed by an inclusion-based points-to analysis. In the proofs, we assume that both the analyses use the modified constraint graph G' (which is equivalent to the original constraint graph G w.r.t. the computation of points-to information).

Theorem 8. *Algorithm 3 is sound.*

Proof. We prove the claim by contradiction. Let there exist a points-to fact f which is computed by an inclusion-based analysis I but not by our dominator-based analysis D. Let it be the iteration in which f was first computed by I. $it > 0$, because 0th iteration corresponds to processing address-of constraints, and the processing of address-of constraints is handled in the same manner in both D and I, . If the fact f was not computed by D in iteration it, then $f{:}src \rightarrow dst$ was not propagated from src to dst. However, since Lines 22–32 ensure that points-to information is propagated in the current constraint graph upto a fixed-point, I and D differ in iteration it with respect to the node src being in the worklist in I and not being in the worklist in D. This suggests that the node src did not receive fact f as a new fact in iteration it of D. In other words, src already had fact f in its points-to set from the previous iteration. Therefore, D and I must differ in iteration $it - 1$. Arguing the same way for iteration $it - 1$ and using the fact that $it > 0$, we prove

We now describe our points-to analysis algorithm in detail, as presented in Algorithm 3. Our algorithm is worklist-based, and in each iteration of the algorithm, the worklist keeps track of the nodes from which the points-to information is to be propagated to its reachable neighbors, i.e., to the target nodes of its outgoing edges.

In Lines 3–8, address-of constraints are processed and all the start nodes are added to the worklist. The `for` loop at Lines 9–12 processes the copy constraints and updates the worklist. Lines 13–20 compute the dominator trees and their representatives. The representative for a dominator tree is an arbitrary but fixed node in the tree. In our analysis we set it to the root of the tree. The `repeat-until` loop at Lines 21–56 is executed until the fixed-point of the points-to information and the number of edges in the constraint graph G'. The `while` loop at Lines 22–32 iterates over each node u of the worklist to propagate information. The information, instead of propagating from u to its neighbors, is propagated from u's representative to the representative of its neighbor. The correctness of this way of propagating information can be easily verified. Propagating information across representatives significantly reduces the amount of points-to information propagated, since otherwise, multiple nodes may try to propagate the same information to a node (or multiple nodes). It also makes sure that the representative of each tree is kept up-to-date with the information. Keeping the representative up-to-date is critical, since later, if a node in a tree ceases to be pointer equivalent with other nodes, the representative's points-to information is used to update the points-to information of the node's new representative (Lines 50–54). Specifically, when the dominator-dominee relationship between two nodes is broken, following steps are performed: (i) dominee's representative is identified, (ii) dominee's new dominator is computed by the incremental dominator update procedure, and (iii) points-to information is scheduled to be propagated from the original representative to the dominee, using difference propagation. The above steps ensure that the dominee retains all of its points-to information from the earlier representative. The `for` loop running across Lines 34–46 processes load and store constraints in a standard way and adds new edges to G'. The set of newly added edges is kept track of in variable `newedges`. Note that edges are added between actual nodes and not between their representatives. This is because, later, when the dominator tree changes, we would want the edges to be present between nodes, rather than their representatives. Thus, our analysis adds the same set of edges as the traditional analysis, but uses a different propagation (via dominator tree representatives). The algorithm then calls a subroutine that detects and collapses cycles in the constraint graph. The subroutine does not actually delete any nodes and edges, but simply marks each node with its cycle representative. Note that a cycle representative is different from a dominator tree representative. The nested

Algorithm 3 Dominator-based points-to analysis.

Require: set C of points-to constraints, set V of variables
Ensure: each variable in V has its points-to set computed

```
1:  worklist = {}
2:  Initialize constraint graph G' = (V, E) with E = φ
3:  for each address-of constraint p = &q ∈ C do
4:      V = V ∪ v_{&q}
5:      E = E ∪ (v_{&q}, p)
6:      pointsto(v_{&q}) = {q}
7:      worklist.add(v_{&q})
8:  end for
9:  for each copy constraint p = q ∈ C do
10:     E = E ∪ (q, p)
11:     worklist.add(q)
12: end for
13: for each node v ∈ V do
14:     compute immediate dominator of v
15:     if v is a start node then
16:         assign v as its own representative
17:     else
18:         assign a randomly chosen but fixed representative within
            v's dominator tree
19:     end if
20: end for
21: repeat
22:     while worklist is not empty do
23:         u = worklist.remove()
24:         r_u = representative of u
25:         for each v ∈ outgoing(u) do
26:             r_v = representative of v
27:             pointsto(r_v) = pointsto(r_v) ∪ pointsto(r_u)
28:             if pointsto(r_v) changed then
29:                 worklist.add(r_v)
30:             end if
31:         end for
32:     end while
33:     newedges = {}
34:     for each load or store constraint c ∈ C do
35:         if c is a load constraint p = *q then
36:             for each v ∈ pointsto(q) do
37:                 E = E ∪ (v, p)
38:                 newedges = newedges ∪ (v, p), if (v, p) was newly
                    added to E
39:             end for
40:         else if c is a store constraint *p = q then
41:             for each v ∈ pointsto(p) do
42:                 E = E ∪ (q, v)
43:                 newedges = newedges ∪ (q, v), if (q, v) was newly
                    added to E
44:             end for
45:         end if
46:     end for
47:     detect and eliminate cycles in G' {from [24]}
48:     for each (u, v) ∈ newedges do
49:         incrementally update immediate dominators of v's domi-
            nator tree {Figure 3.4 from [28]}
50:         for each node w in v's (original) dominator tree do
51:             rold_w = representative of w
52:             compute the new representative rnew_w of w
53:             pointsto(rnew_w)     =     pointsto(rnew_w)     ∪
                pointsto(rold_w)
54:         end for
55:         worklist.add(u)
56:     end for
57: until newedges is empty
```

that if the fact f was computed by I, it must also be computed by D. This completes the proof. ☐

Theorem 9. *Algorithm 3 is precise.*

Proof. The proof is similar to the one for Theorem 8. Let there exist a points-to fact f which is computed by our dominator-based analysis D but not by an inclusion-based analysis I. Let it be the iteration in which f was first computed by D. Since address-of constraints are processed by both D and I in the same manner, $it > 0$. If the fact f was additionally computed by D in iteration it, then $f{:}src \rightarrow dst$ was additionally propagated from src to dst. Thus, I and D differ in iteration it with respect to the node src being in the worklist (Lines 22–32) in D and not being in the worklist in I. This suggests that the node src did not receive fact f as a new fact in iteration it of I. In other words, src already had fact f in its points-to set from the previous iteration. Therefore, D and I must differ in iteration $it - 1$. Arguing the same way for iteration $it - 1$ and using the fact that $it > 0$, we prove that if the fact f was computed by D, it must also be computed by I. This completes the proof. ☐

3.5 Balancing Analysis Cost

Since the dominator information changes with each addition of an edge, it is essential to keep the cost of updating dominators to a minimum. We employ the following optimizations to reduce it.

- Dominators are updated for several edges in a batch, rather than individually for each edge. This helps in reducing the number of changes to the new dominator of a node.

- Points-to information is propagated across dominator tree representatives rather than individual nodes. This essentially propagates information across trees rather than individual edges.

- We prioritize the constraint evaluation [22] so that edges are added near to the start nodes in the initial iterations, in order to reduce the number of changes to the dominator information in the later iterations.

- When the dominator of a node n changes from d_1 to d_2, instead of copying all the points-to information from d_1 to n, we simply maintain an additional pointer with n suggesting that all of the points-to information of d_1 is contained in that of n.

3.6 Avoiding Dominator Update

It should be noted that in certain cases, dominator information of a node need not be updated. Some of these cases are costly to handle as they involve traversing a large part of the constraint graph. We list below some situations which can be quickly checked.

- If v is not address-taken, and v and the nodes on the path between itself and its immediate dominator do not appear as a destination of a load/store constraint.

- If v is not address-taken, v appears as a destination of a load $v = *q$ but q's points to information did not change in this iteration.

- If v is address-taken, but no edge is added to a node on the path between v and its immediate dominator in this iteration.

- If v is address-taken, but edges are added only between the nodes on the path between v and its immediate dominator in this iteration.

4. Context-Sensitive Analysis

We extend the context-insensitive analysis in Algorithm 3 for context-sensitivity using an invocation graph based approach [7].

Algorithm 4 Context-sensitive analysis.

Require: Function f, callchain cc, constraints C, variable set V
1: **for all** statements s ∈ f **do**
2:   **if** s is of the form p = alloc() **then**
3:     **if** inrecursion == false **then**
4:       $V = V \cup (p, cc)$
5:     **end if**
6:   **else if** s is of the form non-recursive call fnr **then**
7:     cc.add(fnr)
8:     add copy constraints to C for actual and formal arguments
9:     call Algorithm 4 with parameters fnr, cc, C
10:     add copy constraints to C for return value of fnr and ℓ-value in s
11:     cc.remove()
12:   **else if** s is of the form recursive call fnr **then**
13:     inrecursion = true
14:     C-cycle = {}
15:     **repeat**
16:       **for all** functions fc ∈ cyclic callchain **do**
17:         call Algorithm 4 with parameters fc, cc, C-cycle
18:       **end for**
19:     **until** no new constraints are added to C-cycle
20:     inrecursion = false
21:     $C = C \cup C\text{-cycle}$
22:   **else if** s is an address-of, copy, load, store statement **then**
23:     c = constraint(s, cc)
24:     $C = C \cup c$
25:   **end if**
26: **end for**

The approach readily disallows non-realizable interprocedural execution paths. The context-sensitive algorithm starts from function *main* and maintains a stack of function invocations, similar to the runtime. Thus, a *return* from a function always matches the function invocation at the top of the stack. Recursion is detected by examining the current call-chain at each function-invocation and checking if the function already exists in the call-chain. We handle recursion, which can introduce potentially unbounded number of contexts, by iterating over the cyclic call-chain and computing a fixed-point of the points-to tuples. Although this reduces analysis precision compared to a k-cfa [30] approach which keeps track of k contexts inside recursion, the reduction is not substantial as we track complete contexts outside recursion. Our analysis is field-insensitive, i.e., we assume that any reference to a field inside a structure is to the whole structure. We also map any references to an array element to the whole array. Our algorithm handles function pointers similar to [7] by gradually refining the target functions. The context-sensitive version is outlined in recursive Algorithm 4, which we explain next.

The algorithm takes four parameters: the function f to be processed, its calling context cc, the set of constraints C to be generated and the set of variables V to be created. The analysis first adds $(g, \{\})$ to V for each global variable g where {} denotes an empty context (not shown in the algorithm). It then makes the first call to the algorithm with parameters *main*, {*main*}, C={}, V. The procedure processes all the statements in the function and generates context-sensitive points-to constraints in C. C is later evaluated using Algorithm 3. Lines 2–5 in Algorithm 4 process memory allocation and create a new variable on encountering an *alloc* statement outside recursion. Lines 6–11 handle a non-recursive call. It first adds the callee to the callchain and then maps the actual arguments to the formal arguments. The algorithm recursively calls itself in Line 9 to process the invocation graph of the callee. The callee is analyzed the same way and the set of constraints C keeps

getting updated. On the callee function's return, its return value is mapped to the ℓ-value in the call statement. Finally, the calling context is updated by removing the callee. A recursive call is handled in Lines 12–21 by iterating over the cyclic call chain and computing a fixed-point of the points-to information by the constraints in C-cycle. Note that the recursive call to Algorithm 4 in Line 17 uses the same callchain. The fixed-point over the constraints C-cycle generated in the cyclic call graph is then merged with C in Line 21. The corresponding context-sensitive constraints for address-of, copy, load and store statements are added in Lines 22–25. A context-sensitive constraint contains variables in a particular context. For instance, a copy constraint is of the form $a_{c_1} = b_{c_2}$ where a and b are variables and c_1 and c_2 are contexts. The two sets, C and V are finally passed on to Algorithm 3 for solving. The reason for designing the analysis as a two step process (generating constraints and solving them) is to have a common constraint solving phase (with minor modifications). Thus, Algorithm 3 is used for both context-insensitive and context-sensitive analysis.

5. Experimental Evaluation

We evaluate the effectiveness of our approach using 16 SPEC C/C++ benchmarks and five large open source programs, namely *httpd, sendmail, ghostscript, gdb* and *wine-server*. The benchmark characteristics are given in Table 2. *KLOC* is the number of kilo lines of unprocessed source code, *Total Inst* is the total number of static LLVM instructions after optimizing at -O2 level, *Pointer Inst* is the number of static pointer-type LLVM instructions processed by the analysis and *Func* is the number of functions in the benchmark. The LLVM intermediate representations of SPEC 2000 benchmarks and open source programs were run using the *opt* tool of LLVM on an Intel Xeon machine with 2 GHz clock and 16 GB RAM running Debian GNU/Linux 5.0.

We have two implementations of our dominator-based points-to analysis: context-insensitive referred to as *doms-ci* and context-sensitive referred to as *doms-cs*. We compare *doms* with the following highly optimized implementations.

- *anders*: This is the base Andersen's algorithm [2] which is field-insensitive, flow-insensitive and context-insensitive (*anders-ci*). We extend it for context-sensitivity using the same approach as for *doms-cs* (see Section 4) and the context-sensitive version is referred to as *anders-cs*. It uses sparse bitmaps to store points-to information.

- *bddlcd*: This is the *Lazy Cycle Detection* (LCD) algorithm implemented using Binary Decision Diagrams (BDD) from Hardekopf and Lin [12]. The base implementation (as downloaded from [10]) is context-insensitive (*bddlcd-ci*). We extend it for context-sensitivity using the same approach as for *doms-cs* (Section 4) and we refer to it as *bddlcd-cs*.

- *deep*: This is the context-insensitive Deep Propagation method from [25] (downloaded from [26]). This method propagates points-to information in the constraint graph to all the reachable nodes in a depth-first manner along a path, before the other paths are considered. It uses a sparse bitmap representation to store points-to sets has been shown to scale well.

We separate the following discussion for context-sensitive (cs) analyses and context-insensitive (ci) analyses.

5.1 Context-sensitive Analysis

Table 2 shows the analysis time and memory requirement for various context-sensitive algorithms. We observe that *doms-cs* is the fastest of the three algorithms. Specifically, it is 39% faster than *anders-cs* and 88% faster than *bddlcd-cs*. Our result adds one more

Benchmark	KLOC	# Total Inst	# Pointer Inst	# Func	Time (seconds)			Memory (MB)		
					anders-cs	bddlcd-cs	doms-cs	anders-cs	bddlcd-cs	doms-cs
176.gcc	222.185	328,425	119,384	1,829	330	17411	284	2859	2534	2168
253.perlbmk	81.442	143,848	52,924	1,067	143	5880	97	2133	1723	1873
254.gap	71.367	118,715	39,484	877	91	4726	71	1857	1358	1550
255.vortex	67.216	75,458	16,114	963	94	2392	76	1276	1425	910
177.mesa	59.255	96,919	26,076	1,040	35	618	24	478	345	422
186.crafty	20.657	28,743	3,467	136	129	330	89	457	362	384
300.twolf	20.461	49,507	15,820	215	30	200	22	735	692	689
175.vpr	17.731	25,851	6,575	228	29	155	21	672	566	601
252.eon	17.679	126,866	43,617	1,723	89	22	62	894	729	820
188.ammp	13.486	26,199	6,516	211	34	55	28	427	336	375
197.parser	11.394	35,814	11,872	356	42	27	33	624	617	483
164.gzip	8.618	8,434	991	90	25	7	17	514	522	446
256.bzip2	4.650	4,832	759	90	23	5	13	633	588	583
181.mcf	2.414	2,969	1,080	42	22	32	12	403	389	381
183.equake	1.515	3,029	985	40	24	4	14	546	527	493
179.art	1.272	1,977	386	43	27	8	18	597	582	519
httpd	125.877	220,552	104,962	2,339	225	47	179	791	825	688
sendmail	113.264	171,413	57,424	1,005	173	118	163	914	851	800
ghostscript	438.204	906,398	488,998	6,991	4384	20613	2935	1958	1672	1627
gdb	474.591	576,624	362,171	7,127	9338	24872	5179	2194	1859	1673
wine-server	178.592	110,785	66,501	2,105	201	37	139	774	690	622
average	92.946	145,874	67,910	1,358	738	3693	451	1035	918	862

Table 2. Benchmark characteristics and comparison with context-sensitive algorithms.

data point to the analysis time efficiency of bitmaps versus BDDs: using sparse bitmaps is much faster than accessing BDDs. In our experience, BDDs are well suited for reducing the storage requirement, but the complex logic in enumerating and updating points-to information of pointers is significantly costly in terms of analysis time.

In terms of memory, the BDD-based implementation *bddlcd-cs* beats our highly optimized *anders-cs*. However, as a pleasant surprise, *doms-cs* consumes lesser memory than *bddlcd-cs* by a non-trivial margin (918 MB versus 862 MB). The larger saving in memory occurs due to detection of more dynamic pointer-equivalences compared to other two methods (see Section 5.3). Although *doms-cs* maintains additional information (like immediate dominators and reachability information), the memory benefits significantly outweigh the costs. This helps our analysis reduce not only the propagation time, but also the number of copies of the points-to sets across variables, since pointer-equivalent variables share only a single copy of points-to information.

5.2 Context-insensitive Analysis

We compare the performance of our context-insensitive dominator-based points-to analysis against Andersen's Analysis *anders-ci* [2], BDD-based Lazy Cycle Detection *bddlcd-ci* [12] and Deep Propagation *deep-ci* [25], in Table 3. From the results, it is clear that *doms-ci* is almost 4×, 3×, and more than 2× faster than *anders-ci*, *bddlcd-ci*, and *deep-ci* respectively. This happens mainly due to the reduction in the number of propagations of points-to sets in the constraint graph by the detection of dynamic pointer-equivalent variables. For the same reason, the memory requirement of *doms-ci* is also relatively smaller than that of *anders-ci* and *deep-ci*. However, in terms of memory requirement, *bddlcd-ci* performs the best for context-insensitive analysis. Our analysis *doms-ci* requires 63% more memory than *bddlcd-ci*. For smaller programs, the memory reduction by identifying pointer equivalence is offset by the additional memory requirement for storing auxiliary information like immediate dominators, the reachability information and the book-keeping for incremental dominator update. However, it is interest-

ing to see that the additional memory required by *doms-ci* goes on reducing with the increasing program size. Specifically, for the two largest benchmarks in our suite, *ghostscript* and *gdb*, the memory requirements of both *bddlcd-ci* and *doms-ci* are almost the same. This suggests that the benefit of identifying pointer-equivalence outweighs the cost of additional bookkeeping especially for larger programs. This is evident from the (lesser) memory requirement of *doms-ci* in case of context-sensitive analysis (see Section 5.1).

In summary, our dominator-based points-to analysis offers significant performance benefits over the state-of-the-art methods.

5.3 Constraint Graph Statistics

We now present our results on applying the dynamic pointer equivalence method on the constraint graph. Figure 5 shows the percentage of the pointer-equivalent variables detected by various methods for our suite of benchmarks. Total number of pointer equivalent variables (i.e., 100%) is calculated by a separate analysis that exhaustively checks for pointer equivalent variables, i.e., pointers with the same points-to set, in the constraint graph and computes the number of *pairs* of such pointer equivalent variables. Then, the percentage of pointer-equivalent variables detected by a method is calculated as

$$100 * \frac{\text{no. of pointer-equivalent pairs detected by the method}}{\text{no. of pointer-equivalent pairs present in constraint graph}}$$

Offline Variable Substitution (*ovs*) [9] is able to detect only 19% of the total pointer equivalence. Hash-based Value Numbering (HVN) with deReference and Union (*hru*) is a powerful offline optimization technique for detecting pointer-equivalent variables [11], and it detects a superset of that detected by *ovs*. It is also able to detect only a quarter of the actual available pointer equivalence. Both these methods are offline, i.e., they are executed prior to running pointer analysis. Online cycle detection (*ocd*) [24] is an online method that periodically identifies and collapses cycles on the fly, while points-to analysis is in progress. We implemented the algorithm with the cycle detection done in every analysis iteration (same as in Algorithm 3). We observe that *ocd* is able to detect more

Benchmark	Time (seconds)				Memory (MB)			
	anders-ci	bddlcd-ci	deep-ci	doms-ci	anders-ci	bddlcd-ci	deep-ci	doms-ci
176.gcc	151.618	5.154	1.740	1.172	1269	27	83	42
253.perlbmk	65.969	3.078	1.744	1.392	669	17	100	56
254.gap	1.457	2.282	0.116	0.088	10	18	16	17
255.vortex	29.625	2.339	11.701	2.280	383	64	248	127
177.mesa	0.831	2.020	0.176	0.072	8	3	4	4
186.crafty	6.689	2.527	0.092	0.040	87	6	8	9
300.twolf	0.465	1.290	0.024	0.008	1	1	2	2
175.vpr	0.453	1.528	0.004	0.004	1	1	1	1
252.eon	1.029	2.231	0.248	0.112	3	4	14	13
188.ammp	0.372	1.347	0.032	0.012	1	2	3	2
197.parser	0.614	2.056	0.032	0.012	3	3	4	4
164.gzip	0.221	0.955	0.004	0.004	1	2	1	1
256.bzip2	0.199	0.889	0.004	0.004	1	2	1	1
181.mcf	0.175	1.228	0.004	0.004	1	1	1	1
183.equake	0.176	0.856	0.004	0.004	1	1	1	1
179.art	0.167	0.643	0.004	0.004	1	1	1	1
httpd	58.624	1.856	53.727	21.720	469	49	674	269
sendmail	37.276	1.521	12.729	9.512	353	64	256	182
ghostscript	425.362	343.579	207.033	124.248	547	177	2871	186
gdb	852.622	758.473	587.829	268.164	631	218	3556	214
wine-server	62.545	45.512	8.165	5.444	444	94	185	99
average	80.785	56.255	42.162	20.681	233	36	382	59

Table 3. Comparison with context-insensitive algorithms.

than half of pointer equivalence. However, it fails to detect a significant portion of pointer equivalence in the program. This happens not because of the frequency of cycle detection, but because cycle detection *cannot* exploit the constraint graph structure beyond a strongly connected component. When we combine *hru + ocd*, their combined effect is only 58%. Our observations about *hru* are in close agreement with those mentioned by Hardekopf and Lin [11]. Our results support our thesis that a combination of offline techniques and online cycle detection have inherent limitation in detecting the pointer equivalence prevalent in programs.

Running our Algorithm 3 improves the pointer equivalence detection percentage to almost 70% (*ocd + doms*). *doms* alone is able to detect additional 15% of the pointer-equivalence. When combined with an offline analysis phase of *hru*, the resultant analysis *hru + ocd + doms* is able to detect almost 75% of the total pointer equivalence. This suggests that existing methods can be combined with our dominator-based analysis for significant benefits.

We observe that around 25% of the pointer-equivalences are not detected by our algorithm. This happens because our algorithm does not try to detect all the variables that are reachable from the same start nodes. Two nodes in the constraint graph that do not have a common dominator nor are in a cycle can still be pointer equivalent if they are reachable from the same set of start (address-of) nodes (see Figure 3). Detecting such nodes is costly in our experience and it reduces the benefits of our optimizations.

In summary, the dominator-based pointer-equivalence algorithm is able to detect significantly larger number of pointer equivalences compared to the previous methods.

6. Related Work

Surveys on pointer analysis techniques are presented by Hind and Pioli [14] and Nasre [20].

Inclusion based algorithms incur cubic computational complexity. A naive implementation of Andersen's analysis turns out to be inefficient in practice. Therefore, several novel techniques have been developed to improve upon the original Andersen's analysis [3, 13, 19, 32]. Binary Decision Diagrams (BDD) [3, 32] are used

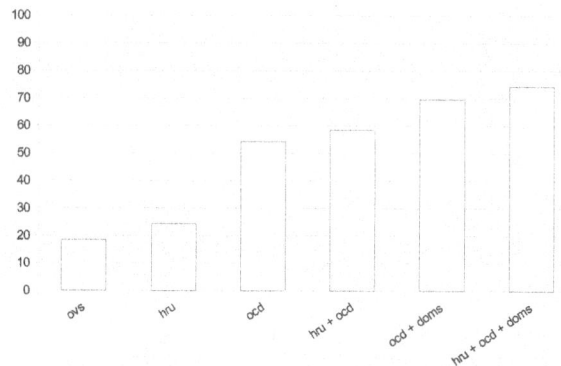

Figure 5. Percentage of pointer equivalence detected across our benchmark suite.

to store points-to information in a succinct manner. Although the space reduction using BDD is significant, it also incurs a performance penalty over sparse bitmaps, since accessing and merging points-to information involve a complex logic. The idea of *bootstrapping* [15] uses a divide-and-conquer strategy to first divide the large problem of pointer analysis by partitioning the set of pointers into disjoint alias sets using a fast and less precise algorithm (e.g., [31]) and later, a more precise algorithm analyzes each partition. Due to the small partition sizes, the overall analysis scales well with the program size. The analysis over the alias partitions can be done in parallel. Nasre et al. [21] convert points-to constraints into a set of linear equations and solve it using a standard linear solver. Storing complete calling context information achieves a good precision, but at the cost of storage and analysis time. For a complete context-sensitive analysis, potentially, the storage requirement and the analysis time can be exponential in the number of functions in the program making it non-scalable. Therefore, approximate representations have been introduced to trade off precision for scalability. Das [6] proposed *one level flow* while Lattner et al. [17]

unified contexts while Nasre et al. [23] hashed contexts to alleviate the need to store the complete context information.

Inclusion based analysis can also be improved using several novel enhancements proposed in literature. Online cycle elimination [8] breaks dependence cycles amongst pointer variables on the fly. Offline variable substitution [29] operates over constraints prior to the constraint evaluation to find out pointer equivalent variables and rewrites constraints with the reduced set of variables to improve the analysis time. Hardekopf and Lin [11] provide a suite of offline analyses based on Hash-based Value Numbering to further improve the effectiveness of offline methods.

Wave and Deep Propagation techniques [25] perform a breadth-wise and depth-wise propagation of points-to information in a constraint graph. Various techniques proposed for worklist management [16] also identify heuristics to reach the fixed-point faster. Prioritized constraint evaluation [22] dynamically orders constraints to produce useful edges early in the constraint graph. Although all of these techniques work on the constraint graph, they are orthogonal to our approach. Our dominator based technique is more comprehensive and provides more opportunities to identify pointer equivalent variables.

However, dominators have been extensively used in other dataflow analysis of programs. Cytron et al. [5] introduced the notion of dominance frontiers to efficiently compute static single assignment (SSA) form and control dependence graph of programs, and showed that their storage requirement is usually linear in the program size. Burke and Torczon [4] used dominators to avoid unnecessary recompilation of modules after a change to the source code. They described several methods to reduce the number of recompilations based on the trade-off between compilation time and the number of spurious recompilations. Agrawal and Horgan [1] reduced the cost of dynamic slicing by using dominators in the program dependence graphs. Ours is the first work that uses dominators for points-to analysis.

7. Conclusion

We defined a new type of dynamic pointer equivalence in this work based on the notion of dominators. Based on this notion, we developed a new context-sensitive points-to analysis which exploits the structure of the constraint graph to improve opportunities to detect more pointer-equivalent variables. We showed that the algorithm is sound and as precise as an inclusion-based analysis. We argued that detecting dominator-based pointer equivalence is critical for improving the efficiency of pointer analysis. Using a suite of benchmarks, we showed that our analysis performs significantly better than the state-of-the-art methods. We believe that dominator-based points-to analysis will find applications in several optimizations.

References

[1] H. Agrawal and J. R. Horgan. Dynamic program slicing. In PLDI, pages 246–256, 1990.

[2] L. O. Andersen. Program analysis and specialization for the C programming language, PhD Thesis, DIKU, University of Copenhagen, 1994.

[3] M. Berndl, O. Lhoták, F. Qian, L. Hendren, and N. Umanee. Points-to analysis using bdds. In PLDI, PLDI '03, pages 103–114, New York, NY, USA, 2003. ACM.

[4] M. Burke and L. Torczon. Interprocedural optimization: eliminating unnecessary recompilation. ACM Trans. Program. Lang. Syst., 15: 367–399, July 1993. ISSN 0164-0925.

[5] R. Cytron, J. Ferrante, B. K. Rosen, M. N. Wegman, and F. K. Zadeck. Efficiently computing static single assignment form and the control dependence graph. ACM Trans. Program. Lang. Syst., 13:451–490, October 1991. ISSN 0164-0925.

[6] M. Das. Unification-based pointer analysis with directional assignments. In PLDI, PLDI '00, pages 35–46, New York, NY, USA, 2000. ACM.

[7] M. Emami, R. Ghiya, and L. J. Hendren. Context-sensitive interprocedural points-to analysis in the presence of function pointers. In PLDI, PLDI '94, pages 242–256, New York, NY, USA, 1994. ACM.

[8] M. Fähndrich, J. S. Foster, Z. Su, and A. Aiken. Partial online cycle elimination in inclusion constraint graphs. In PLDI, PLDI '98, pages 85–96, New York, NY, USA, 1998. ACM.

[9] M. Fähndrich, J. Rehof, and M. Das. Scalable context-sensitive flow analysis using instantiation constraints. In PLDI, PLDI '00, pages 253–263, New York, NY, USA, 2000. ACM.

[10] B. Hardekopf. Homepage, http://www.cs.utexas.edu/users/benh/.

[11] B. Hardekopf and C. Lin. Exploiting pointer and location equivalence to optimize pointer analysis. In H. R. Nielson and G. Filé, editors, SAS, volume 4634 of Lecture Notes in Computer Science, pages 265–280. Springer, 2007.

[12] B. Hardekopf and C. Lin. The ant and the grasshopper: fast and accurate pointer analysis for millions of lines of code. In PLDI, PLDI '07, pages 290–299, New York, NY, USA, 2007. ACM.

[13] N. Heintze and O. Tardieu. Ultra-fast aliasing analysis using cla: a million lines of c code in a second. In PLDI, PLDI '01, pages 254–263, New York, NY, USA, 2001. ACM.

[14] M. Hind and A. Pioli. Which pointer analysis should i use? In ISSTA, ISSTA '00, pages 113–123, New York, NY, USA, 2000. ACM.

[15] V. Kahlon. Bootstrapping: a technique for scalable flow and context-sensitive pointer alias analysis. In PLDI, PLDI '08, pages 249–259, New York, NY, USA, 2008. ACM.

[16] A. Kanamori and D. Weise. Worklist management strategies for dataflow analysis, MSR Technical Report, MSR-TR-94-12, 1994.

[17] C. Lattner, A. Lenharth, and V. Adve. Making context-sensitive points-to analysis with heap cloning practical for the real world. In PLDI, PLDI '07, pages 278–289, New York, NY, USA, 2007. ACM.

[18] T. Lengauer and R. E. Tarjan. A fast algorithm for finding dominators in a flowgraph. ACM Trans. Program. Lang. Syst., 1(1):121–141, Jan. 1979. ISSN 0164-0925. doi: 10.1145/357062.357071. URL http://doi.acm.org/10.1145/357062.357071.

[19] O. Lhoták and L. Hendren. Scaling java points-to analysis using spark. In Proceedings of the 12th international conference on Compiler construction, CC'03, pages 153–169, Berlin, Heidelberg, 2003. Springer-Verlag.

[20] R. Nasre. Scaling context-sensitive points-to analysis, Ph.D. Thesis, CSA, Indian Institute of Science, 2012.

[21] R. Nasre and R. Govindarajan. Points-to analysis as a system of linear equations. In Proceedings of the 17th international conference on Static analysis, SAS'10, pages 422–438, Berlin, Heidelberg, 2010. Springer-Verlag. ISBN 3-642-15768-8, 978-3-642-15768-4. URL http://portal.acm.org/citation.cfm?id=1882094.1882120.

[22] R. Nasre and R. Govindarajan. Prioritizing constraint evaluation for efficient points-to analysis. In CGO, CGO '11, 2011.

[23] R. Nasre, K. Rajan, R. Govindarajan, and U. P. Khedker. Scalable context-sensitive points-to analysis using multi-dimensional bloom filters. In Proceedings of the 7th Asian Symposium on Programming Languages and Systems, APLAS '09, pages 47–62, Berlin, Heidelberg, 2009. Springer-Verlag. ISBN 978-3-642-10671-2.

[24] D. J. Pearce, P. H. J. Kelly, and C. Hankin. Online cycle detection and difference propagation: Applications to pointer analysis. Software Quality Control, 12:311–337, December 2004.

[25] F. M. Q. Pereira and D. Berlin. Wave propagation and deep propagation for pointer analysis. In CGO, CGO '09, pages 126–135, Washington, DC, USA, 2009. IEEE Computer Society.

[26] pereiraweb. Wave propagation / deep propagation website, http://compilers.cs.ucla.edu/fernando/projects/pta/home/.

[27] G. Ramalingam. The undecidability of aliasing. ACM Trans. Program. Lang. Syst., 16:1467–1471, September 1994. ISSN

0164-0925. doi: http://doi.acm.org/10.1145/186025.186041. URL http://doi.acm.org/10.1145/186025.186041.

[28] G. Ramalingam and T. Reps. An incremental algorithm for maintaining the dominator tree of a reducible flowgraph. In PLDI, POPL '94, pages 287–296, New York, NY, USA, 1994. ACM.

[29] A. Rountev and S. Chandra. Off-line variable substitution for scaling points-to analysis. In PLDI, PLDI '00, pages 47–56, New York, NY, USA, 2000. ACM.

[30] O. G. Shivers. Control-flow analysis of higher-order languages, PhD Thesis, Carnegie Mellon University, 1991.

[31] B. Steensgaard. Points-to analysis in almost linear time. In POPL, POPL '96, pages 32–41, New York, NY, USA, 1996. ACM.

[32] J. Whaley and M. S. Lam. An efficient inclusion-based points-to analysis for strictly-typed languages. In Proceedings of the 9th International Symposium on Static Analysis, SAS '02, pages 180–195, London, UK, 2002. Springer-Verlag.

[33] J. Whaley and M. S. Lam. Cloning-based context-sensitive pointer alias analysis using binary decision diagrams. In Proceedings of the ACM SIGPLAN 2004 conference on Programming language design and implementation, PLDI '04, pages 131–144, New York, NY, USA, 2004. ACM. ISBN 1-58113-807-5. doi: http://doi.acm.org/10.1145/996841.996859. URL http://doi.acm.org/10.1145/996841.996859.

Identifying the Sources of Cache Misses in Java Programs Without Relying on Hardware Counters

Hiroshi Inoue and Toshio Nakatani

IBM Tokyo Research Laboratory
1623-14, Shimo-tsuruma, Yamato-shi, Kanagawa-ken, 242-8502, Japan
{inouehrs, nakatani}@jp.ibm.com

Abstract

Cache miss stalls are one of the major sources of performance bottlenecks for multicore processors. A Hardware Performance Monitor (HPM) in the processor is useful for locating the cache misses, but is rarely used in the real world for various reasons. It would be better to find a simple approach to locate the sources of cache misses and apply runtime optimizations without relying on an HPM. This paper shows that pointer dereferencing in hot loops is a major source of cache misses in Java programs. Based on this observation, we devised a new approach to identify the instructions and objects that cause frequent cache misses. Our heuristic technique effectively identifies the majority of the cache misses in typical Java programs by matching the hot loops to simple idiomatic code patterns. On average, our technique selected only 2.8% of the load and store instructions generated by the JIT compiler and these instructions accounted for 47% of the L1D cache misses and 49% of the L2 cache misses caused by the JIT-compiled code. To prove the effectiveness of our technique in compiler optimizations, we prototyped object placement optimizations, which align objects in cache lines or collocate paired objects in the same cache line to reduce cache misses. For comparison, we also implemented the same optimizations based on the accurate information obtained from the HPM. Our results showed that our heuristic approach was as effective as the HPM-based approach and achieved comparable performance improvements in the SPECjbb2005 and SPECpower_ssj2008 benchmark programs.

Categories and Subject Descriptors D.3.4 [**Programming Languages**]: [Programming Languages]: Processors – Compilers, Optimization, Memory management.

General Terms Measurement, Performance, Experimentation.

Keywords Hardware performance monitor, Object placement optimization

1. Introduction

Cache miss stalls are one of the major sources of performance

bottlenecks in high performance processors. Hence, it is important for compilers and language runtime systems to use the processor cache efficiently, especially on multicore processors, which have limited memory bandwidth compared to the huge computation resources. Previous techniques [1-4] showed that cache miss profiles were useful for runtime systems in reducing cache misses and improve the performance of cache-miss-intensive programs. These previous techniques used an HPM (Hardware Performance Monitor) in the processor to obtain cache miss profiles. However, for a compiler to use the HPM in is difficult because the HPM functions are often specific to the processor, the HPM may require a special device driver and super-user privilege, and only one process can use the HPM at a time.

In this paper, we identify the source of cache misses without relying on hardware support. We used an HPM for a thorough study of various Java programs and identified the hot loops that cause frequent cache misses. We found that many of them can be classified into a small set of patterns that can be heuristically detected as simple idioms without relying on an HPM. In general, the idioms correspond to repeated indirect loads from the Java heap in hot loops. Typical object-oriented programs heavily use complicated data structures, such as hashmaps and linked lists, and many cache misses come from accesses to such data structures. Our basic idioms work well for many Java programs because they can effectively capture such accesses. We experimentally showed that our heuristic approach effectively identified a large part of the L1 and L2 cache misses in many Java programs, including SPECjbb2005, SPECpower_ssj2008, SPECjvm2008, and the DaCapo benchmark suite. On average, our technique selected only 2.8% of the load and store instructions generated by the JIT compiler and these instructions accounted for 47.3% of the L1D cache misses and 48.9% of the L2 data cache misses caused by the JIT-compiled code. Compared to the total number of load and store instructions and cache misses caused by hot methods that we apply our analysis, our technique achieved about 63.6% and 69.2% coverage for the L1 and L2 cache misses by selecting 14.2% of the load and store instructions in the hot methods.

We demonstrate the effectiveness of our technique for compiler optimizations. We prototyped two types of object placement optimizations based on our heuristic approach in a Java VM with a JIT compiler. We compared the performance improvements from the optimizations based on our heuristic approach against the similar optimizations based on accurate cache miss statistics obtained from the HPM. Our optimizations showed performance improvements in two benchmarks with many cache misses, SPECjbb2005 and SPECpower_ssj2008. These performance improvements were close to the gains based on the accurate cache miss statistics from the HPM.

The main contributions of this paper are two-fold. (1) We present a technique to identify the instructions and objects that frequently cause cache misses in Java programs without relying on an HPM. (2) We prototyped the online optimizations in a Java JIT compiler using our heuristic approach and compared to the HPM-based approach. Our results showed that our technique is effective in implementing optimizations in dynamic compilers.

The rest of the paper is organized as follows. Section 2 discusses related techniques. Section 3 presents our no-HPM technique to identify the instructions that cause frequent cache misses. Section 4 describes the experimental environment and our results. Section 5 explains how we use the pattern-matching-based heuristic approach in compiler optimizations. We also show the performance gains from our optimizations and compare them to the HPM-based approach. Section 6 summarizes our work.

2. Related Work

In this paper, we identify the instructions and objects that tend to cause many cache misses. Burtscher *et al.* [5] classified load instructions based on the region of memory (stack, heap, or global), the kind of reference (array, field, or scalar) and the type of data (pointer or value). They showed that load instructions for certain classes caused more cache misses than others in C and Java programs. Our technique identifies exactly those load and store instructions that tend to cause many cache misses. Panait *et al.* [6] proposed a technique to statically identify the load instructions that cause many cache misses. They call such a load instruction a delinquent load. Their technique focuses on analyzing program binaries to calculate a weight for each load instruction. They estimate the likelihood each load causes cache misses based on criteria such as the number of dereferences and the base register used to calculate the address to be accessed. Our technique identifies more information for compiler optimizations, such as the target classes, rather than just identifying load instructions that cause cache misses. Therefore we focus on analyzing the compiler IR, which includes more information than the binaries. We demonstrated the practical effectiveness of our technique by implementing two types of optimizations in a Java JIT compiler, in contrast to simply identifying the delinquent load instructions.

There are some techniques that use cache miss profiles from HPMs for optimizations in compilers and runtime systems. Adl-Tabatabai *et al.* [1] exploit cache miss statistics in their Java JIT compiler to insert effective prefetch instructions for the Itanium 2 processor. Schneider *et al.* [2] used cache miss statistics from the garbage collector to optimize the placement of objects in the Jikes RVM on the Pentium 4 processor. Serrano and Zhuang [3] also identified opportunities to reduce cache misses by reordering the objects in the garbage collector in the POWER5 and POWER6 processors. Cuthbertson *et al.* [4] exploited the HPM of the Itanium 2 processor for instruction scheduling and object collocation in the garbage collector. In our work, we use alignment [3] and collocation [2-4] to test the effectiveness of our approach, since they are two of the most proven optimization techniques based on cache miss profiles. Both HPM-based and pattern-matching-based optimizations use approaches similar to the previous techniques [2-4], locating load instructions that cause many cache misses, identifying target classes, and then optimizing the object locations to reduce the cache misses. Though we did not study prefetch injection [1] with our heuristic approach, it could be used to identify the targets for prefetching.

```
ClassA objA;
ClassB objB;
while (!end) { // in a hot loop

    ...
    // 1) first, load a reference of ClassA
    objA = objB.referenceToClassA;

    ...
    // 2) then, access a field of objA
    access to objA.field1;

    ...
}
a) a pattern for frequent cache misses


ClassA objA;
while (!end) { // in a hot loop

    ...
    // 1) first, load a reference of ClassA from
    //     a field of 'this' object
    objA = this.referenceToClassA;

    ...
    // 2) then, access a field of objA
    access to objA.field1;

    ...
}
b) anti-pattern
```

Figure 1. (a) A pattern that tends to cause frequent cache misses and (b) An anti-pattern that does not cause frequent cache misses.

Object placement optimization has a rich history of research and many software-based techniques have been proposed. These techniques use a variety of types of static and dynamic information that can be obtained without special hardware, such as field access profiles at read barriers [7, 8, 9], object lifetimes [10], allocation frequencies for each Java class [11], hints provided by the STL container libraries [12], or static access patterns analyzed at the compilation time [13]. Our heuristic approach is unique in the sense that we try to detect objects and fields that cause many cache misses, not just those that are frequently accessed. In most environments cache misses are transparent to software. Therefore, to predict the number of cache misses we need to use an empirical approach based on pattern matching rather than inserting instrumentation code.

3. Identifying the Instructions and Objects Causing Frequent Cache Misses without an HPM

In this section, we first explain our technique to identify the instructions and objects that frequently cause cache misses to provide effective information for optimizations in the JIT compiler. Our key insight to locate cache misses without using an HPM is that most cache misses identified by an HPM in typical Java workloads are often caused by certain idiomatic code patterns in those programs. This insight allows us to identify the objects that frequently cause cache misses by matching the hot loops with the idiomatic patterns.

Though these patterns look quite simple and standard in many Java programs, we found that the percentage of load instructions selected by matching with this idiom in hot loops was up to 5.9% of the total load and store instructions in the JIT-compiled code (and 2.8% on average). We identified these patterns by investigating the cache miss profiles from the HPM using SPECjbb2005 and SPECjvm2008. As shown later, due to the simplicity and generality of these patterns, pattern matching with them worked well with programs from the DaCapo-9.12 benchmark suite [14]. In Section 4, we also discuss some cache

Table 1. Thresholds for two configurations.

	hot loop threshold			hot method threshold
	hot	veryHot	scorching	
Base	40	20	10	veryHot
Aggressive	16	8	4	hot

misses in multi-threaded programs that we cannot capture with our current technique.

Figure 1(a) shows the most frequently observed pattern that causes many cache misses. In this pattern, there is a load of a reference to objA and a following access to the objA in one highly iterated loop. Here, the access to the objA can be a load or a store to a field of objA, or an operation accessing the object header, such as a monitor enter, a monitor exit, a checkcast, or an instanceof operation. As a variant, a reference to objA can be obtained from a return value of a method call instead of loading from a field of objB. We observed that a hot loop matching this pattern tends to cause a cache miss in each iteration when accessing the objA.field1. Thus we should focus on the objects of ClassA to improve the memory system performance.

In addition to this basic pattern, we used an anti-pattern in our analysis. Figure 1(b) shows this anti-pattern. The code sequence is almost identical to the basic pattern shown in Figure 1(a), but a reference to objA is loaded from the 'this' object. In this case, the 'this' object is loop invariant and thus objA should not cause many cache misses. We observed that this anti-pattern appeared frequently in many programs but rarely caused cache misses. This anti-pattern can be extended to check the loop invariance of the first load in addition to loading from a 'this' object. When we match the pattern after applying the loop optimizations including loop invariant code motion, we do not need to explicitly apply this anti-pattern. We used this approach in our implementation rather than handling 'this' object explicitly.

We do this pattern matching in the JIT compiler. The JIT compiler uses this analysis when it recompiles a method with a higher optimization level than the initial level. We used the execution frequency information obtained by software-based profiling to identify the hot loops for the pattern matching. Many high performance dynamic compilers already provide this information because it is important for many widely used optimizations. We designate a loop as hot if the estimated number of iterations per method invocation (N_{iter}) exceeds a threshold, which we call the *hot loop threshold*. In the current implementation, we adjust the threshold for the hot loops between $N_{iter} = 10$ and 40 based on the hotness of the compiling method. When the method is compiled with the highest optimization level (*scorching*), such a method is typically consuming more than 10% of the total CPU time, and we use 10 as the threshold. When the method is compiled with the second highest level (*veryHot*), typically consuming more than 3% of the CPU time, we use 20 as the threshold. For other hot methods we use 40.

The heuristics based on the number of iterations give good estimates for the hot loops, but in some cases opportunities are missed. If a method is invoked frequently, loops included in the method are also executed frequently, even though the loops do not meet our criteria. To identify such methods, we do pattern matching for the entire method when there are no loops having N_{iter} larger than 3.0 in the method and the method was compiled with veryHot or scorching levels (for the *hot method threshold*). If there are no highly iterated loops within a very hot method, then the method must be invoked quite frequently, typically from inside a very hot loop. We do not use the anti-pattern shown in Figure 1(b) when we match the pattern for the entire method,

```
void method1 (void) {

    for (i=0; i<100; i++) { // N_iter = 100
    ....
    }                                    hot loop

    for (j=0; j<5; j++) { // N_iter = 5
        ....
        for (k=0; k<20; k++) { // N_iter = 100
        ....
        }                                hot loop
    ....
    }                                    cold loop

}

void method2 (Element e) {
                    hot method without hot loops
    ....            (apply the analysis for the entire
                    method instead of hot loops)
}
```

N_{iter}: average number of iterations per method invocation calculated from the block execution frequencies

Threshold of the hot loop depends on the optimization level of the method

Figure 2. Overview of our hot loop criteria.

because in this case 'this' pointer may change in each invocation of the method. Figure 2 summarizes our hot loop detection methods. We also use the execution frequency to exclude cold blocks when we analyze a loop. There can be cold blocks even inside of a hot loop, such as a rarely executed if block.

These thresholds control the aggressiveness of the identification. Using smaller values for these thresholds increase the number of identified targets. To study the effect of the thresholds, we also evaluated another configuration with lower threshold values to pick more loops for analysis. We call these two threshold configurations *Base* and *Aggressive*. Table 1 summarizes the two configurations.

We do the pattern matching after applying most of the code transformation optmizations including method inlining to simplify the implementation of our analyzer. Small methods in hot loops are inlined by method inlining and so we do not need to implement our analysis as a costly interprocedural analysis. In the current implementation, we did not alter the method inlining policy to cooperate with our analyzer.

4. Experimental Results

This section presents our experimental results to evaluate the accuracy of our pattern-matting-based technique in identifying the instructions that frequently cause cache misses. We used standard benchmarks: SPECpower_ssj2008, SPECjbb2005, SPECjbb2000, SPECjvm2008 (excluding the scimark and crypto benchmarks), and the DaCapo-9.12 benchmark suite.

We ran the benchmarks on an IBM BladeCenter JS22 using 2 POWER6 [15] cores running at 4.0 GHz with 2 SMT threads per core. We implemented our technique in the 32-bit JVM included in the IBM SDK for Java 6 SR2. Each POWER6 core has 64 KB of L1 data cache (L1D), 64 KB of L1 instruction cache, and 4 MB of L2 cache. The cache line size of the POWER6 processor is 128 bytes for both L1 and L2 caches. The size of the Java heap was 2 GB using 16-MB pages. We selected the generational garbage collector so that the Java heap was divided into a nursery space and a survivor space for young objects and a tenured space for older objects. The test system had 16 GB of system memory and used RedHat Enterprise Linux 5.2.

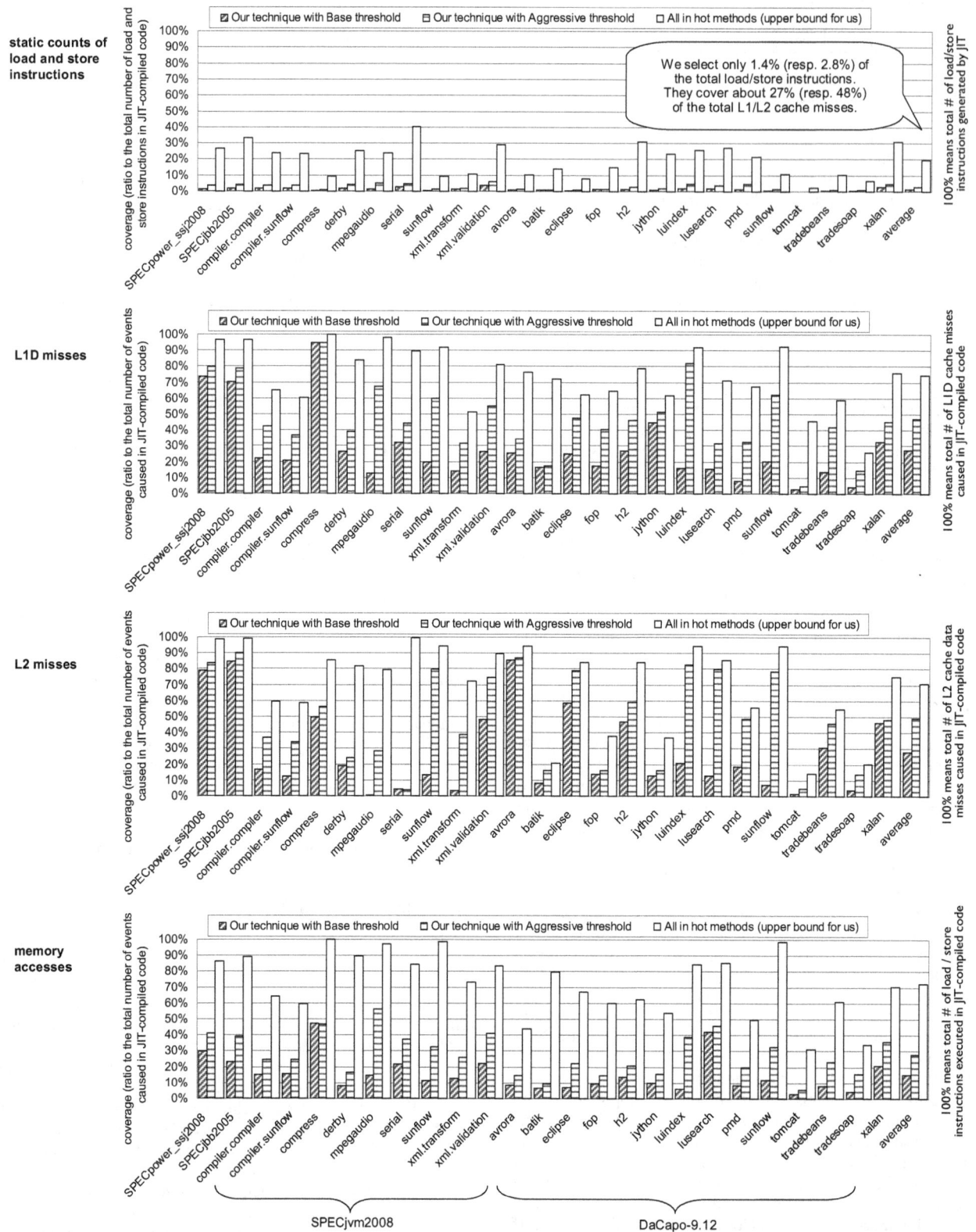

Fig. 3. Coverages of the instructions identified by our technique for the number of L1D cache misses, L2 cache data misses, memory accesses, and the static counts of load and store instructions. Our technique selected only 1.4% and 2.8% of the total load and store instructions, which account for about 27% and 48% of the total L1 cache misses for Base and Aggressive threshold configurations.

Table 2. Summary of the coverage by our technique.

	Base Threshold	Aggressive Threshold
ratio to the total counts in all the JIT-compiled method	coverage: L1D miss 27.3%, L2 miss 27.9% (by selecting 1.4% of load/store instructions)	coverage: L1D miss 47.3%, L2 miss 48.9% (by selecting 2.8% of load/store instructions)
ratio to the total counts in the hot methods that we apply our analysis (against the white bars labeled "All in hot methods" in Figure 3)	coverage: L1D miss 36.7%, L2 miss 39.4% (by selecting 6.9% of load/store instructions)	coverage: L1D miss 63.6%, L2 miss 69.2% (by selecting 14.2% of load/store instructions)

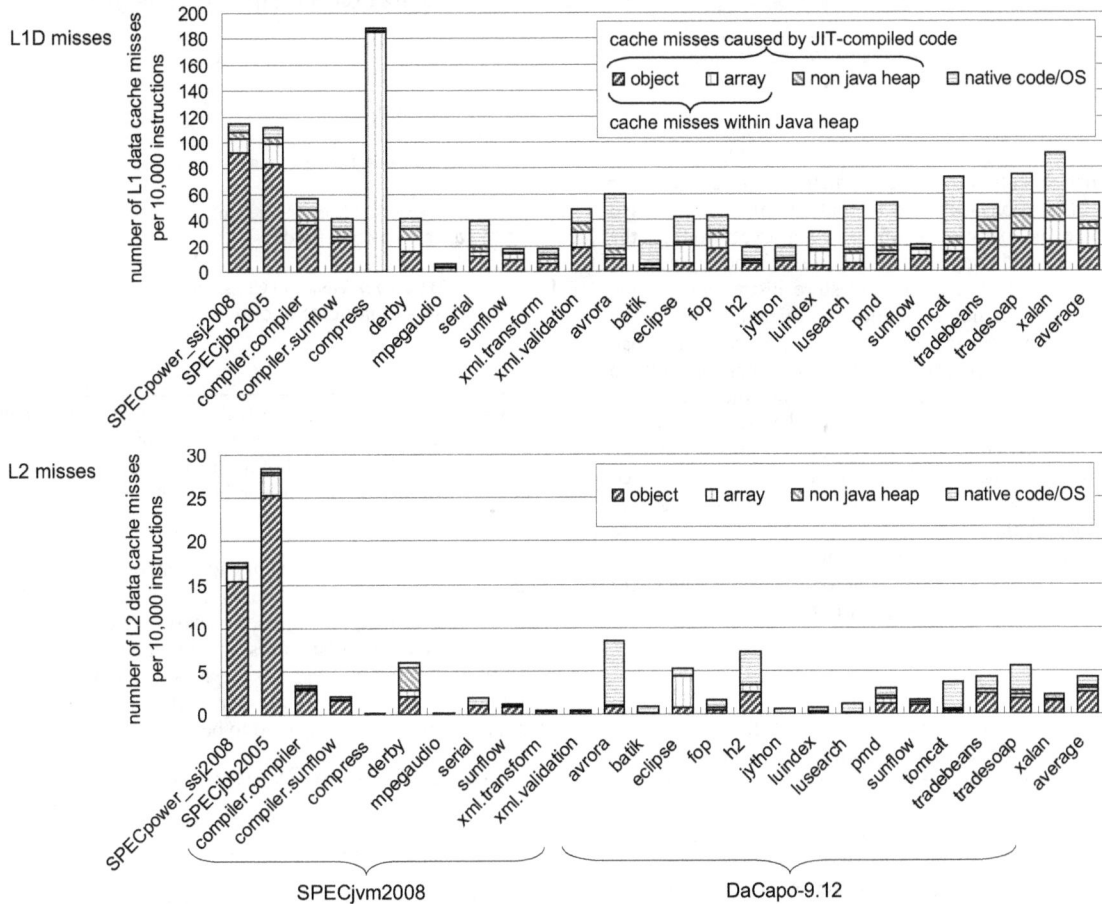

Figure 4. L1 and L2 cache miss ratios and breakdown by code location and access targets. We exclude the cache misses during stop-the-world garbage collection to focus on mutator performance.

4.1 Coverage

The first graph in Figure 3 shows the number of load and store instructions selected by our technique over the total number of load and store instructions generated by the JIT compiler. The other three graphs in Figure 3 show the coverages for the instructions identified by our technique for L1D cache misses, L2 cache data misses and all memory accesses. We measured the number of cache misses and memory accesses by using the HPM. We compare the coverages for our technique using the two threshold configurations (*Base* and *Aggressive*, as shown in Table 1) against the case of selecting all of the load and store instructions in the methods compiled with hot or higher compilation levels (labeled *all in hot methods* in the figure). Here,

we focus on the events caused by JIT-compiled code and hence the results do not include the events caused by the Linux kernel or native code in the JVM such as the garbage collector. We performed the measurements 4 times and averaged the results.

From the figure, our technique selected an average of only 1.4% and 2.8% (and up to 3.7% and 5.9%) of the total load and store instructions generated by the JIT compiler for Base and Aggressive threshold configurations, respectively. These instructions accounted for 27.3% and 47.3% of the total L1D cache misses and 27.9% and 48.9% of the total L2 data cache misses (average values). The coverages for the numbers of memory accesses of the instructions selected by our technique were 15.2% and 27.9%, which were smaller than the coverages of the cache misses. This means that the instructions selected by our technique were not only frequently executed but also caused more

Basic pattern for alignment optimization

```
    ClassA objA;
    ClassB objB;
    while (!end) { // in a hot loop
        ...
        // 1) first, load a reference of ClassA
        objA = objB.referenceToClassA;

        ...
        // 2) then, access at least two different fields of objA
        access to objA.field1;

        ...
        access to objA.field2;
        ...
    }
```

Figure 5. An example of a code sequence for which object alignment optimization is appropriate. Here we select ClassA as a target for alignment.

cache misses per execution than the instructions not selected. For example, the instructions selected by pattern matching caused more than twice as many cache misses per execution as the instructions not selected regardless of the threshold configuration.

When we select all of the load and store instructions in the methods compiled with hot or higher optimization levels, the number of instructions selected was 19.7% of the total of the load and store instructions. Because we apply our analysis only to these hot methods to avoid excessive overhead, the number of total cache misses for the hot methods were the upper bound for our technique. Compared to this upper bound (the white bars labeled "All in hot methods" in Figure 3), our technique achieved 63.6% and 69.2% coverage for the L1 and L2 cache misses with the Aggressive threshold by selecting 14.2% of the load and store instructions in the hot methods. Table 2 summarizes the coverage by our technique. These results show that our technique can cover a large part of the sources of the cache misses without depending on the HPM.

4.2 Discussion

We show the L1 and L2 cache miss statistics for each benchmark in Figure 4. The bar shows the number of cache misses per 10,000 executed instructions and the breakdown by the code location (JIT-compiled code or native code) and the accessed data type (objects, arrays, or non-Java-heap addresses). SPECpower_ssj2008, SPECjbb2005, and compress generated much more frequent cache misses than the other benchmarks in the JIT-compiled code. In these benchmarks, many of these cache misses were caused by only few hot loops. Our technique is effective in identifying such hot loops even with the Base threshold and hence the coverages for these benchmarks are much higher than the average of the other benchmarks. In the other non-cache-miss-intensive programs, no dominant hot loops exist and many code locations were contributing to the cache misses. Hence, the coverages were more dependent on the hot loop thresholds and their coverages were typically smaller than the three cache-miss-intensive programs.

We found one type of frequent cache miss that our technique failed to detect. Such cache misses are caused by conflicting store instructions from multiple threads. For example, the derby benchmark from SPECjvm2008 caused many L2 cache misses when accessing a method's static variable, and our heuristics could not detect this. These cache misses in the derby benchmark were only observed with multi-threaded execution. When we ran the derby benchmark with only one thread, accesses to the static

Additional patterns for alignment optimization

```
    ClassA objA;
    ClassB objB;
    ClassS objS; // ClassS is a super class of ClassA
    while (!end) { // in a hot loop
        ...
        // 1) first, load a reference of a super class of ClassA
        objS = objB.referenceToSuperClass;

        ...
        // 2) next, cast objC to ClassA
        objA = (ClassA) objS;

        ...
        // 3) then, access at least one field of objA
        access to objA.field1;
        ...
    }
```

```
    ClassA objA;
    objA = head;
    while (objA != null) { // in a hot loop
        ...
        // 1) access at least one field of objA
        access to objA.field1;

        ...
        // 2) load a reference to ClassA from objA
        objA = objA.next; or objA = objA.child[nextChild];
        ...
    }
```

Figure 6. Two additional patterns for the object alignment optimization. ClassA is the alignment candidate for both patterns. The first is typical of hashmap or treemap operations. The second appears while traversing a linked list.

variables did not cause frequent cache misses and the coverage of our technique was greatly improved. This type of cache miss is more difficult to capture by static analysis alone. Adding idioms to capture such special cases is our future work. Additional runtime information such as a lock contention profile will potentially help in identifying such cache misses, because objects shared by multiple threads tend to be guarded by monitors.

5. Applications in Runtime Optimization

In this section, we demonstrate the usefulness of our technique to identify the instructions that cause frequent cache misses in compiler optimizations. We evaluated two types of object placement optimizations, an object alignment optimization and an object collocation optimization based on our cache miss identification technique without relying on the HPM. We also describe techniques to exploit the corresponding opportunities based on the accurate cache miss profiles obtained from the HPM to compare with the optimizations based on our technique.

5.1 Our Object Alignment Optimization Without HPM

In the object alignment optimization, we adjust the address of an object to keep two or more hot fields of the object in the same cache line. Here, we describe how we identify the objects that generate frequent cache misses in more than two fields as targets to align based on matching the basic pattern shown in Figure 1. We search for the hot loops with the pattern shown in Figure 5. This pattern is a straightforward extension of the pattern shown in Figure 1(a). In this pattern, there is a load of a reference to objA and two following accesses in one loop. We want to adjust the address of the object to keep these two fields in the same cache

```
ClassA objA;
ClassB objB;
ClassC objC;
while (!end) { // in a hot loop
    ...
    // 1) first, load a reference of ClassA
    objA = objC.referenceToClassA;

    ...
    // 2) next, load a reference of ClassB from objA
    objB = objA.referenceToClassB;

    ...
    // 3) then, access at least one field of objB
    access to objB.field1;
    ...
}
```

Figure 7. An example of a code sequence for the object collocation optimization. The pair of ClassA and ClassB is the target for collocation.

line to reduce the cache misses caused by this code sequence (from two to one). If we find a hot loop that matches this pattern when compiling a method, we can identify the ClassA as a target for the object alignment optimization. Based on the anti-pattern shown in Figure 1(b), we do not select ClassA as a target if a reference to objA is loaded from the 'this' object in the loop.

Figure 6 shows two variant patterns, but still based on the pattern shown in Figure 1, in addition to the most common pattern shown in Figure 5. We use these special patterns to handle collection classes. Because it is known that the objects managed by a collection class, such as hashmaps, frequently cause cache misses and so these patterns are important when identifying likely cache misses [12]. The first pattern in Figure 6 includes a type cast. In this example, objS is converted from ClassS (a superclass of ClassA) to ClassA. In this case, we select ClassA, but not ClassS, as the target. This pattern commonly appears in loops accessing a hashmap (java.util.HashMap) or a treemap (java.util.TreeMap), in which all of the objects are treated as being in java.lang.Object. The second pattern in Figure 6 handles a linked data structure. This code pattern often appears in a loop iterating over all of the objects in a linked list. In this example, a reference to objA is loaded in each iteration and then its fields are accessed in the next iteration. We select objA as the target even though the load of the reference and the following use belong to different iterations of the loop. In the hot loop, two fields of each object (field1 and either next or child) are accessed. Thus we pick ClassA as the target.

After a target is identified, we do the optimizations at both allocation time and GC time. If the objects frequently cause cache misses in the nursery space, we optimize the object locations at allocation time. If they cause cache misses in the survivor or the tenure space, we do the optimization in the garbage collector. From the source code analysis alone, however, we cannot determine where the objects will reside. Hence, we adjust the object locations of each target at both allocation time and GC time.

For the allocation-time optimization, we generate special allocation code in the JIT compiler, which checks the alignment and adds padding before the new object for all of the allocation sites of the class. In the current implementation, all methods having at least one allocation site of the identified target class are recompiled to apply allocation-time optimization.

The generational garbage collector in the JVM copies objects using the parallel hierarchical copying order [16]. When an object to be tenured is marked as a target for the GC-time alignment, we first check whether the size of the remaining cache line is large enough to hold the object. If the remaining space is too small, we add padding and skip to the next cache line to ensure the object fits into one cache line. We did not implement these optimizations for objects in survivor space because additional operations in the frequently executed young GC may impose heavy overhead in the GC pause time.

5.2 Object Collocation Optimization Without HPM

The object collocation optimization collocates two objects that are accessed together into the same cache line. In the current implementation, we do not apply our optimization to array objects nor do we collocate more than two objects at a time. We identify pairs of classes to collocate when the code matches the pattern shown in Figure 7. We selected the pair of ClassA and ClassB as a target for the object collocation in this example. In this example, first a reference to objA is loaded, then a reference to objB is loaded from a field of objA, and finally a field of objB is accessed in the same loop. In such a code sequence, objA and objB often cause cache misses and so we can reduce two cache misses to one by collocating the two objects into one cache line. Based on the anti-pattern shown in Figure 1(b), we do not select the target if the reference to objA is loaded from the 'this' object.

We need the ordering of the two objects to do the allocation-time object collocation. We check their order in the garbage collector. The analyzer sends information on the collocation targets consisting of a referrer class, a referee class, and the field id of the referrer class, which has a reference to the referee. In the example of Figure 7, the referrer is ClassA and the referee is ClassB. The garbage collector checks the order of the two objects of these respective classes when it finds an object of the referrer class and its specified field holds a valid pointer to an object of the referee class.

We check if the referee object resides in front of the location of the corresponding referrer object. This means that the referee object was allocated before the referrer object was allocated, because we allocate the objects in the Java heap by simply incrementing a pointer that tracks the next location to allocate in our JVM. In this situation, we can generate special allocation code to add a reserved area of the size of the referrer object in the same cache line for all of the allocation sites of the referee objects. Also, we generate special allocation code for the allocation sites of the referrer objects to use the reserved area generated when the referee object was allocated. In the current implementation, all methods having at least one allocation site of the identified target classes are recompiled. When the garbage collector counts objects in the Java heap, we do not consider the class hierarchy. For example, in Figure 7 objA is not necessarily an instance of ClassA, but it might be an instance of a subclass of ClassA. In the current implementation, we skip such cases to avoid excessive profiling overhead.

For the identified targets, we calculate the object creation frequencies as the ratios of the number of objects created for each class to the total number of objects created by counting the number of objects in the nursery area. If this ratio exceeds our threshold, 10%, then we do not use the object collocation optimization for the class. This is because the optimization imposes additional overhead for CPU cycles and space proportional to the number of the created objects. We count the number of objects allocated in Java heap in the garbage collector and use this information to avoid applying allocation-time

```
allocateObject(class) {
    allocateByte = size of the class;
    updatedCursor = allocationCursor + allocateByte;

    if (updatedCursor > end_of_heap)  call allocation helper

    allocationCursor = updatedCursor;
    return allocationCursor;
}
```
(a) original object allocation code

```
allocateObject(class) {
    allocateByte = size of the class;

    if (class is marked to use reserved area for collocation ) {
        if (allocateByte < sizeOfReservedArea) {
            sizeOfReservedArea = 0;
            return reservedArea;
        }
    }

    if (class is marked to generate reserved area for collocation) {
        if ((allocateByte + byteToReserve) > remainingBytesInCacheline)
            allocationCursor += remainingBytesInCacheline;
        sizeOfReservedArea = byteToReserve;
        reservedArea = allocationCursor;
        allocationCursor += byteToReserve;
    }                                           for object collocation

    else if (class is marked for alignment) {
        if (allocateByte > remainingBytesInCacheline)
            allocationCursor += remainingBytesInCacheline;
    }                                           for object alignment

    updatedCursor = allocationCursor + allocateByte;

    if (updatedCursor > end_of_heap)  call allocation helper

    allocationCursor = updatedCursor;
    return allocationCursor;
}
```
(b) object allocation code for the allocation-time
    object placement optimization

Figure 8. Pseudocode of the object allocation code sequence used for the allocation-time object-placement optimizations.

optimization for frequently instantiated classes. We also apply the criteria for object alignment optimization described in Section 5.1. Figure 8 is pseudocode for the allocation code sequences for both the alignment and collocation optimizations. The current implementation does not collocate more than two objects. We could support more objects per cache line, but at the price of additional instructions in the allocation code.

5.3 Object Placement Optimizations Using HPM

This section describes the object alignment and collocation optimizations based on the accurate L1 and L2 cache miss profiles obtained from the HPM to contrast them against the technique based on our cache miss identification technique. Note that these optimizations themselves are not the primary focus of this paper though our techniques are much simpler than existing techniques, but still effective. For example, our HPM-based techniques do not require additional metadata to translate the instruction addresses into Java bytecode while previous techniques require huge amounts of additional metadata for this purpose. We implemented a framework to obtain HPM profiles from the JVM by adapting the earlier work [17] to obtain L1 and L2 data cache miss profiles at runtime. To focus on the mutator performance, we do not include the cache misses during stop-the-world GC in the profiles.

Table 3. An example of a cache miss profile for a method in which the object alignment optimization is used.

	class	offset	location	number of samples
1	spec/jbb/Stock	0	tenure	5.1%
2	spec/jbb/Stock	32	tenure	2.1%
3	spec/jbb/Orderline	8	nursery	2.1%
4	spec/jbb/Orderline	56	nursery	1.7%
5	java/math/BigDecimal	24	nursery	1.5%

- L2 cache miss profile for *spec/jbb/*CustomerReportTransaction.process
- number of samples shown in the ratio to the total number of samples

Table 4. An example of a cache miss profile for a method in which the object collocation optimization is used.

	class	offset	location	number of samples
1	java/util/TreeMap$Entry	24	nursery	8.4%
2	spec/jbb/History	0	nursery	4.5%
3	spec/jbb/History	24	nursery	3.8%
4	spec/jbb/Order	0	nursery	2.4%

⋮
- L1 cache miss profile for *spec/jbb/*DeliveryTransaction.preprocess
- number of samples shown in the ratio to the total number of samples

5.3.1 Object Alignment Optimization Using HPM

Based on the accurate cache miss profiles, similar object alignment opportunities can be found. We first use the HPM to generate L1 and L2 cache miss profiles for each method. If multiple fields of one class cause many cache misses in one method, that class is a target for the object alignment optimization. Table 3 shows cache miss profiles that include targets. In this example, we picked two classes, Stock and Orderline, as the targets for the object alignment optimization, because two fields of each class cause cache misses above the threshold. We used 0.5% of the total cache miss samples from the entire program as the threshold for the alignment optimization. Based on our measurements, this simple heuristic identified many targets that did not provide significant cache miss reductions when using a threshold smaller than 0.5%. In the HPM-based optimization, we can get the location of the objects that caused the cache misses directly from the HPM, as shown in Table 3. In the table, the Stock class causes cache misses in the tenure space and so we control the location of the Stock objects when the garbage collector moves them into the tenure space. The Orderline objects cause cache misses in the nursery space and so we optimize at allocation time. We use the same mechanism to control the object location at the allocation time and the GC time.

5.3.2 Object Collocation Optimization Using HPM

For the object collocation optimization, we identify pairs of classes to collocate in a way similar to the alignment optimization. Table 4 shows an example of cache miss profiles that include targets for the object collocation optimization. In this optimization, we count the references from the objects that cause the cache misses for other objects, as well as the cache misses themselves, to select the targets. First we select each pair of two classes that cause more than 0.5% of the total cache misses in one location (such as the nursery). Then we iterate over the objects of those classes that caused the cache misses and count the number of objects that have references to objects in another class. If the

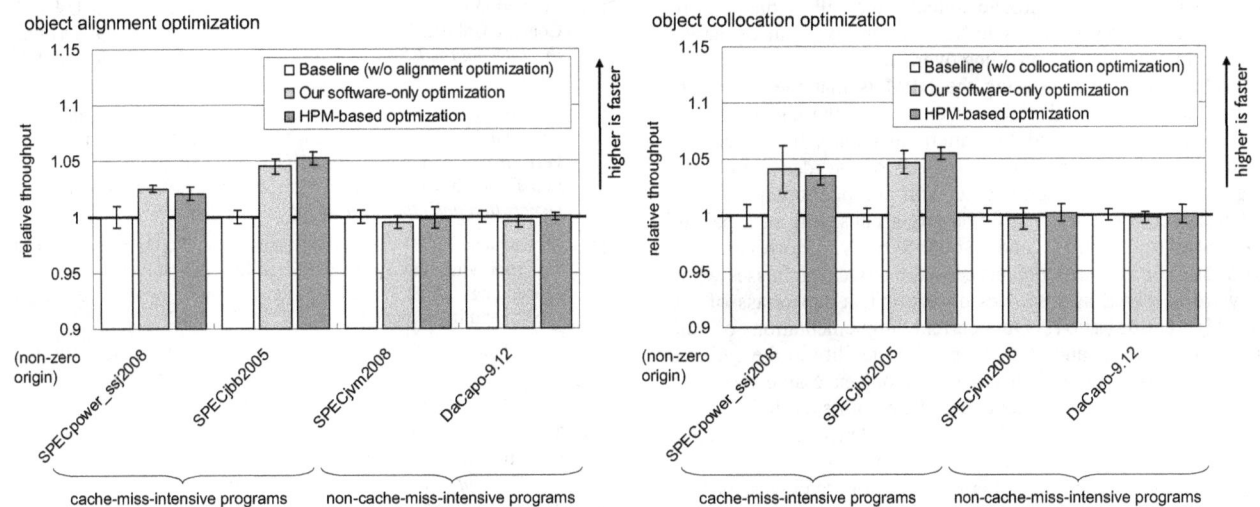

Fig. 9. Performance improvements from object placement optimizations with our approach and with HPM-based approach. The error bars show 95% confidence intervals. We used the Base threshold for pattern matching. Note that the origin of the Y-axis is not zero.

number of objects that have a reference also exceeds 0.5% of the total number of sampled cache misses, then this pair is a target for the object collocation optimization. In Table 4, the `TreeMap$Entry` and `History` classes generate many cache misses and (though the table does not includes this information) many of the `TreeMap$Entry` objects causing cache misses have references to `History` objects, making this pair is a good target. The `TreeMap$Entry` and `History` classes shown in Table 4 both cause cache misses in the nursery space and so we optimize them when they are allocated in the Java heap. If the target objects cause cache misses in the tenure or the survivor space, we collocate the objects in the garbage collector.

For the allocation-time object collocation, we first check the order of the two objects, the `TreeMap$Entry` object that caused the cache miss and the `History` object that is referenced from the `TreeMap$Entry` object as we do in pattern-matching-based approach. To avoid excessive allocation-time overhead, we do not use this object collocation and alignment optimization if the object creation frequency of one of the target classes exceeds 10% based on the object creation profile generated using HPM information [17].

5.4 Performance Improvements by the Optimizations

We implemented the HPM-based and our pattern-matching-based optimizations to compare the two approaches in the object placement optimizations. We implemented both optimizations as online optimizations in Java JIT compiler. We use Base threshold configurations for our pattern-matching used in the evaluations.

Figure 9 shows the performance improvements for SPECpower_ssj2008 and SPECjbb2005 with our pattern-matching-based and the HPM-based optimizations for object alignment and collocation. As shown in Figure 4, the cache miss rates for the other benchmarks are much smaller than these two and hence the effects of the optimizations for the other programs were not significant even when we used the accurate cache miss profile from the HPM. Thus we only show the averages for the SPECjvm2008 and dacapo-9.12 benchmark suites. We ran the performance measurements 8 times and averaged the throughputs. The error bars in the graph show the 95% confidence intervals.

We observed acceleration for SPECpower_ssj2008 and SPECjbb2005. The largest improvements were for SPECjbb2005, with 4.7% for our pattern-matching-based optimization and 5.5% for the HPM-based optimization with collocation. The effects of the optimizations for the non-cache-miss-intensive programs were not significant and the confidence intervals overlap in most cases. On average for the non-cache-miss-intensive programs, we observed small performance degradation with our approach. This performance degradation came from additional runtime overhead caused by additional profiling in garbage collector and also from the extra CPU time for the special allocation code.

We observed significant reduction in both L1 and L2 data cache misses in the two benchmarks that did benefit from our optimizations. In these benchmarks, many of the L1 and L2 cache misses were due to very hot loops, and so it was possible to change the memory access behavior of the entire program by controlling the objects related to these hot loops. In the other programs, many objects were contributing to the data cache misses and thus it was much harder to improve the cache behavior with the object placement changes even when using the precise profiles from the HPM.

These results showed that our pattern-matching-based heuristic approach successfully identified optimization opportunities for object placement optimizations in cache-miss-intensive programs and our techniques achieved similar performance gains by exploiting the same opportunities without depending on the HPM.

5.5 Challenges in Software-Only Optimizations

By comparing the differences between the HPM-based and our pattern-matching-based optimizations in detail, we identified two major remaining challenges in optimizations that do not rely on the HPM.

One obvious advantage is that the HPM can directly identify the location of the objects causing the cache misses. With static analysis alone, we cannot determine the locations of the objects. Hence, for our heuristic approach, we aggressively control the locations of the target objects at both allocation time and GC time. With HPM-based optimizations, we can select the best ways to control the object locations to minimize the additional overhead in CPU time and memory waste. Using the more accurate statistics gathered in the garbage collector may allow the pattern-matching-based optimizations to be location aware in exchange for the additional runtime profiling overhead.

Another advantage of using the HPM is that the HPM can identify the classes of the objects that cause the cache misses. When a class is identified by pattern matching, the objects at runtime might be instances of subclasses of the identified class. We actually observed such a case with compiler.compiler. The HPM-based collocation identified a target consisting of a pair of `Symbol$MethodSymbol` and `Scope$Entry`. However, the `Symbol$MethodSymbol` objects caused many cache misses when they were accessed as instances of `Symbol`, a superclass of the `Symbol$MethodSymbol`. Our current implementation of the source code analysis and also the profiling facility in the garbage collector do not handle such cases to avoid excessive overhead and thus failed to identify this target. To obtain such information without depending on the hardware, we can generate special code for additional profiling in the identified loop.

Another challenge in the pattern-matching-based optimizations was the criteria to select hot loops. In general, picking more loops for analysis increases the opportunities to reduce the cache misses, but also increases the overhead. When using the Aggressive threshold configuration, the number of identified classes was especially increased for the programs from SPECjvm2008. The thresholds play roles similar to the threshold for the cache miss rate to pick the targets in the HPM-based optimizations (0.5% in our implementation).

Future work for the object placement optimizations will implement more sophisticated profiling techniques, such as software-based sampling techniques to capture object creations [18] or techniques to track the allocation site of each object [19] to obtain more accurate information with smaller overhead.

In summary, our pattern-matching-based heuristic approach successfully identified many of the same opportunities for Java object placement optimization as the HPM-based approach. Though the HPM had some advantages, such as dynamic information on objects that caused the cache misses, our results showed that we can achieve comparable performance gains without using the HPM in SPECjbb2005 and SPECpower_ssj2008.

6. Summary

In this paper, we presented our techniques to identify the instructions and objects that frequently cause cache misses without using the HPM of the processor and then showed its effectiveness in compiler optimization using two examples. Our key insight is that the cache misses are often caused by pointer dereferences in hot loops in the Java programs. Thus we can heuristically identify the targets by finding the hot loops with idiomatic patterns often used in Java programs. We showed that our heuristic technique effectively identified many of the cache misses in a variety of Java programs. As a result, optimizations based on our heuristic approach successfully identified many of the same targets that the HPM-based optimizations identified.

References

[1] A. Adl-Tabatabai, R. L. Hudson, M. J. Serrano, and S. Subramoney, "Prefetch injection based on hardware monitoring and object metadata", in *Proceedings of the ACM Conference on Programming Language Design and Implementation*, pp. 267–276, 2004.

[2] F. T. Schneider, M. Payer, and T. R. Gross, "Online optimizations driven by hardware performance monitoring", in *Proceedings of the ACM Conference on Programming Language Design and Implementation*, pp. 373–382, 2007.

[3] M. Serrano and X. Zhuang, "Placement Optimization Using Data Context Collected During Garbage Collection", In *Proceedings of the International Symposium on Memory Management*, pp. 69–78, 2009.

[4] J. Cuthbertson, S. Viswanathan, K. Bobrovsky, A. Astapchuk, E. Kaczmarek, and U. Srinivasan, "A Practical Approach to Hardware Performance Monitoring Based Dynamic Optimizations in a Production JVM", in *Proceedings of the International Symposium on Code Generation and Optimization*, pp. 190–199, 2009.

[5] M. Burtscher, A, Diwan and M. Hauswirth, "Static load classification for improving the value predictability of data cache misses" in Proceedings of the ACM Conference on Programming Language Design and Implementation, pp. 222–233, 2002.

[6] V. M. Panait, A. Sasturkar, and W. F. Wong, "Static Identification of Delinquent Loads", in *Proceedings of the International Symposium on Code Generation and Optimization*, pp. 303–314, 2004.

[7] T. M. Chilimbi, and J. R. Larus, "Using generational garbage collection to implement cache-conscious data placement", in *Proceedings of the ACM International Symposium on Memory Management*, pp. 37-48, 1998.

[8] T. M. Chilimbi, M. D. Hill, and J. R. Larus, "Cache-conscious structure layout", in *Proceedings of the ACM Conference on Programming Language Design and Implementation*, pp. 1–12, 1999.

[9] W. Chen, S. Bhansali, T. M. Chilimbi, X. Gao, and W. Chuang, "Profile-guided proactive garbage collection for locality optimization", in *Proceedings of ACM Conference on Programming Language Design and Implementation*, pp. 332–340, 2006.

[10] M. L. Seidel and B. G. Zorn, "Segregating Heap Objects by Reference Behavior and Lifetime", in *Proceedings of the International Conference on Architectural Support for Programming Languages and Operating Systems*, pp. 12–23, 1998.

[11] Y. Shuf, M. Gupta, R. Bordawekar, and J. P. Singh, Exploiting prolific types for memory management and optimizations, in *Proceedings of the ACM Symposium on Principles of Programming Languages*, pp. 295–306, 2002.

[12] A. Jula and L. Rauchwerger, "Two memory allocators that use hints to improve locality", in *Proceedings of the ACM International Symposium on Memory Management*, pp. 109–118, 2009.

[13] J. Jeon, K. Shin, and H. Han, "Layout transformations for heap objects using static access patterns", in *Proceedings of the International Conference on Compiler Construction*, pp. 187–201, 2007.

[14] S. M. Blackburn *et al.*, "The DaCapo Benchmarks: Java Benchmarking Development and Analysis", in *Proceedings of the ACM conference on Object-Oriented Programming, Systems, Languages, and Applications*, pp. 169–190, 2006.

[15] H. Q. Le, W. J. Starke, J. S. Fields, F. P. O'Connell, D. Q. Nguyen, B. J. Ronchetti, W. M. Sauer, E. M. Schwarz, and M. T. Vaden, "IBM POWER6 microarchitecture", *IBM Journal of Research and Development*, Vol. 51 (6), pp. 639–662, 2007.

[16] D. Siegwart and Martin Hirzel, "Improving locality with parallel hierarchical copying GC", in *Proceedings of the International Symposium on Memory Management*, pp. 52–63, 2006.

[17] H. Inoue and T. Nakatani, "How a Java VM Can Get More from a Hardware Performance Monitor", in *Proceedings of the ACM Conference on Object Oriented Programming Systems Languages and Applications*, pp. 137–154, 2009.

[18] M. Jump, S. M. Blackburn, and K. S. McKinley, "Dynamic object sampling for pretenuring", in *Proceedings of the International Symposium on Memory Management*, pp. 152–162, 2004.

[19] R. Odaira, K. Ogata, K. Kawachiya, T. Onodera, and T. Nakatani, "Efficient Runtime Tracking of Allocation Sites in Java", in *Proceedings of the ACM International Conference on Virtual Execution Environments*, pp. 109–120, 2010.

Author Index

www.ingramcontent.com/pod-product-compliance
Lightning Source LLC
Chambersburg PA
CBHW080557220326
41599CB00032B/6510